Theory Test, Practical Test & Highway Code

Everything you need to know
to help you pass your driving tests

Save £40
on your first 10 lessons*
theaa.com/driving-school

AA Driving
School

CONTENTS

Published by AA Publishing (a trading name of AA Media Ltd, whose registered office is Grove House, Chineham Court, Basingstoke, Hampshire RG24 8AG; registered number 06112600).

© AA Media Ltd 2022
Tenth edition.

AA Media Ltd retains the copyright in the current edition and in all previous editions, reprints and amendments to editions.

Previously published as *Complete Test*.

Parts 3 and 4: Crown Copyright material reproduced under licence from the Driver and Vehicle Standards Agency, which does not accept any responsibility for the accuracy of the reproduction.

Part 7 reproduced from *The Official Highway Code*, Department of Transport and the Driver and Vehicle Standards Agency © Crown Copyright 2022. Contains public sector information licensed under the Open Government Licence v3.0.

ISBN: 978-0-7495-8310-1

Printed in the UK by Bell & Bain Ltd

A05829

For driving lessons, visit AA Driving School at www.theaa.com/driving-school

Getting your licence

You want to pass your driving test and take advantage of the freedom and mobility that driving a car can give you. The following three things will help you to achieve your goal.

- Acquire knowledge of the rules of the road by learning *The Highway Code*.
- Take the right attitude. Be careful, courteous and considerate to all other road users.
- Learn and understand the skills of driving by taking lessons from a trained and qualified driving instructor.

This book has been designed to help you become a careful and safe driver and help you take the first steps towards achieving your goal – preparing for your theory test.

SIX ESSENTIAL STEPS TO GETTING YOUR LICENCE

1 Get your provisional licence

You can apply online for your provisional licence at www.gov.uk/apply-first-provisional-driving-licence or apply using form D1 available from Post Offices.

The driving licence is issued as a photocard.

You must be at least 17 before you can legally begin learning to drive and you must be in possession of the correct licence documents. Take care when completing all the forms. Many licences cannot be issued for the required date because of errors or omissions on the application. You will need to provide proof of identity, such as a UK passport.

2 Learn *The Highway Code*

The Highway Code is essential reading for all drivers and not just those learning to drive. It sets out all the rules for good driving, as well as the rules for other road users such as pedestrians and motorcycle riders. When you have learned the rules you will be able to answer most of the questions in the theory test and be ready to start learning the driving skills you will need to pass your practical test.

3 Apply for and take the theory test

The driving test is in two parts, the theory test and the practical test. Once you have a valid provisional licence you may take the theory test at any time, but you must pass it before you are allowed to apply for the practical test. It is important, however, not to take your theory test too early in your course of practical lessons. This is because you need the experience of meeting real hazards while you are learning to drive, to help you pass the hazard perception element of the theory test.

You can book your theory test online or by phone. You will need your Driver and Vehicle Licensing Agency (DVLA) licence number and your debit or credit card details to hand.

Online: www.gov.uk/book-theory-test
Enquiries and booking support: 0300 200 1122
Welsh speakers: 0300 200 1133
Textphone: 0300 200 1166
Lines are open Monday to Friday, from 8am to 4pm
Post: DVSA, PO Box 381, M50 3UW

4 Learn to drive

It is recommended that you learn to drive with an Approved Driving Instructor (ADI). Only an ADI may legally charge for providing tuition. A fully qualified ADI must display a green badge on the windscreen of the car while teaching you. Some trainee driving instructors display a pink badge on the windscreen.

Choose an instructor or driving school by asking friends or relatives for recommendations. Price is important, so find out whether the school offers any discounts for blocks or lessons paid in advance; if you decide to pay in advance, make sure the driving school is reputable. If lesson prices are very low, ask yourself 'why?' Check how long the lesson will last. Ask about the car you'll be learning to drive in. Is it modern and reliable? Is it insured? Does it have dual controls?

The most efficient and cost-effective way to learn to drive is to accept that there is no short-cut approach to learning the necessary skills. Agree with your instructor on a planned course of tuition suited to your needs, take regular lessons, and don't skip weeks and expect to pick up where you left off. Ensure the full official syllabus is covered and, as your skills develop, get as much driving practice on the road as possible with a relative or friend. Ensure they are legally able to supervise you; they must be over 21 years of age and have held a full driving licence for at least three years.

5 Apply for and take the practical test

Once you have passed the theory test, and with your instructor's guidance based on your progress, you can plan ahead for a suitable test date for the practical test. You can book your practical test online or by phone.

Online: www.gov.uk/book-driving-test
Enquiries and booking support: 0300 200 1122
Welsh speakers: 0300 200 1133
Lines are open Monday to Friday, from 8am to 4pm

Make sure you have the following details to hand when booking your practical test:
- Theory test pass certificate number
- driver number shown on your licence
- driving school code number (if known)
- your preferred date
- unacceptable days or periods
- if you can accept a test at short notice
- disability or any special circumstances
- your credit/debit card details (the person who books the test must be the cardholder).

If you need to, you can change your practical test appointment online.

Saturday and weekday evening tests are available at some driving test centres. The fee is higher than for a driving test during normal working hours on weekdays. Evening tests are available during the summer months only.

6 Apply for your full driving licence

If you have a photocard provisional driving licence issued after 1 March 2004, and pass your driving test, the examiner can issue your full driving licence immediately. The DVLA will send your new full licence by post within four weeks of passing your practical test.

If you don't have a photocard provisional driving licence, you need to send your Pass Certificate and your provisional licence to the DVLA in Swansea, within two years of passing your practical test.

AFTER THE PRACTICAL TEST

Drivers may wish to enhance their basic skills and widen their experience by taking further training in the form of the Pass Plus scheme.

This is a six-module syllabus that covers town and rural driving, night driving, driving in adverse weather conditions and driving on dual carriageways and motorways. It offers you the opportunity to gain more driving experience with the help of an instructor. Insurance companies may be prepared to offer discounts to new drivers who have completed the course. There is no test to take at the end of the course.

MORE INFORMATION

For more information on learning to drive, including the theory test, the practical test and Pass Plus, visit www.gov.uk/browse/driving.

How to use this book

This book is arranged in seven sections.

Part 1 explains what to expect and how to prepare for each part of the test: Theory and Practical.

This section explains how to take the theory test using a touch-screen computer and gives details of the clips used in the hazard perception part of the test. In the Practical section we have included information about the Driver's Record, which your instructor will complete after each lesson.

We tell you what to expect on the day you take your test, details of the documents you must have with you, and tell you what the examiner will be looking for in your general driving. We have also included information on the vehicle safety check questions, which forms part of the practical test.

Part 2 is designed to help you understand each of the 14 topics in the theory test. This section will tell you what type of questions you can expect in each section and we've included lots of helpful tips. Each topic is colour coded to its relevant section in Part 3 of this book, which contains all the revision Theory Questions from the Driver and Vehicle Standards Agency (DVSA).

Experience has taught us that learner drivers find particular theory questions difficult and are often confused when they see questions that are similar. Reading through the background to each topic, before looking at the questions, will help you to avoid the pitfalls and help you to group questions together, as you will often find several questions are asking the same thing in a slightly different way.

Part 3 contains revision questions for car drivers created by the DVSA. The questions in your live test will be unseen and different from the ones shown in this book.

The questions are arranged in topics, such as Safety Margins and Rules of the Road. You will be tested on a range of these topics when you take your touch-screen theory test. Each topic has its own colour band to help you find your way around.

Each question is accompanied by explanatory information to help you understand each question. Most of the theory test questions can be answered if you learn *The Highway Code*. However, you will only find the answers to some questions by talking to your driving instructor and learning about good driving practice on the road.

You'll find all the correct answers to the theory test questions in Part 4 (see pages 255–260), that way, you can easily test yourself to see what you are getting right and what you still need to work on.

Part 4 has all the answers to the theory test questions.

Part 5 is a short glossary, which explains some of the more difficult words and terms used in the theory questions and *The Highway Code*. It's in alphabetical order and you can use this to check if you're not sure what a chicane is, for example, or what brake fade means.

Part 6 contains questions and answers for learner drivers set by a panel of driving experts, as an aid to help you pass your practical test. They are designed to test your knowledge of what is required before you even sit in the driver's seat. Topics include parallel parking, reversing and motorway driving.

Part 7 contains *The Highway Code* with its own index (according to rule number).

PART 1: ABOUT THE THEORY TEST

Revising for the theory test

The theory test is all about making you a safer driver and it is a good idea to prepare for the theory test at the same time as you develop your skills behind the wheel for the practical test. By preparing for both tests at the same time, you will reinforce your knowledge and understanding of all aspects of driving and improve your chances of passing both tests first time.

USING THE THEORY TEST REVISION QUESTIONS

This book is designed to help you prepare for the multiple-choice questions part of the theory test and contains all the recommended revision questions from the DVSA. The test will consist of 50 unseen theory test questions based on the topics shown here (see pages 53–254). The real test questions are not published, but the questions in this book will help you revise for the test.

To help you study for the test, the questions are arranged into the theory test topics. Each topic has its own colour band to help you find your way through the book.

Start your revision by picking a topic; you don't have to study the topics in order. Study each question carefully to make sure you understand what it is asking you. Look carefully at any diagram or photograph before reading the explanatory information and deciding on your answer.

All the correct answers are given in Part 4 (see pages 255–260).

REMEMBER
- Learning *The Highway Code* and taking lessons with an ADI (approved driving instructor) are the best way to prepare for your theory test.
- Don't attempt too many questions at once.
- Don't try to learn the questions and answers by heart; the real test questions are not available for you to practice and are different from the revision questions given in this book.

Questions marked **NI** are **not** found in theory tests in Northern Ireland.

① Study the question carefully and make sure you understand what it is asking you

19 Mark *one* answer
You're travelling along this road. How should you pass the cyclist?

③ Look carefully at any photograph, symbol or diagram given within the question.

☐ **A** Sound your horn as you pass
☐ **B** Keep close to them as you pass
☐ **C** Leave them plenty of room as you pass
☐ **D** Change down one gear before you pass

② Read through all the possible options.

Allow the cyclist plenty of room in case they wobble or swerve around a pothole or raised drain. Look well ahead before you start to overtake, because you'll need to cross the hazard line. Look for entrances where vehicles could be waiting to pull out.

④ Each question in this book is accompanied by an explanation that will help you understand the theory behind the question and what answer may be appropriate. Make sure you read through this text before answering the question. This text will not appear in your actual theory test.

What to expect in the theory test

The theory test consists of two parts: 50 multiple-choice questions and hazard perception (see page 16). You have to pass both parts in order to pass your theory test. You will receive your test scores at the end of the test. Even if you only failed on one part of the theory test, you still have to take both parts again next time.

MULTIPLE-CHOICE QUESTIONS

You will have 57 minutes to complete the question part of the test using a touch-screen and all the questions are multiple-choice. Three questions will be case studies, based on a video clip (see page 14).

The 50 questions appear on the screen one at a time and you can return to any of the questions within the 57 minutes to re-check or change your answers (an example of how they might appear is shown opposite). You have to score a minimum of 43 out of 50 to pass. The Government may change the pass mark from time to time. Your driving school or the DVSA will be able to tell you if there has been a change.

Each question has four possible options. You must select the one correct answer. Don't worry about accidentally missing marking an answer because you'll be reminded that you haven't chosen an answer before moving on to the next question.

Study each question carefully and look carefully at any diagram, drawing or photograph. Before you look at the options given, decide what you think the correct answer might be. Read through the options and then select the answer that matches the one you had decided on. If you follow this system, you will avoid being confused by answers that appear to be similar.

You can answer the questions in any order you choose by moving forwards and backwards through the questions. You can also change your answer if necessary and flag questions you're unsure about. This means that you can go back to them later in the test. In the actual test, the remaining time you have left in the test is shown clearly on the screen.

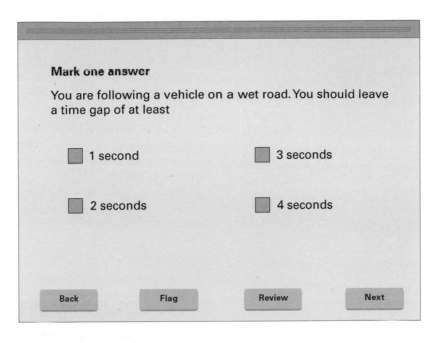

Mark one answer

You are following a vehicle on a wet road. You should leave
a time gap of at least

- 1 second
- 3 seconds
- 2 seconds
- 4 seconds

Back Flag Review Next

Mark one answer

You have just gone through deep water. To dry off
the brakes you should

- accelerate and keep to a
  high speed for a short time
- avoid using the brakes
  at all for a few miles
- go slowly while gently
  applying the brakes
- stop for at least an
  hour to allow them time
  to dry

Back Flag Review Next

CASE STUDY QUESTIONS

Currently, 3 of the 50 questions will take the form of a case study. The case study is based on a short, silent, video clip and you will be asked 3 multiple-choice questions about it. You can watch the video clip as many times as you like during the multiple-choice part of the theory test. For example, you could watch the video, answer a question, and then watch the video again before you answer the next question.

Case studies are designed to test that you not only know your car theory but also that you understand how to apply your knowledge when faced with a given driving situation.

The case study in your theory test could be based on any driving scenario and ask questions from a range of topics in the DVSA's database of questions.

The sample case study on the next page demonstrates how the case study questions may appear in your live test, so you'll know what to expect.

WHAT WILL I SEE?

The video clip (see below) will show you a situation from the driver's viewpoint, such as driving through a town centre or driving on a country road. You'll then be given three questions, such as:

1. Why are motorcyclists considered vulnerable road users?
2. Why should the driver, on the side road, look out for motorcyclists at junctions?
3. In this clip, who can cross the chevrons to overtake other vehicles, when it's safe to do so?

For each of the 3 questions, you'll have to choose the correct answer from 4 possible answers. The left-hand side of The screen will show the video clip much like below with controls to:

– play the video
– pause the video
– move to a specific part of the video on a progress bar
– watch the video using the full screen

The right-hand side of the screen will show the multiple-choice questions.

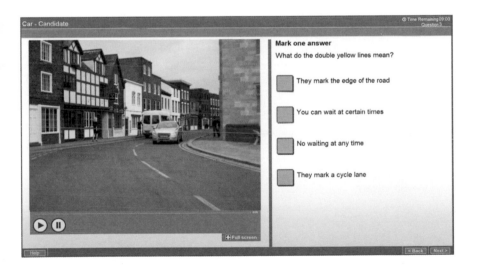

HAZARD PERCEPTION

The second part of the theory test is known as 'hazard perception' and is based on video clips. Its aim is to find out how good you are at noticing hazards developing on the road ahead. The test will also show how much you know about the risks to you as a driver, the risks to your passengers and the risks to other road users.

> Who do you think have the most accidents – new or experienced drivers? New drivers have just had lessons, so they should remember how to drive safely, but in fact statistics show that new drivers have the most accidents.

Learner drivers need training in how to spot hazards because they are often so busy thinking about the car's controls that they forget to watch the road and traffic. Losing concentration for even a second could prove fatal to you or another road user.

Proper training can help you to recognize more of the hazards that you will meet when driving and to spot those hazards earlier, so you are less likely to have an accident.

Your driving instructor has been trained to help you learn hazard perception skills and can give you plenty of practice in what to look out for when driving, how to anticipate hazards, and what action to take to deal with hazards of all kinds.

WHAT IS A HAZARD?

A hazard is anything that might cause you to change speed or direction when driving. The hazard perception element of the theory test is about spotting developing hazards. This is one of the key skills of good driving and is also called 'anticipation'. Anticipating hazards, such as car doors opening or children running into the road, means looking out for them in advance and taking the appropriate action.

As you get more driving experience you will start to learn about the times and places where you are most likely to meet hazards. An example of this is the rush hour. You know people take more risks when they are in a hurry. Maybe they have to drop their children at school before going to work. Perhaps they are late for a meeting or want to get home. So you have to be prepared for bad driving, such as another driver pulling out in front of you.

You won't be able to practise with the real clips used in the official test, of course, but training books and practice videos are widely available.

TAKING THE THEORY TEST: HAZARD PERCEPTION

After answering the multiple-choice questions, you will be given a short break before you begin the hazard perception part of the test. The hazard perception test lasts for about 20 minutes. Before you start you will be given some instructions explaining how the test works; you'll also get a chance to practise with the computer and mouse before you start. This is to make sure that you know what to expect on the test and that you are happy with what you have to do.

Next you will see 14 clips of street scenes with traffic such as cars, pedestrians, cyclists, etc. The scenes are shot from the point of view of a driver in a car. You have to notice potential hazards that are developing on the road ahead – that is, problems that could lead to an incident. As soon as you notice a hazard developing, click the mouse. You will have plenty of time to see the hazard and the sooner you notice it, the more marks you score.

Each clip has at least one hazard in it but some clips may have more than one hazard. You have to score a minimum of 44 out of 75 to pass, but the pass mark may change so check with your instructor or the DVSA before sitting your test.

Note that the computer has checks built in to show anyone trying to cheat – for example someone who keeps clicking the mouse all the time. Be aware that, unlike the theory test questions, you will not have an opportunity to go back to an earlier clip and change your response, so you need to concentrate throughout the test.

Above: Click the mouse when you spot potential hazards – the tractor emerging from the side road (ringed).

About the tests

What to expect in the practical test

The requirements for passing your test are a combination of practical skills and mental understanding. The open road can be a risky environment, and your test result will show whether you're ready to go out there alone or whether you need a little more practice first.

You will need to bring a car to the practical test. Usually people use a car belonging to their driving instructor, but you can use your own car if it meets the quite strict rules. See https://www.gov.uk/driving-test/using-your-own-car

You'll be asked to sign a declaration that the insurance of your car is in order. Without this, the practical test can't proceed.

> Driving test standards are monitored so that whatever examiner you get, or whatever test centre you go to, you should get the same result. You might find a senior officer in the car as well as the examiner; they are not watching you, but checking that the examiner is doing their job properly.

THE PAPERWORK

You'll need to have with you:

- your signed photocard provisional driving licence. If your licence doesn't have a photo (i.e. an older-style paper licence) you'll need to bring a valid passport for photographic identity. No other form of identification will be accepted.
- your theory test pass certificate

EYESIGHT TEST

Your driving test begins with an eyesight test. You have to be able to read a new style number plate at a minimum distance of 20 metres (about 67 feet) or an old style number plate at 20.5 metres (about 67.5 feet). If you fail the eyesight test your driving test will stop at that point and you will have failed.

VEHICLE SAFETY CHECKS

You will have to answer two vehicle safety check questions. The questions fall into three categories:

- identify
- tell me how you would check...
- show me how you would check...

The 'tell me' question will be asked before you start driving, while the 'show me' question will be asked while you're driving.

These questions are designed to make sure that you know how to check that your vehicle is safe to drive.

If you turn up for your test in an unsuitable vehicle, you will forfeit your test fee.

Although some checks may require you to identify where fluid levels should be checked you will not be asked to touch a hot engine or physically check fluid levels. You may refer to vehicle information systems (if fitted) when answering questions on fluid levels and tyre pressures.

All vehicles differ slightly so it is important that you get to know all the safety systems and engine layout in the vehicle in which you plan to take your practical test.

CHECKS AND OBSERVER ON THE TEST

Before you start the test, the examiner will check all of your documents and ask you to sign the marking sheet to declare that the car is insured and that you have lived in the UK for at least 185 days in the last 12 months. He or she will also ask if you would like your accompanying driver to accompany you on the test. This will mean that your accompanying driver (usually your driving instructor) would sit in the back of the car and observe. The accompanying driver would not be able to take part in the test or help you but will be in a better position to discuss the test afterwards and give advice.

ON THE PRACTICAL TEST

During the test you will be expected to drive for about 40 minutes along normal roads following the directions of the examiner. The roads are selected so as to provide a range of different conditions and road situations and a varied density of traffic.

Your examiner will select suitable areas for you to carry out the set exercises. They will tell you to pull up and stop, and will then explain the exercise to you before you do it:

- you may or may not be asked to perform an emergency stop
- you will be asked to perform one reversing exercise selected by the examiner from: reversing round a corner; reverse parking (behind a parked car, or into a marked bay); turning in the road.

The examiner will be assessing:

- whether you are competent at controlling the car
- whether you are making normal progress for the roads you are on
- how you react to any hazards that occur in the course of the test
- whether you are noticing all traffic signs and signals and road markings, and reacting to them in the correct manner.

To pass the driving test, you must:
- not commit any serious faults, and
- commit no more than 15 driving errors of a less serious nature.

If, during the test, you do not understand what the examiner says to you, ask them to repeat the instruction.

Once you have passed your test you will be driving independently without the help of someone giving you directions. This skill is examined during your practical test. In addition, the examiner will ask you to drive without junction-by-junction directions to assess if this skill has been learned. The examiner will continue to assess your driving skills but will not be assessing your ability to remember a route, so you can still ask the Examiner to confirm which direction you should be going in. Your driving instructor will help you to practise this skill.

If you are faced with an unusually difficult or hazardous situation in the course of your test that results in you making a driving fault, the examiner will take the circumstances into account when marking you on that part of the test.

HOW TO PREPARE FOR THE PRACTICAL TEST

Be sure that you are ready to take the test. This is where choosing a reliable qualified driving instructor is vital. You should feel confident:
- about driving in all conditions
- that you know *The Highway Code*
- that you can make decisions on your own about how to cope with hazards, without having to wait for your instructor to tell you what to do.

STAYING UP-TO-DATE

The government may change elements of the practical test from time to time. Your driving instructor or the Driver and Vehicle Standards Agency (DVSA) will be able to tell you if there has been a change.

FURTHER INFORMATION

For more practical information on learning to drive including the theory test, practical test and Pass Plus, visit www.gov.uk/browse/driving.

PART 2: UNDERSTANDING THE THEORY BEHIND THE TEST

Section 1
Alertness

The first section in the theory test revision questions is headed ALERTNESS. Alertness is a short section and is a good place to start.

- Alertness means being wide awake and concentrating on what you are doing – driving – not being distracted by mobile phones or loud music
- Alertness means looking out for hazards
- Alertness means noticing all road signs and road markings, and acting on the instructions and information they give

ARE YOU FIT TO DRIVE?

'Fit' can mean:
- Did you have any alcoholic drinks before you set out?
- Are you under the influence of illegal substances (drugs)?
- Are you feeling groggy or unwell?
- Are you taking prescription medicine that could affect your ability to control the car?
- Are you too tired to drive?

It's unwise to set out on a journey if you're not well, on the basis of 'I'll see how I go – I'll probably be all right':
- Your reactions are likely to be slower
- You may be unable to judge distances properly
- Your actions may be less well co-ordinated than usual and it's not legal

If you are tired, open the window for a few moments to let in some fresh air. If you drive when you are too tired, you risk falling asleep at the wheel – an all too common cause of serious accidents. Driving for long stretches on a motorway at night can be especially dangerous. If you sense that you are losing your concentration, then take a break at a motorway service station. Plan your journey ahead, giving yourself plenty of time for rest stops – at least every couple of hours.

TACKLING THE QUESTIONS

Look at the questions in the Alertness section.

You'll see that the Alertness questions are all about these:
- anticipation
- observation
- signalling
- reversing
- using your mirrors
- concentration
- getting distracted
- feeling sleepy
- using mobile phones

DID YOU KNOW?

The main causes of distraction are:
- Loud music in the car
- Passengers (usually children)
- Events happening outside (such as accidents)
- Using a mobile phone

Now test yourself on the questions on pages 54–60

Section 2

Attitude

The government road safety organisations believe that the ATTITUDE of learner drivers is extremely important for road safety.

ATTITUDE MEANS:
- Your frame of mind when you get in the car
- How you react when you meet hazards on the road
- How you behave towards other drivers

Attitude is a very important part of being a good driver. Your attitude when you are driving plays a big part in ensuring your safety and that of other road users.

Do you aim to be a careful and safe driver or a fast and skilful driver? If you don't want to end up as another road accident statistic, then carefully and safely is the way to go.

Remember that a car is not an offensive weapon, and often people don't realise what a potentially lethal machine they are in control of when they get behind the wheel. You only have to think about this to understand the importance of your attitude when driving.

You'll see that questions in this section are concerned with encouraging you to be a careful and safe driver, and cover:
- Tailgating
- Consideration for other road users, including pedestrians, buses, slow-moving vehicles and horse riders
- Driving at the right speed for the conditions

- When to flash headlights
- The right place, time and way to overtake

And remembering a few dos and don'ts will help you achieve the right attitude for driving and make passing this section of the test much easier.

GOOD DRIVERS DO:
- drive at the right speed for the road and traffic conditions
- observe speed limits
- overtake only when it is safe to do so
- park in correct and safe places
- wait patiently if the driver in front is a learner or elderly or hesitant
- look out for vulnerable road users such as cyclists, pedestrians and children
- concentrate on their driving at all times
- plan their journey so that they have plenty of time to get to their destination

GOOD DRIVERS DON'T:
- allow themselves to become involved in road rage
- break speed limits
- drive too fast, particularly in wet, foggy or icy weather
- accelerate or brake too harshly
- overtake and 'cut in', forcing others to brake sharply
- put pressure on other drivers by driving too close behind them (this is called 'tailgating'), flashing headlights or gesturing
- allow their attention to be distracted by passengers, mobile phones or loud music, or what is happening on the road, such as staring at an accident

TAILGATING

Driving excessively close behind another vehicle is known as tailgating – and it's dangerous! The car in front may stop suddenly (to avoid hitting a child or animal that has dashed out into the road, for example); when this happens the car following runs the risk of crashing into it.

You should always leave enough space between your vehicle and the one in front, so that you can stop safely if the driver in front suddenly slows down or stops.

Rear-end shunts account for a large percentage of all accidents on the road. In these situations, the driver of the car behind is almost always judged to be the guilty party.

So tailgating is potentially expensive as well as dangerous.

Another time when drivers are tempted to tailgate is when attempting to pass a large, slow-moving vehicle. However, keeping well back will improve your view of the road ahead, so that you're better able to judge when it's safe to overtake and the driver of the large vehicle will also be able to see you.

USEFUL TIP

If you are being followed too closely by another driver you should slow down and increase the distance between your vehicle and the one in front. If you slow down or have to stop suddenly, the driver behind may crash into you, but you will have increased your stopping distance and will not be pushed into the vehicle in front of you.

ALWAYS REMEMBER:

- Expect the unexpected, and make provision for the potential errors of other drivers – everyone makes mistakes sometimes.
- Don't create unnecessary stress for other drivers by showing your frustration in an aggressive manner.

If you are driving at the right speed for the road and weather conditions and a driver behind tries to overtake, you should pull back a bit from the vehicle in front so that if the driver behind insists on overtaking, there is less risk of an accident.

Do not try to stop the car behind from overtaking. Do not move into the middle of the road or move up close to the car in front. These actions could be very dangerous.

You should not give confusing signals such as indicating left or waving the other driver on.

Now test yourself on the questions on pages 61–70

Section 3

Safety and your vehicle

When you go through this section you will notice that the questions are a bit of a mixture. They cover a number of topics about SAFETY, including:

- Understanding the controls of your vehicle
- What the car's warning lights tell you
- Tyres – correct inflation, pressures and tread depths
- When to use hazard warning lights
- Passenger safety
- The environment
- Security and crime prevention

Many of the questions in this section are to do with 'legal requirements' and rules regarding parking your car and using lights. Look up all the sections in *The Highway Code* that deal with parking rules. Find out the rules for red routes, white lines and zigzag lines as well as yellow lines.

SEAT BELTS

If any of your passengers are young people under 14, you are responsible for making sure that they wear seat belts or are in the correct car seat. You are responsible for them by law, even if you are still a learner driver yourself.

TIPS FOR THIS SECTION

Learn *The Highway Code* and you will be able to answer most of the questions in this section. In particular make sure you know the rules regarding seat belts, tyres, and when to use your lights, including your hazard warning lights.

A CONFUSING QUESTION

One of the most confusing questions in this section asks what kind of driving results in high fuel consumption. The answer, of course, is bad driving – especially harsh braking and acceleration. This means you will use more fuel than you should and therefore cause more damage to the environment than is necessary.

BUT many people read the word 'high' as meaning 'good' – as in a level of driving skill – and so pick the wrong answer.

Don't let it be you...

Now test yourself on the questions on pages 71–89

Section 4

Safety margins

Experienced drivers are usually better than new or learner drivers at leaving good SAFETY MARGINS. Learner drivers find it harder to keep their vehicle at a safe distance from the one in front. Therefore the questions in this section cover:

- safe stopping distances

and

- safe separation distances (these are the same as safety margins)

WHAT IS A SAFETY MARGIN?

A safety margin is the space that you need to leave between your vehicle and the one in front so that you will not crash into it if it slows downs or stops suddenly. They are also called 'separation distances' and are an important part of anticipating road and traffic hazards. When you are learning to drive, you can feel pressured to speed up by drivers behind you.

Don't let other drivers make you cut down on your safety margins. Stay a safe distance behind the vehicle in front. Then you will have time to anticipate and react to hazards.

THE TWO-SECOND RULE

In traffic that's moving at normal speed, allow at least a two-second gap between you and the vehicle in front.

STOPPING DISTANCES

Many people who are taking their theory test get confused about this. You will notice that some of the questions ask for your overall stopping distance and others ask for your braking distance. These are different.

Overall stopping distance or stopping distance is not the same as braking distance. Stopping distance is made up of thinking distance + braking distance.

In other words, the time it takes to notice that there's a hazard ahead plus the time it takes to brake to deal with it.

THINKING DISTANCE

Thinking distance is sometimes called 'reaction time' or 'reaction distance'. If you are driving at 30mph, your thinking distance will be 30 feet (9 metres). That means your vehicle will travel 30 feet (9 metres) before you start braking.

THE LINK BETWEEN STOPPING DISTANCE AND SAFETY MARGINS

You should always leave enough space between your vehicle and the one in front. If the other driver has to slow down suddenly or stop without warning, you need to be able to stop safely. The space is your safety margin.

20 mph 6 metres + 6 metres
= 12 metres (40 feet) or 3 car lengths

30 mph 9 metres + 14 metres
= 23 metres (75 feet) or 6 car lengths

40 mph 12 metres + 24 metres
= 36 metres (118 feet) or 9 car lengths

50 mph 15 metres + 38 metres
= 53 metres (175 feet) or 13 car lengths

60 mph 18 metres + 55 metres
= 73 metres (240 feet) or 18 car lengths

70 mph 21 metres + 75 metres
= 96 metres (315 feet) or 24 car lengths

Thinking Distance

Braking Distance

SAFETY MARGINS FOR OTHER VEHICLES

Long vehicles and motorcycles need more room to stop – in other words, you must leave a bigger safety margin when following a long vehicle or motorbike. When driving behind a long vehicle, pull back to increase your separation distance and your safety margin so that you get a better view of the road ahead – there could be hazards developing and if you are too close he will be unable to see you in his rear view mirror. Strong winds can blow lorries and motorbikes off course. So leave a bigger safety margin.

DIFFERENT CONDITIONS AND SAFETY MARGINS

You may find that one or more questions in your theory test might be about driving in 'different conditions'. These questions aim to make sure you know what adjustments you should make to your driving when either road conditions are different from normal, for example, when parts of the road are closed off for roadworks, or weather conditions affect your driving.

Roadworks

You should always take extra care when you see a sign warning you that there are roadworks ahead. Remember, roadworks are a hazard and you have to anticipate them.

If you see the driver in front of you slowing down, take this as a sign that you should do the same – even if you can't see a hazard ahead. You still need to keep a safe distance from him. Harassing the driver in front by 'tailgating' is both wrong and dangerous and so is overtaking to fill the gap. It's especially important that you know what to do when you see a sign for roadworks ahead on a motorway.

- There may be a lower speed limit than normal – keep to it
- Use your mirrors and indicators, and get into the correct lane in plenty of time
- Don't overtake the queue and then force your way in at the last minute (this is an example of showing an inconsiderate attitude to other road users)

- Always keep a safe distance from the vehicle in front

Weather conditions

In bad weather (often called 'adverse' weather), you need to increase your safety margins.

When it's raining you need to leave at least twice as much distance between you and the vehicle in front. When there's ice on the road leave an even bigger gap because your stopping distance increases tenfold.

It's amazing how often drivers go too fast in bad weather. In adverse weather motorways have lower speed limits, but some drivers don't take any notice of them.

When it's icy you should multiply your two-second gap by ten.

QUESTIONS THAT LOOK ALIKE

There are a number of questions about anti-lock brakes in this section. Lots of questions look the same. Some are easy and some are hard. Some of them appear to be the same but they are not.

The questions test two things – your knowledge of the rules of the road and your understanding of words to do with driving.

Now test yourself on the questions on pages 90–98

Section 5
Hazard awareness

How often does a motorist protest that the accident happened before they had time to realise the person they hit was there? Some accidents will inevitably happen, but part of your instructor's job while teaching you to drive is to help you learn to anticipate problems before they happen.

WHAT IS THE DIFFERENCE BETWEEN HAZARD AWARENESS AND HAZARD PERCEPTION?

Hazard awareness and hazard perception mean the same thing

- Hazard Perception is the name for the part of the theory test that uses video clips. This test is about spotting developing hazards. One of the key skills of good driving, this is called 'anticipation'
- Anticipating hazards means looking out for them in advance and taking action immediately
- Hazard awareness is about being alert whenever you are driving

That is why some of the questions in the HAZARD AWARENESS section deal with things that might make you less alert. For example feeling tired, feeling ill, taking medicines prescribed by your doctor, drinking alcohol or taking illegal drugs.

Other questions in Hazard Awareness cover noticing road and traffic signs as well as road markings, what to do at traffic lights and when to slow down for hazards ahead.

WHY ARE YOUNG MALE DRIVERS MORE AT RISK?

New drivers have a greater than average chance of being involved in accidents. Statistics show that young male drivers have the most accidents.

- Maybe it's because when they first get their licence they want to show off to other drivers
- Some people think that driving much too fast will earn them 'respect' from their friends
- Some people think that they are such good drivers that the rules of the road should not apply to them

Whatever the reason – drivers who don't watch out for hazards are at risk of being involved in an accident. The problem has a lot to do with people's attitude to driving. You'll find more about this aspect of driving in the Attitude part of the theory test.

We've already said that young drivers often don't learn to anticipate hazards until they are older and more experienced. The Hazard Perception test aims to 'fill the gap' in hazard perception for young drivers and other new drivers by making sure they have some proper training to make up for their lack of experience.

This should make them safer drivers when they start out on the road alone.

LOOKING FOR CLUES TO HAZARDS DEVELOPING ON THE ROAD

As you get more driving experience you will start to learn about the times and places where you are most likely to meet hazards. Think about some of these examples.

Rush hour

You know that people take more risks when driving in the rush hour. Maybe they have to drop their children off at school before going to work. Maybe they are late for a business meeting. So you have to be prepared for bad driving, such as other drivers pulling out in front of you.

Dustbin day

Drivers in a hurry may get frustrated if they are held up in traffic because of a hazard such as a dustcart. They may accelerate and pull out to overtake even though they cannot see clearly ahead. You should not blindly follow the lead of another driver. Check for yourself that there are no hazards ahead.

School children

Young children are often not very good at judging how far away a car is from them, and may run into the road unexpectedly. Always be on the lookout for hazards near a school entrance.

Parked cars

Imagine you are driving on a quiet one-way street with cars parked down each side of the road. You wouldn't expect to meet any vehicles coming the other way – but what about children playing? They might run out into the road after a football. It would be difficult to see them because of the parked cars, until they were in the road in front of you.

MORE EXAMPLES OF HAZARDS

So, what kinds of hazards are we talking about? And what should you do about them?

Road markings and road signs sometimes highlight likely hazards for you.

The list below gives some of the hazards you should look out for when driving along a busy street in town.

After each hazard there are some ideas about what you should be looking out for, and what to do next.

- You see a bus which has stopped in a lay-by ahead
There may be some pedestrians hidden by the bus who are trying to cross the road, or the bus may signal to pull out. Be ready to slow down and stop.

- You see a white triangle painted on the road surface ahead
This is a hazard warning sign. It tells you that there is a 'Give Way' junction just ahead. Slow down and be ready to stop.

- You see a sign for a roundabout on the road ahead
Anticipate that other drivers may need to change lane, and be ready to leave them enough room.

- You come to some road works where the traffic is controlled by temporary traffic lights
Watch out for drivers speeding to get through before the lights change.

- You look in your rear view mirror and see an emergency vehicle with flashing lights coming up behind you
An emergency vehicle wants to pass, so get ready to pull over when it's safe.

- You see a small child standing with an adult near the edge of the pavement
Check if the child is safely holding the adult's hand. Be ready to stop safely if the child suddenly steps into the road.

- You notice dustbins or rubbish bags put out on the pavement
The dustcart could be around the next corner, or the bin men could be crossing the road with bags of rubbish. Be ready to slow down and stop if necessary.

- You hear a siren
Look all around to find out where the emergency vehicle is. You may have to pull over to let it pass.

You will find out more about the different types of hazards you may encounter, including what to look for when driving on narrow country roads, or in bad (adverse) weather conditions, in the Vehicle Handling section of this book.

ALWAYS EXPECT THE UNEXPECTED
Don't forget that not all hazards can be anticipated. There are bound to be some you haven't expected.

RED FLASHING WARNING LIGHTS
Level crossings, ambulance stations, fire stations and swing bridges all have red lights that flash on and off to warn you when you must stop.

OBSERVATION
Another word for taking in information through our eyes is 'observation'. Observation is one of the three key skills needed in hazard perception. The three skills are:
- observation
- anticipation
- planning

An easy way to remember this is **O A P**
Observe
Anticipate
Plan

TALK TO YOURSELF!
It's a good idea to 'talk to yourself' when you're learning to drive – and even after you've passed your test. Talk about all the things you see that could be potential hazards. Your driving instructor might suggest this as a way of making you concentrate and notice hazards ahead.

Even if you don't talk out loud, you can do a 'running commentary' in your head on everything you see around you as you drive.

For example, you might say to yourself – 'I am following a cyclist and the traffic lights ahead are red. *When the lights change I will allow him/her plenty of time and room to move off.'*
or
'The dual carriageway ahead is starting to look very busy. There is a sign showing that the right lane is closing in 800 yards. *I must get ready to check my mirrors and, if safe to do so, drop back to allow other vehicles to move into the left-hand lane ahead of me.'*

Note: Don't forget the mirrors! This way, you will notice more hazards, and you will learn to make more sense of the information that your eyes are taking in.

SCANNING THE ROAD

Learner drivers tend to look straight ahead of their car and may not notice all the hazards that might be building up on both sides. You will spot more hazards when driving if you train yourself to scan the road.

- Practise looking up and ahead as far as possible
- Use all your mirrors to look out for hazards too
- Don't forget that you have 'blind spots' when driving – work out where they are and find safe ways of checking all round for hazards
- Ask your driving instructor to help you with all of this

LEARN YOUR ROAD SIGNS!
Notice the information at the bottom of the first page of traffic signs in *The Highway Code*. It explains that you won't find every road sign shown here.

You can buy a copy of *Know Your Road Signs* from a bookshop to see some of the extra signs that are not in *The Highway Code*.

Note: In Wales, some road signs include the Welsh spelling as well as the English, and in Scotland some signs are written using Gaelic spelling. You'll also see some 'old-style' road signs around, which are slightly different too.

How is learning to scan the road going to help me pass my theory test?
- The idea of the hazard perception element of the test is to encourage you to get some real experience of driving before you take the theory test
- If you meet real hazards on the road and learn how to anticipate them, you'll learn how to pass the hazard perception element of the test
- In the video test you may not be able to look all around you as you would when driving a car; but the clips will be as realistic as possible in giving you a wide 'view' of the road ahead

OBSERVATION QUESTIONS
Study some of the pictures in the Hazard Awareness section.

They include photographs of scenes such as:

- a cyclist at traffic lights, seen from the viewpoint of a driver in a car behind the cyclist

- what you see as a driver when you are approaching a level crossing

- what you see when coming up to a 'blind bend'

- a view of the road ahead with traffic building up where one lane is closing

Look out for situations like these when you are out driving with your instructor, and use the practice to improve your hazard awareness.

As well as photographs, there are pictures of road and traffic signs.

WHAT DO THESE SIGNS MEAN?
What actions should you take when you see these signs?

- If you are not sure, look them up in *The Highway Code*

- Think about why the square yellow sign with the two children is in the Vehicle Markings section and not with the rest of the road signs

> **Now test yourself on the questions on pages 99–120**

Section 6

Vulnerable road users

Today's new vehicles are becoming safer all the time for the driver inside the car, but sadly this is not always the case for the pedestrian or cyclist outside. Many road users who are not driving cars have nothing to protect them if they are in an accident with a motor vehicle.

The questions in the VULNERABLE ROAD USERS section deal with the following:
- why different types of road users are vulnerable
- what you as a driver must do to keep them safe

WHO ARE VULNERABLE ROAD USERS?

You must drive with extra care when you are near the following vulnerable road users:
- pedestrians
- children
- older people
- people with disabilities
- cyclists
- motorcycle riders
- horse riders
- learner drivers, new drivers and older drivers
- animals being herded along the road

CYCLISTS

Give cyclists plenty of room. Remember to keep well back from cyclists when you are coming up to a junction or a roundabout because you cannot be sure what they are going to do. On the roundabout they may go in any direction – left, right or straight ahead. They are allowed to stay in the left lane and signal right if they are going to continue round. Leave them enough room to cross in front of you if they need to. Turn to the section headed Vulnerable Road Users in the theory test questions to see some pictures of this. You must also give way to cyclists at toucan crossings and in cycle lanes (see the rules for cyclists set out in *The Highway Code*).

Look out for cyclists!
- It can be hard to see cyclists in busy town traffic
- It can also be hard to see them coming when you are waiting to turn out at a junction. They can be hidden by other vehicles

Always be on the lookout for cyclists.

Especially, check your mirror to make sure you do not trap a cyclist on your left when you are turning left into a side road. Check your blind spots for cyclists, too.

Controlling your vehicle near cyclists

When you are following a cyclist, you must be able to drive as slowly as they do, and keep your vehicle under control. Only overtake when you can allow them plenty of room, and it is safe to do so.

CYCLE LANES

Cycle lanes are reserved for cyclists and car drivers should not use them. A cycle lane is marked by a white line on the road. A solid white line means you must not drive or park in the cycle lane during the hours it is in use. A broken white line means that you should drive or park in it only if there is no alternative. You should not park there at any time when there are waiting restrictions.

When you overtake a cyclist, a motorcyclist or a horse rider, give them at least as much room as you would give a car.

Cyclists and motorcycle riders

Cyclists and motorcycle riders are more at risk than car drivers because
- they are more affected by strong winds, or by turbulence caused by other vehicles
- they are more affected by an uneven road surface, and they may have to move out suddenly to avoid a pothole
- car drivers often cannot see them

PEDESTRIANS

Pedestrians most at risk include older people and children. Older people and others who cannot move easily may be slower to cross roads – you must give them plenty of time. Children don't have a sense of danger on the road; they can't tell how close a car is, or how fast it is going. They may run out into the road without looking. Or they may step out behind you when you are reversing – you may not see them because they are small.

People who are unable to see and/or hear

A person who is blind will usually carry a white stick to alert you to their presence. If the stick has a red band, this means that the person is also deaf, so will have no warning of an approaching car either visually or from engine noise.

When to give way to pedestrians

At any pedestrian crossing, if a pedestrian has started to cross, wait until they have reached the other side. Do not harass them by revving your engine or edging forward.

At a crossing with lights (pelican, toucan or puffin crossings), pedestrians have priority once they have started to cross even if, when on a pelican crossing, the amber lights start flashing.

Once a pedestrian has stepped on to a zebra crossing, you must stop and wait for them to cross.

Note: It is courteous to stop at a zebra crossing if a pedestrian is waiting to cross.

Vulnerable road users

When you take your practical driving test, you must stop for any pedestrians who are waiting on the pavement at a zebra crossing even if they haven't stepped on to the crossing yet. However, you must not wave to them to cross.

If you want to turn left into a side road, and there are people crossing or waiting to cross, then you should give way until they finish crossing. People on foot have priority over car drivers.

DID YOU KNOW?
If a car hits a pedestrian at 40mph, the pedestrian will probably be killed. Even at 35mph, 50% of pedestrians hit by cars will be killed.

At 20mph, pedestrians have a better chance of surviving. This is why you will find 20mph limits and other things to slow traffic in some residential streets and near school entrances.

OTHER TYPES OF VULNERABLE ROAD USERS
Be prepared to slow down for animals, learner drivers, and other more unusual hazards such as people walking along the road in organised groups or parades (for example, on a demonstration, or a sponsored walk). There are rules in *The Highway Code* that walkers must follow. But even if they break the rules, make sure you keep to them.

Animals
Drive slowly past horses or other animals. Allow them plenty of space on the road. Don't frighten them by sounding your horn or revving your engine.

If you see a flock of sheep or a herd of cattle blocking the road, you must:
- stop
- switch off your engine
- and wait until they have left the road

People riding horses on the road are often children, so you need to take extra care; when you see two riders abreast, it may well be that the one on the outside is shielding a less experienced rider.

TRAFFIC SIGNS
Look up the Traffic Signs and Vehicle Markings sections in *The Highway Code* and find the following signs:
- pedestrians walking in the road ahead (no pavement)
- cycle lane and pedestrian route
- advance warning of school crossing patrol ahead
- school crossing patrol
- frail or disabled people crossing
- sign on back of school bus or coach

Now test yourself on the questions on pages 121–139

Section 7

Other types of vehicle

We have already come across some of the other types of vehicle that share the road with you and your car including motorbikes and bicycles. The questions in this part of the theory test are mostly about long vehicles such as lorries. However, you also need to know what to do about:

- buses
- caravans
- trams
- tractors and other farm vehicles
- special vehicles for disabled drivers (powered invalid carriages)
- slow vehicles such as road gritters
- motorway repair vehicles

Important points to remember about these types of vehicle:

- Many of them can only move very slowly
- They cannot easily stop or change direction
- The driver's field of vision may be restricted – this means that car drivers have to allow them plenty of room

MOTORCYCLES

- Motorcycles are easily blown off course by strong winds. If you see a motorcyclist overtaking a high-sided vehicle such as a lorry, keep well back. The lorry may shield the motorcyclist from the wind as it is overtaking, but then a sudden gust could blow the motorcyclist off-course
- It can be hard to see a motorcyclist when you are waiting at a junction. Always look out for them

- If you see a motorcyclist looking over their shoulder, it could mean that they will soon give a signal to turn right. This applies to cyclists too. Keep back to give them plenty of room
- Motorcyclists and cyclists sometimes have to swerve to avoid hazards such as bumps in the road, patches of ice and drain covers. As before – give them plenty of room

LONG VEHICLES

- Like cyclists, long vehicles coming up to roundabouts may stay in the left lane even if they intend to turn right. This is because they need lots of room to manoeuvre. Keep well back so they have room to turn
- Take great care when overtaking long or high-sided vehicles. Before you pull out to overtake, make sure you have a clear view of the road ahead
- A long vehicle that needs to turn left off a major road into a minor road may prepare to do so by moving out towards the centre of the road, or by moving across to the other side

If you're following them:

- Give way, and don't try to overtake – on the right or the left
- You might need to slow down and stop while the driver of the long vehicle makes the turn

BUSES AND TRAMS

- Always give way to buses when they signal to pull out
- Always give way to trams as they cannot steer to avoid you
- Don't try to overtake a tram

Trams are **quiet** vehicles – you cannot rely on approaching engine noise to warn you that a tram is coming.

 Take extra care when you see this sign, because trams are sometimes allowed to go when car drivers are not.

TRACTORS AND SLOW-MOVING VEHICLES

- Always be patient if you are following a slow vehicle

Drivers of slow vehicles will usually try to find a safe place to pull in to let the traffic go past. In the meantime you should keep well back, so that you can see the road ahead. Allow a safe distance in case they slow down or stop.

Slow vehicles are not allowed on motorways because they cannot keep up with the fast-moving traffic. Vehicles not allowed on motorways include:

- motorcycles under 50cc
- bicycles
- tractors and other farm vehicles
- powered invalid carriages

Now test yourself on the questions on pages 140–145

Section 8
Vehicle handling

The questions in this section test how much you know about controlling your vehicle on different road surfaces and in different weather.

Your control is affected by:
- the road surface – is it rough or smooth? Are there any holes or bumps? Are there any 'traffic-calming' measures, such as humps or chicanes?
- the weather conditions – you have to drive in different ways when there is fog, snow, ice or heavy rain

Other questions in this section cover driving on country roads – on narrow and one-way roads, humpback bridges, steep hills, fords. Other questions need practical knowledge, for example, on engine braking, brake fade, and coasting your vehicle – use the Glossary.

This section also has some questions on overtaking and parking.

ROAD SURFACE

The condition of the road surface can affect the way your vehicle handles. Your vehicle handles better on a smooth surface than on a surface that is damaged, bumpy or full of holes. If you have to drive on an uneven surface, keep your speed down so that you have full control of your vehicle, even if your steering wheel is jolted.

Take care also where there are tramlines on the road. The layout of the road affects the way your vehicle handles.

You may have to adjust your driving for traffic-calming measures, such as traffic humps (sometimes called 'sleeping policemen') and chicanes. These are double bends that have been put into the road layout to slow the traffic down. The sign before the chicane tells you who has priority.

Traffic calming measures are often used in residential areas or near school entrances to make it safer for pedestrians.

WEATHER CONDITIONS

Bad weather (adverse weather) such as heavy rain, ice or snow affects the way your vehicle handles. If you drive too fast in adverse weather, your tyres may lose their grip on the road when you try to brake. This means the car may skid or 'aquaplane'. Aquaplaning means sliding out of control on a wet surface.

Driving in snow

In snow, the best advice is do not drive at all unless you really have to make a journey. If you have to drive in snowy conditions, leave extra time for your journey and keep to the main roads. You can fit snow chains to your tyres to increase their grip in deep snow.

Driving in fog

In fog your field of vision can be down to a few metres. Your vehicle is fitted with fog lights to help you see and be seen in fog. But you must know how and when to use them. Look up the three rules about fog lights in *The Highway Code*. You'll see that the key points to remember are:

* Don't dazzle other road users with your fog lights

* Switch them off as soon as you can see better (as soon as the fog starts to clear)

> **REMEMBER THE TWO-SECOND RULE**
> You should double the two-second gap to four seconds when driving in rain, and increase the gap by as much as ten times when there is ice on the road.

COUNTRY DRIVING

If you have had most of your driving lessons in a town, you need to know how to drive on narrow country roads. Some are only wide enough for one vehicle ('single-track'), and some are on very steep hills.

Your control of the gears, clutch and brakes will be important if you have to follow a tractor very slowly up a hill. On a steep downward slope you have to make sure your vehicle does not 'run away'.

On country roads you might find humpback bridges and fords. The signs below warn you of these hazards.

* Find out what you must do first after you have driven through a ford

TECHNICAL KNOWLEDGE

We have already mentioned engine braking. Understanding how engine braking works is part of good vehicle handling.

Note: If you press the footbrake constantly on a long hill, you may get 'brake fade'. If you're not sure, check what that means in the Glossary near the back of this book.

Use the gears to control your vehicle on a downhill slope (or 'gradient'). If you put the vehicle in 'neutral', or drive with the clutch down (called 'coasting'), your vehicle will increase speed beyond what is safe and will not be under proper control.

This sign warns you of a steep hill downwards.

- Travelling in neutral for long distances (known as coasting) is wrong and dangerous – you should not be tempted to do it and it doesn't save fuel

Remember that if there is sudden heavy rain after a dry hot spell, the road surface can get very slippery.

Now test yourself on the questions on pages 146–157

Section 9
Motorway rules

Learner drivers are only allowed on motorways at the discretion – and under the supervision – of an Approved Driving Instructor, so you might not experience driving on them until after you've passed your test. However, you do need to know all about MOTORWAY RULES before taking your practical test, and your theory test will most likely include a question about motorways.

As soon as you pass your driving test you will be legally allowed to drive on motorways. You need to know all the motorway rules in advance, so that you are confident and ready to cope with motorway driving when you pass your test.

There are some major roads and dual carriageways that learners can drive on which are very much like motorways. You may drive on some of these fast roads during your driving test, so that your examiner can see how well you cope with hazards at higher speeds.

When driving on these fast roads you will need some of the very same skills that you will need for motorway driving – for example, using lanes properly, knowing when it is safe to overtake, and controlling your vehicle at speed.

If you don't have a lesson on motorway driving with your ADI before taking your practical test, it makes sense to arrange one after you have passed before driving on a motorway alone for the first time.

MOTORWAYS AND OTHER ROADS

- On a motorway traffic is moving at high speed all the time
- All lanes are in use
- No stopping is allowed on a motorway – traffic only slows or comes to a stop because of accidents or other types of hold-up
- Some road users are not allowed on motorways. These include:
  - pedestrians, cyclists and learner drivers not accompanied by an ADI in a car with dual controls
  - horses and other animals
  - motorcycles under 50cc
  - slow-moving vehicles, tractors and farm vehicles and invalid carriages
- You always enter and leave a motorway on the left, via a slip road
- To the left of the inside lane (left hand lane) on a motorway is the hard shoulder. You can only drive on this in an emergency
- Special signs and signals are used on motorways. These include signs above the road on overhead gantries, signs on the central reservation, and amber and red flashing lights

CHECKS BEFORE YOUR JOURNEY

Be extra careful about doing all your regular checks before you set out on a motorway journey. You cannot stop on the motorway to fix small problems, and no one wants to break down in the middle of fast traffic.

Always check:
- oil and coolant levels, screen wash container
- tyres and tyre pressure
- fuel gauge
- that the horn works

- that all mirrors and windows are free of dirt and grease

Many of these checks are legally necessary, as well as important for your safety.

HOW TO MOVE ON TO A MOTORWAY

- Join the motorway by building up your speed on the slip road to match the speed of traffic in the left lane of the motorway
- Use MSM (Mirrors – Signal – Manoeuvre) and move into the flow of traffic when it is safe to do so

CHANGING LANES AND OVERTAKING

Driving on a motorway needs all the skills you have learned about anticipation and forward planning.

You should:
- make good use of all mirrors, and check your blind spots
- signal to move out in plenty of time
- look out for hazards ahead in the lane you want to move to
- not go ahead if it will force another vehicle to brake or swerve
- keep a safe distance from the vehicle in front

TAKE A BREAK

When you drive on motorways you will sometimes see signs that say 'Tiredness can kill – take a break!' This is very good advice. Motorways are monotonous – boring to drive, with long stretches of road that look the same for miles. A major cause of accidents is drivers falling asleep at the wheel. Plan your journey so that you have time to get out, stretch your legs and have a drink or snack.

THE RULES YOU NEED TO KNOW:

- Keep to the left-hand lane unless you are overtaking and move back to the left lane as soon as it is safe to do so. Sometimes you need to stay in the centre lane for a time – for example, when a line of lorries is travelling up a hill in the left lane. Stay in the centre lane until you have passed the hazard, then signal left and return to the left lane
- NEVER reverse, park, walk or drive in the wrong direction on a motorway
- Don't exceed the speed limit. This is normally 70mph, but lower speed limits may be signed when the road is busy, or in bad weather
- Keep to the correct separation distance (see Safety Margins)
- Don't overtake on the left. If traffic is moving slowly in all three lanes you may find that the lane on the left is moving faster than the one to its right for a short time. Or the left lane may be signed for traffic turning off at the next junction only. But these are exceptions to the rule
- If luggage falls from your vehicle, do not get out to pick it up. Stop at the next emergency phone and tell the Highways Agency or the police. Posts on the edge of the motorway show the way to the nearest emergency phone. You should use these phones rather than your mobile phone, because the emergency phone connects directly to the Highways Agency or the police and tells them exactly where you are calling from on the motorway
- Don't stop on the hard shoulder except in an emergency. The hard shoulder is an extremely dangerous place, as many as one in eight road deaths happen there.

TRAFFIC SIGNS AND ROAD MARKINGS

Light signals

In *The Highway Code* you'll find the light signals only seen on motorways. Signs above the roadway or on the central reservation are activated as needed to warn of accidents, lane closures or weather conditions. Overhead gantries display arrows or red crosses showing which lanes are open or closed to traffic and which lanes to move to when motorways merge or diverge. They may also show temporary speed limits.

Direction signs

Direction signs on motorways are blue and those on other major roads are green – other direction signs are white with black print.

Reflective studs or 'cat's eyes'

It's useful to know the colours of studs on a motorway; this can help in working out which part of the road you're on if it's dark or foggy. White studs mark lanes or the centre of the road and red studs mark the left edge of the carriageway. Amber studs are used alongside the central reservation and green studs mark the entry to a slip road.

Note: These markings are also found on some dual carriageways.

USING THE HARD SHOULDER IN AN EMERGENCY
Light signals

- Stop as far to the left as possible and, if you can, near an emergency phone
- Emergency phones are situated 1 mile apart and have blue and white marker posts every 100 metres. An arrow on the posts points the direction of the nearest phone
- If you are using a mobile phone you can identify your location from the number on the post, or from a nearby blue 'driver location sign'
- Switch on your hazard warning lights
- Use the left-hand door to get out of the vehicle, and make sure your passengers do too This is also known as a 'Dutch reach'.
- Get everyone away from the road – if possible, behind the barrier or up the bank
- Leave animals in the vehicle unless they aren't safe there

Phone the Highways Agency or the police with full details of where you are, then go back and wait in a safe place near your vehicle

Now test yourself on the questions on pages 158–174

Section 10
Rules of the road

'Rules of the Road' is a good way to describe what is in *The Highway Code*.

The questions that come under this heading in the theory test include several on road signs and road markings. There are many more road sign questions in the section on Road and Traffic Signs. Several of the topics listed in this section have already come up.

Other questions in this section cover:
- speed limits
- overtaking
- parking
- lanes and roundabouts
- clearways
- box junctions
- crossroads
- pedestrian crossings
- towing caravans and trailers

SPEED LIMITS
Driving too fast for the road, traffic or weather conditions causes accidents. Make sure that you keep below the speed limit shown on the signs for the road that you are on.

| 30mph in a built-up area | 50mph on a long, twisty country road | or as low as 20mph in a residential area with speed humps or traffic-calming measures |

The national speed limit for cars on a dual carriageway is 70mph. This is also the maximum speed for motorway driving.

National speed limit
When you leave a built-up area you will usually see this sign.

- This sign tells you that the national speed limit for this type of road applies here
- The national speed limit for cars on a normal road (single carriageway outside a built-up area) is 60mph. So on this road you must drive below 60mph even if it is straight and empty

Street lights usually mean that a 30mph limit applies, unless there are signs showing other limits.

The right speed for the conditions

If it is raining, there is snow and ice on the road, or there is a high wind, you will have to drive more slowly than the maximum speed limit. This will keep you and other road users safe.

- Remember – you have to double the time you allow for stopping and braking in wet weather. Allow even more time in snow and ice
- You need to be extra careful when driving in fog

The right speed for your vehicle

Some other vehicles have lower speed limits than cars. You can find out more about speed limits from the table in *The Highway Code*.

PARKING RULES

There are some general rules about parking that all drivers should know:
- Whenever you can, you should use off-street car parks, or parking bays. These are marked out with white lines on the road
- Never park where your vehicle could be a danger to other road users

Look for special signs that tell you that you cannot park there at certain times of the day or that only certain people may park in that place. Examples include signs showing bus lanes, cycle lanes, residents' parking zones and roads edged with red or yellow lines.

Blue badges are given to people with disabilities. Do not park in a space reserved for a driver with a disability, even if that is the only place left to park. A driver with a disability may need to park there. You will break the law if you park in that space.

Parking at night

- If you park at night on a road that has a speed limit higher than 30mph, you must switch on your parking lights. You must switch on your parking lights even if you have parked in a lay-by on this type of road
- When parking at night, always park facing in the same direction as the traffic flow
- If your vehicle has a trailer, you must switch on parking lights, even if the road has a 30mph speed limit

Where not to park

You are not permitted to park:

- on the pavement
- at a bus stop
- in front of someone's drive
- opposite a traffic island
- near a school entrance
- on a pedestrian crossing (or inside the zigzag lines either side of it)
- near a junction
- on a clearway
- on a motorway

Now test yourself on the questions on pages 175–192

Section 11
Road and traffic signs

When you look up the chapter on ROAD AND TRAFFIC SIGNS in the theory test questions you will see that it takes up a lot of pages. This is because most of the questions have a picture of a road sign or marking. You will also see that a lot of questions ask 'What does this sign mean?'

But however differently the questions are worded, it all comes down to how well you know *The Highway Code*. You can try to learn as much of *The Highway Code* as possible, but there are other ways you can get to know the road signs.

As you walk or drive around, look at the road signs you see in the street, and the different markings painted on the road surface.

ON FOOT

Look at the signs and signals that all road users must obey, whether they are in a car or walking. For example, when you use a pedestrian crossing, check what kind of crossing it is (such as a pelican, toucan or zebra crossing).

CHECK WHETHER YOU KNOW THE FOLLOWING:

- What are the rules for pedestrians and drivers coming up to the crossing?
- What kinds of crossings are controlled by traffic lights?
- What is different about a zebra crossing?

DURING YOUR DRIVING LESSONS

If you are having a driving lesson look well ahead so that you see all the signs that tell you what to do next. Obey them in good time.

DURING YOUR TEST

When you take your test the examiner will tell you when to move off, when to make a turn and when to carry out one of the set manoeuvres. The examiner will expect you to watch out for lane markings on the road, and signs giving directions, and to decide how to react to these yourself.

SIGNS

If you see several signs all on the same post, it can be confusing. The general rule is to start at the top and read down the post. The sign at the top tells you about the first hazard you have to look out for.

If you are a passenger in a car on a motorway, look at the motorway signs, because you need to know them, even though you can't drive on a motorway yet yourself.

Check that you can answer the following:
- What colour are the signs at the side of the motorway?
- What do the light signals above the road tell you?
- What signs tell you that you are coming to an exit?

Shapes of signs

Road and traffic signs come in three main shapes. Get to know them. You must learn what the signs mean.

Circles
Signs in circles tell you to do (blue) or not do (red) something – they give orders.

Triangles
Signs in triangles tell you of a hazard ahead – they give warnings.

Rectangles
Signs in rectangles tell you about where you are or where you are going – they give information.

There is only one sign which is octagonal – that is, it has eight sides. This is the sign for STOP. The eight-sided shape makes the sign stand out.

Now test yourself on the questions on pages 193–229

Section 12

Documents

This is quite a short section in the theory test. It is also different from the other sections, because it does not deal with either your driving skills or knowledge of *The Highway Code*.

It covers all the paperwork and the laws that you need to know about when you start learning to drive.

In this section there are questions about:
- driving licences
- insurance
- MOT certificate
- Vehicle Excise Duty (road tax)
- Vehicle Registration Document (log book)

This section also covers who can supervise a learner driver and changes you must tell the licensing authority about.

DRIVING LICENCE

If you are learning to drive, you'll need a provisional licence.
- You must have a valid licence to drive legally
- The driving licence consists of a photocard (see example, above) – keep it with you at all times
- Your signature appears on the licence
- Take good care of your provisional licence. If you lose it, you can get another one but you will have to pay a fee, and wait for the new licence to come before you can drive again
- When you pass your test you can apply for a full licence

INSURANCE

You must have a valid insurance certificate that covers you at least for third party liability. If you are learning with a driving school, you are covered by their insurance while you are in the driving school car. When you are in your own or anybody else's car, you must have insurance. Third party insurance cover usually comes as 'Third Party, Fire and Theft'. It is a basic insurance policy that will pay for repairs to another person's car and allows you to claim on the other driver's insurance if you are in an accident that was not your fault. If you have comprehensive insurance, the policy will pay for repairs to your vehicle even when the accident was your fault.

MOT CERTIFICATE

Cars and motorcycles must have their first MOT test three years (four years in Northern Ireland) after they are new and first registered. After that, they must have an MOT test every year.

The MOT test checks that your vehicle:
- is roadworthy – that is, all the parts work properly and the vehicle is safe to drive
- keeps to the legal limits for exhaust emissions – that is, the level of poisons in the gas that comes from the exhaust of your vehicle

If your vehicle is more than three years old you must not drive it without a valid MOT certificate – unless you are on your way to get an MOT and you have booked it in advance.

VEHICLE EXCISE DUTY

Vehicle Excise Duty is the tax that the government charges you to drive your vehicle on the roads. It is also sometimes called 'road tax'.

To drive or keep a vehicle on the road you must pay vehicle tax. The DVLA will send you a reminder when your tax is due to expire. When you buy a vehicle, any existing tax cannot be transferred with the vehicle.

Your vehicle must have valid insurance cover before you can tax it. If required, it will also need to have a valid MOT certificate. You can tax your vehicle online, by phone or at certain post offices.

If you want to keep a vehicle off the public road you must inform the DVLA by completing a Statutory Off Road Notification (SORN). It is an offence not to do so. You then won't have to pay Vehicle Excise Duty. The SORN is valid until your vehicle is taxed, sold or scrapped.

VEHICLE REGISTRATION CERTIFICATE

The Vehicle Registration Certificate (also known as a V5C) has all the important details about you and your vehicle, such as the make and model of the vehicle. It also has your name and address as the registered keeper of the vehicle. It is a record of the vehicle's history and is sometimes called 'the log book'.

DVLA

The Driver and Vehicle Licensing Agency is known as the DVLA. You must tell the DVLA if you are going to keep your car off road and are not renewing your Vehicle Excise Duty, when you buy or sell a car and if you change your name or your address.

This is because your details go on to the Vehicle Registration Certificate and you are legally responsible for the vehicle (car tax, parking fines, etc) until you have notified the DVLA that it is off road or you have sold it.

SUPERVISING A LEARNER DRIVER

As a learner driver you cannot drive on your own. If you are not with your driving instructor, you must be supervised by a person who is at least 21 years old, has a full licence for the kind of car you drive and has had that licence for at least three years. Note that if a person has a licence to drive an automatic car only, they cannot supervise a learner in a manual car.

Now test yourself on the questions on pages 230–237

Section 13

Incidents, accidents and emergencies

Most of the questions in this section are about helping anyone who is hurt in a road accident. Some people think they might do more harm than good if they try to help. But if you have a basic knowledge of first aid you won't panic and if you are first on the scene at an accident, you could even save a life. Look up 'First Aid on the road' in *The Highway Code.*

The theory test questions in this section cover:

- what to do when warning lights come on in your vehicle
- what to do if you break down
- safety equipment to carry with you
- when to use hazard warning lights
- what to do – and what not to do – at the scene of an accident
- what to do in tunnels

BASIC FIRST AID

What to do at an accident scene:

- Check that you are not putting yourself in danger before you go to help somebody else. You may need to warn other drivers of the accident
- Check all vehicle engines are switched off
- Make sure no one is smoking
- Move people who are not injured to a safe place. If the accident has happened on a motorway, if possible get uninjured people away from the hard shoulder, behind the barrier or on to the bank
- Call the emergency services. You will need to tell them exactly where you

are, and how many vehicles are involved in the accident. On motorways, use the emergency phone which connects directly to the Highways Agency or the police and tells them exactly where you are

- Do not move injured people – unless there is a risk of fire or of an explosion
- Give essential first aid to injured people (see Annexe 7 of *The Highway Code*)
- Stay there until the emergency services arrive

Other ways to help:

- Do speak in a calm way to the injured person
- Do try to keep them warm and as comfortable as possible
- Do not give them anything to drink
- Do not give them a cigarette
- Don't let injured people wander into the road

ADVICE ON SAFETY IF YOU BREAK DOWN

If you are on a non-motorway road:

- Try to get your vehicle off the main road. At least, get it right to the side of the road or on to the verge
- If the vehicle is in a place where it might be hit by another vehicle, get any passengers out and to a safer place
- Switch on the hazard warning lights to warn other drivers
- If you have a red warning triangle, place it at least 45 metres behind your car to warn other traffic (but don't use it on a motorway)
- If you are a member of a motoring organisation, call them and tell them where you are and what has happened. Wait with your vehicle until the patrol arrives

If you are on a motorway:

- If possible, leave the motorway at the next exit. If you can't get that far, drive on to the hard shoulder. Stop far over to the left, and switch on your hazard warning lights
- Get everyone out of the vehicle, using the nearside doors (but leave pets in the vehicle). Get them to sit on the bank, well away from the traffic
- Use the nearest orange emergency phone to call the emergency services and tell them where you are and what has happened (for your safety, face the oncoming traffic while you are on the phone)
- Go back to your vehicle and wait on the bank near by until help arrives
- Do not cross the motorway on foot or try to do repairs yourself – even changing a wheel. This is too dangerous on a motorway

DID YOU KNOW?

Before driving into a tunnel you should tune into a local radio station and listen to the traffic reports in case there are any accidents or problems in the tunnel.

Now test yourself on the questions on pages 238–250

Section 14

Vehicle loading

This last section, called VEHICLE LOADING, is the shortest of all. It covers a mixture of the following:

- how to load your vehicle safely
- using a roof rack
- towing caravans and trailers
- child restraints and safety locks

When you have passed your test you can tow a trailer, if the combined weight of the vehicle and trailer is less than 3,500kg. So you need to know the rules about towing.

TOWING

When you get your first full driving licence, check it to see how much you are allowed to tow. Do not tow any trailer that comes to more than that weight. The weight of a trailer should be no more than 85% of the weight of the car that is to pull it. But it is best to stay well below that top weight, because towing a trailer will affect the way your vehicle handles. When you are towing, you need to allow more room when overtaking and more time to brake and stop.

When towing a heavy load, you might need to blow your tyres up to more than the normal pressures. Check your vehicle's handbook for advice. Remember to change back to the normal tyre pressures when you finish your journey.

When you are turning at a roundabout or junction you will need to think about where you are on the road.

ROOF RACKS

If you attach a roof rack to your car, it will make a difference to the way in which your vehicle handles. Any load that is carried on a roof rack must be tied down securely.

- The roof rack makes your vehicle taller, so more vulnerable to strong winds
- You will increase your fuel consumption
- You need to change the way you drive to allow for the extra weight

To find out more, look up the parts of *The Highway Code* that deal with 'Loads and Towing'.

LOADING A TRAILER

If the weight of the load is arranged properly, this should cut down the risk of losing control, swerving and snaking.

- Try to spread the weight evenly when you load your trailer. Do not put more weight towards the front, or the back, or to one side
- It is against the law to have a load that is sticking out in a dangerous way
- Don't forget that if you park a vehicle with a trailer overnight, it must have lights

A vehicle towing a trailer:
- must not go over a maximum speed limit of 60mph
- must not use the right (outside) lane on a motorway

If you are going to buy a trailer, make sure it fits your car's tow bar. Tow bars must keep to EU regulations, and must have electric sockets to connect to the lights on the trailer.

SNAKING

'Snaking' means moving from side to side. A caravan will snake if it is not properly attached or loaded, or if the car pulling it is going too fast.

If you are towing a caravan or trailer and it starts to snake:
- slow down – stop pressing the accelerator (do not brake suddenly)
- get back in control of the steering
- then brake gently

YOU ARE RESPONSIBLE FOR PASSENGERS IN YOUR VEHICLE

There are also questions in the Vehicle Loading section about the safety of passengers. As the driver, you are responsible for making sure your vehicle is not overloaded – and this applies to people and animals as well as to luggage. Remember that all passengers must wear a seat belt (unless they have a medical certificate saying they should not wear one) and that all children under the age of 14 must wear a seat belt or be strapped into a child seat or other 'restraint' suitable for their age. (See the section on 'Child Restraints' in *The Highway Code*).

Children

Children must not sit in the space behind the back seat of a hatchback car, and no passengers should sit in a caravan while it is being towed.

Pets

Pets should be kept under careful control. You might keep them and you safe with a special harness, or if they are kept behind a screen in a hatchback which would stop them being thrown forward in the event of an accident.

Now test yourself on the questions on pages 251–254

PART 3: THEORY TEST REVISION QUESTIONS

1 Mark *one* answer
What should you do before making a U-turn?

☐ **A** Give an arm signal as well as using your indicators
☐ **B** Check road markings to see that U-turns are permitted
☐ **C** Look over your shoulder for a final check
☐ **D** Select a higher gear than normal

If you have to make a U-turn, slow down and ensure that the road is clear in both directions. Make sure that the road is wide enough for you to carry out the manoeuvre safely. Use your mirrors and look round to check it's safe before turning across the road.

2 Mark *one* answer
What should you do as you approach this bridge?

☐ **A** Move to the right
☐ **B** Slow down
☐ **C** Change gear
☐ **D** Keep to 30 mph

You should slow down and be cautious. Hump bridges are often narrow and there may not be enough room for you to pass an oncoming vehicle at this point. Also, there's no footpath, so be aware of pedestrians in the road.

3 Mark *one* answer
Where should you avoid overtaking?

☐ **A** Just after a bend
☐ **B** In a one-way street
☐ **C** On a 30 mph road
☐ **D** Approaching a dip in the road

Oncoming vehicles or other hazards can be hidden from view by dips in the road. If you can't see into the dip, wait until you have a clear view and can see that it's safe before starting to overtake.

4 Mark *one* answer
What does this curved arrow road marking mean?

☐ **A** Heavy vehicles should take the next road on the left to avoid a weight limit
☐ **B** The road ahead bends to the left
☐ **C** Overtaking traffic should move back to the left
☐ **D** The road ahead has a camber to the left

In this picture, the road marking shows that overtaking drivers or riders need to return to the left. These markings show the direction drivers must pass hatch markings or solid double white lines. They're also used to show the route that high vehicles should take under a low arched bridge.

5 Mark *one* answer

What should you do if your mobile phone rings while you're driving or riding?

- ☐ **A** Stop immediately
- ☐ **B** Answer it immediately
- ☐ **C** Leave it until you have stopped in a safe place
- ☐ **D** Pull up at the nearest kerb

It's illegal to use a hand-held mobile or similar device when driving or riding, except in a genuine emergency. The safest option is to switch off your mobile phone before you set off, and use a message service. If you've forgotten to switch your phone off and it rings, you should leave it. When you've stopped in a safe place, you can see who called and return the call if necessary.

6 Mark *one* answer

Why are these yellow lines painted across the road?

- ☐ **A** To help you choose the correct lane
- ☐ **B** To help you keep the correct separation distance
- ☐ **C** To make you aware of your speed
- ☐ **D** To tell you the distance to the roundabout

These lines are often found on the approach to a roundabout or a dangerous junction. They give you extra warning to adjust your speed. Look well ahead and do this in good time.

7 Mark *one* answer

What should you do when you're approaching traffic lights that have been green for some time?

- ☐ **A** Accelerate hard
- ☐ **B** Maintain your speed
- ☐ **C** Be ready to stop
- ☐ **D** Brake hard

The longer traffic lights have been green, the sooner they'll change. Allow for this as you approach traffic lights that you know have been green for a while. They're likely to change soon, so you should be prepared to stop.

8 Mark *one* answer

What should you do before slowing down or stopping your vehicle?

- ☐ **A** Sound the horn
- ☐ **B** Use the mirrors
- ☐ **C** Select a higher gear
- ☐ **D** Flash the headlights

Before slowing down or stopping, check the mirrors to see what's happening behind you. Also assess what's ahead and make sure you give the correct signal if it will help other road users.

9 Mark *one* answer
You're following a large vehicle. Why should you stay a safe distance behind it?

- ☐ **A** You'll be able to corner more quickly
- ☐ **B** You'll help the large vehicle to stop more easily
- ☐ **C** You'll give the driver a chance to see you in their mirrors
- ☐ **D** You'll keep out of the wind better

If you're following a large vehicle but are so close to it that you can't see its exterior mirrors, the driver won't be able to see you. Keeping well back will also allow you to see the road ahead by looking past the large vehicle.

10 Mark *one* answer
Why should you use your mirrors when you see a hazard ahead?

- ☐ **A** Because you'll need to accelerate out of danger
- ☐ **B** To assess how your actions will affect the traffic behind
- ☐ **C** Because you'll need to brake sharply and stop
- ☐ **D** To check what's happening on the road ahead

You should be constantly scanning the road for clues about what's going to happen next. Check your mirrors regularly, particularly as soon as you spot a hazard. What's happening behind may affect how you respond to hazards ahead.

11 Mark *one* answer
You're waiting to turn right at the end of a road. What should you do if your view is obstructed by parked vehicles?

- ☐ **A** Stop and then move forward slowly and carefully for a clear view
- ☐ **B** Move quickly to where you can see so you only block traffic from one direction
- ☐ **C** Wait for a pedestrian to let you know when it's safe for you to emerge
- ☐ **D** Turn your vehicle around immediately and find another junction to use

At junctions, your view is often restricted by buildings, trees or parked cars. You need to be able to see in order to judge a safe gap. Edge forward slowly and keep looking all the time. Don't cause other road users to change speed or direction as you emerge.

12 Mark *one* answer
There are objects hanging from your interior mirror. Why could this be a hazard?

- ☐ **A** Your view could be obstructed
- ☐ **B** Your sun visor might get tangled
- ☐ **C** Your radio reception might be affected
- ☐ **D** Your windscreen could mist up more easily

Ensure that you can see clearly through the windscreen of your vehicle. Stickers or hanging objects could obstruct your view or draw your attention away from the road.

13 Mark *one* answer

You're on a long motorway journey. What should you do if you start to feel sleepy?

☐ **A** Play some loud music

☐ **B** Stop on the hard shoulder for a rest

☐ **C** Drive faster to complete your journey sooner

☐ **D** Leave the motorway and stop in a safe place

If you feel sleepy, you should leave the motorway at a service area or at the next exit and stop in a safe place to rest. A supply of fresh air can help to keep you alert before you reach the exit, but it isn't a substitute for stopping and resting.

14 Mark *one* answer

Why should you switch your headlights on when it first starts to get dark?

☐ **A** To make your dials easier to see

☐ **B** So others can see you more easily

☐ **C** So that you blend in with other drivers

☐ **D** Because the street lights are lit

Your headlights and tail lights help others on the road to see you. It may be necessary to turn on your headlights during the day if visibility is reduced; for example, due to heavy rain. In these conditions, the light might fade before the street lights are timed to switch on. Be seen to be safe.

15 Mark *one* answer

What's most likely to distract you while you're driving?

☐ **A** Using a mobile phone

☐ **B** Using the windscreen wipers

☐ **C** Using the demisters

☐ **D** Using the mirrors

Except for emergencies, it's illegal to use a hand-held mobile phone while you're driving. Even using a hands-free kit can severely distract your attention.

16 Mark *one* answer

You're driving your car. When may you use a hand-held mobile phone?

☐ **A** When you're receiving a call

☐ **B** When you've parked safely

☐ **C** When you're driving at less than 30 mph

☐ **D** When your car has automatic transmission

It's illegal to use a hand-held mobile phone while you're driving, except in a genuine emergency. Even using a hands-free kit can distract your attention. Park in a safe and convenient place before receiving or making a call or using text messaging. Then you'll also be free to take notes or refer to papers.

17 Mark *one* answer

You're driving on a wet road. What should you do if you have to stop your vehicle in an emergency?

- ☐ **A** Apply the parking brake and footbrake together
- ☐ **B** Keep both hands on the steering wheel
- ☐ **C** Select reverse gear
- ☐ **D** Give an arm signal

As you drive, look well ahead and all around so that you're ready for any hazards that might develop. If you have to stop in an emergency, react as soon as you can while keeping control of the vehicle. Keep both hands on the steering wheel so you can control the vehicle's direction of travel.

---

18 Mark *one* answer

What should you do when you move off from behind a parked car?

- ☐ **A** Give a signal after moving off
- ☐ **B** Look around before moving off
- ☐ **C** Look around after moving off
- ☐ **D** Use the exterior mirrors only

Before moving off, you should use both the interior and exterior mirrors to check that the road is clear. Look around to check the blind spots and, if necessary, give a signal to warn other road users of your intentions. Also look well ahead as you'll have to steer out into the road to pass the parked car.

19 Mark *one* answer

You're travelling along this road. How should you pass the cyclist?

- ☐ **A** Sound your horn as you pass
- ☐ **B** Keep close to them as you pass
- ☐ **C** Leave them plenty of room as you pass
- ☐ **D** Change down one gear before you pass

Allow the cyclist plenty of room in case they wobble or swerve around a pothole or raised drain. Look well ahead before you start to overtake, because you'll need to cross the hazard line. Look for entrances where vehicles could be waiting to pull out.

20 Mark *one* answer
When do windscreen pillars cause a serious obstruction to your view?

- ☐ **A** When you're driving on a motorway
- ☐ **B** When you're driving on a dual carriageway
- ☐ **C** When you're approaching a one-way street
- ☐ **D** When you're approaching bends and junctions

Windscreen pillars can obstruct your view, particularly at bends and junctions. Look out for other road users – especially cyclists, motorcyclists and pedestrians who can easily be overlooked.

21 Mark *one* answer
What should you do if you can't see clearly behind when you're reversing?

- ☐ **A** Open the window to look behind
- ☐ **B** Open the door to look behind
- ☐ **C** Look in the nearside mirror
- ☐ **D** Ask someone to guide you

If you want to turn your car around, try to find a place where you have good all-round vision. If this isn't possible, and you're unable to see clearly, then get someone to guide you.

22 Mark *one* answer
What does the term 'blind spot' mean?

- ☐ **A** An area covered by your right-hand mirror
- ☐ **B** An area not covered by your headlights
- ☐ **C** An area covered by your left-hand mirror
- ☐ **D** An area not visible to the driver

Modern vehicles provide the driver with a good view of both the road ahead and behind using well-positioned mirrors. However, the mirrors can't see every angle of the scene behind and to the sides of the vehicle. It's essential that you know when and how to check the vehicle's blind spots, so that you're aware of any hidden hazards.

23 Mark *one* answer
What's likely to happen if you use a hands-free phone while you're driving?

- ☐ **A** It will improve your safety
- ☐ **B** It will increase your concentration
- ☐ **C** It will reduce your view
- ☐ **D** It will divert your attention

Talking to someone while you're driving can distract you and, unlike when someone is in the car with you, the person on the other end of a mobile phone is unable to see the traffic situations you're dealing with. They won't stop speaking to you even if you're approaching a hazardous situation. You need to concentrate on your driving at all times.

24 Mark *one* answer

You're turning right onto a dual carriageway. What should you do before emerging?

☐ **A** Stop, apply the parking brake and then select a low gear

☐ **B** Position your vehicle well to the left of the side road

☐ **C** Check that the central reservation is wide enough for your vehicle

☐ **D** Make sure that you leave enough room for a vehicle behind

Before emerging right onto a dual carriageway, make sure that the central reservation is deep enough to protect your vehicle. If it isn't, you should treat the dual carriageway as one road and check that it's clear in both directions before pulling out. Neglecting to do this could place part or all of your vehicle in the path of approaching traffic and cause a collision.

25 Mark *one* answer

You're waiting to emerge from a junction. The windscreen pillar is restricting your view. What should you be particularly aware of?

☐ **A** Lorries

☐ **B** Buses

☐ **C** Motorcyclists

☐ **D** Coaches

Windscreen pillars can completely block your view of pedestrians, motorcyclists and cyclists. You should make a particular effort to look for these road users; don't just rely on a quick glance.

---

26 Mark *one* answer

How can you make sure that a satellite navigation (satnav) system doesn't distract you when you're driving?

☐ **A** Turn it off while you're driving in built-up areas

☐ **B** Choose a voice that you find calming

☐ **C** Only set the destination when you're lost

☐ **D** Set it before starting your journey

Satnavs can be useful when driving on unfamiliar routes. However, they can also distract you and cause you to lose control if you look at or adjust them while you're driving. Set the satnav before starting your journey, or pull up in a safe place before making any changes to it.

27 Mark *one* answer
What must you do when the amber light is flashing at a pelican crossing?

☐ **A** Stop and wait for the green light
☐ **B** Stop and wait for the red light
☐ **C** Give way to pedestrians waiting to cross
☐ **D** Give way to pedestrians already on the crossing

Pelican crossings are signal-controlled crossings operated by pedestrians. Push-button controls change the signals. Pelican crossings have no red-and-amber stage before green; instead, they have a flashing amber light. This means you must give way to pedestrians who are on the crossing but if the crossing is clear you can continue.

28 Mark *one* answer
Why should you never wave people across at pedestrian crossings?

☐ **A** Another vehicle may be coming
☐ **B** They may not be looking
☐ **C** It's safer for you to carry on
☐ **D** They may not be ready to cross

If people are waiting to use a pedestrian crossing, slow down and be prepared to stop. Don't wave them across the road, because another driver may not have seen them, may not have seen your signal, and may not be able to stop safely.

29 Mark *one* answer
Why is it dangerous to drive too close to the vehicle ahead?

☐ **A** Your engine will overheat
☐ **B** Your mirrors will need adjusting
☐ **C** Your view of the road ahead will be restricted
☐ **D** Your satnav will be confused

'Tailgating' is the term used when a driver or rider follows the vehicle in front too closely. It's dangerous because it restricts your view of the road ahead and leaves no safety margin if the vehicle in front needs to slow down or stop suddenly. Tailgating is often the underlying cause of rear-end collisions or multiple pile-ups.

30 Mark *one* answer
What will happen if you follow this vehicle too closely?

☐ **A** Your brakes will overheat
☐ **B** Your fuel consumption will be increased
☐ **C** Your engine will overheat
☐ **D** Your view ahead will be reduced

Staying back will increase your view of the road ahead. This will help you to see any hazards that might occur and give you more time to react.

31 Mark *one* answer
What's the minimum time gap you should leave when following a vehicle on a wet road?

☐ **A** One second
☐ **B** Two seconds
☐ **C** Three seconds
☐ **D** Four seconds

Water will reduce your tyres' grip on the road. The safe separation gap of at least two seconds in dry conditions should be doubled, to at least four seconds, in wet weather.

32 Mark *one* answer
You're being overtaken by a long, heavily laden lorry. What should you do if it's taking a long time for it to overtake?

☐ **A** Speed up
☐ **B** Slow down
☐ **C** Hold your speed
☐ **D** Change direction

A long lorry with a heavy load will need more time to pass you than a car, especially on an uphill stretch of road. Slow down and allow the lorry to pass.

33 Mark *one* answer
Which vehicle will use a blue flashing beacon?

☐ **A** Motorway maintenance
☐ **B** Bomb disposal
☐ **C** Snow plough
☐ **D** Breakdown recovery

Emergency vehicles use blue flashing lights. If you see or hear one, move out of its way as soon as it's safe and legal to do so.

34 Mark *one* answer
What should you do if you're being followed by an ambulance showing flashing blue lights?

☐ **A** Pull over as soon as it's safe to do so
☐ **B** Accelerate hard to get away from it
☐ **C** Maintain your speed and course
☐ **D** Brake harshly and stop well out into the road

Pull over in a place where the ambulance can pass safely. Check that there are no bollards or obstructions in the road that will prevent it from passing.

35 Mark *one* answer
What type of emergency vehicle is fitted with a green flashing beacon?

☐ **A** Fire engine
☐ **B** Road gritter
☐ **C** Ambulance
☐ **D** Doctor's car

A green flashing beacon on a vehicle means the driver or passenger is a doctor on an emergency call. Give way to them if it's safe to do so. Be aware that the vehicle may be travelling quickly or may stop in a hurry.

36 Mark *one* answer
Who should obey diamond-shaped traffic signs?

☐ **A** Tram drivers
☐ **B** Bus drivers
☐ **C** Lorry drivers
☐ **D** Taxi drivers

These signs apply only to tram drivers, but you should know their meaning so that you're aware of the priorities and are able to anticipate the actions of the driver.

37 Mark *one* answer
On a road where trams operate, which vehicles will be most at risk from the tram rails?

☐ **A** Cars
☐ **B** Cycles
☐ **C** Buses
☐ **D** Lorries

The narrow wheels of a bicycle can become stuck in the tram rails, causing the cyclist to stop suddenly, wobble or even lose balance altogether. The tramlines are also slippery, which could cause a cyclist to slide or fall off.

38 Mark *one* answer
When should you use your vehicle's horn?

☐ **A** To alert others to your presence
☐ **B** To allow you right of way
☐ **C** To greet other road users
☐ **D** To signal your annoyance

You mustn't use your vehicle's horn between 11.30 pm and 7 am in a built-up area or when you're stationary, unless a moving vehicle poses a danger. Its function is to alert other road users to your presence.

39 Mark *one* answer

You're in a one-way street and want to turn right. Where should you position your vehicle when there are two lanes?

- ☐ **A** In the right-hand lane
- ☐ **B** In the left-hand lane
- ☐ **C** In either lane, depending on the traffic
- ☐ **D** Just left of the centre line

When you're in a one-way street and want to turn right, you should take up a position in the right-hand lane. This will allow other road users, not wishing to turn, to pass on the left. Indicate your intention and take up the correct position in good time.

40 Mark *one* answer

You wish to turn right ahead. Why should you take up the correct position in good time?

- ☐ **A** To allow other drivers to pull out in front of you
- ☐ **B** To give you a better view into the road that you're joining
- ☐ **C** To help other road users know what you intend to do
- ☐ **D** To allow drivers to pass you on the right

If you wish to turn right into a side road, take up your position in good time. Move to the centre of the road when it's safe to do so. This will allow vehicles to pass you on the left. Early planning will show other traffic what you intend to do.

41 Mark *one* answer

Which type of crossing allows cyclists to ride across while pedestrians are also crossing?

- ☐ **A** Toucan
- ☐ **B** Puffin
- ☐ **C** Pelican
- ☐ **D** Zebra

A toucan crossing is designed to allow pedestrians and cyclists to cross at the same time. Look out for cyclists approaching the crossing at speed.

42 Mark *one* answer

You're travelling at the legal speed limit. What should you do if the vehicle behind approaches quickly, flashing its headlights?

- ☐ **A** Accelerate to make a gap behind you
- ☐ **B** Touch the brakes sharply to show your brake lights
- ☐ **C** Maintain your speed to prevent the vehicle from overtaking
- ☐ **D** Allow the vehicle to overtake

Don't enforce the speed limit by blocking another vehicle's progress. This will only cause frustration. Allow the other vehicle to pass when you can do so safely.

43 Mark *one* answer
When should you flash your headlights at other road users?

☐ **A** When showing that you're giving way
☐ **B** When showing that you're about to turn
☐ **C** When telling them that you have right of way
☐ **D** When letting them know that you're there

You should only flash your headlights to warn others of your presence. Don't use them to greet others, show impatience or give priority to other road users, because they could misunderstand your signal.

44 Mark *one* answer
You're approaching an unmarked crossroads. How should you deal with the junction?

☐ **A** Accelerate and keep to the middle
☐ **B** Slow down and keep to the right
☐ **C** Accelerate and look to the left
☐ **D** Slow down and look both ways

Be cautious, especially when your view is restricted by hedges, bushes, walls, large vehicles, etc. In the summer months, these junctions can become more difficult to deal with, because growing foliage may further obscure your view.

45 Mark *one* answer
The conditions are good and dry. When should you use the 'two-second rule'?

☐ **A** Before restarting the engine after it has stalled
☐ **B** When checking your gap from the vehicle in front
☐ **C** Before using the 'Mirrors – Signal – Manoeuvre' routine
☐ **D** When traffic lights change to green

In good conditions, the 'two-second rule' can be used to check the distance between your vehicle and the one in front. This technique works on roads carrying faster traffic. Choose a fixed object, such as a bridge, sign or tree. When the vehicle ahead passes this object, say to yourself 'Only a fool breaks the two-second rule.' If you reach the object before you finish saying this, you're too close.

46 Mark *one* answer
Which colour follows the green signal at a puffin crossing?

☐ **A** Steady red
☐ **B** Flashing amber
☐ **C** Steady amber
☐ **D** Flashing green

Puffin crossings have infra-red sensors that detect when pedestrians are crossing and hold the red traffic signal until the crossing is clear. The use of a sensor means there's no flashing amber phase as there is with a pelican crossing.

47 Mark *one* answer

You're in a line of traffic. What action should you take if the driver behind is following very closely?

☐ **A** Ignore the driver behind and continue to travel within the speed limit

☐ **B** Slow down, gradually increasing the gap between you and the vehicle in front

☐ **C** Signal left and wave the driver behind to come past

☐ **D** Move over to a position just left of the centre line of the road

If the driver behind is following too closely, there's a danger they'll collide with the back of your vehicle if you stop suddenly. You can reduce this risk by slowing down and increasing the safety margin in front of you. This reduces the chance that you'll have to stop suddenly and allows you to spread your braking over a greater distance. This is an example of defensive driving.

48 Mark *one* answer

You're driving on a clear night. Which lights should you use if the national speed limit applies and there's a steady stream of oncoming traffic?

☐ **A** Full-beam headlights
☐ **B** Sidelights
☐ **C** Dipped headlights
☐ **D** Fog lights

Use the full-beam headlights only when you can be sure that you won't dazzle other road users.

49 Mark *one* answer

You're driving behind a large goods vehicle. What should you do if it signals left but steers to the right?

☐ **A** Slow down and let the vehicle turn
☐ **B** Drive on, keeping to the left
☐ **C** Overtake on the right of it
☐ **D** Hold your speed and sound your horn

Large, long vehicles need extra room when making turns at junctions. They may move out to the right in order to make a left turn. Keep well back and don't attempt to pass them on their left.

50 Mark *one* answer

You're driving along this road. What should you do if the red car cuts in close in front of you?

☐ **A** Accelerate to get closer to the red car
☐ **B** Give a long blast on the horn
☐ **C** Drop back to leave the correct separation distance
☐ **D** Flash your headlights several times

There are times when other drivers make incorrect or ill-judged decisions. Be tolerant and try not to retaliate or react aggressively. Always consider the safety of other road users, your passengers and yourself.

51 Mark *one* answer
You're waiting in a traffic queue at night. How can you avoid dazzling drivers behind you?

☐ **A** Use the parking brake and release the footbrake
☐ **B** Keep your foot on the footbrake
☐ **C** Balance the clutch with the accelerator
☐ **D** Use the parking brake and footbrake together

In queuing traffic, your brake lights can dazzle drivers behind you. If you apply your parking brake, you can take your foot off the footbrake. This will turn off the brake lights so that they can't dazzle the driver behind you.

52 Mark *one* answer
You're driving in traffic at the speed limit for the road. What should you do if the driver behind is trying to overtake?

☐ **A** Move closer to the car ahead, so the driver behind has no room to overtake
☐ **B** Wave the driver behind to overtake when it's safe
☐ **C** Keep a steady course and allow the driver behind to overtake
☐ **D** Accelerate to get away from the driver behind

Keep a steady course to give the driver behind an opportunity to overtake safely. If necessary, slow down. Reacting incorrectly to another driver's impatience can lead to danger.

53 Mark *one* answer
What does it mean if the signs at a bus lane show no times of operation?

☐ **A** The lane isn't in operation
☐ **B** The lane is only in operation at peak times
☐ **C** The lane is in operation 24 hours a day
☐ **D** The lane is only in operation in daylight hours

Bus-lane signs show the vehicles allowed to use the lane and its times of operation. Where no times are shown, the bus lane is in operation 24 hours a day.

54 Mark *one* answer
What should you do when a person herding sheep asks you to stop?

☐ **A** Ignore them as they have no authority
☐ **B** Stop and switch off your engine
☐ **C** Continue on but drive slowly
☐ **D** Try to get past quickly

If someone in charge of animals asks you to stop, you should do so and switch off your engine. Animals are unpredictable and startle easily; they could turn and run into your path or into the path of another moving vehicle.

55 Mark *one* answer
What should you do when you're overtaking a horse and rider?

☐ **A** Sound your horn as a warning
☐ **B** Go past as quickly as possible
☐ **C** Flash your headlights as a warning
☐ **D** Go past slowly and carefully

Horses can be startled by the sound of a car engine or the rush of air caused by a vehicle passing too closely. Keep well back and only pass when it's safe. Leave them plenty of room; you may have to use the other side of the road to go past safely.

56 Mark *one* answer
You're approaching a zebra crossing. What should you do if pedestrians are waiting to cross?

☐ **A** Give way to older and infirm people only
☐ **B** Slow down and prepare to stop
☐ **C** Use your headlights to indicate they can cross
☐ **D** Wave at them to cross the road

As you approach a zebra crossing, look for pedestrians waiting to cross. Where you can see them, slow down and prepare to stop. Be especially careful of children and older people, who may have difficulty judging when it's safe to cross.

57 Mark *one* answer
What should you do if a vehicle pulls out in front of you at a junction?

☐ **A** Swerve past it and sound your horn
☐ **B** Flash your headlights and drive up close behind
☐ **C** Slow down and be ready to stop
☐ **D** Accelerate past it immediately

Try to anticipate what other drivers might do. Look and plan ahead so that you're ready to respond safely if a hazard develops. Be tolerant of road users who make mistakes.

58 Mark *one* answer
You're approaching a red light at a puffin crossing. Pedestrians are on the crossing. When will the red light change?

☐ **A** When you start to edge forward onto the crossing
☐ **B** When the pedestrians have cleared the crossing
☐ **C** When the pedestrians push the button on the far side of the crossing
☐ **D** When a driver from the opposite direction reaches the crossing

A sensor will automatically detect that the pedestrians have reached a safe position. Don't drive on until the green light shows and it's safe for you to do so.

59 Mark *one* answer
Which instrument-panel warning light would show that headlights are on main beam?

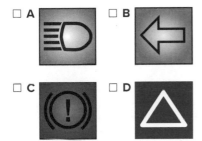

☐ A   ☐ B

☐ C   ☐ D

You should be aware of all the warning lights and visual aids on the vehicle you're driving. If you're driving a vehicle for the first time, you should familiarise yourself with all the controls, warning lights and visual aids before you set off.

60 Mark *one* answer
When should you leave a two-second gap between your vehicle and the one in front?

☐ A When it's raining
☐ B When it's dry
☐ C When it's icy
☐ D When it's foggy

In good, dry conditions, a driver needs to keep a distance of at least two seconds from the car in front. This should allow enough space for you to stop if the driver in front has to stop suddenly.

61 Mark *one* answer
You're driving at night on an unlit road. What should you do if you're following another vehicle?

☐ A Flash your headlights
☐ B Use dipped headlights
☐ C Switch off your headlights
☐ D Use full-beam headlights

If you follow another vehicle with your headlights on full beam, they could dazzle the driver. Leave a safe distance and make sure that the light from your dipped beam falls short of the vehicle in front.

62 Mark *one* answer
What should you do if you're driving a slow-moving vehicle on a narrow winding road?

☐ A Keep well out to stop vehicles overtaking dangerously
☐ B Wave the vehicles behind to come past you if you think they can overtake quickly
☐ C Pull in when you can, to let the vehicles behind overtake
☐ D Give a left signal when it's safe for vehicles to overtake you

If you're driving a slow-moving vehicle along a narrow road, try not to hold up faster traffic. If you see vehicles following behind, pull over in a safe place and let the traffic pass before continuing. Don't wave other traffic past – this could be dangerous if you or they haven't noticed a hazard ahead.

63 Mark *one* answer

You're driving a car that has a diesel engine. What can a loose filler cap on your fuel tank cause?

☐ **A** It can make the engine difficult to start

☐ **B** It can make the roads slippery for other road users

☐ **C** It can improve your vehicle's fuel consumption

☐ **D** It can increase the level of exhaust emissions

Diesel fuel can spill out if your filler cap isn't secured properly. This is most likely to occur on bends, junctions and roundabouts, where it will make the road slippery, especially if it's wet. At the end of a spell of dry weather, road surfaces may be especially slippery where diesel has been spilled but it hasn't been washed away by rain.

64 Mark *one* answer

What should you do to avoid fuel spillage?

☐ **A** Check that your tank is only three-quarters full

☐ **B** Check that you've used a locking filler cap

☐ **C** Check that your fuel gauge is working

☐ **D** Check that your filler cap is securely fastened

When learning to drive, it's a good idea to practise filling your car with fuel. Ask your instructor if you can use a petrol station and fill the fuel tank yourself. You need to know where the filler cap is on the car you're driving, so you know which side of the pump to park at. Take care not to overfill the tank and make sure you secure the filler cap correctly, so that no fuel leaks onto the road while you're driving.

65 Mark *one* answer

What style of driving causes increased risk to everyone?

☐ **A** Considerate

☐ **B** Defensive

☐ **C** Competitive

☐ **D** Responsible

Competitive driving increases the risks to everyone and is the opposite of responsible, considerate and defensive driving. Defensive driving is about questioning the actions of other road users and being prepared for the unexpected. Don't be taken by surprise.

66 Mark *one* answer
How would under-inflated tyres affect your vehicle?

☐ **A** The vehicle's stopping distance would increase
☐ **B** The flash rate of the vehicle's indicators would increase
☐ **C** The vehicle's gear change mechanism would become stiff
☐ **D** The vehicle's headlights would aim high

Your tyres are your only contact with the road. To prevent problems with braking and steering, keep your tyres free from defects; they must have sufficient tread depth and be correctly inflated. Correct tyre pressures help reduce the risk of skidding and provide a safer and more comfortable drive or ride.

67 Mark *one* answer
When are you not allowed to sound your vehicle's horn?

☐ **A** Between 10.00 pm and 6.00 am in a built-up area
☐ **B** At any time in a built-up area
☐ **C** Between 11.30 pm and 7.00 am in a built-up area
☐ **D** Between 11.30 pm and 6.00 am on any road

Every effort must be made to prevent excessive noise, especially in built-up areas at night. Don't rev your engine or sound the horn unnecessarily. It's illegal to sound your horn in a built-up area between 11.30 pm and 7.00 am, except when another road user poses a danger.

68 Mark *one* answer
What makes the vehicle in the picture 'environmentally friendly'?

☐ **A** It's powered by gravity
☐ **B** It's powered by diesel
☐ **C** It's powered by electricity
☐ **D** It's powered by unleaded petrol

Trams are powered by electricity and therefore don't emit exhaust fumes. They ease traffic congestion by offering drivers an alternative to using their car, particularly in busy cities and towns.

69 Mark *one* answer
Why have 'red routes' been introduced in major cities?

☐ **A** To raise the speed limits
☐ **B** To help the traffic flow
☐ **C** To provide better parking
☐ **D** To allow lorries to load more freely

Inconsiderate parking can obstruct the flow of traffic and so make traffic congestion worse. Red routes are designed to prevent this by enforcing strict parking restrictions. Driving slowly in traffic increases fuel consumption and causes a build-up of exhaust fumes.

70 Mark *one* answer

What's the purpose of road humps, chicanes and narrowings?

☐ **A** To separate lanes of traffic
☐ **B** To increase traffic speed
☐ **C** To allow pedestrians to cross
☐ **D** To reduce traffic speed

Traffic-calming measures help to keep vehicle speeds low in congested areas where there are pedestrians and children. A pedestrian is much more likely to survive a collision with a vehicle travelling at 20 mph than they are with a vehicle travelling at 40 mph.

71 Mark *one* answer

What's the purpose of a catalytic converter?

☐ **A** To reduce fuel consumption
☐ **B** To reduce the risk of fire
☐ **C** To reduce harmful exhaust gases
☐ **D** To reduce engine wear

Catalytic converters reduce a large percentage of harmful exhaust emissions. They work more efficiently when the engine has reached its normal working temperature.

72 Mark *one* answer

When should tyre pressures be checked?

☐ **A** After any lengthy journey
☐ **B** After travelling at high speed
☐ **C** When tyres are hot
☐ **D** When tyres are cold

Check the tyre pressures when the tyres are cold. This will give you a more accurate reading. The heat generated on a long journey will raise the pressure inside the tyre.

73 Mark *one* answer

When will your vehicle use more fuel?

☐ **A** When its tyres are under-inflated
☐ **B** When its tyres are of different makes
☐ **C** When its tyres are over-inflated
☐ **D** When its tyres are new

Check your tyre pressures frequently – normally once a week. If they're lower than those recommended by the manufacturer, there will be more 'rolling resistance'. The engine will have to work harder to overcome this, leading to increased fuel consumption.

74 Mark *one* answer

How should you dispose of a used vehicle battery?

☐ **A** Bury it in your garden
☐ **B** Put it in the dustbin
☐ **C** Take it to a local-authority disposal site
☐ **D** Leave it on waste land

Batteries contain acid, which is hazardous, and they must be disposed of safely. This means taking them to an appropriate disposal site.

75 Mark *one* answer

What's most likely to increase fuel consumption?

☐ **A** Poor steering control
☐ **B** Accelerating around bends
☐ **C** Staying in high gears
☐ **D** Harsh braking and accelerating

Accelerating and braking gently and smoothly will help to save fuel and reduce wear on your vehicle. This makes it better for the environment too.

76 Mark *one* answer

The fluid level in your battery is low. What fluid should you use to top it up?

☐ **A** Battery acid
☐ **B** Distilled water
☐ **C** Engine oil
☐ **D** Engine coolant

Some modern batteries are maintenance free. Check your vehicle handbook and, if necessary, make sure that the plates in each battery cell are covered with fluid.

77 Mark *one* answer

You're parked on the road at night. When must you use parking lights?

☐ **A** When there are continuous white lines in the middle of the road
☐ **B** When the speed limit exceeds 30 mph
☐ **C** When you're facing oncoming traffic
☐ **D** When you're near a bus stop

When parking at night, park in the direction of the traffic. This will enable other road users to see the reflectors on the rear of your vehicle. Use your parking lights if the speed limit is over 30 mph.

78 Mark *one* answer

How can you reduce the environmental harm caused by your motor vehicle?

☐ **A** Only use it for short journeys
☐ **B** Don't service it
☐ **C** Drive faster than normal
☐ **D** Keep engine revs low

Engines that burn fossil fuels produce exhaust emissions that are harmful to health. The harder you make the engine work, the more emissions it will produce. Engines also use more fuel and produce higher levels of emissions when they're cold. Anything you can do to reduce your use of fossil fuels will help the environment.

79 Mark *one* answer

What can cause excessive or uneven tyre wear?

☐ **A** A faulty gearbox
☐ **B** A faulty braking system
☐ **C** A faulty electrical system
☐ **D** A faulty exhaust system

If you see that parts of the tread on your tyres are wearing before others, it may indicate a brake, suspension or wheel-alignment fault. Regular servicing will help to detect faults at an early stage and this will avoid the risk of minor faults becoming serious or even dangerous.

80 Mark *one* answer

You need to top up your battery with distilled water. What level should you fill it to?

☐ **A** The top of the battery
☐ **B** Halfway up the battery
☐ **C** Just below the cell plates
☐ **D** Just above the cell plates

Top up the battery with distilled water and make sure each cell plate is covered.

81 Mark *one* answer

How can you plan your route before starting a long journey?

☐ **A** Check your vehicle handbook
☐ **B** Ask your local garage
☐ **C** Use a route planner on the internet
☐ **D** Consult a travel agent

Various route planners are available on the internet. Most of them give you several options, allowing you to choose between the most direct route and quieter roads. They may also identify rest and fuel stops. Print off the directions and take them with you.

82 Mark *one* answer

Why is it a good idea to plan your journey to avoid busy times?

☐ **A** You'll have an easier journey
☐ **B** You'll have a more stressful journey
☐ **C** Your journey time will be longer
☐ **D** It will cause more traffic congestion

No-one likes to spend time in traffic queues. Try to avoid busy times related to school or work travel.

83 Mark *one* answer
How will your journey be affected by travelling outside the busy times of day?

☐ **A** Your journey will use more fuel
☐ **B** Your journey will take longer
☐ **C** Your journey will be more hazardous
☐ **D** Your journey will have fewer delays

If possible, avoid the early morning, late afternoon and early evening 'rush hour'. Doing this should allow you to have a better journey, with fewer delays. This should help you to arrive at your destination feeling less stressed.

84 Mark *one* answer
You plan your route before starting a journey. Why should you also plan an alternative route?

☐ **A** Your original route may be blocked
☐ **B** Your maps may have different scales
☐ **C** You may find you have to pay a congestion charge
☐ **D** You may get held up by a tractor

It can be frustrating and worrying to find your planned route is blocked by roadworks or diversions. If you've planned an alternative, you'll feel less stressed and more able to concentrate fully on your driving or riding. If your original route is mostly on motorways, it's a good idea to plan an alternative using non-motorway roads. Always carry a map with you just in case you need to refer to it.

85 Mark *one* answer
You have to arrive on time for an appointment. How should you plan for the journey?

☐ **A** Allow plenty of time for the trip
☐ **B** Plan to travel at busy times
☐ **C** Avoid roads with the national speed limit
☐ **D** Prevent other drivers from overtaking

Always allow plenty of time for your journey in case of unforeseen problems. Anything can happen; for example, punctures, breakdowns, road closures, diversions and delays. You'll feel less stressed and less inclined to take risks if you aren't 'pushed for time'.

86 Mark *one* answer
What can you expect if you drive using rapid acceleration and heavy braking?

☐ **A** Reduced pollution
☐ **B** Increased fuel consumption
☐ **C** Reduced exhaust emissions
☐ **D** Increased road safety

Using the controls smoothly can reduce fuel consumption by about 15%, as well as reducing wear and tear on your vehicle. Plan ahead and anticipate changes of speed well in advance. This will reduce the need to accelerate rapidly or brake sharply.

87 Mark *one* answer

What could cause you to crash if the level is allowed to get too low?

- ☐ **A** Anti-freeze level
- ☐ **B** Brake-fluid level
- ☐ **C** Battery-water level
- ☐ **D** Radiator-coolant level

You should carry out frequent checks on all fluid levels but particularly brake fluid. As the brake pads or shoes wear down, the brake-fluid level will drop. If it drops below the minimum mark on the fluid reservoir, air could enter the hydraulic system and lead to a loss of braking efficiency or even complete brake failure.

88 Mark *one* answer

What should you do if your anti-lock brakes (ABS) warning light stays on?

- ☐ **A** Check the brake-fluid level
- ☐ **B** Check the footbrake free play
- ☐ **C** Check that the parking brake is released
- ☐ **D** Have the brakes checked immediately

Consult the vehicle handbook or a garage before driving the vehicle any further. Only drive to a garage if it's safe to do so. If you aren't sure, get expert help.

89 Mark *one* answer

What does it mean if this light comes on while you're driving?

- ☐ **A** A fault in the braking system
- ☐ **B** The engine oil is low
- ☐ **C** A rear light has failed
- ☐ **D** Your seat belt isn't fastened

If this light comes on, you should have the brake system checked immediately. A faulty braking system could have dangerous consequences.

90 Mark *one* answer

Why is it important to wear suitable shoes when you're driving?

- ☐ **A** To prevent wear on the pedals
- ☐ **B** To maintain control of the pedals
- ☐ **C** To enable you to adjust your seat
- ☐ **D** To enable you to walk for assistance if you break down

When you're going to drive, make sure that you're wearing suitable clothing. Comfortable shoes will ensure that you have proper control of the foot pedals.

91 Mark *one* answer

If you're involved in a collision, what will reduce the risk of neck injury?

- ☐ **A** An air-sprung seat
- ☐ **B** Anti-lock brakes
- ☐ **C** A collapsible steering wheel
- ☐ **D** A properly adjusted head restraint

If you're involved in a collision, head restraints will reduce the risk of neck injury. They must be properly adjusted. Make sure they aren't positioned too low: in a crash, this could cause damage to the neck.

92 Mark *one* answer

What does it mean if your vehicle keeps bouncing after you sharply press down and release on the bodywork over a wheel?

- ☐ **A** The tyres are worn
- ☐ **B** The tyres are under inflated
- ☐ **C** The vehicle is on soft ground
- ☐ **D** The shock absorbers are worn

If you find that your vehicle bounces as you drive around a corner or bend in the road, the shock absorbers might be worn. To test your shock absorbers, sharply press down and release above each wheel. If the vehicle continues to bounce, take it to be checked by a qualified mechanic.

93 Mark *one* answer

How will a roof rack affect your car?

- ☐ **A** There will be less wind noise
- ☐ **B** The engine will use more oil
- ☐ **C** The car will accelerate faster
- ☐ **D** Fuel consumption will increase

A roof rack increases your car's wind resistance. This will cause an increase in fuel consumption, so you should remove it when it isn't being used. An aerodynamically designed roof rack or box will help reduce wind resistance to a minimum, but the rack or box should still be removed when it isn't in use.

94 Mark *one* answer

What makes your tyres illegal?

- ☐ **A** If they were bought second-hand
- ☐ **B** If they have any large, deep cuts in the side wall
- ☐ **C** If they're of different makes
- ☐ **D** If they have different tread patterns

Your tyres may be of different treads and makes. They can even be second-hand, as long as they're in good condition. They must, however, be intact, without cuts or tears. When checking the side walls for cuts and bulges, don't forget to check the side of the tyre that's hidden from view, under the car.

95 Mark *one* answer
What's the legal minimum depth of tread for car tyres?

- ☐ **A** 1 mm
- ☐ **B** 1.6 mm
- ☐ **C** 2.5 mm
- ☐ **D** 4 mm

Car tyres must have sufficient depth of tread to give them a good grip on the road surface. The legal minimum for cars is 1.6 mm. This depth should be across the central three-quarters of the breadth of the tyre and around the entire circumference.

96 Mark *one* answer
You're carrying two 13-year-old children and their parents in your car. Who's responsible for seeing that the children wear seat belts?

- ☐ **A** The children's parents
- ☐ **B** You, the driver
- ☐ **C** The front-seat passenger
- ☐ **D** The children

Seat belts save lives and reduce the risk of injury. If you're carrying passengers under 14 years old, it's your responsibility as the driver to ensure that their seat belts are fastened or they're seated in an approved child restraint.

97 Mark *one* answer
How can drivers help the environment?

- ☐ **A** By accelerating harshly
- ☐ **B** By accelerating gently
- ☐ **C** By using leaded fuel
- ☐ **D** By driving faster

Rapid acceleration and heavy braking lead to increased
- fuel consumption
- wear on your vehicle.

Having your vehicle serviced regularly will maintain its efficiency, produce cleaner emissions and reduce the risk of a breakdown.

98 Mark *one* answer
How can you avoid wasting fuel?

- ☐ **A** By having your vehicle serviced regularly
- ☐ **B** By revving the engine in the lower gears
- ☐ **C** By keeping an empty roof rack on your vehicle
- ☐ **D** By driving at higher speeds where possible

If you don't have your vehicle serviced regularly, the engine will gradually become less efficient. This will cause increased fuel consumption and, in turn, an increase in the amount of harmful emissions it produces.

99 Mark *one* answer

What could you do to reduce the volume of traffic on the roads?

- ☐ **A** Drive in a bus lane
- ☐ **B** Use a car with a smaller engine
- ☐ **C** Walk or cycle on short journeys
- ☐ **D** Travel by car at all times

Try not to use your car as a matter of routine. For shorter journeys, consider walking or cycling instead - this is much better for both you and the environment.

100 Mark *one* answer

What's most likely to waste fuel?

- ☐ **A** Reducing your speed
- ☐ **B** Driving on motorways
- ☐ **C** Using different brands of fuel
- ☐ **D** Under-inflated tyres

Wasting fuel costs you money and also causes unnecessary pollution. Ensuring your tyres are correctly inflated, avoiding carrying unnecessary weight and removing a roof rack that's not in use will all help to reduce your fuel consumption.

101 Mark *one* answer

What part of the car does the law require you to keep in good condition?

- ☐ **A** The gearbox
- ☐ **B** The transmission
- ☐ **C** The door locks
- ☐ **D** The seat belts

Unless exempt, you and your passengers must wear a seat belt (or suitable child restraint). The seat belts in your car must be in good condition and working properly; they'll be checked during its MOT test.

102 Mark *one* answer

How much more fuel will you use by driving at 70 mph, compared with driving at 50 mph?

- ☐ **A** About 5%
- ☐ **B** About 15%
- ☐ **C** About 75%
- ☐ **D** About 100%

Your vehicle will use less fuel if you avoid heavy acceleration. The higher the engine revs, the more fuel you'll use. Using the same gear, and covering the same distance, a vehicle travelling at 70 mph will use about 15% more fuel than it would at 50 mph. However, don't travel so slowly that you inconvenience or endanger other road users.

103 Mark *one* answer

What should you do if your vehicle pulls to one side when you use the brakes?

- ☐ **A** Increase the pressure in your tyres
- ☐ **B** Have the brakes checked as soon as possible
- ☐ **C** Change gear and pump the brake pedal
- ☐ **D** Use your parking brake at the same time

The brakes on your vehicle must be effective and properly adjusted. If your vehicle pulls to one side when braking, take it to be checked by a qualified mechanic as soon as you can.

104 Mark *one* answer

What will happen if your car's wheels are unbalanced?

- ☐ **A** The steering will pull to one side
- ☐ **B** The steering will vibrate
- ☐ **C** The brakes will fail
- ☐ **D** The tyres will deflate

If your wheels are out of balance, it will cause the steering to vibrate at certain speeds. This isn't a fault that will put itself right, so take your vehicle to a garage or tyre fitter to have the wheels rebalanced.

105 Mark *one* answer

What can be damaged if you turn the steering wheel when the car isn't moving?

- ☐ **A** The gearbox
- ☐ **B** The engine
- ☐ **C** The brakes
- ☐ **D** The tyres

Turning the steering wheel when the car isn't moving is known as dry steering. It can cause unnecessary wear to the tyres and steering mechanism.

106 Mark *one* answer

What's the safest thing to do if you have to leave valuables in your car?

- ☐ **A** Put them in a carrier bag
- ☐ **B** Park near a school entrance
- ☐ **C** Lock them out of sight
- ☐ **D** Park near a bus stop

If you have to leave valuables in your car, lock them out of sight. This is the best way to deter an opportunist thief.

107 Mark *one* answer

What may help to deter a thief from stealing your car?

☐ **A** Always keeping the headlights on
☐ **B** Fitting reflective glass windows
☐ **C** Always keeping the interior light on
☐ **D** Etching the registration number on the windows

Having your car registration number etched on all your windows is a cheap and effective way to deter professional car thieves.

108 Mark *one* answer

What should you remove from your car before leaving it unattended?

☐ **A** The car dealer's details
☐ **B** The owner's manual
☐ **C** The service record
☐ **D** The vehicle registration document

Never leave the vehicle registration document inside your car. This document would help a thief to dispose of your car more easily.

109 Mark *one* answer

What should you do when leaving your vehicle parked and unattended?

☐ **A** Park near a busy junction
☐ **B** Park in a housing estate
☐ **C** Lock it and remove the key
☐ **D** Leave the left indicator on

An unlocked car is an open invitation to thieves. Leaving the keys in the ignition not only makes your car easy to steal but could also invalidate your insurance.

110 Mark *one* answer

What will reduce fuel consumption?

☐ **A** Driving more slowly
☐ **B** Accelerating rapidly
☐ **C** Late and heavy braking
☐ **D** Staying in lower gears

Harsh braking, frequent gear changes and harsh acceleration increase fuel consumption. A car uses less fuel when travelling at a constant low speed in an appropriate high gear. You need to look well ahead so you're able to anticipate hazards early. Easing off the accelerator and timing your approach at junctions, for example, can reduce the fuel consumption of your vehicle.

111 Mark *one* answer

You service your own vehicle. How should you dispose of the old engine oil?

☐ **A** Take it to a local-authority site
☐ **B** Pour it down a drain
☐ **C** Tip it into a hole in the ground
☐ **D** Put it in your dustbin

It's illegal to pour engine oil down any drain. Oil is a pollutant and harmful to wildlife. Dispose of it safely at an authorised site.

112 Mark *one* answer

Why do MOT tests include an exhaust emission test?

☐ **A** To recover the cost of expensive garage equipment
☐ **B** To help protect the environment against pollution
☐ **C** To discover which fuel supplier is used the most
☐ **D** To make sure diesel and petrol engines emit the same fumes

Emission tests are carried out to make sure your vehicle's engine is operating efficiently. This ensures the pollution produced by the engine is kept to a minimum. If your vehicle isn't serviced regularly, it may fail the MOT emissions test.

113 Mark *one* answer

How can you reduce the damage your vehicle causes to the environment?

☐ **A** Use narrow side streets
☐ **B** Brake heavily
☐ **C** Use busy routes
☐ **D** Anticipate well ahead

By looking well ahead and recognising hazards in good time, you can avoid late and heavy braking. Watch the traffic flow and look well ahead for potential hazards so you can control your speed in good time. Avoid over-revving the engine and accelerating harshly, as this increases wear to the engine and uses more fuel.

114 Mark *one* answer

How will you benefit from following the manufacturer's service schedule for your vehicle?

☐ **A** Your vehicle will be cheaper to insure
☐ **B** Your vehicle tax will be lower
☐ **C** Your vehicle will remain reliable
☐ **D** Your journey times will be reduced

All vehicles need to be serviced to keep working efficiently. An efficient engine uses less fuel and produces fewer harmful emissions than an engine that's running inefficiently. Keeping the vehicle serviced to the manufacturer's schedule should also keep it reliable and reduce the chance of it breaking down.

115 Mark *one* answer
How should you drive when you're driving along a road that has road humps?

☐ **A** Maintain a reduced speed throughout
☐ **B** Accelerate quickly between the humps
☐ **C** Always keep to the maximum legal speed
☐ **D** Drive slowly at school times only

Road humps are there for a reason – to protect vulnerable road users by reducing the speed of traffic. Don't accelerate harshly between the humps. Put the safety of others first and maintain a reduced speed throughout the zone.

116 Mark *one* answer
When should you check the engine oil level?

☐ **A** Before a long journey
☐ **B** When the engine is hot
☐ **C** Early in the morning
☐ **D** Every time you drive the car

An engine can use more oil during long journeys than on shorter trips. Insufficient engine oil is potentially dangerous: it can lead to excessive wear, mechanical breakdown and expensive repairs. Most cars have a dipstick to allow the oil level to be checked. If not, you should refer to the vehicle handbook.

117 Mark *one* answer
You're having difficulty finding a parking space in a busy town. Can you park on the zigzag lines of a zebra crossing?

☐ **A** No, not unless you stay with your car
☐ **B** Yes, in order to drop off a passenger
☐ **C** Yes, if you don't block people from crossing
☐ **D** No, not under any circumstances

It's an offence to park on the zigzag lines of a zebra crossing. You'll be causing an obstruction by obscuring the view of both pedestrians and drivers.

118 Mark *one* answer
What should you do when you leave your car unattended for a few minutes?

☐ **A** Leave the engine running
☐ **B** Switch the engine off but leave the key in
☐ **C** Lock it and remove the key
☐ **D** Park near a traffic warden

Always switch off the engine, remove the key and lock your car, even if you're only leaving it for a few minutes.

119 Mark *one* answer
Why should you try and park in a secure car park?

☐ **A** It makes it easy to find your car
☐ **B** It helps deter thieves
☐ **C** It stops the car being exposed to bad weather
☐ **D** It doesn't cost anything to park here

Whenever possible, leave your car in a secure car park. This will help deter thieves.

120 Mark *one* answer
Where would parking your vehicle cause an obstruction?

☐ **A** Alongside a parking meter
☐ **B** In front of a property entrance
☐ **C** On your driveway
☐ **D** In a marked parking space

Don't park your vehicle where it may obstruct access to a business or property. Think carefully before you slow down and stop. Look at road markings and signs to ensure that you aren't parking illegally.

121 Mark *one* answer
What's the most important reason for having a properly adjusted head restraint?

☐ **A** To make you more comfortable
☐ **B** To help you avoid neck injury
☐ **C** To help you relax
☐ **D** To help you maintain your driving position

In a collision, rapid deceleration will violently throw vehicle occupants forward and then backwards as the vehicle stops. Seat belts and airbags protect occupants against the forward movement. Head restraints should be adjusted so they give maximum protection to the head and neck during the backward movement.

122 Mark *one* answer
What can you do to reduce environmental damage caused by your vehicle?

☐ **A** Avoid using the cruise control
☐ **B** Use the air conditioning whenever you drive
☐ **C** Use the gears to slow the vehicle
☐ **D** Avoid making a lot of short journeys

Avoid using your car for short journeys. On a short journey, the engine is unlikely to warm up fully and will therefore be running less efficiently. This will result in the car using more fuel and emitting higher levels of harmful emissions.

123 Mark *one* answer

What can people who live or work in towns and cities do to help reduce urban pollution levels?

☐ **A** Drive more quickly
☐ **B** Over-rev in a low gear
☐ **C** Walk or cycle
☐ **D** Drive short journeys

Using a vehicle for short journeys means the engine doesn't have time to reach its normal operating temperature. When an engine is running below its normal operating temperature, it produces increased amounts of pollution. Walking and cycling don't create pollution and have health benefits as well.

124 Mark *one* answer

How can you reduce the chances of your car being broken into when leaving it unattended?

☐ **A** Take all valuables with you
☐ **B** Park near a taxi rank
☐ **C** Place any valuables on the floor
☐ **D** Park near a fire station

When leaving your car, take all valuables with you if you can. Otherwise, lock them out of sight.

125 Mark *one* answer

How can you help to prevent your car radio being stolen?

☐ **A** Park in an unlit area
☐ **B** Leave the radio turned on
☐ **C** Park near a busy junction
☐ **D** Install a security-coded radio

A security-coded radio can deter thieves, as it's likely to be of little use when removed from the vehicle.

126 Mark *one* answer

How can you reduce the risk of your vehicle being broken into at night?

☐ **A** Leave it in a well-lit area
☐ **B** Park in a quiet side road
☐ **C** Don't engage the steering lock
☐ **D** Park in a poorly lit area

Having your vehicle broken into or stolen can be very distressing and inconvenient. Avoid leaving your vehicle unattended in poorly lit areas.

127 Mark *one* answer
What will help you to keep your car secure?

☐ **A** Being a member of a vehicle breakdown organisation
☐ **B** Registering with a Vehicle Watch scheme
☐ **C** Passing an advanced driving test
☐ **D** Taking car maintenance classes

The Vehicle Watch scheme helps to reduce the risk of your car being stolen. By displaying high-visibility Vehicle Watch stickers in your car, you're inviting the police to stop your vehicle if it's seen in use between midnight and 5 am.

128 Mark *one* answer
On a vehicle, where would you find a catalytic converter?

☐ **A** In the fuel tank
☐ **B** In the air filter
☐ **C** On the cooling system
☐ **D** On the exhaust system

Although carbon dioxide is still produced, a catalytic converter fitted to the exhaust system reduces the toxic and polluting gases by up to 90%.

129 Mark *one* answer
What can you achieve if you drive smoothly?

☐ **A** Reduction in journey times by about 15%
☐ **B** Increase in fuel consumption by about 15%
☐ **C** Reduction in fuel consumption by about 15%
☐ **D** Increase in journey times by about 15%

By driving smoothly, you'll not only save about 15% of your fuel but will also reduce the amount of wear and tear on your vehicle and the level of pollution it produces. You're also likely to feel more relaxed and have a more pleasant journey.

130 Mark *one* answer
Which driving technique can help you save fuel?

☐ **A** Using lower gears as often as possible
☐ **B** Accelerating sharply in each gear
☐ **C** Using each gear in turn
☐ **D** Missing out some gears

Missing out intermediate gears, when appropriate, helps to reduce the amount of time spent accelerating and decelerating - the times when your vehicle uses the most fuel.

131 Mark *one* answer
How can driving in a fuel-efficient manner help protect the environment?

- ☐ **A** Through the legal enforcement of speed regulations
- ☐ **B** By increasing the number of cars on the road
- ☐ **C** Through increased fuel bills
- ☐ **D** By reducing exhaust emissions

Fuel-efficient driving is all about looking and planning further ahead. This helps raise your hazard awareness and reduces the need for late and heavy braking. This will make your journeys more comfortable, as well as considerably reducing your fuel bills and reducing emissions that can damage the environment.

132 Mark *one* answer
What does fuel-efficient driving achieve?

- ☐ **A** Increased fuel consumption
- ☐ **B** Improved road safety
- ☐ **C** Damage to the environment
- ☐ **D** Increased exhaust emissions

The emphasis is on hazard awareness and planning ahead. By looking well ahead, you'll have plenty of time to deal with hazards safely and won't need to brake sharply. This will also reduce damage to the environment.

133 Mark *one* answer
What's the legal minimum tread depth for tyres on your trailer or caravan?

- ☐ **A** 1 mm
- ☐ **B** 1.6 mm
- ☐ **C** 2 mm
- ☐ **D** 2.6 mm

Trailers and caravans may be left in storage over the winter months, and tyres can deteriorate. It's important to check their tread depth and also their pressures and general condition. The legal tread depth of 1.6 mm applies to the central three-quarters of a tyre's breadth, over its entire circumference.

134 Mark *one* answer
When is fuel consumption at its highest?

- ☐ **A** When you're braking
- ☐ **B** When you're coasting
- ☐ **C** When you're accelerating
- ☐ **D** When you're turning sharply

Accelerating uses a lot of fuel, so always try to use the accelerator smoothly. Taking your foot off the accelerator allows the momentum of the car to take you forward, especially when going downhill. This can save a considerable amount of fuel without any loss of control over the vehicle.

135 Mark *one* answer
When may a passenger travel in a car without wearing a seat belt?

☐ **A** When they're under 14 years old
☐ **B** When they're under 1.5 metres (5 feet) in height
☐ **C** When they're sitting in the rear seat
☐ **D** When they're exempt for medical reasons

If you have adult passengers, it's their responsibility to wear a seat belt, but you should still remind them to use one as they get in the car. It's your responsibility to make sure that all children in your car are secured with an appropriate restraint. Exemptions are allowed for those with a medical exemption certificate.

136 Mark *one* answer
You're driving a friend's children home from school. They're both under 14 years old. Who's responsible for making sure they wear a seat belt or approved child restraint where required?

☐ **A** An adult passenger
☐ **B** The children
☐ **C** You, the driver
☐ **D** Your friend

Passengers should always be secured and safe. Children should be encouraged to fasten their seat belts or approved restraints themselves from an early age, so that it becomes a matter of routine. As the driver, you must check that they're fastened securely. It's your responsibility.

137 Mark *one* answer
What's likely to happen if you put too much oil in your engine?

☐ **A** The clutch pedal will lock
☐ **B** The air intake will become blocked
☐ **C** The timing belt will slip
☐ **D** The oil seals will leak

Too much oil will lead to increased pressure in the engine. This could damage oil seals and lead to oil leaks. Any excess oil should be drained off.

138 Mark *one* answer
You have to make an unexpected journey. You're carrying a five-year-old child on the back seat of your car. They're under 1.35 metres (4 feet 5 inches) tall. How should you seat them if a correct child restraint isn't available?

☐ **A** Behind the passenger seat
☐ **B** Using an adult seat belt
☐ **C** Sharing a belt with an adult
☐ **D** Between two other children

In journeys of unexpected necessity, and when a correct child restraint isn't available, the child must sit on the rear seat and use an adult seat belt. In a collision, unrestrained objects and people can cause serious injury or even death.

139 Mark *one* answer

You're carrying an 11-year-old child on the front seat of your car. They're under 1.35 metres (4 feet 5 inches) tall. What seat belt security must be in place?

☐ **A** They must use an adult seat belt
☐ **B** They must be able to fasten their own seat belt
☐ **C** They must use a suitable child restraint
☐ **D** They must be able to see clearly out of the front window

As the driver, it's your responsibility to make sure that children are secure and safe in your vehicle. Make yourself familiar with the rules. When children are carried on the back seat, there are a few very exceptional cases when an adult seat belt can be used instead of a correct child restraint.

140 Mark *one* answer

You're stopped at the side of the road. What must you do if you'll be waiting there for some time?

☐ **A** Switch off the engine
☐ **B** Apply the steering lock
☐ **C** Switch off the radio
☐ **D** Use your headlights

If your vehicle is stationary and is likely to remain so for some time, you must switch off the engine unless you're stationary in traffic or diagnosing a fault.

141 Mark *one* answer

You want to put a rear-facing baby seat on the front passenger seat. What must you do if the passenger seat is protected by a frontal airbag?

☐ **A** Deactivate the airbag
☐ **B** Turn the seat to face sideways
☐ **C** Ask a passenger to hold the baby
☐ **D** Put the child in an adult seat belt

It's illegal to fit a rear-facing baby seat into a passenger seat protected by an active frontal airbag. If the airbag activates, it could cause serious injury or even death to the child. You must secure it in a different seat or deactivate the relevant airbag. Follow the manufacturer's advice when fitting a baby seat.

142 Mark *one* answer

You're leaving your vehicle parked on a road and unattended. When may you leave the engine running?

☐ **A** If you'll be parking for less than five minutes
☐ **B** If the battery keeps going flat
☐ **C** When parked in a 20 mph zone
☐ **D** Never if you're away from the vehicle

When you leave your vehicle parked on a road, switch off the engine and secure the vehicle. Make sure no valuables are visible, shut all the windows, lock the vehicle, and set the alarm if the vehicle has one.

143 Mark *one* answer
How much can stopping distances increase in icy conditions?

- ☐ **A** Two times
- ☐ **B** Three times
- ☐ **C** Five times
- ☐ **D** Ten times

Tyre grip is greatly reduced in icy conditions. For this reason, you need to allow up to ten times the stopping distance you would allow on dry roads.

144 Mark *one* answer
What requires extra care when you're driving or riding in windy conditions?

- ☐ **A** Using the brakes
- ☐ **B** Moving off on a hill
- ☐ **C** Turning into a narrow road
- ☐ **D** Passing pedal cyclists

Always give cyclists plenty of room when overtaking them. You need to give them even more room when it's windy. A sudden gust could easily blow them off course and into your path.

145 Mark *one* answer
Why should you keep well to the left as you approach a right-hand bend?

- ☐ **A** To improve your view of the road
- ☐ **B** To overcome the effect of the road's slope
- ☐ **C** To let faster traffic from behind overtake
- ☐ **D** To be positioned safely if you skid

Keeping to the left as you approach right-hand bends will give you an earlier view around the bend and enable you to see any hazards sooner. It also reduces the risk of collision with any oncoming vehicle that may have drifted over the centre line while taking the bend.

146 Mark *one* answer

You've just gone through flood water. What should you do to make sure your brakes are working properly?

- ☐ **A** Accelerate and keep to a high speed for a short time
- ☐ **B** Go slowly while gently applying the brakes
- ☐ **C** Avoid using the brakes at all for a few miles
- ☐ **D** Stop for at least an hour to allow them time to dry

Water on the brakes will act as a lubricant, causing them to work less efficiently. Using the brakes lightly as you go along will quickly dry them out.

147 Mark *one* answer

What will be affected if the road surface becomes soft in very hot weather?

- ☐ **A** The suspension
- ☐ **B** The exhaust emissions
- ☐ **C** The fuel consumption
- ☐ **D** The tyre grip

If the road surface becomes very hot, it can soften. Tyres are unable to grip a soft surface as well as they can a firm dry one. Take care when cornering and braking.

148 Mark *one* answer

Where is your vehicle most likely to be affected by side winds?

- ☐ **A** On a narrow country lane
- ☐ **B** On an open stretch of road
- ☐ **C** On a busy stretch of road
- ☐ **D** On a long, straight road

In windy conditions, care must be taken on exposed roads. A strong gust of wind can blow you off course. Watch out for other road users who are particularly likely to be affected, such as cyclists, motorcyclists, high-sided lorries and vehicles towing trailers.

149 Mark *one* answer

You're following a vehicle on a wet road. You stay a safe distance behind it. What should you do if a driver overtakes you and pulls into the gap you've left?

- ☐ **A** Flash your headlights as a warning
- ☐ **B** Try to overtake safely as soon as you can
- ☐ **C** Drop back to regain a safe distance
- ☐ **D** Stay close to the other vehicle until it moves on

Wet weather will affect the time it takes for you to stop and can affect your control. Your speed should allow you to stop safely and in good time. If another vehicle pulls into the gap you've allowed, ease back until you've regained your stopping distance.

150 Mark *one* answer

You're travelling on the motorway. How can you lower the risk of a collision when the vehicle behind is following too closely?

- ☐ **A** Increase your distance from the vehicle in front
- ☐ **B** Brake sharply
- ☐ **C** Switch on your hazard warning lights
- ☐ **D** Move onto the hard shoulder and stop

On busy roads, traffic may still travel at high speeds. Don't follow the vehicle in front too closely. If a driver behind seems to be 'pushing' you, gradually increase your distance from the vehicle in front by slowing down gently. This will give you more space in front if you have to brake, and will reduce the risk of a collision involving several vehicles.

151 Mark *one* answer

You're following other vehicles in fog. You have your headlights on dipped beam. What else can you do to reduce the chances of being in a collision?

- ☐ **A** Keep close to the vehicle in front
- ☐ **B** Use main beam instead of dipped headlights
- ☐ **C** Keep up with the faster vehicles
- ☐ **D** Keep a safe distance from the vehicle in front

When it's foggy, use your headlights on dipped beam. This will help you see and be seen by other road users. If visibility is seriously reduced, consider using front and rear fog lights if you have them. Keep to a sensible speed and don't follow the vehicle in front too closely. If the road is wet and slippery, you'll need to allow twice the normal stopping distance.

152 Mark *one* answer

What should you do when you're using a contraflow system?

- ☐ **A** Choose an appropriate lane in good time
- ☐ **B** Switch lanes to make better progress
- ☐ **C** Increase speed to get through the contraflow more quickly
- ☐ **D** Follow other motorists closely to avoid long queues

In a contraflow system, you'll be travelling close to oncoming traffic and sometimes in narrow lanes. You should get into the correct lane in good time, obey any temporary speed-limit signs and keep a safe separation distance from the vehicle ahead.

153 Mark *one* answer

How can you avoid wheelspin when you're driving on an icy road?

- ☐ **A** Drive at a slow speed in the highest gear possible
- ☐ **B** Use the parking brake if the wheels start to slip
- ☐ **C** Brake gently and repeatedly
- ☐ **D** Drive in a low gear at all times

If you're travelling on an icy road, extra caution will be required to avoid loss of control. Keeping your speed down and using the highest gear possible will reduce the risk of the tyres losing their grip on this slippery surface.

– Section 4

154 Mark *one* answer
What's the main cause of skidding?

☐ **A** The weather
☐ **B** The driver
☐ **C** The vehicle
☐ **D** The road

Skidding is usually caused by driver error. You should always adjust your driving to take account of the road and weather conditions.

155 Mark *one* answer
You're driving in freezing conditions. What should you do as you approach a sharp bend?

☐ **A** Coast into the bend
☐ **B** Apply your parking brake
☐ **C** Firmly use your footbrake
☐ **D** Slow down gently

Harsh use of the accelerator, brakes or steering is likely to lead to skidding, especially on slippery surfaces. Avoid steering and braking at the same time. In icy conditions, it's very important that you constantly assess what's ahead so that you can take appropriate action in plenty of time.

156 Mark *one* answer
You're about to start a journey in freezing weather. What part of your vehicle should you clear of ice and snow?

☐ **A** The aerial
☐ **B** The windows
☐ **C** The bumper
☐ **D** The boot

Driving in bad weather increases your risk of having a collision. If you absolutely have to travel, clear your lights, mirrors, number plates and windows of any snow or ice, so that you can see and be seen.

157 Mark *one* answer
What will help you to move off on a snowy surface?

☐ **A** Using the car's lowest gear
☐ **B** Using a higher gear than normal
☐ **C** Using a high engine speed
☐ **D** Using the parking brake and footbrake together

If you attempt to move off in a low gear, there'll be more torque (turning force) at the driven wheels than if you use a higher gear. More torque makes it easier for the tyres to lose grip and so spin the wheels.

158 Mark *one* answer
What should you do when you're driving in snowy conditions?

☐ **A** Brake firmly and quickly
☐ **B** Be ready to steer sharply
☐ **C** Use sidelights only
☐ **D** Brake gently in plenty of time

In snowy conditions, be careful with the steering, accelerator and brakes. Braking sharply while you're driving on snow is likely to make your car skid.

159 Mark *one* answer
What's the main benefit of driving a four-wheel-drive vehicle?

☐ **A** Improved grip on the road
☐ **B** Lower fuel consumption
☐ **C** Shorter stopping distances
☐ **D** Improved passenger comfort

By driving all four wheels, the vehicle has maximum grip on the road. This grip is especially helpful when travelling on slippery or uneven surfaces. However, having four-wheel drive doesn't replace the skills you need to drive safely.

160 Mark *one* answer
You're about to go down a steep hill. What should you do to control the speed of your vehicle?

☐ **A** Select a high gear and use the brakes carefully
☐ **B** Select a high gear and use the brakes firmly
☐ **C** Select a low gear and use the brakes carefully
☐ **D** Select a low gear and avoid using the brakes

When driving down a steep hill, gravity will cause your vehicle to speed up. This will make it more difficult for you to stop. To help keep your vehicle's speed under control, select a lower gear to give you more engine braking and make careful use of the brakes.

161 Mark *one* answer
What should you do when you park a car facing downhill?

☐ **A** Turn the steering wheel towards the kerb
☐ **B** Park close to the bumper of another car
☐ **C** Park with two wheels on the kerb
☐ **D** Turn the steering wheel away from the kerb

Turning the wheels towards the kerb will allow them to act as a chock, preventing any forward movement of the vehicle. It will also help to leave your car in gear, or select 'Park' if you have an automatic.

162 Mark *one* answer

You're driving in a built-up area that has traffic-calming measures. What should you do when you approach a road hump?

☐ **A** Move across to the left-hand side of the road
☐ **B** Wait for any pedestrians to cross
☐ **C** Check your mirror and slow down
☐ **D** Stop and check both pavements

Many towns have road humps as part of traffic-calming measures, designed to slow down traffic. Reduce your speed when driving over them. If you go too fast, you could lose control or damage your car. Look out for pedestrians or cyclists while you're driving in these areas.

163 Mark *one* answer

On what type of road surface may anti-lock brakes be ineffective?

☐ **A** Dry
☐ **B** Loose
☐ **C** Firm
☐ **D** Smooth

Poor contact with the road surface could cause one or more of the tyres to lose grip on the road. This is more likely to happen when braking in poor weather conditions and when the road has a loose, slippery or uneven surface.

164 Mark *one* answer

You're driving a vehicle that has anti-lock brakes. How should you apply the footbrake when you need to stop in an emergency?

☐ **A** Slowly and gently
☐ **B** Slowly but firmly
☐ **C** Rapidly and gently
☐ **D** Rapidly and firmly

You may have to stop in an emergency due to a misjudgement by another driver or a hazard arising suddenly, such as a child running out into the road. If your vehicle has anti-lock brakes, you should apply the brakes immediately and keep them firmly applied until you stop.

165 Mark *one* answer

You're driving along a country road. You see this sign. What should you do after dealing safely with the hazard?

☐ **A** Check your tyre pressures
☐ **B** Switch on your hazard warning lights
☐ **C** Accelerate briskly
☐ **D** Test your brakes

If your brakes have been thoroughly soaked, you should check that they're working properly before you build up speed again. Before you do this, remember to check your mirrors and consider what's behind you.

166 Mark *one* answer
What would suggest you're driving on an icy road?

☐ **A** There's less wind noise
☐ **B** There's less tyre noise
☐ **C** There's less transmission noise
☐ **D** There's less engine noise

Drive extremely carefully when the roads are icy. When travelling on ice, tyres make virtually no noise and the steering feels light and unresponsive. In icy conditions, be very gentle when braking, accelerating and steering.

167 Mark *one* answer
You're driving along a wet road. How can you tell if your vehicle's tyres are losing their grip on the surface?

☐ **A** The engine will stall
☐ **B** The steering will feel very heavy
☐ **C** The engine noise will increase
☐ **D** The steering will feel very light

If you drive at speed in very wet conditions, your steering may suddenly feel lighter than usual. This means that the tyres have lifted off the surface of the road and are floating on the surface of the water. This is known as aquaplaning. Reduce speed but don't brake until your steering returns to normal.

168 Mark *one* answer
In which conditions will your overall stopping distance increase?

☐ **A** In the rain
☐ **B** In fog
☐ **C** At night
☐ **D** In strong winds

Extra care should be taken in wet weather. On wet roads, your stopping distance could be double that in dry conditions.

169 Mark *one* answer
You're driving on an open road in dry weather. What distance should you keep from the vehicle in front?

☐ **A** A two-second time gap
☐ **B** One car length
☐ **C** Two metres (6 feet 6 inches)
☐ **D** Two car lengths

One way of checking there's a safe distance between you and the vehicle in front is to use the two-second rule. To check for a two-second time gap, choose a stationary object ahead, such as a bridge or road sign. When the car in front passes the object, say 'Only a fool breaks the two-second rule'. If you reach the object before you finish saying the phrase, you're too close and need to increase the gap.

170 Mark *one* answer
How can you use your vehicle's engine as a brake?

☐ **A** By changing to a lower gear
☐ **B** By selecting reverse gear
☐ **C** By changing to a higher gear
☐ **D** By selecting neutral gear

When driving on downhill stretches of road, selecting a lower gear gives increased engine braking. This will prevent excessive use of the brakes, which become less effective if they overheat.

171 Mark *one* answer
How should you use anti-lock brakes when you need to stop in an emergency?

☐ **A** Keep pumping the footbrake to prevent skidding
☐ **B** Brake normally but grip the steering wheel tightly
☐ **C** Brake promptly and firmly until you've stopped
☐ **D** Apply the parking brake to reduce the stopping distance

If you have ABS and need to stop in an emergency, keep your foot firmly on the brake pedal until the vehicle has stopped. When the ABS operates, you may hear a grating sound and feel vibration through the brake pedal. This is normal and you should maintain pressure on the brake pedal until the vehicle stops.

172 Mark *one* answer
What lights should you use when you're driving on a wet motorway and vehicles are throwing up surface spray?

☐ **A** Hazard warning lights
☐ **B** Dipped headlights
☐ **C** Rear fog lights
☐ **D** Sidelights

When surface spray reduces visibility, switch on your headlights on dipped beam. This will help other road users to see you.

173 Mark *one* answer
What can result when you travel for long distances in neutral (known as coasting)?

☐ **A** Improvement in control
☐ **B** Easier steering
☐ **C** Reduction in control
☐ **D** Increased fuel consumption

Coasting is the term used when the clutch is held down, or the gear lever is in neutral, and the vehicle is allowed to freewheel. This reduces the driver's control of the vehicle. When you coast, the engine can't drive the wheels to stabilise you through a corner, or give the assistance of engine braking to help slow the car.

174 Mark *one* answer
What should you do before starting a journey in foggy weather?

☐ **A** Wear a hi-visibility jacket
☐ **B** Have a caffeinated drink
☐ **C** Allow more time
☐ **D** Reduce your tyre pressures

Don't venture out if your journey isn't necessary. If you have to travel and someone is expecting you at the other end, let them know that you'll be taking longer than usual for your journey. This will stop them worrying if you don't turn up on time and will also take the pressure off you, so you don't feel you have to rush.

---

175 Mark *one* answer
What should you do when you're overtaking a motorcyclist on a windy day?

☐ **A** Pass closely
☐ **B** Pass very slowly
☐ **C** Pass widely
☐ **D** Pass immediately

In strong winds, riders of two-wheeled vehicles are particularly vulnerable. When you overtake them, allow plenty of room. Check to the left as you pass to make sure they're safe.

176 Mark *one* answer
What does it mean if the Electronic Stability Control (ESC) indicator lamp lights up while you're driving?

☐ **A** The ESC system has activated
☐ **B** The ESC system has a fault
☐ **C** The ESC system is running a routine test
☐ **D** The ESC system is switched off

ESC is a computer controlled technology that detects reduced traction and automatically makes corrective adjustments to prevent loss of control. The ESC lamp comes on to alert the driver that the system has activated and the car is approaching its handling limits. It's a powerful driver aid but it cannot save a car once its traction limits have been exceeded.

177 Mark *one* answer
Where would you expect to see these markers?

☐ **A** On a motorway sign
☐ **B** On a railway bridge
☐ **C** On a large goods vehicle
☐ **D** On a diversion sign

These markers must be fitted to vehicles over 13 metres long, large goods vehicles, and rubbish skips placed in the road. They're reflective to make them easier to see in the dark.

---

178 Mark *one* answer
What's the main hazard shown in this picture?

☐ **A** Vehicles turning right
☐ **B** Vehicles doing U-turns
☐ **C** The cyclist crossing the road
☐ **D** Parked cars around the corner

Look at the picture carefully and try to imagine you're there. The cyclist in this picture appears to be trying to cross the road. You must be able to deal with the unexpected, especially when you're approaching a hazardous junction. Look well ahead to give yourself time to deal with any hazards.

179 Mark *one* answer
Which road user has caused a hazard?

☐ **A** The parked car (arrowed A)
☐ **B** The pedestrian waiting to cross (arrowed B)
☐ **C** The moving car (arrowed C)
☐ **D** The car turning (arrowed D)

The car arrowed A is parked within the area marked by zigzag lines at the pedestrian crossing. Parking here is illegal. It also
- blocks the view for pedestrians wishing to cross the road
- restricts the view of the crossing for approaching traffic.

180 Mark *one* answer
What should the driver of the car approaching the crossing do?

☐ **A** Continue at the same speed
☐ **B** Sound the horn
☐ **C** Drive through quickly
☐ **D** Slow down and get ready to stop

Look well ahead to see whether any hazards are developing. This will give you more time to deal with them in the correct way. The man in the picture is clearly intending to cross the road. You should be travelling at a speed that allows you to check your mirror, slow down and stop in good time. You shouldn't have to brake harshly.

181 Mark *one* answer
What should the driver of the dark grey car be especially aware of?

☐ **A** The uneven road surface
☐ **B** Traffic following behind
☐ **C** Doors opening on parked cars
☐ **D** Empty parking spaces

When passing parked cars, there's a risk that a driver or passenger may not check before opening the door into the road. A defensive driver will drive slowly and be looking for people who may be about to get out of their car.

182 Mark *one* answer
What should you expect if you see this sign ahead?

☐ **A** The road will go steeply uphill
☐ **B** The road will go steeply downhill
☐ **C** The road will bend sharply to the left
☐ **D** The road will bend sharply to the right

This sign indicates that the road will bend sharply to the left. Slow down in plenty of time and select the correct gear before you start to turn. Braking hard and late, while also sharply changing direction, is likely to cause a skid.

183 Mark *one* answer
What should you do as you approach this cyclist?

- ☐ **A** Try to overtake before the cyclist gets to the junction
- ☐ **B** Flash your headlights at the cyclist
- ☐ **C** Slow down and allow the cyclist to turn
- ☐ **D** Rev your engine so the cyclist knows you're following behind

Keep well back and give the cyclist time and room to turn safely. Don't intimidate them by getting too close or trying to squeeze past.

184 Mark *one* answer
Why must you take great care when emerging from this junction?

- ☐ **A** The road surface is poor
- ☐ **B** The footpath is narrow
- ☐ **C** The kerbs are high
- ☐ **D** The view is restricted

You may have to pull forward slowly until you can see up and down the road. Be aware that the traffic approaching the junction can't see you either. If you don't know that it's clear, don't go.

185 Mark *one* answer
Which type of vehicle should you be ready to give way to as you approach this bridge?

- ☐ **A** Bicycles
- ☐ **B** Buses
- ☐ **C** Motorcycles
- ☐ **D** Cars

A bus or high-sided lorry will have to take a position in the centre of the road to clear the bridge. There's normally a sign to show this. Look well ahead, past the bridge and be ready to stop and give way to large oncoming vehicles.

186 Mark *one* answer
What type of vehicle could you expect to meet in the middle of the road?

- ☐ **A** Lorry
- ☐ **B** Bicycle
- ☐ **C** Car
- ☐ **D** Motorcycle

The highest point of the bridge is in the centre, so a large vehicle might have to move to the centre of the road to have enough room to pass safely under the bridge.

187 Mark *one* answer
What must you do at this junction?

- ☐ **A** Stop behind the line, then edge forward to see clearly
- ☐ **B** Stop beyond the line, at a point where you can see clearly
- ☐ **C** Stop only if there's traffic on the main road
- ☐ **D** Stop only if you're turning right

The 'stop' sign has been put here because the view into the main road is poor. sYou must stop because it won't be possible to take proper observation while you're moving.

188 Mark *one* answer
What should you do if a driver pulls out of a side road in front of you, causing you to brake hard?

- ☐ **A** Ignore the error and stay calm
- ☐ **B** Flash your lights to show your annoyance
- ☐ **C** Sound your horn to show your annoyance
- ☐ **D** Overtake as soon as possible

Be tolerant if a vehicle emerges and you have to brake quickly. Anyone can make a mistake, so don't react aggressively. Be alert where there are side roads and be especially careful where there are parked vehicles, because these can make it difficult for emerging drivers to see you.

189 Mark *one* answer
How would age affect an older person's driving ability?

- ☐ **A** They won't be able to obtain car insurance
- ☐ **B** They'll need glasses to read road signs
- ☐ **C** They'll take longer to react to hazards
- ☐ **D** They won't signal at junctions

As people age, their reaction time gets slower. The rate of decline varies from person to person but you can expect them to take longer to react to a hazard and they may be hesitant in some situations – for example, at a junction.

190 Mark *one* answer
Do you need to plan rest stops when you're planning a long journey?

- ☐ **A** Yes, you should plan to stop every half an hour
- ☐ **B** Yes, regular stops help concentration
- ☐ **C** No, you'll be less tired if you get there as soon as possible
- ☐ **D** No, only fuel stops will be needed

Try to plan your journey so that you can take rest stops. It's recommended that you take a break of at least 15 minutes after every two hours of driving or riding. This should help to maintain your concentration.

191 Mark *one* answer
What should you do if the red lights start flashing as you approach a level crossing?

- ☐ **A** Go over it quickly
- ☐ **B** Go over it carefully
- ☐ **C** Stop before the barrier
- ☐ **D** Switch on your hazard warning lights

At level crossings, the red lights flash before and while the barrier is down. At most crossings, an amber light will precede the red lights. You must stop behind the white line unless you've already crossed it when the amber light comes on. Don't be tempted to zigzag around half-barriers.

192 Mark *one* answer
You're approaching a crossroads. What should you do if the traffic lights have failed?

- ☐ **A** Brake and stop only for large vehicles
- ☐ **B** Brake sharply to a stop before looking
- ☐ **C** Be prepared to brake sharply to a stop
- ☐ **D** Be prepared to stop for any traffic

When approaching a junction where the traffic lights have failed, you should proceed with caution. Treat the situation as an unmarked junction and be prepared to stop.

193 Mark *one* answer

What should the driver of the red car (arrowed) do?

☐ **A** Wave towards the pedestrians who are waiting to cross

☐ **B** Wait for the pedestrian in the road to cross

☐ **C** Quickly drive behind the pedestrian in the road

☐ **D** Tell the pedestrian in the road she shouldn't have crossed

Some people might take a long time to cross the road. They may be older or have a disability. Be patient and don't hurry them by showing your impatience. If pedestrians are standing at the side of the road, don't signal or wave them to cross. Other road users might not have seen your signal and this could lead the pedestrians into a hazardous situation.

194 Mark *one* answer

You're following a slower-moving vehicle. What should you do if there's a junction just ahead on the right?

☐ **A** Overtake after checking your mirrors and signalling

☐ **B** Only consider overtaking when you're past the junction

☐ **C** Accelerate quickly to overtake before reaching the junction

☐ **D** Slow down and prepare to overtake on the left

You should never overtake as you approach a junction. If a vehicle emerged from the junction while you were overtaking, a dangerous situation could develop very quickly.

195 Mark *one* answer
What should you do as you approach this overhead bridge?

- ☐ **A** Move out to the centre of the road before going through
- ☐ **B** Find another route; this one is only for high vehicles
- ☐ **C** Be prepared to give way to large vehicles in the middle of the road
- ☐ **D** Move across to the right-hand side before going through

Oncoming large vehicles may need to move to the middle of the road to pass safely under the bridge. There won't be enough room for you to continue, so you should be ready to stop and wait.

196 Mark *one* answer
Why are vehicle mirrors often slightly curved (convex)?

- ☐ **A** They give a wider field of vision
- ☐ **B** They totally cover blind spots
- ☐ **C** They make it easier to judge the speed of the traffic behind
- ☐ **D** They make the traffic behind look bigger

Although a convex mirror gives a wide view of the scene behind, you should be aware that it won't show you everything behind or to the side of your vehicle. Before you move off, you'll need to look over your shoulder to check for anything not visible in the mirrors.

197 Mark *one* answer
You're on a three-lane motorway. How should you overtake a slow-moving lorry in the middle lane if it's showing this sign?

- ☐ **A** Cautiously approach the lorry, then overtake on either side
- ☐ **B** Follow the lorry until you can leave the motorway
- ☐ **C** Use the right-hand lane and overtake the lorry normally
- ☐ **D** Approach with care and overtake on the left of the lorry

This sign is found on slow-moving or stationary works vehicles. If you wish to overtake it, do so on the left, as indicated. Be aware that there might be workmen in the area.

198 Mark *one* answer
What should you do if you think the driver of the vehicle in front has forgotten to cancel their right indicator?

- ☐ **A** Flash your lights to alert the driver
- ☐ **B** Sound your horn before overtaking
- ☐ **C** Overtake on the left if there's room
- ☐ **D** Stay behind and don't overtake

Be cautious and don't attempt to overtake. The driver may be unsure of the location of a junction and may turn suddenly.

199 Mark *one* answer
What's the main hazard the driver of the red car (arrowed) should be aware of?

- ☐ **A** Glare from the sun may affect the driver's vision
- ☐ **B** The black car may stop suddenly
- ☐ **C** The bus may move out into the road
- ☐ **D** Oncoming vehicles will assume the driver is turning right

If you can do so safely, give way to buses signalling to move off at bus stops. Try to anticipate the actions of other road users around you. The driver of the red car should be prepared for the bus pulling out. As you approach a bus stop, look to see how many passengers are waiting to board. If the last one has just got on, the bus is likely to move off.

200 Mark *one* answer
What type of vehicle displays this yellow sign?

- ☐ **A** A broken-down vehicle
- ☐ **B** A school bus
- ☐ **C** An ice-cream van
- ☐ **D** A private ambulance

Buses which carry children to and from school may stop at places other than scheduled bus stops. Be aware that they might pull over at any time to allow children to get on or off. This will normally be when traffic is heavy during rush hour.

201 Mark *one* answer
What hazard should you be aware of when travelling along this street?

- ☐ **A** Glare from the sun
- ☐ **B** Lack of road markings
- ☐ **C** Children running out between vehicles
- ☐ **D** Large goods vehicles

On roads where there are many parked vehicles, you might not be able to see children between parked cars and they may run out into the road without looking.

202 Mark *one* answer
What's the main hazard you should be aware of when following this cyclist?

- ☐ **A** The cyclist may move to the left and dismount
- ☐ **B** The cyclist may swerve into the road
- ☐ **C** The cyclist may get off and push their bicycle
- ☐ **D** The cyclist may wish to turn right at the end of the road

When following a cyclist, be aware that they have to deal with the hazards around them. They may wobble or swerve to avoid a pothole in the road or see a potential hazard and change direction suddenly. Don't follow them too closely or rev your engine impatiently.

203 Mark *one* answer
A driver's behaviour has upset you. How can you get over this incident safely?

- ☐ **A** Stop and take a break
- ☐ **B** Shout abusive language
- ☐ **C** Gesture to them with your hand
- ☐ **D** Follow them, flashing your headlights

If you feel yourself becoming tense or upset, stop in a safe place and take a break. Tiredness can make things worse and may cause a different reaction to upsetting situations.

204 Mark *one* answer
How should you drive in areas with traffic-calming measures?

- ☐ **A** At a reduced speed
- ☐ **B** At the speed limit
- ☐ **C** In the centre of the road
- ☐ **D** With headlights on dipped beam

Traffic-calming measures such as road humps, chicanes and narrowings are intended to slow drivers down to protect vulnerable road users. Don't speed up until you reach the end of the traffic-calmed zone.

205 Mark *one* answer
Why should you slow down as you approach this hazard?

- ☐ **A** Because of the level crossing
- ☐ **B** Because it's hard to see to the right
- ☐ **C** Because of approaching traffic
- ☐ **D** Because of animals crossing

You should be slowing down and selecting the correct gear in case you have to stop at the level crossing. Look for the signals and be prepared to stop if necessary.

206 Mark *one* answer
Why are place names painted on the road surface?

☐ **A** To restrict the flow of traffic
☐ **B** To warn of oncoming traffic
☐ **C** To help you select the correct lane in good time
☐ **D** To prevent you from changing lanes

The names of towns and cities may be painted on the road at busy junctions and complex road systems. They guide you into the correct lane in good time, allowing traffic to flow more freely.

207 Mark *one* answer
Some two-way roads are divided into three lanes. Why are they particularly dangerous?

☐ **A** Traffic in both directions can use the middle lane to overtake
☐ **B** Traffic can travel faster in poor weather conditions
☐ **C** Traffic can overtake on the left
☐ **D** Traffic uses the middle lane for emergencies only

If you intend to overtake, you must consider that approaching traffic could be planning the same manoeuvre. When you've considered the situation and decided it's safe, indicate your intentions early. This will show the approaching traffic that you intend to pull out.

208 Mark *one* answer
What type of vehicle uses an amber flashing beacon on a dual carriageway?

☐ **A** An ambulance
☐ **B** A fire engine
☐ **C** A doctor on call
☐ **D** A tractor

An amber flashing beacon on a vehicle indicates that it's moving slowly or stopped and a possible hazard. Look well ahead on a dual carriageway and you should be able to see and respond to these vehicles in good time.

209 Mark *one* answer
What does this signal from a police officer mean to oncoming traffic?

☐ **A** Go ahead
☐ **B** Stop
☐ **C** Turn left
☐ **D** Turn right

Police officers may need to direct traffic; for example, at a junction where the traffic lights have broken down. Check your copy of *The Highway Code* for the signals that they use.

210 Mark *one* answer
Why should you be cautious when going past this bus waiting at a bus stop?

- ☐ **A** There's a zebra crossing ahead
- ☐ **B** There are driveways on the left
- ☐ **C** People may cross the road in front of it
- ☐ **D** The road surface will be slippery

A bus at a bus stop can hide pedestrians who might try to cross the road just in front of it. Drive at a speed that will enable you to respond safely if you have to.

211 Mark *one* answer
Where would it be unsafe to overtake?

- ☐ **A** On a single carriageway
- ☐ **B** On a one-way street
- ☐ **C** Approaching a junction
- ☐ **D** Travelling up a long hill

You should overtake only when it's really necessary and you can see it's clear ahead. Look out for road signs and markings that show it's illegal or would be unsafe to overtake; for example, approaching junctions or bends. In many cases, overtaking is unlikely to significantly improve your journey time.

212 Mark *one* answer
How can drinking alcohol affect your ability to drive?

- ☐ **A** Your ability to judge speed will be reduced
- ☐ **B** Your confidence will be reduced
- ☐ **C** Your reactions will be faster
- ☐ **D** Your awareness of danger will be improved

Alcohol will severely reduce your ability to drive or ride safely and there are serious consequences if you're caught over the drink-drive limit. It's known that alcohol can

- • affect your judgement
- • cause overconfidence
- • reduce coordination and control.

213 Mark *one* answer
What does the solid white line at the side of the road indicate?

- ☐ **A** Traffic lights ahead
- ☐ **B** Edge of the carriageway
- ☐ **C** Footpath on the left
- ☐ **D** Cycle path

The continuous white line shows the edge of the carriageway. It can be especially useful when visibility is restricted, such as at night or in bad weather. It's discontinued in some places; for example, at junctions, lay-bys, entrances or other openings.

214 Mark *one* answer
You're driving towards this level crossing. What would be the first warning of an approaching train?

- ☐ **A** Both half-barriers down
- ☐ **B** A steady amber light
- ☐ **C** One half-barrier down
- ☐ **D** Twin flashing red lights

The steady amber light will be followed by twin flashing red lights that mean you must stop. An alarm will also sound to alert you to the fact that a train is approaching.

215 Mark *one* answer
You're behind this cyclist. When the traffic lights change, what should you do?

- ☐ **A** Try to move off before the cyclist
- ☐ **B** Allow the cyclist time and room
- ☐ **C** Turn right but give the cyclist room
- ☐ **D** Tap your horn and drive through first

Hold back and allow the cyclist to move off. Some junctions have special areas marked across the front of the traffic lane. These allow cyclists to wait for the lights to change and move off ahead of other traffic.

216 Mark *one* answer
You intend to turn left at the traffic lights. What should you do just before turning?

- ☐ **A** Check your right mirror
- ☐ **B** Move up closer to the car ahead
- ☐ **C** Move out to the right
- ☐ **D** Check for bicycles on your left

If you've been in a queue of traffic and are about to turn left, check your nearside for cyclists as they often filter past on the nearside of slow-moving or stationary vehicles.

217 Mark *one* answer
Why should you reduce your speed here?

- ☐ **A** A staggered junction is ahead
- ☐ **B** A low bridge is ahead
- ☐ **C** The road surface changes ahead
- ☐ **D** The road narrows ahead

Traffic could be turning off or pulling out ahead of you, to the left or right. Vehicles turning left will be slowing down before the junction, and any vehicles turning right may have to stop to allow oncoming traffic to clear. Be prepared for this, as you might have to slow down or stop behind them.

218 Mark *one* answer
What might you expect to happen in this situation?

- ☐ **A** Traffic will move into the right-hand lane
- ☐ **B** Traffic speed will increase
- ☐ **C** Traffic will move into the left-hand lane
- ☐ **D** Traffic won't need to change position

Be courteous and allow the traffic to merge into the left-hand lane.

219 Mark *one* answer
You're driving on a road with several lanes. What do these signs above the lanes mean?

- ☐ **A** The two right lanes are open
- ☐ **B** The two left lanes are open
- ☐ **C** Traffic in the left lanes should stop
- ☐ **D** Traffic in the right lanes should stop

On some busy roads, lane control signals are used to vary the number of lanes available to give priority to the main traffic flow. A green arrow indicates that the lane is available to traffic facing the signal. A white diagonal arrow means that the lane is closed ahead and traffic should move to the next lane on the left. A red cross means that the lane is closed to traffic facing the signal.

220 Mark *one* answer
You're invited to a pub lunch. What should you do if you know that you'll have to drive in the evening?

- ☐ **A** Avoid mixing your alcoholic drinks
- ☐ **B** Don't drink any alcohol at all
- ☐ **C** Have some milk before drinking alcohol
- ☐ **D** Eat a hot meal with your alcoholic drinks

Alcohol will stay in your body for several hours and may make you unfit to drive later in the day. Drinking during the day will also affect your performance at work or study.

221 Mark *one* answer

What will become more expensive after you've been convicted of driving while unfit through drink or drugs?

- ☐ **A** Road fund licence
- ☐ **B** Insurance premiums
- ☐ **C** Vehicle test certificate
- ☐ **D** Driving licence

You've shown that you're a risk to yourself and others on the road. For this reason, insurance companies may charge you a higher premium.

222 Mark *one* answer

What advice should you give to a driver who has had a few alcoholic drinks at a party?

- ☐ **A** Have a strong cup of coffee and then drive home
- ☐ **B** Drive home carefully and slowly
- ☐ **C** Go home by public transport
- ☐ **D** Wait a short while and then drive home

Drinking black coffee or waiting a few hours won't make any difference. Alcohol takes time to leave the body. A driver who has been drinking should go home by public transport or taxi. They might even be unfit to drive the following morning.

223 Mark *one* answer

What should you do about driving if you've been taking medicine that causes drowsiness?

- ☐ **A** Only drive if your journey is necessary
- ☐ **B** Drive on quiet roads
- ☐ **C** Ask someone to come with you
- ☐ **D** Avoid driving and check with your doctor

You aren't fit to drive if you're taking medicine that makes you drowsy. Check with your doctor if you're unsure. You mustn't put other road users, your passengers or yourself at risk.

224 Mark *one* answer

What should you do if a doctor prescribes drugs that are likely to affect your driving?

- ☐ **A** Only drive if someone is with you
- ☐ **B** Avoid driving on motorways
- ☐ **C** Get someone else to drive
- ☐ **D** Never drive at more than 30 mph

You shouldn't drive if you're taking medicine that could cause you to feel drowsy at the wheel. Ask someone else to drive or, if that isn't possible, find another way to get home.

225 Mark *one* answer
What must you do if your ability to drive is impaired during a period of illness?

☐ **A** See your doctor each time before you drive
☐ **B** Take smaller doses of any medicines
☐ **C** Stop driving until you're fit to drive again
☐ **D** Take all your medicines with you when you drive

Only drive if you're fit to do so. Driving when you're ill or taking some medicines can affect your concentration and judgement. It may also cause you to become drowsy or even fall asleep.

226 Mark *one* answer
What should you do if you begin to feel drowsy while you're driving?

☐ **A** Stop and rest as soon as possible
☐ **B** Turn the heater up to keep you warm and comfortable
☐ **C** Close the car windows to help you concentrate
☐ **D** Continue with your journey but drive more slowly

You'll be putting other road users at risk if you continue to drive when you're drowsy. Pull over and stop in a safe place for a rest. If you're driving a long distance, think about finding some accommodation so you can rest for longer before continuing your journey.

227 Mark *one* answer
What should you do if you become tired while you're driving on a motorway?

☐ **A** Pull up on the hard shoulder and change drivers
☐ **B** Leave the motorway at the next exit and rest
☐ **C** Increase your speed and turn up the radio volume
☐ **D** Close all your windows and set the heating to warm

If you feel yourself becoming tired or sleepy, you should leave the motorway at the next exit or services and stop for a rest. If you have to drive a long way, leave earlier and plan your journey to include rest stops. That way, you're less likely to become tired while driving and you'll still arrive in good time.

228 Mark *one* answer
You're about to drive home. What should you do if you feel very tired and have a severe headache?

☐ **A** Wait until you're fit and well before driving
☐ **B** Drive home, but take a tablet for headaches
☐ **C** Drive home if you can stay awake for the journey
☐ **D** Wait for a short time, then drive home slowly

All of your concentration should be on your driving. Any pain you feel will distract you, and you should avoid driving when drowsy. The safest course of action is to wait until you've rested and are feeling better before starting your journey.

229 Mark *one* answer
What can you do to help prevent tiredness on a long journey?

☐ **A** Eat a large meal before driving
☐ **B** Take regular refreshment breaks
☐ **C** Play loud music in the car
☐ **D** Complete the journey without stopping

Long-distance driving can be boring. This, coupled with a stuffy, warm vehicle, can make you feel tired and sleepy. Make sure you take rest breaks to help you stay awake and alert. Stop in a safe place before you get to the stage of fighting sleep.

230 Mark *one* answer
You take some cough medicine given to you by a friend. What should you do before driving your car?

☐ **A** Ask your friend if taking the medicine affected their driving
☐ **B** Drink some strong coffee one hour before driving
☐ **C** Check the label to see if the medicine will affect your driving
☐ **D** Drive a short distance to see if the medicine is affecting your driving

If you've taken medicine, never drive without first checking what the side effects might be; they might affect your judgement and perception, and therefore endanger lives.

231 Mark *one* answer
You're driving on a one-way street. What should you do if you realise you've taken the wrong route?

☐ **A** Reverse out of the road
☐ **B** Turn around in a side road
☐ **C** Continue and find another route
☐ **D** Reverse into a driveway

Never reverse or turn your vehicle around in a one-way street. It's illegal and could even cause a collision. If you've taken a wrong turn, carry on along the one-way street and find another route, checking the direction signs as you drive. Stop in a safe place if you need to check a map.

232 Mark *one* answer
What will be a serious distraction while you're driving?

☐ **A** Looking at road maps
☐ **B** Switching on your demister
☐ **C** Using your windscreen washers
☐ **D** Looking in your door mirror

Looking at road maps while driving is very dangerous. If you aren't sure of your route, stop in a safe place and check the map. You must not allow anything to take your attention away from the road while you're driving.

233 Mark *one* answer
What should you do if the vehicle starts reversing off the driveway?

- ☐ **A** Move to the opposite side of the road
- ☐ **B** Drive through as you have priority
- ☐ **C** Sound your horn and be prepared to stop
- ☐ **D** Speed up and drive through quickly

White lights at the rear of a car show that the driver has selected reverse gear. The driver is hidden from view so can't see you approaching. Sound your horn to warn of your presence, and be ready to stop if the car reverses into your path.

234 Mark *one* answer
**You've been involved in an argument that's made you feel angry.
What should you do before starting your journey?**

- ☐ **A** Open a window
- ☐ **B** Turn on your radio
- ☐ **C** Have an alcoholic drink
- ☐ **D** Calm down

If you're feeling upset or angry, you'll find it much more difficult to concentrate on your driving. You should wait until you've calmed down before starting a journey.

235 Mark *one* answer
You're driving on this dual carriageway. Why may you need to slow down?

- ☐ **A** There's a broken white line in the centre
- ☐ **B** There are solid white lines on either side
- ☐ **C** There are roadworks ahead of you
- ☐ **D** There are no footpaths

Look well ahead and read any road signs as you drive. They're there to inform you of what's ahead. In this case, you may need to slow down and change direction. Check your mirrors so you know what's happening around you before you change speed or direction.

236 Mark *one* answer

You've just been overtaken by this motorcyclist. What should you do if the rider cuts in sharply?

- ☐ **A** Sound the horn
- ☐ **B** Brake firmly
- ☐ **C** Keep a safe gap
- ☐ **D** Flash your lights

If another vehicle cuts in sharply, ease off the accelerator and drop back to allow a safe separation distance. Try not to overreact by braking sharply or swerving, as you could lose control. If vehicles behind you are too close or unprepared, it could lead to a crash.

237 Mark *one* answer

You're about to drive your car. What should you do if you can't find the glasses you need to wear?

- ☐ **A** Drive home slowly, keeping to quiet roads
- ☐ **B** Borrow a friend's glasses and use those
- ☐ **C** Drive home at night, so that the lights will help you
- ☐ **D** Find a way of getting home without driving

If you need to wear glasses for driving, it's illegal to drive without them. You must be able to see clearly when you're driving.

238 Mark *one* answer

How does drinking alcohol affect your driving behaviour?

- ☐ **A** It improves judgement skills
- ☐ **B** It increases confidence
- ☐ **C** It leads to faster reactions
- ☐ **D** It increases concentration

Alcohol can increase confidence to a point where your driving behaviour might become 'out of character'. Sensible behaviour might change to risk-taking behaviour. Never let yourself or your friends get into this situation.

239 Mark *one* answer

Why should you check the information leaflet before taking any medicine?

- ☐ **A** Drug companies want customer feedback on their products
- ☐ **B** You may have to let your insurance company know about the medicine
- ☐ **C** Some types of medicine can affect your ability to drive safely
- ☐ **D** The medicine you take may affect your hearing

Always check the label or information leaflet for any medication you take. The medicine might affect your driving. If you aren't sure, ask your doctor or pharmacist.

240 Mark *one* answer
You need glasses to read a vehicle number plate at the required distance. When must you wear them?

☐ **A** Only in bad weather conditions
☐ **B** Whenever you're driving
☐ **C** When you think it's necessary
☐ **D** Only at night time

Have your eyesight tested before you start your practical training. Then, throughout your driving life, have checks periodically, as your vision may change.

241 Mark *one* answer
Which type of glasses would make driving at night more difficult?

☐ **A** Half-moon
☐ **B** Round
☐ **C** Bifocal
☐ **D** Tinted

If you're driving at night or in poor visibility, tinted lenses will reduce the efficiency of your vision by reducing the amount of light reaching your eyes.

242 Mark *one* answer
What can seriously reduce your ability to concentrate?

☐ **A** Drugs
☐ **B** Busy roads
☐ **C** Tinted windows
☐ **D** Weather conditions

Both recreational drugs and prescribed medicine can affect your concentration. It's also an offence to drive with certain drugs in your body and a positive test could lead to a conviction.

243 Mark *one* answer
What must you do if your eyesight has become very poor and you're no longer able to meet the driver's eyesight requirements?

☐ **A** Tell the driver licensing authority
☐ **B** Tell your doctor
☐ **C** Tell the police
☐ **D** Tell your optician

Having very poor eyesight will have a serious effect on your ability to drive safely. If you can't meet the driver's eyesight requirements, you must tell DVLA (or DVA in Northern Ireland).

244 Mark *one* answer
When should you use hazard warning lights?

☐ **A** When you're double-parked on a two-way road
☐ **B** When your direction indicators aren't working
☐ **C** When warning oncoming traffic that you intend to stop
☐ **D** When your vehicle has broken down and is causing an obstruction

Hazard warning lights are an important safety feature and should be used if you've broken down and are causing an obstruction. Don't use them as an excuse to park illegally. You may also use them on motorways to warn traffic behind you of danger ahead.

245 Mark *one* answer

You want to turn left at this junction. What should you do if your view of the main road is restricted?

- ☐ **A** Stay well back and wait to see if anything comes
- ☐ **B** Build up your speed so that you can emerge quickly
- ☐ **C** Stop and apply the parking brake even if the road is clear
- ☐ **D** Approach slowly and edge out until you can see more clearly

You should slow right down, and stop if necessary, at any junction where your view is restricted. Edge forward until you can see properly. Only then can you decide whether it's safe to go.

246 Mark *one* answer

You're driving a car fitted with automatic transmission. When would you use 'kick down'?

- ☐ **A** To engage cruise control
- ☐ **B** To accelerate quickly
- ☐ **C** To brake progressively
- ☐ **D** To improve fuel economy

'Kick down' selects a lower gear, enabling the vehicle to accelerate faster.

247 Mark *one* answer

What should you do if it's raining and you're following this lorry on a motorway?

- ☐ **A** Allow a two-second separation gap
- ☐ **B** Switch your headlights onto main beam
- ☐ **C** Move into a lane that has less spray
- ☐ **D** Be aware of spray reducing your vision

The usual two-second time gap increases to four seconds when the roads are wet. If you stay well back, you'll
- be able to see past the vehicle
- be out of the spray thrown up by the lorry's tyres
- give yourself more time to stop if the need arises
- increase your chances of being seen by the lorry driver.

248 Mark *one* answer
You're driving towards this left-hand bend. What danger should you be anticipating?

- ☐ **A** A vehicle overtaking you
- ☐ **B** Mud on the road
- ☐ **C** The road getting narrower
- ☐ **D** Pedestrians walking towards you

Pedestrians walking on a road with no pavement should walk against the direction of the traffic. You can't see around this bend and if pedestrians are in the road you need to be able to deal with the situation safely. Always keep this in mind and give yourself time to react if a hazard does appear.

249 Mark *one* answer
What should you do if the traffic in the left-hand lane is slowing?

- ☐ **A** Slow down, keeping a safe separation distance
- ☐ **B** Accelerate past the vehicles in the left-hand lane
- ☐ **C** Pull up on the left-hand verge
- ☐ **D** Move across and continue in the right-hand lane

Allow the traffic to merge into the left-hand lane. Leave enough room so that you can maintain a safe separation distance, even if vehicles pull in ahead of you.

250 Mark *one* answer
When may you use hazard warning lights?

- ☐ **A** When driving on a motorway to warn traffic behind of a hazard ahead
- ☐ **B** When you're double-parked on a two-way road
- ☐ **C** When your direction indicators aren't working
- ☐ **D** When warning oncoming traffic that you intend to stop

Hazard warning lights are an important safety feature. Use them when driving on a motorway to warn traffic behind you of danger ahead. You should also use them if your vehicle has broken down and is causing an obstruction.

251 Mark *one* answer

You're waiting to emerge at a junction. Your view is restricted by parked vehicles. What can help you to see traffic on the road you're joining?

☐ **A** Looking for traffic behind you
☐ **B** Reflections of traffic in windows
☐ **C** Making eye contact with other road users
☐ **D** Checking for traffic in your interior mirror

You must be completely sure it's safe to emerge. Try to look for traffic through the windows of the parked cars or in the reflections in windows. Keep looking in all directions as you slowly edge forwards until you can see it's safe.

252 Mark *one* answer

What must you do if poor health affects your driving?

☐ **A** Inform your local police
☐ **B** Avoid using motorways
☐ **C** Always drive accompanied
☐ **D** Inform the licensing authority

You must tell DVLA (or DVA in Northern Ireland) if your health is likely to affect your ability to drive. The licensing authority will investigate your situation and then make a decision on whether you're fit enough to drive safely.

253 Mark *one* answer

Why should the junction on the left be kept clear?

☐ **A** To allow vehicles to enter and emerge
☐ **B** To allow the bus to reverse
☐ **C** To allow vehicles to make a U-turn
☐ **D** To allow vehicles to park

You should always try to keep junctions clear. If you're in queuing traffic, make sure that when you stop you leave enough space for traffic to flow in and out of the junction.

254 Mark *one* answer

What should you do if you start to feel drowsy while you're driving on a motorway?

☐ **A** Stop on the hard shoulder for a sleep
☐ **B** Open a window and stop as soon as it's safe and legal
☐ **C** Speed up to arrive at your destination sooner
☐ **D** Slow down and let other drivers overtake

Never stop on the hard shoulder to rest. If there's no service area for several miles, leave the motorway at the next exit and find somewhere safe and legal to pull over.

255 Mark *one* answer
Which sign means that there may be people walking along the road?

☐ A   ☐ B

☐ C   ☐ D

Always check the road signs. Triangular signs are warning signs: they inform you about hazards ahead and help you to anticipate any problems. There are a number of different signs showing pedestrians. Learn the meaning of each one.

256 Mark *one* answer
What should you do if you want to turn left at a junction where pedestrians have started to cross?

☐ A Go around them, leaving plenty of room
☐ B Stop and wave at them to cross
☐ C Sound your horn and proceed
☐ D Give way to them

When you're turning into a side road, pedestrians who are crossing have priority. You should wait to allow them to finish crossing safely. Be patient if they're slow or unsteady. Don't try to rush them by sounding your horn, flashing your lights, revving your engine or giving any other inappropriate signal.

257 Mark *one* answer
What hazard should you be especially aware of if you're turning left into a side road?

☐ A One-way street
☐ B Pedestrians
☐ C Traffic congestion
☐ D Parked vehicles

Make sure that you've reduced your speed and are in the correct gear for the turn. Look into the road before you turn and always give way to any pedestrians who are crossing.

258 Mark *one* answer
Why should you check for motorcyclists just before turning right into a side road?

- ☐ **A** They may be overtaking on your left
- ☐ **B** They may be following you closely
- ☐ **C** They may be emerging from the side road
- ☐ **D** They may be overtaking on your right

Never attempt to change direction to the right without first checking your right-hand mirror and blind spot. A motorcyclist might not have seen your signal and could be hidden by other traffic. This observation should become a matter of routine.

259 Mark *one* answer
Why is a toucan crossing different from other crossings?

- ☐ **A** Moped riders can use it
- ☐ **B** It's controlled by a traffic warden
- ☐ **C** It's controlled by two flashing lights
- ☐ **D** Cyclists can use it

Toucan crossings are shared by pedestrians and cyclists, who are permitted to cycle across. They're shown the green light together. The signals are push-button-operated and there's no flashing amber phase.

260 Mark *one* answer
How will a school crossing patrol signal you to stop?

- ☐ **A** By pointing to children waiting to cross
- ☐ **B** By displaying a red light
- ☐ **C** By displaying a 'stop' sign
- ☐ **D** By giving you an arm signal

If a school crossing patrol steps out into the road with a 'stop' sign, you must stop. Don't wave anyone across the road and don't get impatient or rev your engine.

261 Mark *one* answer
Where would you see this sign?

- ☐ **A** In the window of a car taking children to school
- ☐ **B** At the side of the road
- ☐ **C** At playground areas
- ☐ **D** On the rear of a school bus or coach

Vehicles that are used to carry children to and from school will be travelling at busy times of the day. If you're following a vehicle with this sign, be prepared for it to make frequent stops. It might pick up or set down passengers in places other than normal bus stops.

262 Mark *one* answer
What does this sign mean?

- ☐ **A** No route for pedestrians and cyclists
- ☐ **B** A route for pedestrians only
- ☐ **C** A route for cyclists only
- ☐ **D** A route for pedestrians and cyclists

This sign shows a shared route for pedestrians and cyclists: when it ends, the cyclists will be rejoining the main road.

---

263 Mark *one* answer
You see a pedestrian carrying a white stick that also has a red band. What does this mean?

- ☐ **A** They have limited mobility
- ☐ **B** They're deaf
- ☐ **C** They're blind
- ☐ **D** They're deaf and blind

When someone is deaf as well as blind, they may carry a white stick with a red reflective band or bands. They may not be aware that you're approaching and they may not be able to hear anything; so, for example, your horn would be ineffective as a warning to them.

264 Mark *one* answer
What would you do if you see older people crossing the road ahead?

- ☐ **A** Wave them across so they know that you've seen them
- ☐ **B** Be patient and allow them to cross in their own time
- ☐ **C** Rev the engine to let them know that you're waiting
- ☐ **D** Tap the horn in case they're hard of hearing

Be aware that older people might take a long time to cross the road. They might also be hard of hearing and not hear you approaching. Don't hurry older people across the road by getting too close to them or revving your engine.

---

265 Mark *one* answer
What should you do when you see an older person about to cross the road ahead?

- ☐ **A** Expect them to wait for you to pass
- ☐ **B** Speed up to get past them quickly
- ☐ **C** Stop and wave them across the road
- ☐ **D** Be careful; they may misjudge your speed

Older people may have impaired hearing, vision, concentration and judgement. They may also walk slowly and so could take a long time to cross the road.

266 Mark *one* answer
You're approaching a roundabout. What should you do if a cyclist ahead is signalling to turn right?

- ☐ **A** Overtake on the right
- ☐ **B** Give a warning with your horn
- ☐ **C** Signal the cyclist to move across
- ☐ **D** Give the cyclist plenty of room

If you're following a cyclist who's signalling to turn right at a roundabout, leave plenty of room. Give them space and time to get into the correct lane.

267 Mark *one* answer
Which vehicle should you allow extra room as you overtake them?

- ☐ **A** Lorry
- ☐ **B** Tractor
- ☐ **C** Bicycle
- ☐ **D** Road-sweeper

Don't pass cyclists too closely, as they may
- need to veer around a pothole, drain or other hazard
- be buffeted by side windbe made unsteady by your vehicle.

Always leave as much room as you would for a car, and don't cut in front of them.

268 Mark *one* answer
Why should you look carefully for motorcyclists and cyclists at junctions?

- ☐ **A** They may want to turn into the side road
- ☐ **B** They may slow down to let you turn
- ☐ **C** They're harder to see
- ☐ **D** They might not see you turn

Cyclists and motorcyclists are smaller than other vehicles and so are more difficult to see. They can easily be hidden from your view by cars parked near a junction.

269 Mark *one* answer
You're waiting to come out of a side road. Why should you look carefully for motorcycles?

- ☐ **A** Motorcycles are usually faster than cars
- ☐ **B** Police patrols often use motorcycles
- ☐ **C** Motorcycles can easily be hidden behind obstructions
- ☐ **D** Motorcycles have right of way

If you're waiting to emerge from a side road, look carefully for motorcycles: they can be difficult to see. Be especially careful if there are parked vehicles or other obstructions restricting your view.

270 Mark *one* answer

Why do motorcyclists use dipped headlights in daylight?

☐ **A** So that the rider can be seen more easily
☐ **B** To stop the battery overcharging
☐ **C** To improve the rider's vision
☐ **D** The rider is inviting you to proceed

A motorcycle can be lost from sight behind another vehicle. The use of headlights helps to make it more conspicuous and therefore more easily seen.

271 Mark *one* answer

Why do motorcyclists wear bright clothing?

☐ **A** They must do so by law
☐ **B** It helps keep them cool in summer
☐ **C** The colours are popular
☐ **D** To make them more visible

Motorcycles and scooters are generally smaller than other vehicles and can be difficult to see. Wearing bright clothing makes it easier for other road users to see a motorcyclist approaching, especially at junctions.

272 Mark *one* answer

Why do motorcyclists often look round over their right shoulder just before turning right?

☐ **A** To listen for traffic behind them
☐ **B** Motorcycles don't have mirrors
☐ **C** It helps them balance as they turn
☐ **D** To check for traffic in their blind area

When you see a motorcyclist take a glance over their shoulder, they're probably about to change direction. Recognising a clue like this helps you to anticipate their next action. This can improve road safety for you and others.

273 Mark *one* answer

Which is the most vulnerable road user?

☐ **A** Car driver
☐ **B** Tractor driver
☐ **C** Lorry driver
☐ **D** Motorcyclist

Pedestrians and riders on two wheels can be harder to see than other road users. Make sure you look for them, especially at junctions. Effective observation, coupled with appropriate action, can save lives.

274 Mark *one* answer
You're approaching a roundabout. What should you do if there are horses being ridden in front of you?

☐ **A** Sound your horn as a warning
☐ **B** Treat them like any other vehicle
☐ **C** Give them plenty of room
☐ **D** Accelerate past as quickly as possible

Horse riders often keep to the outside of the roundabout even if they're turning right. Give them plenty of room and remember that they may have to cross lanes of traffic.

---

275 Mark *one* answer
As you approach a pelican crossing, the lights change to green. What should you do if older people are still crossing?

☐ **A** Wave them to cross as quickly as they can
☐ **B** Rev your engine to make them hurry
☐ **C** Flash your lights in case they haven't noticed you
☐ **D** Wait patiently while they cross

If the lights turn to green, wait for any pedestrians to clear the crossing. Allow them to finish crossing the road in their own time, and don't try to hurry them by revving your engine.

276 Mark *one* answer
What action should you take when you see flashing amber lights under a school warning sign?

☐ **A** Reduce speed until you're clear of the area
☐ **B** Keep up your speed and sound the horn
☐ **C** Increase your speed to clear the area quickly
☐ **D** Wait at the lights until they stop flashing

The flashing amber lights are switched on to warn you that children may be crossing near a school. Slow down and take extra care, as you may have to stop.

277 Mark *one* answer

Why should these road markings be kept clear?

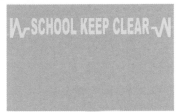

☐ **A** To allow children to be dropped off at school

☐ **B** To allow teachers to park

☐ **C** To allow children to be picked up after school

☐ **D** To allow children to see and be seen when they're crossing the road

The markings are there to show that the area should be kept clear. This is to allow an unrestricted view for
- approaching drivers and riders
- children wanting to cross the road.

278 Mark *one* answer

Where would you see this sign?

☐ **A** Near a school crossing

☐ **B** At a playground entrance

☐ **C** On a school bus

☐ **D** At a 'pedestrians only' area

School buses can stop to pick up or drop off schoolchildren at places that aren't designated bus stops. Watch out for children crossing the road to catch the bus or from the far side of the bus if they've just been dropped off.

279 Mark *one* answer

You're following two cyclists as they approach a roundabout in the left-hand lane. Where would you expect the cyclists to go?

☐ **A** Left

☐ **B** Right

☐ **C** Any direction

☐ **D** Straight ahead

Cyclists approaching a roundabout in the left-hand lane may be turning right but may not have been able to get into the correct lane due to heavy traffic. They may also feel safer keeping to the left all the way around the roundabout. Be aware of them and give them plenty of room.

Section 6 – **Vulnerable road users**

280 Mark *one* answer

You're travelling behind a moped. What should you do if you want to turn left a short distance ahead?

- ☐ **A** Overtake the moped before the junction
- ☐ **B** Pull alongside the moped and stay level until just before the junction
- ☐ **C** Sound your horn as a warning and pull in front of the moped
- ☐ **D** Stay behind until the moped has passed the junction

Passing the moped and turning into the junction could mean that you cut across the front of the rider. This might force them to slow down, stop or even lose control. Stay behind the moped until it has passed the junction and then you can turn without affecting the rider.

281 Mark *one* answer

You see a horse rider as you approach a roundabout. What should you do if they're signalling right but keeping well to the left?

- ☐ **A** Proceed as normal
- ☐ **B** Keep close to them
- ☐ **C** Cut in front of them
- ☐ **D** Stay well back

Allow the horse rider to enter and exit the roundabout in their own time. They may feel safer keeping to the left all the way around the roundabout. Don't get up close behind or alongside them, because that would probably upset the horse and create a dangerous situation.

282 Mark *one* answer

How should you react to inexperienced drivers?

- ☐ **A** Sound your horn to warn them of your presence
- ☐ **B** Be patient and prepare for them to react more slowly
- ☐ **C** Flash your headlights to indicate that it's safe for them to proceed
- ☐ **D** Overtake them as soon as possible

Learners might not have confidence when they first start to drive. Allow them plenty of room and don't react adversely to their hesitation. We all learn from experience, but new drivers will have had less practice in dealing with all the situations that might occur.

283 Mark *one* answer

What should you do when you're following a learner driver who stalls at a junction?

- ☐ **A** Be patient, as you expect them to make mistakes
- ☐ **B** Stay very close behind and flash your headlights
- ☐ **C** Start to rev your engine if they take too long to restart
- ☐ **D** Immediately steer around them and drive on

Learning to drive is a process of practice and experience. Try to understand this and tolerate those who make mistakes while they're learning.

284 Mark *one* answer

You're on a country road. What should you expect to see coming towards you on your side of the road?

☐ **A** Motorcycles
☐ **B** Bicycles
☐ **C** Pedestrians
☐ **D** Horse riders

On a quiet country road, always be aware that there may be a hazard just around the next bend, such as a slow-moving vehicle or pedestrians. Pedestrians are advised to walk on the right-hand side of the road if there's no pavement, so they may be walking towards you on your side of the road.

285 Mark *one* answer

You're following a cyclist. What should you do when you wish to turn left a short distance ahead?

☐ **A** Overtake the cyclist before you reach the junction
☐ **B** Pull alongside the cyclist and stay level until after the junction
☐ **C** Hold back until the cyclist has passed the junction
☐ **D** Go around the cyclist on the junction

Make allowances for cyclists, and give them plenty of room. Don't overtake and then immediately turn left. Be patient and turn behind them when they've passed the junction.

286 Mark *one* answer

A horse rider is in the left-hand lane approaching a roundabout. Where should you expect the rider to go?

☐ **A** In any direction
☐ **B** To the right
☐ **C** To the left
☐ **D** Straight ahead

Horses and their riders move more slowly than other road users. They might not have time to cut across heavy traffic to take up a position in the right-hand lane. For this reason, a horse and rider may approach a roundabout in the left-hand lane even though they're turning right.

287 Mark *one* answer

Powered vehicles used by disabled people are small and can be hard to see. What must they display if they're travelling on a dual carriageway?

☐ **A** Flashing red beacon
☐ **B** Flashing green beacon
☐ **C** Flashing blue beacon
☐ **D** Flashing amber beacon

Powered vehicles used by disabled people are small and low making them hard to see on the road. They also travel very slowly. On an unrestricted dual carriageway, they must display a flashing amber beacon to warn other road users of their presence.

288 Mark *one* answer
What does it mean when a moving vehicle is showing a flashing amber beacon?

☐ **A** The vehicle is slow moving
☐ **B** The vehicle has broken down
☐ **C** The vehicle is a doctor's car
☐ **D** The vehicle belongs to a school crossing patrol

Different coloured beacons warn of different types of vehicle needing special attention. Blue beacons are used on emergency vehicles that need priority. Green beacons are found on doctors' cars. Amber beacons generally denote slower moving vehicles, which are often large. These vehicles are usually involved in road maintenance or local amenities and make frequent stops.

289 Mark *one* answer
What does this sign mean?

☐ **A** Contraflow cycle lane
☐ **B** With-flow cycle lane
☐ **C** Cycles and buses only
☐ **D** No cycles or buses

Usually, a picture of a cycle will also be painted on the road, and sometimes the lane will have a different coloured surface. Leave these areas clear for cyclists and don't pass too closely when you overtake.

290 Mark *one* answer
What should you do when you see these horse riders in front?

☐ **A** Pull out to the middle of the road
☐ **B** Slow down and be ready to stop
☐ **C** Switch on your hazard warning lights
☐ **D** Give a right-turn signal

Be particularly careful when approaching horse riders – slow down and be prepared to stop. Always pass wide and slowly, and look out for signals given by the riders. Horses are unpredictable: always treat them as potential hazards and take great care when passing them.

291 Mark *one* answer
What's the purpose of these road markings?

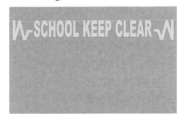

- [ ] **A** To ensure children can see and be seen when they're crossing the road
- [ ] **B** To enable teachers to have clear access to the school
- [ ] **C** To ensure delivery vehicles have easy access to the school
- [ ] **D** To enable parents to pick up or drop off children safely

These markings are found on the road outside schools. Don't stop or park on them, even to set down or pick up children. The markings are there to ensure that drivers, riders, children and other pedestrians have a clear view of the road in all directions.

292 Mark *one* answer
What should you do if the left-hand pavement is closed due to street repairs?

- [ ] **A** Watch out for pedestrians walking in the road
- [ ] **B** Use your right-hand mirror more often
- [ ] **C** Speed up to get past the roadworks more quickly
- [ ] **D** Position close to the left-hand kerb

Where street repairs have closed off pavements, proceed carefully and slowly, as pedestrians might have to walk in the road.

293 Mark *one* answer
What should you do when you're following a motorcyclist along a road that has a poor surface?

- [ ] **A** Follow closely so they can see you in their mirrors
- [ ] **B** Overtake immediately to avoid delays
- [ ] **C** Allow extra room in case they swerve to avoid potholes
- [ ] **D** Allow the same room as normal to avoid wasting road space

To avoid being unbalanced, a motorcyclist might swerve to avoid potholes and bumps in the road. Be prepared for this and allow them extra space.

294 Mark *one* answer
What does this sign mean?

- [ ] **A** No cycling
- [ ] **B** Cycle route ahead
- [ ] **C** Cycle parking only
- [ ] **D** End of cycle route

More people are cycling today and cycle routes are being extended in our towns and cities to provide safe cycling routes. Respect the presence of cyclists on the road and give them plenty of room if you need to pass.

295 Mark *one* answer
You're approaching this roundabout. What should you do when a cyclist is keeping to the left while signalling to turn right?

☐ **A** Sound your horn
☐ **B** Overtake them
☐ **C** Assume they're turning left
☐ **D** Allow them space to turn

Cycling in today's heavy traffic can be hazardous. Some cyclists may not feel safe crossing the path of traffic to take up a position in an outside lane. Be aware of this and understand that, although they're in the left-hand lane, the cyclist might be turning right.

296 Mark *one* answer
What should you do when you're approaching this crossing?

☐ **A** Prepare to slow down and stop
☐ **B** Stop and wave the pedestrians across
☐ **C** Speed up and pass by quickly
☐ **D** Continue unless the pedestrians step out

Be courteous and prepare to stop. Don't wave people across, because this could be dangerous if another vehicle is approaching the crossing.

297 Mark *one* answer
What does it mean if you see a pedestrian with a dog that has a yellow or burgundy coat?

☐ **A** The pedestrian is an older person
☐ **B** The pedestrian is a dog trainer
☐ **C** The pedestrian is colour-blind
☐ **D** The pedestrian is deaf

Dogs trained to help deaf people have a yellow or burgundy coat. If you see one, you should take extra care, as the pedestrian may not be aware of vehicles approaching.

298 Mark *one* answer
Who may use toucan crossings?

- ☐ **A** Motorcyclists and cyclists
- ☐ **B** Motorcyclists and pedestrians
- ☐ **C** Only cyclists
- ☐ **D** Cyclists and pedestrians

There are some crossings where cycle routes lead cyclists to cross at the same place as pedestrians. These are called toucan crossings. Always look out for cyclists, as they're likely to be approaching faster than pedestrians.

299 Mark *one* answer
This junction, controlled by traffic lights, has a marked area between two stop lines. What's this for?

- ☐ **A** To allow taxis to position in front of other traffic
- ☐ **B** To allow people with disabilities to cross the road
- ☐ **C** To allow cyclists and pedestrians to cross the road together
- ☐ **D** To allow cyclists to position in front of other traffic

These are known as advanced stop lines. When the lights are red (or about to become red), you should stop at the first white line. However, if you've crossed that line as the lights change, you must stop at the second line even if it means you're in the area reserved for cyclists.

300 Mark *one* answer
You're about to overtake a cyclist. Why should you leave them as much room as you would give to a car?

- ☐ **A** The cyclist might speed up
- ☐ **B** The cyclist might get off their bicycle
- ☐ **C** The cyclist might be unsettled if you pass too near them
- ☐ **D** The cyclist might have to make a left turn

Before overtaking, assess the situation. Look well ahead to see whether the cyclist will need to change direction. Be especially aware of a cyclist approaching parked vehicles, as they'll need to alter course. Don't pass too closely or cut in sharply as this could unsettle the rider.

301 Mark *one* answer
What should you do when you're passing loose sheep on the road?

- ☐ **A** Briefly sound your horn
- ☐ **B** Go very slowly
- ☐ **C** Pass quickly but quietly
- ☐ **D** Herd them to the side of the road

Slow down and be ready to stop if you see animals in the road ahead. Animals are easily frightened by noise and vehicles passing too close to them. Stop if you're signalled to do so by the person in charge.

302 Mark *one* answer

At night, what does it mean if you see a pedestrian wearing reflective clothing and carrying a bright red light?

☐ **A** You're approaching roadworks
☐ **B** You're approaching an organised walk
☐ **C** You're approaching a slow-moving vehicle
☐ **D** You're approaching a traffic danger spot

The people on the walk should be keeping to the left, but don't assume this. Pass carefully, making sure you have time to do so safely. Be aware that the pedestrians have their backs to you and may not know that you're there.

303 Mark *one* answer

You've just passed your driving test. How can you reduce your risk of being involved in a collision?

☐ **A** By always staying close to the vehicle in front
☐ **B** By never going over 40 mph
☐ **C** By staying in the left-hand lane on all roads
☐ **D** By taking further training

New drivers and riders are often involved in a collision or incident early in their driving career. Due to a lack of experience, they may not react to hazards appropriately. Approved training courses are offered by driver and rider training schools for people who have passed their test but want extra training.

304 Mark *one* answer

You're turning right from a main road into a side road. There's no oncoming traffic. What should you do if pedestrians are standing on the pavement waiting to cross the side road?

☐ **A** Turn in because the pedestrians are safe on the pavement
☐ **B** Wave at the pedestrians, inviting them to cross the road
☐ **C** Wait and give way to the pedestrians
☐ **D** Sound your horn to alert the pedestrians to your presence

You should give way to pedestrians crossing or waiting to cross the road into which or from which you're turning. Be patient if they're cautious and take their time checking that it's safe before they step into the road.

305 Mark *one* answer

You're travelling on a narrow section of road. What should you do if a horse rider ahead is riding in the centre of the lane?

☐ **A** Sound your horn to alert them to your presence
☐ **B** Stay behind and allow them to ride in this position
☐ **C** Move across to the right and try to ease past them
☐ **D** Get up close behind to encourage them to move aside

On narrow sections of road, horse riders may ride in the centre of the lane. This is for their own safety as it makes them more visible. You should be patient and only pass when it's safe to do so.

306 Mark *one* answer
You're about to overtake a cyclist on a road that has a 30 mph speed limit. How much room should you leave them as you overtake?

☐ **A** At least as much room as you would if you were overtaking a car
☐ **B** At least a car's width
☐ **C** At least a car's length
☐ **D** At least 2 car widths

You should leave cyclists at least as much room as you would if you were overtaking a car. Leave them more room if you're overtaking at speeds over 30 mph.

307 Mark *one* answer
You're turning left from a main road into a side road. What should you do if there's a pedestrian on the pavement waiting to cross the side road?

☐ **A** Flash your lights to encourage the pedestrian to cross
☐ **B** Carry on turning into the side road
☐ **C** Sound your horn to let the pedestrian know you're there
☐ **D** Wait and give way to the pedestrian

You should give way to pedestrians crossing or waiting to cross the road into which or from which you're turning. Be patient if they're cautious, and let them check that it's safe from all directions before they step into the road. Do not signal or wave them to cross.

308 Mark *one* answer
You want to reverse into a side road. What should you do if you aren't sure that the area behind your car is clear?

☐ **A** Look through the rear window only
☐ **B** Get out and check
☐ **C** Check the mirrors only
☐ **D** Carry on, assuming it's clear

If you can't tell whether there's anything behind you, it's always safest to check before reversing. There may be a small child or a low obstruction close behind your car.

309 Mark *one* answer
You're about to reverse into a side road. What should you do if a pedestrian is waiting to cross behind your car?

☐ **A** Wave to the pedestrian to stop
☐ **B** Give way to the pedestrian
☐ **C** Sound your horn to warn the pedestrian
☐ **D** Reverse before the pedestrian starts to cross

If you need to reverse into a side road, try to find a place that's free from traffic and pedestrians. Look all around before and during the manoeuvre. Stop and give way to any pedestrians who want to cross behind you. Avoid waving them across, sounding the horn, flashing your lights or giving any signals that could mislead them and create a dangerous situation.

310 Mark *one* answer
Which road users are most difficult to see when you're reversing your car?

- ☐ **A** Motorcyclists
- ☐ **B** Car drivers
- ☐ **C** Cyclists
- ☐ **D** Children

It may not be possible to see a small child through the rear windscreen of your vehicle. Be aware of this before you reverse. If there are children about, get out and check that it's clear before reversing.

311 Mark *one* answer
You want to turn right from a junction. What should you do if your view is restricted by parked vehicles?

- ☐ **A** Move out quickly, but be prepared to stop
- ☐ **B** Sound your horn and pull out if there's no reply
- ☐ **C** Stop, then move forward slowly until you have a clear view
- ☐ **D** Stop, get out and look along the main road to check

If you want to turn right from a junction and your view is restricted, stop. Ease forward until you can see – something might be approaching. If you don't know, don't go.

312 Mark *one* answer
You're at the front of a queue of traffic waiting to turn right into a side road. Why is it important to check your right mirror just before turning?

- ☐ **A** To look for pedestrians about to cross
- ☐ **B** To check for overtaking vehicles
- ☐ **C** To make sure the side road is clear
- ☐ **D** To check for emerging traffic

A motorcyclist could be riding along the outside of the queue. Always check your mirror before turning, as situations behind you can change while you've been waiting to turn.

313 Mark *one* answer
You've driven up to a pelican crossing. What must you do while the amber light is flashing?

- ☐ **A** Signal the pedestrian to cross
- ☐ **B** Always wait for the green light before proceeding
- ☐ **C** Give way to any pedestrians on the crossing
- ☐ **D** Wait for the red-and-amber light before proceeding

The flashing amber light allows pedestrians already on the crossing to get to the other side before a green light shows to the traffic. Be aware that some pedestrians, such as older people and young children, need longer to cross. Let them do this at their own pace.

314 Mark *one* answer
You've stopped at a pelican crossing. What should you do if a disabled person is crossing slowly in front of you and the lights change to green?

- [ ] **A** Wait for them to finish crossing
- [ ] **B** Drive in front of them
- [ ] **C** Edge forward slowly
- [ ] **D** Sound your horn

At a pelican crossing, the green light means you may proceed as long as the crossing is clear. If someone hasn't finished crossing, be patient and wait for them, whether they're disabled or not.

315 Mark *one* answer
You're driving past a line of parked cars. What should you do if a ball bounces out into the road ahead?

- [ ] **A** Continue driving at the same speed and sound your horn
- [ ] **B** Continue driving at the same speed and flash your headlights
- [ ] **C** Slow down and be prepared to stop for children
- [ ] **D** Stop and wave the children across to fetch their ball

Beware of children playing in the street and running out into the road. If a ball bounces out from the pavement, slow down and be prepared to stop. Don't encourage anyone to retrieve it. Other road users may not see your signal and you might lead a child into a dangerous situation.

316 Mark *one* answer
You want to turn right from a main road into a side road. What should you do just before turning?

- [ ] **A** Cancel your right-turn signal
- [ ] **B** Select first gear
- [ ] **C** Check for traffic overtaking on your right
- [ ] **D** Stop and set the parking brake

In some circumstances, your indicators may be difficult to see and another road user may not realise you're about to turn. A final check in your mirror and blind spot can help you to see an overtaking vehicle, so that you can avoid turning across their path.

317 Mark *one* answer
You're driving in a slow-moving queue of traffic. What should you do just before changing lane?

- [ ] **A** Sound the horn and flash your lights
- [ ] **B** Look for motorcyclists filtering through the traffic
- [ ] **C** Give a 'slowing down' arm signal
- [ ] **D** Change down to first gear

In queuing traffic, motorcyclists could be passing you on either side. Use your mirrors and check your blind area before changing lanes or changing direction.

318 Mark *one* answer

You're driving in town. Why should you be careful if there's a bus at a bus stop on the other side of the road?

- ☐ **A** The bus might have broken down
- ☐ **B** Pedestrians might come from behind the bus
- ☐ **C** The bus might move off suddenly
- ☐ **D** The bus might remain stationary

If you see a bus ahead, watch out for pedestrians. They might not be able to see you if they're behind the bus.

319 Mark *one* answer

How should you overtake horse riders?

- ☐ **A** Drive up close and overtake as soon as possible
- ☐ **B** Speed isn't important but allow plenty of room
- ☐ **C** Use your horn just once to warn them
- ☐ **D** Drive slowly and leave plenty of room

When you decide to overtake a horse rider, make sure you can do so safely before you move out. Leave them plenty of room and pass slowly. Passing too close could startle the horse and unseat the rider.

320 Mark *one* answer

Why should you allow extra room while overtaking a motorcyclist on a windy day?

- ☐ **A** The rider may turn off suddenly to get out of the wind
- ☐ **B** The rider may be blown in front of you
- ☐ **C** The rider may stop suddenly
- ☐ **D** The rider may be travelling faster than normal

If you're driving in high winds, be aware that the conditions might make a motorcyclist (or cyclist) swerve or wobble. Take this into consideration if you're following or wish to overtake a two-wheeled vehicle.

321 Mark *one* answer

Where should you take particular care to look for motorcyclists and cyclists?

- ☐ **A** On dual carriageways
- ☐ **B** At junctions
- ☐ **C** At zebra crossings
- ☐ **D** On one-way streets

Motorcyclists and cyclists are often more difficult to see at junctions. They're easily hidden from view and you may not be able to see them approaching a junction if your view is partially blocked; for example, by other traffic.

322 Mark *one* answer

The road outside this school is marked with yellow zigzag lines. What do these lines mean?

- ☐ **A** You may park on the lines when dropping off schoolchildren
- ☐ **B** You may park on the lines when picking up schoolchildren
- ☐ **C** You shouldn't wait or park your vehicle here
- ☐ **D** You must stay with your vehicle if you park here

Parking here would block other road users' view of the school entrance and would endanger the lives of children on their way to and from school.

323 Mark *one* answer

You're driving past parked cars. What should you do if you see a bicycle wheel sticking out between the cars?

- ☐ **A** Accelerate past quickly and sound your horn
- ☐ **B** Slow down and wave the cyclist across
- ☐ **C** Brake sharply and flash your headlights
- ☐ **D** Slow down and be prepared to stop for a cyclist

Scan the road as you drive. Try to anticipate hazards by being aware of the places where they're likely to occur. You'll then be able to react in good time.

324 Mark *one* answer

You're driving at night. What should you do if you're dazzled by a vehicle behind you?

- ☐ **A** Set your mirror to the anti-dazzle position
- ☐ **B** Set your mirror to dazzle the other driver
- ☐ **C** Brake sharply to a stop
- ☐ **D** Switch your rear lights on and off

The interior mirror of most vehicles can be set to an anti-dazzle position. You'll still be able to see the lights of the traffic behind you, but the dazzle will be greatly reduced.

325 Mark *one* answer

You're driving towards a zebra crossing. What should you do if a person in a wheelchair is waiting to cross?

- ☐ **A** Continue on your way
- ☐ **B** Wave to the person to cross
- ☐ **C** Wave to the person to wait
- ☐ **D** Be prepared to stop

You should slow down and be prepared to stop, as you would for an able-bodied person. Don't wave them across, as other traffic may not stop.

326 Mark *one* answer
You're about to overtake a slow-moving motorcyclist. Which sign would make you take special care?

☐ A ☐ B

☐ C ☐ D

In windy weather, watch out for motorcyclists and also cyclists, as they can be blown sideways into your path. When you pass them, leave plenty of room and check their position in your mirror before pulling back in.

327 Mark *one* answer
You're waiting to turn right out of a minor road. It's clear to the left but a lorry is coming from the right. Why should you wait, even if you have enough time to turn?

☐ **A** Anything overtaking the lorry will be hidden from view
☐ **B** The lorry could suddenly speed up
☐ **C** The lorry might be slowing down
☐ **D** The load on the lorry might be unstable

Large vehicles can hide other vehicles that are overtaking – especially motorcycles. You need to be aware of the possibility of hidden vehicles and not assume that it's safe to turn.

328 Mark *one* answer
You're following a long vehicle as it approaches a crossroads. What should you do if it signals left but moves out to the right?

☐ **A** Get closer in order to pass it quickly
☐ **B** Stay well back and give it room
☐ **C** Assume the signal is wrong and that it's turning right
☐ **D** Overtake it as it starts to slow down

A long vehicle may need to swing out in the opposite direction as it approaches a turn, to allow the rear wheels to clear the kerb. Don't try to filter through if you see a gap; as the lorry turns, the gap will close.

329 Mark *one* answer
You're following a long vehicle approaching a crossroads. What should you do if the driver signals right but moves close to the left-hand kerb?

☐ **A** Warn the driver about the wrong signal
☐ **B** Wait behind the long vehicle
☐ **C** Report the driver to the police
☐ **D** Overtake on the right-hand side

When a long vehicle is going to turn right, it may need to keep close to the left-hand kerb. This is to prevent the rear end of the trailer cutting the corner. You need to be aware of how long vehicles behave in such situations. Don't overtake the lorry, because it could turn as you're alongside. Stay behind and wait for it to turn.

330 Mark *one* answer

You're approaching a mini-roundabout. What should you do if a long vehicle in front signals left but positions over to the right?

- ☐ **A** Sound your horn
- ☐ **B** Overtake on the left
- ☐ **C** Follow the same course as the lorry
- ☐ **D** Keep well back

At mini-roundabouts, there isn't much room for a long vehicle to manoeuvre. It will have to swing out wide so that it can complete the turn safely. Keep well back and don't try to move up alongside it.

331 Mark *one* answer

You're driving on a single carriageway road. Why should you keep well back while you're following a large vehicle?

- ☐ **A** To give yourself acceleration space if you decide to overtake
- ☐ **B** To get the best view of the road ahead
- ☐ **C** To leave a gap in case the vehicle stops and rolls back
- ☐ **D** To offer other drivers a safe gap if they want to overtake you

When following a large vehicle, keep well back. If you're too close, you won't be able to see the road ahead and the driver of the long vehicle might not be able to see you in their mirrors.

332 Mark *one* answer

You're travelling behind a bus. What should you do if it pulls up at a bus stop?

- ☐ **A** Accelerate past the bus
- ☐ **B** Look for pedestrians
- ☐ **C** Sound your horn
- ☐ **D** Pull in closely behind the bus

People may be running to catch the bus or passengers leaving the bus might wish to cross the road in front of the bus. Look out for them if you intend to go past it. Consider how many people are waiting to get on the bus – check the queue if you can. The bus might move off straight away if no-one is waiting to get on. If a bus is signalling to pull out, give it priority if it's safe to do so.

333 Mark *one* answer

You're following a lorry on a wet road. What should you do when spray makes it difficult to see the road ahead?

- ☐ **A** Drop back until you can see better
- ☐ **B** Put your headlights on full beam
- ☐ **C** Keep close to the lorry, away from the spray
- ☐ **D** Speed up and overtake quickly

Large vehicles can throw up a lot of spray when it's wet. This makes it difficult for drivers behind to see the road ahead. You'll be able to see more by dropping back further, out of the spray. This will also increase your separation distance, giving you more room to stop if you have to.

334 Mark *one* answer

You're leaving a safe gap as you follow a large vehicle. What should you do if a car moves into this gap?

- ☐ **A** Sound your horn
- ☐ **B** Drop back further
- ☐ **C** Flash your headlights
- ☐ **D** Start to overtake

Sometimes your separation distance is shortened by a driver moving into the gap you've allowed. When this happens, react positively, stay calm and drop further back to re-establish a safe following distance.

335 Mark *one* answer

What should you do when you're approaching a bus that's signalling to move away from a bus stop?

- ☐ **A** Get past before it moves
- ☐ **B** Allow it to pull away, if it's safe to do so
- ☐ **C** Flash your headlights as you approach
- ☐ **D** Signal left and wave the bus on

Try to give way to buses if you can do so safely, especially when the driver signals to pull away from a bus stop. Look out for people getting off the bus or running to catch it, because they may cross the road without looking. Don't accelerate to get past the bus, and don't flash your lights, as this could mislead other road users.

336 Mark *one* answer
What should you do if you want to overtake a long, slow-moving vehicle on a busy road?

- ☐ **A** Follow it closely and keep moving out to see the road ahead
- ☐ **B** Flash your headlights for the oncoming traffic to give way
- ☐ **C** Stay behind until the driver waves you past
- ☐ **D** Keep well back so that you get a good view of the road ahead

When you're following a long vehicle, stay well back so that you can get a better view of the road ahead. The closer you get, the less you'll be able to see of the road. Be patient and don't take a gamble. Only overtake when you're certain that you can complete the manoeuvre safely.

337 Mark *one* answer
Which vehicles are least likely to be affected by side wind?

- ☐ **A** Cyclists
- ☐ **B** Motorcyclists
- ☐ **C** High-sided vehicles
- ☐ **D** Cars

Although cars are the least likely to be affected, side winds can take anyone by surprise. This is most likely to happen after overtaking a large vehicle, when passing gaps between hedges or buildings, and on exposed sections of road.

338 Mark *one* answer
What should you do as you approach this lorry?

- ☐ **A** Slow down and be prepared to wait
- ☐ **B** Make the lorry wait for you
- ☐ **C** Flash your lights at the lorry
- ☐ **D** Move to the right-hand side of the road

When turning, long vehicles need much more room on the road than other vehicles. At junctions, they may take up the whole of the road space, so be patient and allow them the room they need.

339 Mark *one* answer
You're following a large vehicle as it approaches a crossroads. What should you do if the driver signals to turn left?

- ☐ **A** Overtake if you can leave plenty of room
- ☐ **B** Overtake if there are no oncoming vehicles
- ☐ **C** Wait for the driver to cancel their signal
- ☐ **D** Wait for the vehicle to finish turning

Hold back and wait until the vehicle has turned before proceeding. Don't overtake, because the vehicle turning left could hide another vehicle emerging from the same junction.

340 Mark *one* answer
Why is it more difficult to overtake a large vehicle than a car?

- ☐ **A** It will take longer to overtake a large vehicle
- ☐ **B** A large vehicle will be fitted with a speed limiter
- ☐ **C** A large vehicle will have air brakes
- ☐ **D** It will take longer for a large vehicle to accelerate

Depending on relative speed, it will usually take you longer to pass a lorry than other vehicles. Hazards to watch for include oncoming traffic, junctions ahead, bends or dips that could restrict your view, and signs or road markings that prohibit overtaking. Make sure you can see that it's safe to complete the manoeuvre before you start to overtake.

341 Mark *one* answer
It's very windy. What should you do if you're behind a motorcyclist who's overtaking a high-sided vehicle?

- ☐ **A** Overtake the motorcyclist immediately
- ☐ **B** Keep well back
- ☐ **C** Stay level with the motorcyclist
- ☐ **D** Keep close to the motorcyclist

Windy weather affects motorcyclists more than other vehicles. In windy conditions, high-sided vehicles cause air turbulence. You should keep well back, as the motorcyclist could be blown off course.

342 Mark *one* answer
What should you do if there's a bus at a bus stop ahead of you?

- ☐ **A** Flash your lights to warn the driver of your presence
- ☐ **B** Continue at the same speed but sound your horn as a warning
- ☐ **C** Watch carefully for the sudden appearance of pedestrians
- ☐ **D** Pass the bus as quickly as you possibly can

As you approach, look out for any signal the driver might make. If you pass the vehicle, watch out for pedestrians attempting to cross the road from behind the bus. They'll be hidden from view until the last moment.

343 Mark *one* answer
What should you be prepared to do in this situation?

- ☐ **A** Sound your horn and continue
- ☐ **B** Slow down and give way
- ☐ **C** Report the driver to the police
- ☐ **D** Squeeze through the gap

Sometimes, large vehicles may need more space than other road users. If a vehicle needs more time and space to turn, be prepared to stop and wait.

344 Mark *one* answer
Why should drivers be more careful on roads where trams also operate?

☐ **A** Because trams don't have a horn
☐ **B** Because trams can't stop for cars
☐ **C** Because trams don't have lights
☐ **D** Because trams can't steer to avoid obstructions

You should take extra care when you first encounter trams. You'll have to get used to dealing with a different traffic system. Be aware that trams can accelerate and travel very quickly, and they can't change direction to avoid obstructions.

345 Mark *one* answer
You're towing a caravan. Which is the safest type of rear-view mirror to use?

☐ **A** Interior wide-angle mirror
☐ **B** Extended-arm side mirrors
☐ **C** Ordinary door mirrors
☐ **D** Ordinary interior mirror

Towing a large trailer or caravan can greatly reduce your view of the road behind. You may need to fit extended-arm side mirrors so that you can see clearly behind and down both sides of the caravan or trailer.

346 Mark *one* answer
You're driving in heavy traffic on a wet road. Which lights should you use if there's a lot of surface spray?

☐ **A** Main-beam headlights
☐ **B** Sidelights only
☐ **C** Rear fog lights if visibility is more than 100 metres (328 feet)
☐ **D** Dipped headlights

You must make sure that other road users can see you, but you don't want to dazzle them. Use your dipped headlights during the day if visibility is poor. If visibility falls below 100 metres (328 feet), you may use your rear fog lights, but don't forget to turn them off when the visibility improves.

347 Mark *one* answer
What should you do if you overtake a cyclist when it's very windy?

☐ **A** Overtake very slowly
☐ **B** Keep close as you pass
☐ **C** Sound your horn repeatedly
☐ **D** Allow extra room

Cyclists, and motorcyclists, are very vulnerable in high winds. They can easily be blown well off course and veer into your path. Always allow plenty of room when overtaking them. Passing too close could cause a draught and unbalance the rider.

348 Mark *one* answer
When may you overtake another vehicle on their left?

- ☐ **A** When you're in a one-way street
- ☐ **B** When approaching a motorway slip road where you'll be turning off
- ☐ **C** When the vehicle in front is signalling to turn left
- ☐ **D** When a slower vehicle is travelling in the right-hand lane of a dual carriageway

You may pass slower vehicles on their left while travelling along a one-way street. Be aware of drivers who may need to change lanes and may not expect faster traffic passing on their left.

349 Mark *one* answer
You're travelling in very heavy rain. How is this likely to affect your overall stopping distance?

- ☐ **A** It will be doubled
- ☐ **B** It will be halved
- ☐ **C** It will be ten times greater
- ☐ **D** It will be no different

The road will be very wet and spray from other vehicles will reduce your visibility. Tyre grip will also be reduced, increasing your stopping distance. You should at least double your separation distance to make sure you can stop safely in the space you've allowed.

350 Mark *one* answer
What should you do when you're overtaking at night?

- ☐ **A** Wait until a bend so that you can see oncoming headlights
- ☐ **B** Sound your horn twice before moving out
- ☐ **C** Go past slowly so that you can react to unseen hazards
- ☐ **D** Beware of bends in the road ahead

Don't overtake if there's a possibility of a road junction, bend or brow of a bridge or hill ahead. There are many hazards that are difficult to see in the dark. Only overtake if you're certain that the road ahead is clear. Don't take a chance.

351 Mark *one* answer
When may you wait in a box junction?

- ☐ **A** When you're stationary in a queue of traffic
- ☐ **B** When approaching a pelican crossing
- ☐ **C** When approaching a zebra crossing
- ☐ **D** When oncoming traffic prevents you turning right

The purpose of a box junction is to keep the junction clear by preventing vehicles from stopping in the path of crossing traffic. You mustn't enter a box junction unless your exit is clear. However, you may enter the box and wait if you want to turn right and are only prevented from doing so by oncoming traffic.

352 Mark *one* answer

Which plate may appear with this road sign?

☐ **A** Humps for ½ mile ☐ **B** Hump Bridge

☐ **C** Low Bridge ☐ **D** Soft Verge

Road humps are used to slow down traffic. They're found in places where there are often pedestrians, such as

- shopping areas
- near schools
- residential areas.

Watch out for people close to the kerb or crossing the road.

353 Mark *one* answer

What's the reason for traffic-calming measures?

☐ **A** To stop road rage
☐ **B** To make overtaking easier
☐ **C** To slow traffic down
☐ **D** To make parking easier

Traffic-calming measures make the roads safer for vulnerable road users, such as cyclists, pedestrians and children. These can be designed as chicanes, road humps or other obstacles that encourage drivers and riders to slow down.

354 Mark *one* answer

What colour are the reflective studs along the left-hand edge of the motorway?

☐ **A** Green
☐ **B** Amber
☐ **C** Red
☐ **D** White

Reflective studs are used to help you in poor visibility. Different colours are used so that you'll know which lane you're in. These are

- red on the left-hand edge of the carriageway
- white between lanes
- amber on the right-hand edge of the carriageway
- green between the carriageway and slip roads.

355 Mark *one* answer
What's a rumble device designed to do?

- ☐ **A** Give directions
- ☐ **B** Prevent cattle escaping
- ☐ **C** Alert you to low tyre pressure
- ☐ **D** Alert you to a hazard

A rumble device consists of raised markings or strips, designed to give drivers an audible, visual and tactile warning. These devices are used in various locations, including in the line separating the hard shoulder and the left-hand lane on the motorway and on the approach to some hazards, to alert drivers to the need to slow down.

356 Mark *one* answer
What should you do if you have to make a journey in foggy conditions?

- ☐ **A** Follow other vehicles' tail lights closely
- ☐ **B** Avoid using dipped headlights
- ☐ **C** Leave plenty of time for your journey
- ☐ **D** Keep two seconds behind the vehicle ahead

If you're planning to make a journey when it's foggy, listen to the weather reports. If visibility is very poor, avoid making unnecessary journeys. If you do travel, leave plenty of time – and if someone is waiting for you to arrive, let them know that your journey will take longer than normal. This will also take off any pressure you may feel to rush.

357 Mark *one* answer
What must you do when you're overtaking a car at night?

- ☐ **A** Flash your headlights before overtaking
- ☐ **B** Select a higher gear
- ☐ **C** Switch your headlights to main beam before overtaking
- ☐ **D** Make sure you don't dazzle other road users

To prevent your headlights from dazzling the driver of the car in front, wait until you've passed them before switching to main beam.

358 Mark *one* answer
You're travelling on a road that has road humps. What should you do when the driver in front is travelling more slowly than you?

- ☐ **A** Sound your horn
- ☐ **B** Overtake as soon as you can
- ☐ **C** Flash your headlights
- ☐ **D** Slow down and stay behind

Be patient and stay behind the car in front. You shouldn't normally overtake other vehicles in areas subject to traffic calming. If you overtake here, you may easily exceed the speed limit, defeating the purpose of the traffic-calming measures.

359 Mark *one* answer
What's the purpose of the yellow lines painted across the road?

☐ **A** To show a safe distance between vehicles
☐ **B** To keep the area clear of traffic
☐ **C** To make you aware of your speed
☐ **D** To warn you to change direction

These lines may be painted on the road on the approach to a roundabout, a village or a particular hazard. The lines are raised and painted yellow, and their purpose is to make you aware of your speed. Reduce your speed in good time so that you avoid having to brake harshly over the last few metres before reaching the junction.

360 Mark *one* answer
What should you do when you meet an oncoming vehicle on a single-track road?

☐ **A** Reverse back to the main road
☐ **B** Carry out an emergency stop
☐ **C** Stop at a passing place
☐ **D** Switch on your hazard warning lights

Take care when using single-track roads. It can be difficult to see around bends, because of hedges or fences, so expect to meet oncoming vehicles. Drive carefully and be ready to pull into or stop opposite a passing place, where you can pass each other safely.

361 Mark *one* answer
The road is wet. Why would a motorcyclist steer around drain covers while they were cornering?

☐ **A** To avoid puncturing the tyres on the edge of the drain covers
☐ **B** To prevent the motorcycle sliding on the metal drain covers
☐ **C** To help judge the bend using the drain covers as marker points
☐ **D** To avoid splashing pedestrians on the pavement

Other drivers or riders may have to change course due to the size or characteristics of their vehicle. Understanding this will help you to anticipate their actions. Motorcyclists and cyclists will be checking the road ahead for uneven or slippery surfaces, especially in wet weather. They may need to move across their lane to avoid surface hazards such as potholes and drain covers.

362 Mark *one* answer

Why should you test your brakes after this hazard?

- ☐ **A** You'll be on a slippery road
- ☐ **B** Your brakes will be wet
- ☐ **C** You'll be going down a long hill
- ☐ **D** You'll have just crossed a long bridge

A ford is a crossing over a stream that's shallow enough to drive or ride through. After you've gone through a ford or deep puddle, your brakes will be wet and they won't work as well as usual. To dry them out, apply a light brake pressure while moving slowly. Don't travel at normal speeds until you're sure your brakes are working properly again.

363 Mark *one* answer

Why should you reduce your speed when you're driving or riding in fog?

- ☐ **A** The brakes don't work as well
- ☐ **B** You'll be dazzled by other headlights
- ☐ **C** The engine will take longer to warm up
- ☐ **D** It's more difficult to see what's ahead

You won't be able to see as far ahead in fog as you can on a clear day. You'll need to reduce your speed so that, if a hazard looms out of the fog, you have the time and space to take avoiding action. Travelling in fog is hazardous. If you can, try to delay your journey until it has cleared.

364 Mark *one* answer

What will happen to your car when you drive up a steep hill?

- ☐ **A** The high gears will pull better
- ☐ **B** The steering will feel heavier
- ☐ **C** Overtaking will be easier
- ☐ **D** The engine will work harder

The engine will need more power to pull the vehicle up the hill. When approaching a steep hill you should select a lower gear to help maintain your speed. You should do this without hesitation, so that you don't lose too much speed before engaging the lower gear.

365 Mark *one* answer

You're driving on the motorway in windy conditions. What should you do as you overtake a high-sided vehicle?

- ☐ **A** Increase your speed
- ☐ **B** Be wary of a sudden gust
- ☐ **C** Drive alongside very closely
- ☐ **D** Expect normal conditions

The draught caused by other vehicles – particularly those with high sides – could be strong enough to push you out of your lane. Be prepared for a sudden gust of wind as you overtake large vehicles. Keep both hands on the steering wheel to help you keep full control.

366 Mark *one* answer
You're driving in fog. Why should you keep well back from the vehicle in front?

- ☐ **A** In case it changes direction suddenly
- ☐ **B** In case its fog lights dazzle you
- ☐ **C** In case it stops suddenly
- ☐ **D** In case its brake lights dazzle you

If you're following another road user in fog, stay well back. The driver in front won't be able to see hazards until they're close and might need to brake suddenly. Also, the road surface is likely to be wet and could be slippery.

367 Mark *one* answer
What should you do if you park on the road when it's foggy?

- ☐ **A** Leave parking lights switched on
- ☐ **B** Leave dipped headlights and fog lights switched on
- ☐ **C** Leave dipped headlights switched on
- ☐ **D** Leave main-beam headlights switched on

If you have to park your vehicle in foggy conditions, try to find a place to park off the road. If this isn't possible, park on the road facing in the same direction as the traffic. Leave your parking lights switched on and make sure they're clean.

368 Mark *one* answer
You're driving at night. What should you do if you're dazzled by headlights coming towards you?

- ☐ **A** Pull down your sun visor
- ☐ **B** Slow down or stop
- ☐ **C** Flash your main-beam headlights
- ☐ **D** Shade your eyes with your hand

If the headlights of an oncoming vehicle dazzle you, slow down or, if necessary, stop. Don't close your eyes or swerve, as you'll increase your chances of having a collision. Don't flash your headlights either, as this could dazzle other drivers and make the situation worse.

369 Mark *one* answer
When may front fog lights be used?

- ☐ **A** When visibility is seriously reduced
- ☐ **B** When they're fitted above the bumper
- ☐ **C** When they aren't as bright as the headlights
- ☐ **D** When an audible warning device is used

Your fog lights must only be used when visibility is reduced to 100 metres (328 feet) or less. You need to be familiar with the layout of your dashboard so you're aware if your fog lights have been switched on in error, or you've forgotten to switch them off.

370 Mark *one* answer
You're driving with your front fog lights switched on. What should you do if the fog has cleared?

- [ ] **A** Leave them on if other drivers have their lights on
- [ ] **B** Switch them off as long as visibility remains good
- [ ] **C** Flash them to warn oncoming traffic that it's foggy
- [ ] **D** Drive with them on instead of your headlights

Switch off your fog lights if the weather improves, but be prepared to use them again if visibility reduces to less than 100 metres (328 feet).

371 Mark *one* answer
Why should you switch off your rear fog lights when the fog has cleared?

- [ ] **A** To allow your headlights to work
- [ ] **B** To stop draining the battery
- [ ] **C** To stop the engine losing power
- [ ] **D** To prevent dazzling drivers behind

Don't forget to switch off your fog lights when the weather improves. You could be prosecuted for driving with them on in good visibility. The high intensity of rear fog lights can dazzle drivers behind and make your brake lights difficult to notice.

372 Mark *one* answer
What will happen if you use rear fog lights in good conditions?

- [ ] **A** They'll make it safer when towing a trailer
- [ ] **B** They'll protect you from larger vehicles
- [ ] **C** They'll dazzle other drivers
- [ ] **D** They'll make drivers behind keep back

Rear fog lights shine more brightly than normal rear lights, so that they show up in reduced visibility. When the visibility improves, you must switch them off; this stops them dazzling the driver behind.

373 Mark *one* answer
Why would you fit chains to your wheels?

- [ ] **A** To help prevent damage to the road surface
- [ ] **B** To help prevent wear to the tyres
- [ ] **C** To help prevent skidding in deep snow
- [ ] **D** To help prevent the brakes locking

Chains can be fitted to your wheels in snowy conditions. They can help you to move off without wheelspin, or to keep moving in deep snow. You'll still need to adjust your driving to suit these conditions.

374 Mark *one* answer
How can you use your vehicle's engine to control your speed?

☐ **A** By changing to a lower gear
☐ **B** By selecting reverse gear
☐ **C** By changing to a higher gear
☐ **D** By selecting neutral

You should brake and slow down before selecting a lower gear. The gear can then be used to keep the speed low and help you control the vehicle. This is particularly helpful on long downhill stretches, where brake fade can occur if the brakes overheat.

375 Mark *one* answer
Why could it be dangerous to keep the clutch down, or select neutral, for long periods of time while you're driving?

☐ **A** Fuel spillage will occur
☐ **B** Engine damage may be caused
☐ **C** You'll have less steering and braking control
☐ **D** It will wear tyres out more quickly

Letting your vehicle roll or coast in neutral reduces your control over steering and braking. This can be dangerous on downhill slopes, where your vehicle could pick up speed very quickly.

376 Mark *one* answer
You're driving on an icy road. What distance from the car in front should you drive?

☐ **A** Four times the normal distance
☐ **B** Six times the normal distance
☐ **C** Eight times the normal distance
☐ **D** Ten times the normal distance

Don't travel in icy or snowy weather unless your journey is essential. Drive extremely carefully when roads are or may be icy. Stopping distances can be ten times greater than on dry roads.

377 Mark *one* answer
Which lights must you use if you're driving on a well-lit motorway at night?

☐ **A** Use only your sidelights
☐ **B** Use your headlights
☐ **C** Use rear fog lights
☐ **D** Use front fog lights

If you're driving on a motorway at night or in poor visibility, you must always use your headlights, even if the road is well lit. Other road users must be able to see you, but you should avoid causing dazzle.

378 Mark *one* answer

You're driving on a motorway at night. Which lights should you have on if there are other vehicles just ahead of you?

- ☐ **A** Front fog lights
- ☐ **B** Main-beam headlights
- ☐ **C** Sidelights only
- ☐ **D** Dipped headlights

If you're driving behind other traffic on the motorway at night, use dipped headlights. Main-beam headlights will dazzle the other drivers. Your headlights' dipped beam should fall short of the vehicle in front.

379 Mark *one* answer

What will affect your vehicle's stopping distance?

- ☐ **A** The speed limit
- ☐ **B** The street lighting
- ☐ **C** The time of day
- ☐ **D** The condition of the tyres

Having tyres correctly inflated and in good condition will ensure they have maximum grip on the road; how well your tyres grip the road has a significant effect on your car's stopping distance.

380 Mark *one* answer

When will you feel the effects of engine braking?

- ☐ **A** When you only use the parking brake
- ☐ **B** When you're in neutral
- ☐ **C** When you change to a lower gear
- ☐ **D** When you change to a higher gear

When you take your foot off the accelerator, engines have a natural resistance to turn, caused mainly by the cylinder compression. Changing to a lower gear requires the engine to turn faster and so it will have greater resistance than when it's made to turn more slowly. When going downhill, changing to a lower gear will therefore help to keep the vehicle's speed in check.

381 Mark *one* answer

Which lights should you switch on when daytime visibility is poor but not seriously reduced?

- ☐ **A** Headlights and fog lights
- ☐ **B** Front fog lights
- ☐ **C** Dipped headlights
- ☐ **D** Rear fog lights

Only use your fog lights when visibility is seriously reduced. Use dipped headlights in poor conditions because this helps other road users to see you without the risk of causing dazzle.

382 Mark *one* answer
Why are vehicles fitted with rear fog lights?

☐ **A** To make them more visible when driving at high speed
☐ **B** To show when they've broken down in a dangerous position
☐ **C** To make them more visible in thick fog
☐ **D** To warn drivers following closely to drop back

Rear fog lights make it easier to spot a vehicle ahead in foggy conditions. Avoid the temptation to use other vehicles' lights as a guide, as they may give you a false sense of security.

383 Mark *one* answer
There's been a heavy fall of snow. What should you consider before driving in these conditions?

☐ **A** Whether you should fit an amber flashing beacon to your car
☐ **B** Whether you should drive without wearing your seat belt
☐ **C** Whether you should wear sunglasses to reduce the glare
☐ **D** Whether your journey is essential

Consider whether the increased risk is worth it. If the weather conditions are bad and your journey isn't essential, then don't drive. If you have to drive, make sure you're well prepared in case you get stuck.

384 Mark *one* answer
What should you check before you start a journey in foggy weather?

☐ **A** The radiator has enough anti-freeze
☐ **B** You have a warning triangle in the vehicle
☐ **C** The windows and lights are clean and clear
☐ **D** You have a mobile phone with you

If you have to drive in fog, switch your dipped headlights on and keep all your windows clear. You should always be able to pull up within the distance you can see ahead.

385 Mark *one* answer
You've been driving in fog. What must you do when the visibility improves?

☐ **A** Switch off your fog lights
☐ **B** Keep your rear fog lights switched on
☐ **C** Keep your front fog lights switched on
☐ **D** Leave your fog lights switched on in case the fog returns

You must turn off your fog lights if visibility is more than 100 metres (328 feet). Be prepared for the fact that the fog may be patchy and you may need to turn them on again if the fog returns.

386 Mark *one* answer
Why is it dangerous to leave rear fog lights switched on after the fog has cleared?

☐ **A** They may be confused with brake lights
☐ **B** The bulbs would fail
☐ **C** Electrical systems could be overloaded
☐ **D** Direction indicators may not work properly

If your rear fog lights are left on when it isn't foggy, the glare they cause makes it difficult for road users behind to know whether you're braking or you've just forgotten to turn off your rear fog lights. This can be a particular problem on wet roads and on motorways. If you leave your rear fog lights on at night, road users behind you are likely to be dazzled and this could put them at risk.

387 Mark *one* answer
What will happen if you hold the clutch pedal down or roll in neutral for too long?

☐ **A** It will use more fuel
☐ **B** It will cause the engine to overheat
☐ **C** It will reduce your control
☐ **D** It will improve tyre wear

Holding the clutch down or staying in neutral for too long will cause your vehicle to freewheel. This is known as 'coasting' and it's dangerous because it reduces your control of the vehicle.

388 Mark *one* answer
Why is it bad technique to coast when you're driving downhill?

☐ **A** The fuel consumption will increase
☐ **B** The engine will overheat
☐ **C** The tyres will wear more quickly
☐ **D** The vehicle will gain speed more quickly

Coasting is when you allow the vehicle to freewheel in neutral or with the clutch pedal depressed. When travelling downhill, this will cause the vehicle to gain speed more quickly as you lose the benefits of engine braking; it may even lead to a loss of control. You shouldn't coast, especially when approaching hazards such as junctions or bends and when travelling downhill.

389 Mark *one* answer
What should you do when dealing with this hazard?

- ☐ **A** Switch on your hazard warning lights
- ☐ **B** Use a low gear and drive slowly
- ☐ **C** Use a high gear to prevent wheelspin
- ☐ **D** Switch on your windscreen wipers

In normal conditions, a ford can be crossed quite safely by driving through it slowly. The water may affect your brakes, so when you're clear of the ford, test them before you resume normal driving.

390 Mark *one* answer
Why is travelling in neutral for long distances (known as coasting) bad driving technique?

- ☐ **A** It will cause the car to skid
- ☐ **B** It will make the engine stall
- ☐ **C** The engine will run faster
- ☐ **D** There won't be any engine braking

Try to look and plan well ahead. Plan your approach to hazards and select the correct gear in good time. This will help give you the control you need to deal with anything unexpected that may occur.

391 Mark *one* answer
When must you use dipped headlights during the day?

- ☐ **A** All the time you're driving
- ☐ **B** When you're driving along narrow streets
- ☐ **C** When you're driving in poor visibility
- ☐ **D** When you're parking

You must use dipped headlights when daytime visibility is seriously reduced, generally to 100 metres (328 feet) or less. You may also use front or rear fog lights, but they must be switched off when visibility improves.

392 Mark *one* answer

You're joining a motorway from a slip road. How should you deal with traffic already on the motorway?

- ☐ **A** Carry on along the hard shoulder until you see a safe gap
- ☐ **B** Stop at the end of the slip road and look for a safe gap
- ☐ **C** Use the slip road to accelerate until you're moving much faster than the motorway traffic
- ☐ **D** Match your speed to traffic in the left-hand lane and filter into a safe gap

You should give way to traffic already on the motorway. Where possible, traffic may move over to let you in, but don't force your way into the traffic stream. Traffic could be travelling at high speed, so try to match your speed to filter in without affecting the traffic flow.

393 Mark *one* answer

What's the national speed limit on motorways for cars and motorcycles?

- ☐ **A** 30 mph
- ☐ **B** 50 mph
- ☐ **C** 60 mph
- ☐ **D** 70 mph

Travelling at the national speed limit doesn't allow you to hog the right-hand lane. Always use the left-hand lane whenever possible. When leaving a motorway, get into the left-hand lane well before your exit. Reduce your speed on the slip road and look out for sharp bends or curves and traffic queuing at roundabouts.

394 Mark *one* answer

Which vehicles should use the left-hand lane on a three-lane motorway?

- ☐ **A** Any vehicle that isn't overtaking
- ☐ **B** Large vehicles only
- ☐ **C** Emergency vehicles only
- ☐ **D** Slow vehicles only

On a motorway, all traffic should use the left-hand lane unless overtaking. When overtaking a number of slower vehicles, move back to the left-hand lane when you're safely past. Check your mirrors frequently and don't stay in the middle or right-hand lane if the left-hand lane is free.

395 Mark *one* answer

Which vehicles aren't allowed to use the right-hand lane of a three-lane motorway?

- ☐ **A** Small delivery vans
- ☐ **B** Motorcycles
- ☐ **C** Vehicles towing a trailer
- ☐ **D** Motorcycle and sidecar outfits

On the motorway, any vehicle towing a trailer is restricted to 60 mph. It isn't allowed in the right-hand lane, as it might hold up faster-moving traffic that wishes to overtake in that lane.

396 Mark *one* answer

Your vehicle breaks down on a motorway and you need to call for help. Why might it be better to use an emergency roadside telephone rather than a mobile phone?

- ☐ **A** It connects you to a local garage
- ☐ **B** Using a mobile phone will distract other drivers
- ☐ **C** It allows easy location by the emergency services
- ☐ **D** Mobile phones don't work on motorways

On a motorway, it's best to use a roadside emergency telephone so that the emergency services are able to find you easily. The location of the nearest telephone is shown by an arrow on marker posts at the edge of the hard shoulder. If you use a mobile, find out the number on the nearest marker post before you call. This number will let the operator know where you are and in which direction you're travelling.

397 Mark *one* answer

Your vehicle broke down on the hard shoulder of a motorway, but has now been repaired. How should you rejoin the main carriageway?

- ☐ **A** Move out onto the carriageway, then build up your speed
- ☐ **B** Move out onto the carriageway using your hazard warning lights
- ☐ **C** Gain speed on the hard shoulder before moving out onto the carriageway
- ☐ **D** Wait on the hard shoulder until someone flashes their headlights at you

Signal your intention and build up sufficient speed on the hard shoulder so that you can filter into a safe gap in the traffic. Don't push your way into a small gap or cause other traffic to alter speed or direction.

398 Mark *one* answer

You're travelling along a motorway. Where would you find a crawler or climbing lane?

- ☐ **A** On a steep gradient
- ☐ **B** Before a service area
- ☐ **C** Before a junction
- ☐ **D** Along the hard shoulder

Large, slow-moving vehicles can hinder the progress of other traffic. On a steep gradient, an extra crawler lane may be provided for slow-moving vehicles to allow faster-moving traffic to flow more easily.

399 Mark *one* answer

What do these motorway signs mean?

- ☐ **A** They're countdown markers to a bridge
- ☐ **B** They're distance markers to the next telephone
- ☐ **C** They're countdown markers to the next exit
- ☐ **D** They warn of a police control ahead

The exit from a motorway is indicated by countdown markers. These are positioned 90 metres (100 yards) apart, the first being 270 metres (300 yards) from the start of the slip road. Move into the left-hand lane well before you reach the start of the slip road.

400 Mark *one* answer

Where are amber reflective studs found on a motorway?

- ☐ **A** Between the hard shoulder and the carriageway
- ☐ **B** Between the acceleration lane and the carriageway
- ☐ **C** Between the central reservation and the carriageway
- ☐ **D** Between each pair of lanes

On motorways, reflective studs of various colours are fixed in the road between the lanes. These help you to identify which lane you're in when it's dark or in poor visibility. Amber-coloured studs are found on the right-hand edge of the main carriageway, next to the central reservation.

401 Mark *one* answer

What colour are the reflective studs between the lanes on a motorway?

- ☐ **A** Green
- ☐ **B** Amber
- ☐ **C** White
- ☐ **D** Red

White studs are found between the lanes on motorways. They reflect back the light from your headlights. This is especially useful in bad weather, when visibility is restricted.

402 Mark *one* answer

What colour are the reflective studs between a motorway and a slip road?

- ☐ **A** Amber
- ☐ **B** White
- ☐ **C** Green
- ☐ **D** Red

The studs between the carriageway and the hard shoulder are normally red. These change to green where there's a slip road, helping you to identify slip roads when visibility is poor or when it's dark.

403 Mark *one* answer

Your vehicle has broken down on a motorway. In which direction should you walk to find the nearest emergency telephone?

- ☐ **A** With the traffic flow
- ☐ **B** Facing oncoming traffic
- ☐ **C** In the direction shown on the marker posts
- ☐ **D** In the direction of the nearest exit

Along the hard shoulder there are marker posts at 100-metre intervals. These will direct you to the nearest emergency telephone.

404 Mark *one* answer

Why is it important to make full use of the slip road as you join a motorway?

- ☐ **A** Because there's space available to turn round if you need to
- ☐ **B** To allow you direct access to the overtaking lanes
- ☐ **C** To allow you to fit safely into the traffic flow in the left-hand lane
- ☐ **D** Because you can continue on the hard shoulder

Try to join the motorway without affecting the progress of the traffic in the left-hand lane and always give way to traffic already on the motorway. At busy times, you may have to slow down to merge into slow-moving traffic.

405 Mark *one* answer
How should you position yourself when you use the emergency telephone on a motorway?

- ☐ **A** Stay close to the carriageway
- ☐ **B** Face the oncoming traffic
- ☐ **C** Keep your back to the traffic
- ☐ **D** Stand on the hard shoulder

Traffic is passing you at speed. If the draught from a large lorry catches you by surprise, it could blow you off balance and even onto the carriageway. By facing the oncoming traffic, you can see approaching lorries and so be prepared for their draught. You'll also be in a position to see any other hazards approaching.

406 Mark *one* answer
What colour are the reflective studs between the hard shoulder and the left-hand lane of a motorway?

- ☐ **A** Green
- ☐ **B** Red
- ☐ **C** White
- ☐ **D** Amber

Red studs are placed between the edge of the carriageway and the hard shoulder. Where slip roads leave or join the motorway, the studs are green.

407 Mark *one* answer
On a three-lane motorway, which lane should you use if there's no traffic ahead?

- ☐ **A** Left
- ☐ **B** Right
- ☐ **C** Centre
- ☐ **D** Either the right or centre

On a three-lane motorway, you should travel in the left-hand lane unless you're overtaking. This applies regardless of the speed at which you're travelling.

408 Mark *one* answer
What should you do when going through a contraflow system on a motorway?

- ☐ **A** Use dipped headlights
- ☐ **B** Keep a good distance from the vehicle ahead
- ☐ **C** Switch lanes to keep the traffic flowing
- ☐ **D** Stay close to the vehicle ahead to reduce queues

At roadworks, and especially where a contraflow system is operating, a speed restriction is likely to be in place. Keep to the lower speed limit and don't
- switch lanes
- get too close to the vehicle in front of you.

Be aware that there will be no permanent barrier between you and the oncoming traffic.

409 Mark *one* answer
You're on a three-lane motorway. Which lane are you in if there are red reflective studs on your left and white ones to your right?

- ☐ **A** In the right-hand lane
- ☐ **B** In the middle lane
- ☐ **C** On the hard shoulder
- ☐ **D** In the left-hand lane

The colours of the reflective studs on the motorway and their locations are
- red – between the hard shoulder and the carriageway
- white – between lanes
- amber – between the carriageway and the central reservation
- green – along slip-road exits and entrances
- bright green/yellow – at roadworks and contraflow systems.

410 Mark *one* answer
What should you do when you're approaching roadworks on a motorway?

- ☐ **A** Speed up to clear the area quickly
- ☐ **B** Always use the hard shoulder
- ☐ **C** Obey the speed limit
- ☐ **D** Stay very close to the vehicle in front

Be aware of reduced speed limits at roadworks. Speed limits shown inside a red circle are mandatory and cameras are often used to enforce the reduced limit. Slow down in good time and keep your distance from the vehicle in front.

411 Mark *one* answer
Which vehicles are prohibited from using the motorway?

- ☐ **A** Powered mobility scooters
- ☐ **B** Motorcycles over 50 cc
- ☐ **C** Double-deck buses
- ☐ **D** Cars with automatic transmission

Motorways mustn't be used by pedestrians, cyclists, motorcycles under 50 cc, certain slow-moving vehicles without permission, and powered wheelchairs/mobility scooters.

412 Mark *one* answer
What should you do while you're driving or riding along a motorway?

- ☐ **A** Look much further ahead than you would on other roads
- ☐ **B** Travel much faster than you would on other roads
- ☐ **C** Maintain a shorter separation distance than you would on other roads
- ☐ **D** Concentrate more than you would on other roads

Traffic on motorways usually travels faster than on other roads. You need to be looking further ahead to give yourself more time to react to any hazard that may develop.

413 Mark *one* answer
What should you do immediately after joining a motorway?

☐ **A** Try to overtake
☐ **B** Re-adjust your mirrors
☐ **C** Position your vehicle in the centre lane
☐ **D** Stay in the left-hand lane

When you've just joined a motorway, stay in the left-hand lane long enough to get used to the higher speeds of motorway traffic before considering overtaking.

414 Mark *one* answer
When would you use the right-hand lane on a three-lane motorway?

☐ **A** When you're turning right
☐ **B** When you're overtaking
☐ **C** When you're travelling above the speed limit
☐ **D** When you're trying to save fuel

The right-hand lane of the motorway is for overtaking. Sometimes you may be directed into a right-hand lane as a result of roadworks or a traffic incident. This will be indicated by signs or officers directing the traffic.

415 Mark *one* answer
You're on a motorway that isn't subject to smart motorway regulations. When should you use the hard shoulder?

☐ **A** When you're stopping in an emergency
☐ **B** When you're leaving the motorway
☐ **C** When you're stopping for a rest
☐ **D** When you're joining the motorway

Don't use the hard shoulder for stopping unless it's an emergency. If you want to stop for any other reason, go to the next exit or service area.

416 Mark *one* answer
You're in the right-hand lane of a three-lane motorway. What do these overhead signs mean?

☐ **A** Move to the left and reduce your speed to 50 mph
☐ **B** There are roadworks 50 metres (55 yards) ahead
☐ **C** Use the hard shoulder until you've passed the hazard
☐ **D** Leave the motorway at the next exit

You must obey these signs even if there appear to be no problems ahead. There could be queuing traffic or another hazard that you can't see yet.

417 Mark *one* answer
When are you allowed to stop on a motorway?

☐ **A** When you need to walk and get fresh air
☐ **B** When you wish to pick up hitchhikers
☐ **C** When you're signalled to do so by traffic signals
☐ **D** When you need to use a mobile telephone

You must stop if overhead gantry signs show a red cross above every lane on the motorway. If any of the other lanes doesn't show a red cross, you may move into that lane and continue if it's safe to do so.

418 Mark *one* answer
You're travelling in the left-hand lane of a three-lane motorway. How should you react to traffic joining from a slip road?

☐ **A** Increase your speed to ensure they join behind you
☐ **B** Adjust your speed or change lane if you can do so safely
☐ **C** Maintain a steady speed
☐ **D** Switch on your hazard warning lights

Plan well ahead when approaching a slip road. If you see traffic joining the motorway, be prepared to adjust your speed or move to another lane if it's safe to do so. This can help the flow of traffic joining the motorway, especially at peak times.

419 Mark *one* answer
How should you use the lanes on a motorway?

☐ **A** Use the lane that has the least traffic
☐ **B** Keep to the left-hand lane unless you're overtaking
☐ **C** Overtake using the lane that's clearest
☐ **D** Stay in one lane until you reach your exit

You should normally travel in the left-hand lane unless you're overtaking a slower-moving vehicle. When you've finished overtaking, move back into the left-hand lane, but don't cut across in front of the vehicle that you've overtaken.

420 Mark *one* answer
You're travelling along a motorway. When are you allowed to overtake on the left?

☐ **A** When you can see well ahead that the hard shoulder is clear
☐ **B** When the traffic in the right-hand lane is signalling right
☐ **C** When you warn drivers behind by signalling left
☐ **D** When in queues and traffic to your right is moving more slowly than you are

Never overtake on the left, unless the traffic is moving in queues and the queue on your right is moving more slowly than the one you're in.

421 Mark *one* answer
When would you use an emergency refuge area on a smart motorway?

☐ **A** In cases of emergency or breakdown
☐ **B** If you think you'll be involved in a road rage incident
☐ **C** To stop and check where you are
☐ **D** To make a private phone call

On smart motorways, emergency refuge areas are built at the side of the hard shoulder. If you break down, try to get your vehicle into the refuge, where there's an emergency telephone. The phone connects directly to a control centre. Remember to take care when rejoining the motorway, especially if the hard shoulder is being used as a running lane.

422 Mark *one* answer
Traffic officers operate on motorways and some primary routes in England and Wales. What are they authorised to do?

☐ **A** Stop and arrest drivers who break the law
☐ **B** Repair broken-down vehicles on the motorway
☐ **C** Issue fixed penalty notices
☐ **D** Stop and direct anyone on a motorway

Traffic officers don't have enforcement powers but are able to stop and direct people on motorways and some 'A' class roads. They operate in England and Wales and work in partnership with the police at incidents, providing a highly trained and visible service. They're recognised by an orange-and-yellow jacket and their vehicle has yellow-and-black markings.

423 Mark *one* answer
You're on a smart motorway. What does it mean when a red cross is displayed above the hard shoulder?

- ☐ **A** Pull up in this lane to answer your mobile phone
- ☐ **B** Use this lane as a running lane
- ☐ **C** This lane can be used if you need a rest
- ☐ **D** You must not travel in this lane

Some motorways have been redesigned as smart motorways. At certain times, the hard shoulder will be open as a running lane. However, a red cross above the hard shoulder shows that it isn't open as a running lane and should only be used for emergencies and breakdowns.

424 Mark *one* answer
You're on a smart motorway. What does it mean when a mandatory speed limit is displayed above the hard shoulder?

- ☐ **A** You shouldn't travel in this lane
- ☐ **B** The hard shoulder can be used as a running lane
- ☐ **C** You can park on the hard shoulder if you feel tired
- ☐ **D** You can pull up in this lane to answer a mobile phone

A mandatory speed-limit sign above the hard shoulder shows that this part of the road can be used as a running lane between junctions. You must stay within the speed limit. Look out for vehicles that may have broken down and could be blocking the hard shoulder.

425 Mark *one* answer
How do smart motorways prevent traffic bunching?

☐ **A** By using higher speed limits
☐ **B** By using advisory speed limits
☐ **C** By using minimum speed limits
☐ **D** By using variable speed limits

When a smart motorway is operating, you must follow the mandatory signs on the gantries above each lane, including the hard shoulder. Variable speed limits help keep the traffic moving and also help to prevent bunching.

426 Mark *one* answer
What helps to reduce traffic bunching on a motorway?

☐ **A** Variable speed limits
☐ **B** Contraflow systems
☐ **C** National speed limits
☐ **D** Lane closures

Congestion can be reduced by keeping traffic at a constant speed. At busy times, maximum speed limits are displayed on overhead gantries. These can be varied quickly, depending on the amount of traffic. By keeping to a constant speed on busy sections of motorway, overall journey times are normally improved.

427 Mark *one* answer
When may you stop on a motorway?

☐ **A** If you have to read a map
☐ **B** When you're tired and need a rest
☐ **C** If your mobile phone rings
☐ **D** In an emergency or breakdown

You shouldn't normally stop on a motorway, but there may be occasions when you need to do so. If your vehicle breaks down or there's an emergency, stop on the hard shoulder and use the emergency telephones to call for assistance.

428 Mark *one* answer
What's the national speed limit for a car or motorcycle on a motorway?

☐ **A** 50 mph
☐ **B** 60 mph
☐ **C** 70 mph
☐ **D** 80 mph

The national speed limit for a car or motorcycle on a motorway is 70 mph. Lower speed limits may be in force; for example, at roadworks. Variable speed limits also operate in some areas when the motorway is very busy. Cars or motorcycles towing trailers are subject to a lower speed limit.

429 Mark *one* answer
You stop on the hard shoulder of a motorway and use the emergency telephone. Where's the best place to wait for help to arrive?

☐ **A** Next to the phone
☐ **B** Well away from the carriageway
☐ **C** With your vehicle
☐ **D** On the hard shoulder

When you're on the hard shoulder, you're at risk of being injured by motorway traffic. The safest place to wait is away from the carriageway, but near enough to see the emergency services arriving.

430 Mark *one* answer
You're on a motorway. What must you do if there's a red cross showing above every lane?

☐ **A** Pull onto the hard shoulder
☐ **B** Slow down and watch for further signals
☐ **C** Leave at the next exit
☐ **D** Stop and wait

A red cross signal above all lanes means you must stop and wait. Don't change lanes and don't try to continue any further along the motorway.

431 Mark *one* answer
You're on a smart motorway. What does it mean if a red cross is showing above the hard shoulder and mandatory speed limits above all other lanes?

☐ **A** The hard shoulder can be used as a rest area if you feel tired
☐ **B** The hard shoulder is for emergency or breakdown use only
☐ **C** The hard shoulder can be used as a normal running lane
☐ **D** The hard shoulder has a speed limit of 50 mph

A red cross above the hard shoulder shows that it's closed as a running lane and should only be used for emergencies or breakdowns. On a smart motorway, the hard shoulder may be used as a running lane at busy times. This will be shown by a mandatory speed limit on the gantry above the hard shoulder.

432 Mark *one* answer
On a smart motorway, what does this sign mean?

☐ **A** Use any lane except the hard shoulder
☐ **B** Use the hard shoulder only
☐ **C** Use the three right-hand lanes only
☐ **D** Use all the lanes, including the
      hard shoulder

You must obey mandatory speed-limit signs above motorway lanes, including the hard shoulder. In this case, you can use the hard shoulder as a running lane but you should look for any vehicles that may have broken down and may be blocking the hard shoulder.

433 Mark *one* answer
Where should you stop to rest if you feel tired while you're travelling along a motorway?

☐ **A** On the hard shoulder
☐ **B** At the nearest service area
☐ **C** On a slip road
☐ **D** On the central reservation

If you feel tired, stop at the nearest service area. If that's too far away, leave the motorway at the next exit and find a safe place to stop. You mustn't stop on the carriageway or hard shoulder of a motorway except in an emergency, when in a traffic queue, or when signalled to do so by a police officer, a traffic officer or traffic signals. Plan your journey so that you have regular rest stops.

434 Mark *one* answer
You have stopped in an emergency refuge area. What must you do before you rejoin the carriageway?

☐ **A** Use the emergency telephone
☐ **B** Give an arm signal as you are
      moving off
☐ **C** Switch on your vehicle's headlights
☐ **D** Switch on your vehicle's headlights

To rejoin the carriageway from an emergency refuge area, you must use the emergency telephone and follow the operator's advice. A lane may have to be closed so that you can rejoin the carriageway safely.

435 Mark *one* answer
How should you rejoin the motorway after a breakdown on the hard shoulder?

- ☐ **A** Build up speed on the hard shoulder before looking for a safe gap in the traffic
- ☐ **B** Move straight out into the left-hand lane as you are not allowed to drive on the hard shoulder
- ☐ **C** Wait until a vehicle in the left-hand lane signals to you that it's safe to rejoin
- ☐ **D** Keep your hazard lights flashing until you have safely rejoined the carriageway.

To rejoin a motorway from the hard shoulder, you first need to build up speed on the hard shoulder. You can then look for a safe gap in the traffic in the left-hand lane. Watch for traffic that may be returning from a lane on the right into the left-hand lane.

436 Mark *one* answer
What's the speed limit for a car towing a trailer on a motorway?

- ☐ **A** 40 mph
- ☐ **B** 50 mph
- ☐ **C** 60 mph
- ☐ **D** 70 mph

If you're towing a small, light trailer, it won't reduce your vehicle's performance by very much and it may not be visible in your mirrors. However, strong winds or buffeting from large vehicles might cause the trailer to snake from side to side. Be aware of your speed and don't exceed the reduced speed limit imposed on vehicles towing trailers.

437 Mark *one* answer
When should you use the left-hand lane of a motorway?

- ☐ **A** When your vehicle breaks down
- ☐ **B** When you're overtaking slower traffic in the other lanes
- ☐ **C** When you're making a phone call
- ☐ **D** When the road ahead is clear

You should drive in the left-hand lane whenever possible. Only use the other lanes for overtaking or when directed to do so by signals. Using other lanes when the left-hand lane is empty can frustrate drivers behind you.

438 Mark *one* answer
You're driving on a motorway and have to slow down suddenly due to a hazard ahead. How can you warn drivers behind of the hazard?

- ☐ **A** Switch on your hazard warning lights
- ☐ **B** Switch on your headlights
- ☐ **C** Sound your horn
- ☐ **D** Flash your headlights

Using your hazard warning lights, as well as your brake lights, will give the traffic behind an extra warning of the problem ahead. Only use them for long enough for your warning to be seen.

439 Mark *one* answer

Your car gets a puncture while you're driving on the motorway. What should you do when you've stopped on the hard shoulder?

- ☐ **A** Carefully change the wheel yourself
- ☐ **B** Use an emergency telephone and call for help
- ☐ **C** Try to wave down another vehicle for help
- ☐ **D** Only change the wheel if you have a passenger to help you

Park as far to the left as you can and leave the vehicle by the nearside door. Don't attempt even simple repairs. Instead, walk to an emergency telephone on your side of the road and phone for help. While waiting for help to arrive, stay by your car, keeping well away from the carriageway and hard shoulder.

440 Mark *one* answer

What should you do if you're driving on a motorway and you miss the exit that you wanted to take?

- ☐ **A** Carefully reverse along the hard shoulder
- ☐ **B** Carry on to the next exit
- ☐ **C** Carefully reverse in the left-hand lane
- ☐ **D** Make a U-turn at the next gap in the central reservation

It's illegal to reverse, cross the central reservation or drive against the traffic flow on a motorway. If you miss your exit, carry on until you reach the next one. Ask yourself why you missed your exit – if you think that your concentration is fading, take a break before continuing your journey.

441 Mark *one* answer

Your vehicle has broken down on a motorway. What should you do if you aren't able to get onto the hard shoulder?

- ☐ **A** Switch on your hazard warning lights
- ☐ **B** Stop the traffic behind and ask for help
- ☐ **C** Attempt to repair your vehicle quickly
- ☐ **D** Stand behind your vehicle to warn others

If you can't get your vehicle onto the hard shoulder, use your hazard warning lights to warn others. Leave your vehicle only when you can safely get clear of the carriageway. Don't try to repair the vehicle or attempt to place any warning device on the carriageway.

442 Mark *one* answer
Why is it particularly important to check your vehicle before making a long motorway journey?

☐ **A** You'll have to do more harsh braking on motorways
☐ **B** Motorway services areas don't deal with breakdowns
☐ **C** The road surface will wear down the tyres faster
☐ **D** Continuous high speeds increase the risk of your vehicle breaking down

Before you start your journey, make sure that your vehicle can cope with the demands of high-speed driving. You should check a number of things; the main ones being fuel, oil, water and tyres. You also need to plan rest stops if you're making a long journey.

443 Mark *one* answer
You're driving on a motorway. What does it mean if the car in front shows its hazard warning lights for a short time?

☐ **A** The driver wants you to overtake
☐ **B** The other car is going to change lanes
☐ **C** Traffic ahead is slowing or stopping suddenly
☐ **D** There's a police speed check ahead

If the vehicle in front shows its hazard warning lights, there may be an incident, stopped traffic or queuing traffic ahead. By keeping a safe distance from the vehicle in front, you're able to look beyond it and see any hazards well ahead.

444 Mark *one* answer
You're driving on the motorway. Which lane should you get into well before you reach your exit?

☐ **A** The middle lane
☐ **B** The left-hand lane
☐ **C** The hard shoulder
☐ **D** The right-hand lane

You'll see the first advance direction sign one mile from a motorway exit. If you're travelling at 60 mph in the right-hand lane, you'll only have about 50 seconds before you reach the countdown markers. There'll be another sign at the half-mile point. Don't cut across lanes of traffic at the last moment – move to the left-hand lane in good time.

445 Mark *one* answer
What restrictions apply to people who have a provisional driving licence?

☐ **A** They can't drive over 30 mph
☐ **B** They can't drive at night
☐ **C** They can't drive unaccompanied
☐ **D** They can't drive with more than one passenger

You won't be able to drive unaccompanied until you've passed your practical driving test. If you haven't driven on the motorway while you were learning, ask your instructor to take you for a lesson on the motorway when you've passed your test. Alternatively, you could take part in the Pass Plus scheme. This has been created for new drivers and includes motorway driving. Ask your instructor for details.

446 Mark *one* answer

Your vehicle breaks down on a motorway and you manage to stop on the hard shoulder. What should you do if you use your mobile phone to call for help?

☐ **A** Stand at the rear of the vehicle while making the call

☐ **B** Phone a friend and ask them to come and collect you

☐ **C** Wait in the car for the emergency services to arrive

☐ **D** Check your location from the nearest marker posts beside the hard shoulder

You should use an emergency telephone when you break down on the motorway; only use your mobile if this isn't possible. The emergency services need to know your exact location so they can reach you as quickly as possible. Look for a number on the nearest marker post beside the hard shoulder. Give this number when you call the emergency services.

447 Mark *one* answer   NI

You're towing a trailer along a three-lane motorway. When may you use the right-hand lane?

☐ **A** When there are lane closures

☐ **B** When there's slow-moving traffic

☐ **C** When you can maintain a high speed

☐ **D** When large vehicles are in the left and centre lanes

If you're towing a caravan or trailer, you mustn't use the right-hand lane of a motorway with three or more lanes except in certain specified circumstances, such as when lanes are closed.

448 Mark *one* answer

What would you expect to find at a contraflow system on a motorway?

☐ **A** Temporary traffic lights

☐ **B** Lower speed limits

☐ **C** Wider lanes than normal

☐ **D** Road humps

When approaching a contraflow system, reduce speed in good time and obey all speed limits. You may be travelling in a narrower lane than normal, with no permanent barrier between you and the oncoming traffic. Be aware that the hard shoulder may be used for traffic and the road ahead could be obstructed by slow-moving or broken-down vehicles.

449 Mark *one* answer
What's the meaning of this sign?

- ☐ **A** Local speed limit applies
- ☐ **B** No waiting on the carriageway
- ☐ **C** National speed limit applies
- ☐ **D** No entry for vehicles

This sign doesn't tell you the speed limit in figures. You should know the speed limit for the type of road that you're on and the type of vehicle that you're driving. Study your copy of *The Highway Code*.

450 Mark *one* answer
What's the national speed limit for cars and motorcycles on a dual carriageway?

- ☐ **A** 30 mph
- ☐ **B** 50 mph
- ☐ **C** 60 mph
- ☐ **D** 70 mph

Make sure that you know the speed limit for the road that you're on. The speed limit on a dual carriageway or motorway is 70 mph for cars and motorcycles, unless signs indicate otherwise. The speed limits for different types of vehicle are listed in *The Highway Code*.

451 Mark *one* answer
There are no speed-limit signs on the road. How is a 30 mph limit generally indicated?

- ☐ **A** By hazard warning lines
- ☐ **B** By street lighting
- ☐ **C** By pedestrian islands
- ☐ **D** By double or single yellow lines

There's a 30 mph speed limit where there are street lights unless signs show another limit.

452 Mark *one* answer
What will the speed limit usually be where you can see street lights but no speed-limit signs?

- ☐ **A** 30 mph
- ☐ **B** 40 mph
- ☐ **C** 50 mph
- ☐ **D** 60 mph

The presence of street lights generally indicates that there's a 30 mph speed limit, unless signs tell you otherwise.

453 Mark *one* answer
What does this sign mean?

- ☐ **A** Minimum speed 30 mph
- ☐ **B** End of maximum speed
- ☐ **C** End of minimum speed
- ☐ **D** Maximum speed 30 mph

The red slash through the sign indicates that the restriction has ended. In this case, the restriction was a minimum speed limit of 30 mph.

454 Mark *one* answer
What should you do if you want to overtake a tractor but aren't sure that it's safe?

- ☐ **A** Follow another vehicle as it overtakes the tractor
- ☐ **B** Sound your horn to make the tractor driver pull over
- ☐ **C** Speed past, flashing your lights at oncoming traffic
- ☐ **D** Stay behind it if you're in any doubt

Following a tractor can be frustrating, but never overtake if you're unsure whether it's safe. Ask yourself: 'Can I see far enough down the road to ensure that I can complete the manoeuvre safely?' It's better to be delayed for a minute or two than to take a chance that may cause a collision.

455 Mark *one* answer
Which vehicle is most likely to take an unusual course at a roundabout?

- ☐ **A** Estate car
- ☐ **B** Milk float
- ☐ **C** Delivery van
- ☐ **D** Long vehicle

Long vehicles might have to take a slightly different position when approaching the roundabout or going around it. This is to stop the rear of the vehicle cutting in and mounting the kerb.

456 Mark *one* answer
When may you stop on a clearway?

- ☐ **A** Never
- ☐ **B** When it's busy
- ☐ **C** In the rush hour
- ☐ **D** During daylight hours

Clearways are in place so that traffic can flow without the obstruction of parked vehicles. Just one parked vehicle can cause an obstruction for all other traffic. You mustn't stop where a clearway is in force, not even to pick up or set down passengers.

457 Mark *one* answer
What's the meaning of this sign?

- ☐ **A** No entry
- ☐ **B** Waiting restrictions
- ☐ **C** National speed limit
- ☐ **D** School crossing patrol

This sign indicates that there are waiting restrictions. It's normally accompanied by details of when the restrictions are in force. Details of most signs in common use are shown in *The Highway Code*. For more comprehensive coverage, see *Know Your Traffic Signs*.

458 Mark *one* answer
You're looking for somewhere to park at night. When may you park on the right-hand side of the road?

- ☐ **A** When you're in a one-way street
- ☐ **B** When you have your sidelights on
- ☐ **C** When you're more than 10 metres (32 feet) from a junction
- ☐ **D** When you're under a lamppost

Red rear reflectors show up when headlights shine on them. These are useful when you're parked at night, but they'll only reflect if you park in the same direction as the traffic flow. Normally you should park on the left, but in a one-way street you may also park on the right-hand side of the road.

459 Mark *one* answer
When should you use the right-hand lane of a three-lane dual carriageway?

- ☐ **A** When you're overtaking only
- ☐ **B** When you're overtaking or turning right
- ☐ **C** When you're using cruise control
- ☐ **D** When you're turning right only

You should normally use the left-hand lane on any dual carriageway unless you're overtaking or turning right. When overtaking on a dual carriageway, look for vehicles ahead that are turning right. They may be slowing or stopped. You need to see them in good time so that you can take appropriate action.

460 Mark *one* answer
You're approaching a busy junction. What should you do when, at the last moment, you realise you're in the wrong lane?

- ☐ **A** Continue in that lane
- ☐ **B** Force your way into the lane you need
- ☐ **C** Stop until the area has cleared
- ☐ **D** Use arm signals to help you change lane

There are times when road markings are obscured by queuing traffic, or you're unsure which lane to use. If, at the last moment, you find you're in the wrong lane, don't cut across or bully other drivers to let you in. Follow the lane you're in and find somewhere safe to turn around and rejoin your route.

461 Mark *one* answer
Where may you overtake on a one-way street?

- ☐ **A** Only on the left-hand side
- ☐ **B** Overtaking isn't allowed
- ☐ **C** Only on the right-hand side
- ☐ **D** On either the right or the left

You can overtake other traffic on either side when travelling in a one-way street. Make full use of your mirrors and ensure it's clear all around before you attempt to overtake. Look for signs and road markings, and use the most suitable lane for your destination.

462 Mark *one* answer
What signal should you give when you're going straight ahead at a roundabout?

- ☐ **A** Signal left before leaving the roundabout
- ☐ **B** Don't signal at any time
- ☐ **C** Signal right when you're approaching the roundabout
- ☐ **D** Signal left when you're approaching the roundabout

When going straight ahead at a roundabout, don't signal as you approach it. Signal left just after passing the exit before the one you wish to take.

463 Mark *one* answer
Which vehicle might have to take a different course from normal at a roundabout?

- ☐ **A** Sports car
- ☐ **B** Van
- ☐ **C** Estate car
- ☐ **D** Long vehicle

A long vehicle may have to straddle lanes either on or approaching a roundabout so that the rear wheels don't mount the kerb. If you're following a long vehicle, stay well back and give it plenty of room.

464 Mark *one* answer
When may you enter a box junction?

- ☐ **A** When there are fewer than two vehicles ahead
- ☐ **B** When signalled by another road user
- ☐ **C** When your exit road is clear
- ☐ **D** When traffic signs direct you

Yellow box junctions are marked on the road to prevent the road becoming blocked. Don't enter the box unless your exit road is clear. You may wait in the box if you want to turn right and your exit road is clear but oncoming traffic or other vehicles waiting to turn right are preventing you from making the turn.

465 Mark *one* answer
When may you stop and wait in a box junction?

- ☐ **A** When oncoming traffic prevents you from turning right
- ☐ **B** When you're in a queue of traffic turning left
- ☐ **C** When you're in a queue of traffic going ahead
- ☐ **D** When you're on a roundabout

The purpose of yellow box markings is to keep junctions clear of queuing traffic. You may only wait in the marked area when you're turning right and your exit lane is clear but you can't complete the turn because of oncoming traffic or other traffic waiting to turn right.

466 Mark *one* answer
Who is authorised to signal you to stop?

- ☐ **A** A motorcyclist
- ☐ **B** A pedestrian
- ☐ **C** A police officer
- ☐ **D** A bus driver

You must obey signals to stop given by police and traffic officers, traffic wardens and school crossing patrols. Failure to do so is an offence and could lead to prosecution.

467 Mark *one* answer
What should you do if you see a pedestrian waiting at a zebra crossing?

- ☐ **A** Go on quickly before they step onto the crossing
- ☐ **B** Stop before you reach the zigzag lines and let them cross
- ☐ **C** Be ready to slow down or stop to let them cross
- ☐ **D** Ignore them as they're still on the pavement

By standing on the pavement, the pedestrian is showing an intention to cross. By looking well ahead, you'll give yourself time to see the pedestrian, check your mirrors and respond safely.

468 Mark *one* answer
Which road users benefit from toucan crossings?

- ☐ **A** Car drivers and motorcyclists
- ☐ **B** Cyclists and pedestrians
- ☐ **C** Bus and lorry drivers
- ☐ **D** Tram and train drivers

Toucan crossings are similar to pelican crossings but there's no flashing amber phase. Cyclists share the crossing with pedestrians and are allowed to cycle across when the green cycle symbol is shown.

469 Mark *one* answer
You're waiting at a pelican crossing. What does it mean when the red light changes to flashing amber?

- ☐ **A** Give way to pedestrians on the crossing
- ☐ **B** Move off immediately without any hesitation
- ☐ **C** Wait for the green light before moving off
- ☐ **D** Get ready and go when the continuous amber light shows

This light allows pedestrians already on the crossing to get to the other side in their own time, without being rushed. Don't rev your engine or start to move off while they're still crossing.

470 Mark *one* answer
You see these double white lines along the centre of the road. When may you park on the left?

- ☐ **A** If the line nearest to you is broken
- ☐ **B** When there are no yellow lines
- ☐ **C** To pick up or set down passengers
- ☐ **D** During daylight hours only

You mustn't park or stop on a road marked with double white lines (even where one of the lines is broken) except to pick up or set down passengers.

471 Mark *one* answer
You're turning right at a crossroads. An oncoming driver is also turning right. What's the advantage of turning behind the oncoming vehicle?

- ☐ **A** You'll have a clearer view of any approaching traffic
- ☐ **B** You'll use less fuel because you can stay in a higher gear
- ☐ **C** You'll have more time to turn
- ☐ **D** You'll be able to turn without stopping

When turning right at a crossroads where oncoming traffic is also turning right, it's generally safer to turn behind the approaching vehicle. This allows you a clear view of approaching traffic and is called 'turning offside to offside'. However, some junctions, usually controlled by traffic-light filters - are marked for vehicles to turn nearside to nearside.

472 Mark *one* answer
You're travelling along a residential street. There are parked vehicles on the left-hand side. Why should you keep your speed down?

- ☐ **A** So that oncoming traffic can see you more clearly
- ☐ **B** You may set off car alarms
- ☐ **C** There may be delivery lorries on the street
- ☐ **D** Children may run out from between the vehicles

Travel slowly and carefully near parked vehicles. Beware of
- vehicles pulling out, especially bicycles and motorcycles
- pedestrians, especially children, who may run out from between cars
- drivers opening their doors.

473 Mark *one* answer
What should you do when there's an obstruction on your side of the road?

- ☐ **A** Carry on, as you have priority
- ☐ **B** Give way to oncoming traffic
- ☐ **C** Wave oncoming vehicles through
- ☐ **D** Accelerate to get past first

Take care if you have to pass an obstruction, such as a parked vehicle, on your side of the road. Give way to oncoming traffic if there isn't enough room for you both to continue safely.

474 Mark *one* answer
When would you use the right-hand lane of a two-lane dual carriageway?

- ☐ **A** When you're turning right or overtaking
- ☐ **B** When you're passing a side road on the left
- ☐ **C** When you're staying at the minimum allowed speed
- ☐ **D** When you're travelling at a constant high speed

Normally you should travel in the left-hand lane and only use the right-hand lane for overtaking or turning right. Move back into the left lane as soon as it's safe but don't cut in across the path of the vehicle you've just passed.

475 Mark *one* answer
Who has priority at an unmarked crossroads?

- ☐ **A** The larger vehicle
- ☐ **B** No-one has priority
- ☐ **C** The faster vehicle
- ☐ **D** The smaller vehicle

Practise good observation in all directions before you emerge or make a turn. Proceed only when you're sure it's safe to do so.

476 Mark *one* answer · NI
What's the nearest you may park to a junction?

- ☐ **A** 10 metres (32 feet)
- ☐ **B** 12 metres (39 feet)
- ☐ **C** 15 metres (49 feet)
- ☐ **D** 20 metres (66 feet)

Don't park within 10 metres (32 feet) of a junction (unless in an authorised parking place). This is to allow drivers emerging from, or turning into, the junction a clear view of the road they're joining. It also allows them to see hazards such as pedestrians or cyclists at the junction.

477 Mark *one* answer
You're looking for somewhere to safely park your vehicle. Where would you choose to park?

- ☐ **A** At or near a bus stop
- ☐ **B** In a designated parking space
- ☐ **C** Near the brow of a hill
- ☐ **D** On the approach to a level crossing

It may be tempting to park where you shouldn't while you run a quick errand. Careless parking is a selfish act and could endanger other road users.

478 Mark *one* answer
You're waiting at a level crossing. What must you do if a train passes but the lights keep flashing?

- ☐ **A** Carry on waiting
- ☐ **B** Phone the signal operator
- ☐ **C** Edge over the stop line and look for trains
- ☐ **D** Park and investigate

If the lights at a level crossing keep flashing after a train has passed, you should continue to wait, because another train might be coming. Time seems to pass slowly when you're held up in a queue. Be patient and wait until the lights stop flashing.

479 Mark *one* answer
What does this sign mean?

- ☐ **A** No through road
- ☐ **B** End of traffic-calming zone
- ☐ **C** Free-parking zone ends
- ☐ **D** End of controlled parking zone

This sign shows that you're leaving a controlled parking zone and those restrictions no longer apply.

480 Mark *one* answer
What must you do if you come across roadworks that have a temporary speed limit displayed?

- ☐ **A** Obey the speed limit
- ☐ **B** Obey the limit, but only during rush hour
- ☐ **C** Ignore the displayed limit
- ☐ **D** Use your own judgment; the limit is only advisory

Where there are extra hazards, such as at roadworks, it's often necessary to slow traffic by imposing a lower speed limit. These speed limits aren't advisory; they must be obeyed.

481 Mark *one* answer
You're in a built-up area at night and the road is well lit. Why should you use dipped headlights?

☐ **A** So that you can see further along the road

☐ **B** So that you can go at a much faster speed

☐ **C** So that you can switch to main beam quickly

☐ **D** So that you can be easily seen by others

You may be difficult to see when you're travelling at night, even on a well-lit road. If you use dipped headlights rather than sidelights, other road users should be able to see you more easily.

482 Mark *one* answer
You're turning right onto a dual carriageway. What should you do if the central reservation is too narrow to contain your vehicle?

☐ **A** Proceed to the central reservation and wait

☐ **B** Wait until the road is clear in both directions

☐ **C** Stop in the first lane so that other vehicles give way

☐ **D** Emerge slightly to show your intentions

When the central reservation is narrow, it may not be able to contain your vehicle. In this case, you should treat a dual carriageway as one road. Wait until the road is clear in both directions before emerging to turn right. If you try to treat it as two separate roads and wait in the middle, your vehicle will stick out and cause an obstruction that may lead to a collision.

483 Mark *one* answer
What's the national speed limit on a single carriageway road for cars and motorcycles?

☐ **A** 30 mph
☐ **B** 50 mph
☐ **C** 60 mph
☐ **D** 70 mph

Exceeding the speed limit is dangerous and can result in you receiving penalty points on your licence. It isn't worth it. You should know the speed limit for the road that you're on by observing the road signs. Different speed limits apply if you're towing a trailer.

484 Mark *one* answer
What should you do when you park at night on a road that has a 40 mph speed limit?

☐ **A** Park facing the traffic
☐ **B** Leave parking lights switched on
☐ **C** Leave dipped headlights switched on
☐ **D** Park near a street light

You must use parking lights when parking at night on a road or in a lay-by on a road with a speed limit greater than 30 mph. You must also park in the direction of the traffic flow and not close to a junction.

485 Mark *one* answer
Where will you see these red and white markers?

- ☐ **A** Approaching the end of a motorway
- ☐ **B** Approaching a concealed level crossing
- ☐ **C** Approaching a concealed speed-limit sign
- ☐ **D** Approaching the end of a dual carriageway

If there's a bend just before a level crossing, you may not be able to see the level-crossing barriers or waiting traffic. These signs give you an early warning that you may find these hazards just around the bend.

486 Mark *one* answer
You're travelling on a motorway in England. When must you stop your vehicle?

- ☐ **A** When signalled to stop by a roadworks supervisor
- ☐ **B** When signalled to stop by a traffic officer
- ☐ **C** When signalled to stop by a pedestrian on the hard shoulder
- ☐ **D** When signalled to stop by a driver who has broken down

You'll find traffic officers on motorways and some primary routes in England and Wales. They work in partnership with the police, helping to keep traffic moving and helping to make your journey as safe as possible. It's an offence not to comply with the directions given by a traffic officer.

487 Mark *one* answer
How should you signal if you're going straight ahead at a roundabout?

- ☐ **A** Signal right on the approach and then left to leave the roundabout
- ☐ **B** Signal left after you leave the roundabout and enter the new road
- ☐ **C** Signal right on the approach to the roundabout and keep the signal on
- ☐ **D** Signal left just after you pass the exit before the one you're going to take

To go straight ahead at a roundabout, you should normally approach in the left-hand lane, but check the road markings. At some roundabouts, the left lane on approach is marked 'left turn only', so make sure you use the correct lane to go ahead. You won't normally need to signal as you approach, but signal before you leave the roundabout, as other road users need to know your

488 Mark *one* answer
When may you drive over a pavement?

- ☐ **A** To overtake slow-moving traffic
- ☐ **B** When the pavement is very wide
- ☐ **C** If there are no pedestrians nearby
- ☐ **D** To gain access to a property

It's illegal to drive on or over a pavement, except to gain access to a property. If you need to cross a pavement, give priority to pedestrians.

489 Mark *one* answer
A single carriageway road has this sign. What's the maximum permitted speed for a car towing a trailer?

- ☐ **A** 30 mph
- ☐ **B** 40 mph
- ☐ **C** 50 mph
- ☐ **D** 60 mph

When you're towing a trailer, a reduced speed limit also applies on dual carriageways and motorways. These lower speed limits apply to vehicles pulling all sorts of trailers, including caravans and horse boxes.

490 Mark *one* answer
What's the speed limit for a car towing a caravan on a dual carriageway?

- ☐ **A** 50 mph
- ☐ **B** 40 mph
- ☐ **C** 70 mph
- ☐ **D** 60 mph

The speed limit for cars towing caravans or trailers on dual carriageways or motorways is 60 mph. Due to the increased weight and size of the combination, you should plan further ahead. Take care in windy weather, as a strong side wind can make a caravan or large trailer unstable.

491 Mark *one* answer
You want to park and you see this sign. What should you do on the days and times shown?

Meter
ZONE

Mon - Fri
8.30 am - 6.30 pm
Saturday
8.30 am - 1.30 pm

- ☐ **A** Park in a bay and not pay
- ☐ **B** Park on yellow lines and pay
- ☐ **C** Park on yellow lines and not pay
- ☐ **D** Park in a bay and pay

Parking restrictions apply in a variety of places and situations. Make sure you know the rules and understand where and when restrictions apply. Controlled parking areas will be indicated by signs and road markings. Parking in the wrong place could cause an obstruction and danger to other traffic. It can also result in a fine.

492 Mark *one* answer

A cycle lane, marked by a solid white line, is in operation. What does this mean for car drivers?

- ☐ **A** They may park in the lane
- ☐ **B** They may drive in the lane at any time
- ☐ **C** They may use the lane when necessary
- ☐ **D** They mustn't drive along the lane

While it's in operation, other vehicles must not use this part of the carriageway except to pick up or set down passengers. At other times, when the lane isn't in operation, you should still be aware that there may be cyclists using the lane. Give them plenty of room as you pass and allow for their movement from side to side, especially in windy weather or on a bumpy road.

493 Mark *one* answer

You're going to turn left from a main road into a minor road. What should you do as you approach the junction?

- ☐ **A** Keep just left of the middle of the road
- ☐ **B** Keep in the middle of the road
- ☐ **C** Swing out to the right just before turning
- ☐ **D** Keep well to the left of the road

Your road position can help other road users to anticipate your actions. Keep to the left as you approach a left turn and don't swing out into the centre of the road in order to make the turn easier. This could endanger oncoming traffic and may cause other road users to misunderstand your intentions.

494 Mark *one* answer

You're waiting at a level crossing. What should you do if the red warning lights continue to flash after a train has passed by?

- ☐ **A** Get out and investigate
- ☐ **B** Telephone the signal operator
- ☐ **C** Continue to wait
- ☐ **D** Drive across carefully

At a level crossing, flashing red lights mean you must stop. If the train passes but the lights keep flashing, wait. Another train may be coming.

495 Mark *one* answer

What should you do if the amber lights come on and a warning sounds while you're driving over a level crossing?

- ☐ **A** Get everyone out of the vehicle immediately
- ☐ **B** Stop and reverse back to clear the crossing
- ☐ **C** Keep going and clear the crossing
- ☐ **D** Stop immediately and use your hazard warning lights

Keep going; don't stop on the crossing. If the warning sounds and the amber lights come on as you're approaching the crossing, you must stop unless it's unsafe to do so. Red flashing lights together with the audible warning mean you must stop.

496 Mark *one* answer

You're driving on a busy main road. What should you do if you find that you're driving in the wrong direction?

- ☐ **A** Turn into a side road on the right and reverse into the main road
- ☐ **B** Make a U-turn in the main road
- ☐ **C** Make a 'three-point' turn in the main road
- ☐ **D** Turn around in a side road

Don't turn around in a busy street or reverse from a side road into a main road. Find a quiet side road and choose a place to turn around where you won't obstruct an entrance or exit. Look out for pedestrians and cyclists as well as other traffic.

497 Mark *one* answer

When may you drive without wearing your seat belt?

- ☐ **A** When you're carrying out a manoeuvre that includes reversing
- ☐ **B** When you're moving off on a hill
- ☐ **C** When you're testing your brakes
- ☐ **D** When you're driving slowly in queuing traffic

You may remove your seat belt while you're carrying out a manoeuvre that includes reversing. However, you must remember to put it back on again before you resume driving.

498 Mark *one* answer
How far are you allowed to reverse?

- ☐ **A** No further than is necessary
- ☐ **B** No more than a car's length
- ☐ **C** As far as it takes to reverse around a corner
- ☐ **D** The length of a residential street

You mustn't reverse further than is necessary. You may decide to turn your vehicle around by reversing into an opening or side road. When you reverse, always look all around you and watch for pedestrians. Don't reverse from a side road into a main road.

499 Mark *one* answer
What should you do when you're unsure whether it's safe to reverse your vehicle?

- ☐ **A** Sound your horn
- ☐ **B** Rev your engine
- ☐ **C** Get out and check
- ☐ **D** Reverse slowly

A small child could be hidden directly behind you, so, if you can't see all around your vehicle, get out and have a look. You could also ask someone reliable outside the vehicle to guide you.

500 Mark *one* answer
Why could it be dangerous to reverse from a side road into a main road?

- ☐ **A** Your reverse sensors will beep
- ☐ **B** Your view will be restricted
- ☐ **C** Your reversing lights will be hidden
- ☐ **D** Your mirrors will need adjusting

Don't reverse into a main road from a side road because your view will be restricted. The main road is likely to be busy and the traffic on it moving quickly.

501 Mark *one* answer
You want to turn right at a box junction. What should you do if there's oncoming traffic?

- ☐ **A** Wait in the box junction if your exit is clear
- ☐ **B** Wait before the junction until it's clear of all traffic
- ☐ **C** Drive on; you can't turn right at a box junction
- ☐ **D** Drive slowly into the box junction when signalled by oncoming traffic

You can wait in the box junction as long as your exit is clear. At some point there'll be a gap in the oncoming traffic, or the traffic lights will change, allowing you to proceed.

502 Mark *one* answer
You're reversing into a side road. When would your vehicle be the greatest hazard to passing traffic?

- ☐ **A** After you've completed the manoeuvre
- ☐ **B** Just before you begin to manoeuvre
- ☐ **C** After you've entered the side road
- ☐ **D** When the front of your vehicle swings out

Always check in all directions before reversing. Keep a good lookout throughout the manoeuvre and remember that the front will swing out as you reverse into the side road. Act on what you see and wait if necessary.

503 Mark *one* answer
Where's the safest place to park your vehicle at night?

- ☐ **A** In a garage
- ☐ **B** On a busy road
- ☐ **C** In a quiet car park
- ☐ **D** Near a red route

If you have a garage, use it. Your vehicle is less likely to be a victim of car crime if it's in a garage. Also, in winter, the windows will be kept free from ice and snow.

504 Mark *one* answer
When may you stop on an urban clearway?

- ☐ **A** To set down and pick up passengers
- ☐ **B** To use a mobile telephone
- ☐ **C** To ask for directions
- ☐ **D** To load or unload goods

Urban clearways have their times of operation clearly signed. You may only stop to pick up or set down passengers.

505 Mark *one* answer
You're looking for somewhere to park your vehicle. Neither you nor your passenger are disabled. What should you do if the only free spaces are marked for disabled drivers?

- ☐ **A** Use one of these spaces
- ☐ **B** Park in one of these spaces but stay with your vehicle
- ☐ **C** Use one of the spaces as long as one is kept free
- ☐ **D** Wait for a regular parking space to become free

It's illegal to park in a space reserved for disabled drivers unless you're permitted to do so. These spaces are provided for people with limited mobility, who may need extra space to get in and out of their vehicle.

506 Mark *one* answer
You're on a road that's only wide enough for one vehicle. What should you do if a car is coming towards you?

- ☐ **A** Pull into a passing place on your right
- ☐ **B** Force the other driver to reverse
- ☐ **C** Pull into a passing place if your vehicle is wider
- ☐ **D** Pull into a passing place on your left

Pull into the nearest passing place on the left if you meet another vehicle on a narrow road. If the nearest passing place is on the right, wait opposite it.

507 Mark *one* answer
You're driving at night with your headlights on main beam. A vehicle is overtaking you. When should you dip your headlights?

- ☐ **A** Some time after the vehicle has passed you
- ☐ **B** Before the vehicle starts to pass you
- ☐ **C** Only if the other driver dips their headlights
- ☐ **D** As soon as the vehicle passes you

On main beam, your lights could dazzle the driver in front. Dip your headlights as soon as the driver passes you and drop back so that the dipped beam falls short of the vehicle in front.

508 Mark *one* answer
When may you drive a car in this bus lane?

- ☐ **A** Outside its hours of operation
- ☐ **B** To get to the front of a traffic queue
- ☐ **C** You may not use it at any time
- ☐ **D** To overtake slow-moving traffic

Some bus lanes operate only during peak hours and other vehicles may use them outside these hours. Make sure you check the sign for the hours of operation before driving in a bus lane.

509 Mark *one* answer
Other than direction indicators, how can you give signals to other road users?

- ☐ **A** By using brake lights
- ☐ **B** By using sidelights
- ☐ **C** By using fog lights
- ☐ **D** By using interior lights

Your brake lights will give an indication to traffic behind that you're slowing down. Good anticipation will allow you time to check your mirrors before slowing.

510 Mark *one* answer
You're parked in a busy high street. What's the safest way to turn your vehicle around so you can drive in the opposite direction?

☐ **A** Turn around in a quiet side road
☐ **B** Drive into a side road and reverse out into the main road
☐ **C** Ask someone to stop the traffic
☐ **D** Carry out a U-turn

Make sure you carry out the manoeuvre without causing a hazard to other vehicles. Choose a place to turn that's safe and considers other road users.

511 Mark *one* answer
Where should you park your vehicle at night?

☐ **A** Near a police station
☐ **B** In a quiet road
☐ **C** On a red route
☐ **D** In a well-lit area

When you're parking at night, park in a well-lit area. This can help deter criminals from targeting your vehicle.

512 Mark *one* answer
You're driving in the right-hand lane of a dual carriageway. What should you do if you see a sign showing that the right-hand lane is closed 800 yards ahead?

☐ **A** Keep in that lane until you reach the queue
☐ **B** Move to the left immediately
☐ **C** Wait and see which lane is moving faster
☐ **D** Move to the left in good time

Keep a lookout for traffic signs. If you're directed to change lanes, do so in good time. Don't

- push your way into traffic in another lane
- try to gain advantage by delaying changing lanes.

513 Mark *one* answer

You're driving on a road that has a cycle lane. What does it mean if the lane is marked by a broken white line?

- ☐ **A** You shouldn't drive in the lane unless it's unavoidable
- ☐ **B** There's a reduced speed limit for motor vehicles using the lane
- ☐ **C** Cyclists can travel in both directions in that lane
- ☐ **D** The lane must be used by motorcyclists in heavy traffic

Cycle lanes are marked with either a solid or a broken white line. If the line is solid, you should check the times of operation shown on the signs, and not drive or park in the lane during those times. If the line is broken, you shouldn't drive or park in the lane unless it's unavoidable.

514 Mark *one* answer

When are you allowed to park in a parking bay for disabled drivers?

- ☐ **A** When you have a Blue Badge
- ☐ **B** When you have a wheelchair
- ☐ **C** When you have an advanced driver certificate
- ☐ **D** When you have an adapted vehicle

Don't park in a space reserved for disabled people unless you or your passenger are a Blue Badge holder. The badge must be displayed on the dashboard or facia panel, where it can be clearly read through the front windscreen.

515 Mark *one* answer

When must you stop your vehicle?

- ☐ **A** If you're involved in an incident that causes damage or injury
- ☐ **B** At a junction where there are 'give way' lines
- ☐ **C** At the end of a one-way street
- ☐ **D** Before merging onto a motorway

You must stop your vehicle when signalled to do so by a
- police, DVSA or traffic officer
- traffic warden
- school crossing patrol
- red traffic light.

You must also stop if you're involved in an incident that causes damage or injury to any other person, vehicle, animal or property.

516 Mark *one* answer
How can you identify traffic signs that give orders?

☐ **A** They're rectangular with a yellow border
☐ **B** They're triangular with a blue border
☐ **C** They're square with a brown border
☐ **D** They're circular with a red border

There are three basic types of traffic sign: those that warn, those that inform and those that give orders. Generally, triangular signs warn, rectangular signs give information or directions and circular signs give orders. An exception is the eight-sided 'stop' sign.

---

517 Mark *one* answer
What shape are traffic signs giving orders?

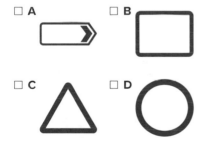

☐ **A**   ☐ **B**

☐ **C**   ☐ **D**

Road signs in the shape of a circle give orders. Those with a red circle are mostly prohibitive. The 'stop' sign is octagonal to give it greater prominence. Signs giving orders must always be obeyed.

518 Mark *one* answer
Which type of sign tells you what you must not do?

☐ **A**   ☐ **B**

☐ **C**   ☐ **D**

Signs in the shape of a circle give orders. A sign with a red circle means that you aren't allowed to do something. Study *Know Your Traffic Signs* to ensure that you understand what the different traffic signs mean.

519 Mark *one* answer
What does this sign mean?

- ☐ **A** Maximum speed limit with traffic calming
- ☐ **B** Minimum speed limit with traffic calming
- ☐ **C** '20 cars only' parking zone
- ☐ **D** Only 20 cars allowed at any one time

If you're in a place where there are likely to be pedestrians (for example, outside a school, near a park, in a residential area or in a shopping area), you should be cautious and keep your speed down. Many local authorities have taken steps to slow traffic down by creating traffic-calming measures such as road humps. They're there for a reason; slow down.

520 Mark *one* answer
What does this sign mean?

- ☐ **A** New speed limit 20 mph
- ☐ **B** No vehicles over 30 tonnes
- ☐ **C** Minimum speed limit 30 mph
- ☐ **D** End of 20 mph zone

Where you see this sign, the 20 mph restriction ends and a 30 mph restriction starts. Check all around for possible hazards and only increase your speed if it's safe to do so.

521 Mark *one* answer
What does this sign mean?

- ☐ **A** No overtaking
- ☐ **B** No motor vehicles
- ☐ **C** Clearway (no stopping)
- ☐ **D** Cars and motorcycles only

A sign will indicate which types of vehicles are prohibited from certain roads. Make sure that you know which signs apply to the vehicle you're using.

522 Mark *one* answer
What does this sign mean?

- ☐ **A** No parking
- ☐ **B** No road markings
- ☐ **C** No through road
- ☐ **D** No entry

'No entry' signs are used in places such as one-way streets to prevent vehicles driving against the traffic. To ignore one would be dangerous, both for yourself and for other road users, as well as being against the law.

523 Mark *one* answer
What does this sign mean?

- ☐ **A** Bend to the right
- ☐ **B** Road on the right closed
- ☐ **C** No traffic from the right
- ☐ **D** No right turn

The 'no right turn' sign may be used to warn road users that there's a 'no entry' prohibition on a road to the right ahead.

524 Mark *one* answer
Which sign means 'no entry'?

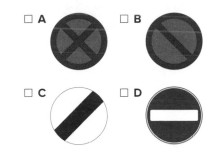

- ☐ A
- ☐ B
- ☐ C
- ☐ D

Look for and obey traffic signs. Disobeying or not seeing a sign could be dangerous. It may also be an offence for which you could be prosecuted.

525 Mark *one* answer
What does this sign mean?

- ☐ **A** Route for trams only
- ☐ **B** Route for buses only
- ☐ **C** Parking for buses only
- ☐ **D** Parking for trams only

Avoid blocking tram routes. Trams are fixed on their route and can't manoeuvre around other vehicles or pedestrians. Modern trams travel quickly and are quiet, so you might not hear them approaching.

526 Mark *one* answer

Which type of vehicle does this sign apply to?

- ☐ **A** Wide vehicles
- ☐ **B** Long vehicles
- ☐ **C** High vehicles
- ☐ **D** Heavy vehicles

The triangular shapes above and below the dimensions indicate a height restriction that applies to the road ahead.

527 Mark *one* answer

Which sign means no motor vehicles allowed?

This sign is used to enable pedestrians to walk free from traffic. It's often found in shopping areas.

528 Mark *one* answer

What does this sign mean?

- ☐ **A** You have priority
- ☐ **B** No motor vehicles
- ☐ **C** Two-way traffic
- ☐ **D** No overtaking

Road signs that prohibit overtaking are placed in locations where passing the vehicle in front is dangerous. If you see this sign, don't attempt to overtake. The sign is there for a reason; you must obey it.

529 Mark *one* answer

What does this sign mean?

- ☐ **A** Waiting restrictions apply
- ☐ **B** Waiting permitted
- ☐ **C** National speed limit applies
- ☐ **D** Clearway (no stopping)

There'll be a plate or additional sign to tell you when the restrictions apply.

530 Mark *one* answer
What does this sign mean?

- ☐ **A** End of restricted speed area
- ☐ **B** End of restricted parking area
- ☐ **C** End of clearway
- ☐ **D** End of cycle route

Even though you've left the restricted area, make sure that you park where you won't endanger other road users or cause an obstruction.

531 Mark *one* answer
Which sign means 'no stopping'?

- ☐ A
- ☐ B
- ☐ C
- ☐ D

Stopping where this clearway restriction applies is likely to cause congestion. Allow the traffic to flow by obeying the signs.

532 Mark *one* answer
What does this sign mean?

- ☐ **A** National speed limit applies
- ☐ **B** Waiting restrictions apply
- ☐ **C** No stopping
- ☐ **D** No entry

This is the sign for a clearway. Clearways are stretches of road where you aren't allowed to stop unless it's an emergency. Stopping where these restrictions apply may be dangerous and is likely to cause an obstruction. Restrictions might apply for several miles and this may be indicated on the sign.

533 Mark *one* answer
What does this sign mean?

- ☐ **A** Distance to parking place ahead
- ☐ **B** Distance to public telephone ahead
- ☐ **C** Distance to public house ahead
- ☐ **D** Distance to passing place ahead

If you intend to stop and rest, this sign allows you time to reduce speed and pull over safely.

534 Mark *one* answer
What does this sign mean?

☐ **A** Vehicles may not park on the verge or footway
☐ **B** Vehicles may park on the left-hand } side of the road only
☐ **C** Vehicles may park fully on the verge or footway
☐ **D** Vehicles may park on the right-hand side of the road only

In order to keep roads free from parked cars, there are some areas where you're allowed to park on the verge. Only do this where you see the sign. Parking on verges or footways anywhere else could lead to a fine.

535 Mark *one* answer
What does this traffic sign mean?

☐ **A** No overtaking allowed
☐ **B** Give priority to oncoming traffic
☐ **C** Two-way traffic
☐ **D** One-way traffic only

Priority signs are normally shown where the road is narrow and there isn't enough room for two vehicles to pass. Examples are narrow bridges, roadworks and where there's a width restriction. Make sure you know who has priority; don't force your way through. Show courtesy and consideration to other road users.

536 Mark *one* answer
What's the meaning of this traffic sign?

- ☐ **A** End of two-way road
- ☐ **B** Give priority to vehicles coming towards you
- ☐ **C** You have priority over vehicles coming towards you
- ☐ **D** Bus lane ahead

Don't force your way through. Show courtesy and consideration to other road users. Although you have priority, make sure oncoming traffic is going to give way before you continue.

537 Mark *one* answer
What shape is a 'stop' sign?

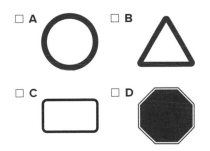

- ☐ **A**
- ☐ **B**
- ☐ **C**
- ☐ **D**

To make it easy to recognise, the 'stop' sign is the only sign of this shape. You must stop and take effective observation before proceeding.

538 Mark *one* answer
In winter, road signs can become covered by snow. What does this sign mean?

- ☐ **A** Crossroads
- ☐ **B** Give way
- ☐ **C** Stop
- ☐ **D** Turn right

The 'stop' sign is the only road sign that's octagonal. This is so that it can be recognised and obeyed even if it's obscured (for example, by snow).

539 Mark *one* answer
What does this sign mean?

- ☐ **A** Service area 30 miles ahead
- ☐ **B** Maximum speed 30 mph
- ☐ **C** Minimum speed 30 mph
- ☐ **D** Lay-by 30 miles ahead

This sign is shown where slow-moving vehicles would impede the flow of traffic; for example, in tunnels. However, if you need to slow down or even stop to avoid an incident or potential collision, you should do so.

540 Mark *one* answer
What does this sign mean?

- ☐ **A** Give way to oncoming vehicles
- ☐ **B** Approaching traffic passes you on both sides
- ☐ **C** Turn off at the next available junction
- ☐ **D** Pass either side to get to the same destination

These signs are often seen in one-way streets that have more than one lane. When you see this sign, use the route that's the most convenient and doesn't require a late change of direction.

541 Mark *one* answer
What does this sign mean?

- ☐ **A** Route for trams
- ☐ **B** Give way to trams
- ☐ **C** Route for buses
- ☐ **D** Give way to buses

Take extra care when you encounter trams. Look out for road markings and signs that alert you to them. Modern trams are very quiet and you may not hear them approaching.

542 Mark *one* answer
What messages are given by circular traffic signs that have a blue background?

- ☐ **A** They give temporary directions during a diversion
- ☐ **B** They give directions to car parks
- ☐ **C** They give motorway information
- ☐ **D** They give mandatory instructions

Signs with blue circles generally give mandatory instruction. These are often found in urban areas and include signs for mini-roundabouts and directional arrows.

543 Mark *one* answer
Where would you see a contraflow bus lane?

- ☐ **A** On a dual carriageway
- ☐ **B** On a roundabout
- ☐ **C** On an urban motorway
- ☐ **D** On a one-way street

The traffic permitted to use a contraflow lane travels in the opposite direction to traffic in the other lanes on the road.

544 Mark *one* answer
What does this sign mean?

- ☐ **A** Bus station on the right
- ☐ **B** Contraflow bus lane
- ☐ **C** With-flow bus lane
- ☐ **D** Give way to buses

There will also be markings on the road surface to indicate the bus lane. You mustn't use this lane for parking or overtaking.

545 Mark *one* answer
What does a sign with a brown background show?

- ☐ **A** Tourist directions
- ☐ **B** Primary roads
- ☐ **C** Motorway routes
- ☐ **D** Minor roads

Signs with a brown background give directions to places of interest. They're often seen on a motorway, directing you along the easiest route to the attraction.

546 Mark *one* answer
What does this sign mean?

- ☐ **A** Tourist attraction
- ☐ **B** Beware of trains
- ☐ **C** Level crossing
- ☐ **D** Beware of trams

These signs indicate places of interest and are designed to guide you by the easiest route. They're particularly useful when you're unfamiliar with the area.

547 Mark *one* answer
What's the purpose of triangular shaped signs?

- ☐ **A** To give warnings
- ☐ **B** To give information
- ☐ **C** To give orders
- ☐ **D** To give directions

Triangular signs warn you of hazards ahead. Make sure you look at each sign that you pass on the road, so that you don't miss any vital instructions or information.

548 Mark *one* answer
What does this sign mean?

- ☐ **A** Turn left ahead
- ☐ **B** T-junction
- ☐ **C** No through road
- ☐ **D** Give way

This type of sign warns you of hazards ahead. Make sure you look at each sign and road marking that you pass, so that you don't miss any vital instructions or information. This sign shows there's a T-junction with priority over vehicles from the right.

549 Mark *one* answer
What does this sign mean?

- ☐ **A** Multi-exit roundabout
- ☐ **B** Risk of ice
- ☐ **C** Six roads converge
- ☐ **D** Place of historical interest

It will take up to 10 times longer to stop when it's icy. Where there's a risk of icy conditions, you need to be aware of this and take extra care. If you think the road may be icy, don't brake or steer harshly, as your tyres could lose their grip on the road.

550 Mark *one* answer
What does this sign mean?

- ☐ **A** Crossroads
- ☐ **B** Level crossing with gate
- ☐ **C** Level crossing without gate
- ☐ **D** Ahead only

The priority through the junction is shown by the broader line. You need to be aware of the hazard posed by traffic crossing or pulling out onto a major road.

551 Mark *one* answer
What does this sign mean?

- ☐ **A** Ring road
- ☐ **B** Mini-roundabout
- ☐ **C** No vehicles
- ☐ **D** Roundabout

As you approach a roundabout, look well ahead and check all signs. Decide which exit you wish to take and move into the correct position as you approach the roundabout, signalling as required.

552 Mark *one* answer
What information would be shown in a triangular road sign?

- ☐ **A** Road narrows
- ☐ **B** Ahead only
- ☐ **C** Keep left
- ☐ **D** Minimum speed

Warning signs are there to make you aware of potential hazards on the road ahead. Take note of the signs so you're prepared and can take whatever action is necessary.

553 Mark *one* answer
What does this sign mean?

- ☐ **A** Cyclists must dismount
- ☐ **B** Cycles aren't allowed
- ☐ **C** Cycle route ahead
- ☐ **D** Cycle in single file

Where there's a cycle route ahead, a sign will show a bicycle in a red warning triangle. Watch out for children on bicycles and cyclists rejoining the main road.

554 Mark *one* answer
Which sign means that pedestrians may be walking along the road?

☐ **A**   ☐ **B**

☐ **C**   ☐ **D**

When you pass pedestrians in the road, leave plenty of room. You might have to use the right-hand side of the road, so look well ahead, as well as in your mirrors, before pulling out. Take great care if a bend in the road obscures your view ahead.

555 Mark *one* answer
Which sign means there's a double bend ahead?

☐ **A**   ☐ **B**

☐ **C**   ☐ **D**

Triangular signs give you a warning of hazards ahead. They're there to give you time to prepare for the hazard; for example, by adjusting your speed.

556 Mark *one* answer
What does this sign mean?

- ☐ **A** Wait at the barriers
- ☐ **B** Wait at the crossroads
- ☐ **C** Give way to trams
- ☐ **D** Give way to farm vehicles

Obey the 'give way' signs. Trams are unable to steer around you if you misjudge when it's safe to enter the junction.

557 Mark *one* answer
What does this sign mean?

- ☐ **A** Hump bridge
- ☐ **B** Humps in the road
- ☐ **C** Entrance to tunnel
- ☐ **D** Soft verges

These humps have been put in place to slow the traffic down. They're usually found in residential areas. Slow down to an appropriate speed.

558 Mark *one* answer
Which sign means the end of a dual carriageway?

☐ **A**   ☐ **B**

☐ **C**   ☐ **D**

If you're overtaking, make sure you move back safely into the left-hand lane before you reach the end of the dual carriageway.

559 Mark *one* answer
What does this sign mean?

- ☐ **A** End of dual carriageway
- ☐ **B** Tall bridge
- ☐ **C** Road narrows
- ☐ **D** End of narrow bridge

Don't wait until the last moment before moving into the left-hand lane. Plan ahead and don't rely on other traffic letting you in.

560 Mark *one* answer
What does this sign mean?

☐ **A** Side winds
☐ **B** Road noise
☐ **C** Airport
☐ **D** Adverse camber

A warning sign with a picture of a windsock indicates that there may be strong side winds. This sign is often found on exposed roads.

561 Mark *one* answer
What does this traffic sign mean?

☐ **A** Slippery road ahead
☐ **B** Tyres liable to punctures ahead
☐ **C** Danger ahead
☐ **D** Service area ahead

This sign is there to alert you to the likelihood of danger ahead. It may be accompanied by a plate indicating the type of hazard. Be ready to reduce your speed and take avoiding action.

562 Mark *one* answer
You're about to overtake. What should you do when you see this sign?

Hidden dip

☐ **A** Overtake the other driver as quickly as possible
☐ **B** Move to the right to get a better view
☐ **C** Switch your headlights on before overtaking
☐ **D** Hold back until you can see clearly ahead

You won't be able to see any hazards that might be hidden in the dip. As well as oncoming traffic, the dip may conceal
- cyclists
- horse riders
- parked vehicles
- pedestrians in the road.

563 Mark *one* answer
What does this sign mean?

- ☐ **A** Level crossing with gate or barrier
- ☐ **B** Gated road ahead
- ☐ **C** Level crossing without gate or barrier
- ☐ **D** Cattle grid ahead

Some crossings have gates but no attendant or signals. You should stop, look both ways, listen and make sure that no train is approaching. If there's a telephone, contact the signal operator to make sure it's safe to cross.

564 Mark *one* answer
What does this sign mean?

- ☐ **A** No trams ahead
- ☐ **B** Oncoming trams
- ☐ **C** Trams crossing ahead
- ☐ **D** Trams only

This sign tells you to beware of trams. If you don't usually drive in a town where there are trams, remember to look out for them at junctions and look for tram rails, signs and signals.

565 Mark *one* answer
What does this sign mean?

- ☐ **A** Adverse camber
- ☐ **B** Steep hill downwards
- ☐ **C** Uneven road
- ☐ **D** Steep hill upwards

This sign gives you an early warning that the road ahead will slope downhill. Prepare to alter your speed and gear. Looking at the sign from left to right will show you whether the road slopes uphill or downhill.

566 Mark *one* answer
What does this sign mean?

- ☐ **A** Uneven road surface
- ☐ **B** Bridge over the road
- ☐ **C** Road ahead ends
- ☐ **D** Water across the road

This sign is found where a shallow stream crosses the road. Heavy rainfall could increase the flow of water. If the water looks too deep or the stream has spread over a large distance, stop and find another route.

567 Mark *one* answer
What does this sign mean?

- ☐ **A** Turn left for parking area
- ☐ **B** No through road on the left
- ☐ **C** No entry for traffic turning left
- ☐ **D** Turn left for ferry terminal

This sign shows you that you can't get through to another route by turning left at the junction ahead.

568 Mark *one* answer
What does this sign mean?

- ☐ **A** T-junction
- ☐ **B** No through road
- ☐ **C** Telephone box ahead
- ☐ **D** Toilet ahead

You won't be able to find a through route to another road. Use this road only for access.

569 Mark *one* answer
Which is the sign for a ring road?

☐ **A** ☐ **B**

☐ **C** ☐ **D**

Ring roads are designed to relieve congestion in towns and city centres.

570 Mark *one* answer
What does this sign mean?

- ☐ **A** The right-hand lane ahead is narrow
- ☐ **B** Right-hand lane for buses only
- ☐ **C** Right-hand lane for turning right
- ☐ **D** The right-hand lane is closed

Yellow-and-black temporary signs may be used to inform you about roadworks or lane restrictions. Look well ahead. If you have to change lanes, do so in good time.

571 Mark *one* answer
What does this sign mean?

- ☐ **A** Change to the left-hand lane
- ☐ **B** Leave at the next exit
- ☐ **C** Contraflow system
- ☐ **D** One-way street

If you use the right-hand lane in a contraflow system, you'll be travelling with no permanent barrier between you and the oncoming traffic. Observe speed limits and keep a good distance from the vehicle ahead.

572 Mark *one* answer
What does this sign mean?

- ☐ **A** Leave motorway at next exit
- ☐ **B** Lane for heavy and slow vehicles
- ☐ **C** All lorries use the hard shoulder
- ☐ **D** Rest area for lorries

Where there's a long, steep, uphill gradient on a motorway, a crawler lane may be provided. This helps the traffic to flow by diverting the slower heavy vehicles into a dedicated lane on the left.

573 Mark *one* answer
What does a red traffic light mean?

- ☐ **A** You should stop unless turning left
- ☐ **B** Stop, if you're able to brake safely
- ☐ **C** You must stop and wait behind the stop line
- ☐ **D** Proceed with care

Whatever light is showing, you should know which light is going to appear next and be able to take appropriate action. For example, when amber is showing on its own, you'll know that red will appear next. This should give you ample time to anticipate and respond safely.

574 Mark *one* answer
At traffic lights, what does it mean when the amber light shows on its own?

- ☐ **A** Prepare to go
- ☐ **B** Go if the way is clear
- ☐ **C** Go if no pedestrians are crossing
- ☐ **D** Stop at the stop line

When the amber light is showing on its own, the red light will follow next. The amber light means stop, unless you've already crossed the stop line or you're so close to it that stopping may cause a collision.

575 Mark *one* answer
You're at a junction controlled by traffic lights. When should you wait at a green light?

☐ **A** When pedestrians are waiting to cross
☐ **B** When your exit from the junction is blocked
☐ **C** When you think the lights may be about to change
☐ **D** When you intend to turn right

As you approach the traffic lights, look into the road you wish to take. Only proceed if your exit road is clear. If the road is blocked, hold back, even if you have to wait for the next green signal.

576 Mark *one* answer
You're in the left-hand lane at traffic lights, waiting to turn left. Which signal means you must wait?

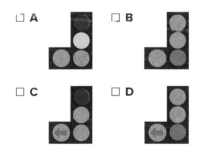

☐ **A**   ☐ **B**

☐ **C**   ☐ **D**

At some junctions, there may be separate signals for different lanes. These are called 'filter' lights. They're designed to help traffic flow at major junctions. Make sure that you're in the correct lane and proceed if the way is clear and the green light shows for your lane.

577 Mark *one* answer
What does this sign mean?

☐ **A** Traffic lights out of order
☐ **B** Amber signal out of order
☐ **C** Temporary traffic lights ahead
☐ **D** New traffic lights ahead

You might see this sign where traffic lights are out of order. Proceed with caution, as nobody has priority at the junction.

578 Mark *one* answer
Who has priority when traffic lights are out of order?

☐ **A** Traffic going straight on
☐ **B** Traffic turning right
☐ **C** Nobody
☐ **D** Traffic turning left

When traffic lights are out of order, you should treat the junction as an unmarked crossroads. Be cautious, as you may need to give way or stop. Look for traffic attempting to cross the junction, unaware that it doesn't have priority.

579 Mark *one* answer
Where would you find these flashing red light signals?

☐ **A** Pelican crossings
☐ **B** Motorway exits
☐ **C** Zebra crossings
☐ **D** Level crossings

These signals are found at level crossings, swing or lifting bridges, some airfields and emergency access sites. The flashing red lights mean stop whether or not the way seems to be clear.

580 Mark *one* answer
What do these zigzag white lines mean?

☐ **A** No parking at any time
☐ **B** Parking allowed only for a short time
☐ **C** Slow down to 20 mph
☐ **D** Sounding horns isn't allowed

The approach to, and exit from, a pedestrian crossing is marked with zigzag lines. You mustn't park on them or overtake the leading vehicle when approaching the crossing. Parking here would block the view for pedestrians and approaching traffic.

581 Mark *one* answer
When may you cross a double solid white line in the middle of the road?

☐ **A** To pass traffic that's queuing back at a junction
☐ **B** To pass a car signalling to turn left ahead
☐ **C** To pass a road maintenance vehicle travelling at 10 mph or less
☐ **D** To pass a vehicle that's towing a trailer

You may cross the solid white line to pass a stationary vehicle or to pass a pedal cycle, horse or road maintenance vehicle if it's travelling at 10 mph or less. You may also cross the solid white line to enter a side road or access a property.

582 Mark *one* answer
What does this road marking mean?

- ☐ **A** Don't cross the line
- ☐ **B** No stopping allowed
- ☐ **C** You're approaching a hazard
- ☐ **D** No overtaking allowed

A single broken line along the centre of the road, with long markings and short gaps, is a hazard warning line. Don't cross it unless you can see that the road is clear well ahead.

583 Mark *one* answer
Where would you see this road marking?

- ☐ **A** At traffic lights
- ☐ **B** On road humps
- ☐ **C** Near a level crossing
- ☐ **D** At a box junction

Because the road has a dark colour, changes in level aren't easily seen. White triangles painted on the road surface give you an indication of where there are road humps.

584 Mark *one* answer
Which diagram shows a hazard warning line?

☐ **A**   ☐ **B**

☐ **C**   ☐ **D**

You need to know the difference between the normal centre line and a hazard warning line. If there's a hazard ahead, the markings are longer and the gaps shorter. This gives you advance warning of an unspecified hazard.

585 Mark *one* answer
Why does this junction have a 'stop' sign and a stop line on the road?

- ☐ **A** Speed on the major road is derestricted
- ☐ **B** It's a busy junction
- ☐ **C** Visibility along the major road is restricted
- ☐ **D** The junction is on a downhill gradient

Where emerging traffic has a very restricted view of the main road, you may find a 'stop' sign and a solid white stop line. You must stop at the line and then check carefully before you emerge.

586 Mark *one* answer

What does this line across the road at the entrance to a roundabout mean?

- ☐ **A** Give way to traffic from the right
- ☐ **B** Traffic from the left has right of way
- ☐ **C** You have right of way
- ☐ **D** Stop at the line

Slow down as you approach the roundabout and check for traffic from the right. If you need to stop and give way, stay behind the broken line until it's safe to emerge onto the roundabout.

---

587 Mark *one* answer

How will a police officer in a patrol vehicle signal for you to stop?

- ☐ **A** Flash the headlights, indicate left and point to the left
- ☐ **B** Overtake and give a slowing down arm signal
- ☐ **C** Use the siren, overtake, cut in front and stop
- ☐ **D** Pull alongside you, use the siren and wave you to stop

You must obey signals given by the police. If a police officer in a patrol vehicle wants you to pull over, they'll indicate this without causing danger to you or other traffic.

588 Mark *one* answer

You're approaching a junction where the traffic lights aren't working. What should you do when a police officer gives this signal?

- ☐ **A** Turn left only
- ☐ **B** Turn right only
- ☐ **C** Continue ahead only
- ☐ **D** Stop at the stop line

When a police officer or traffic warden is directing traffic, you must obey them. They'll use the arm signals shown in *The Highway Code*. Learn what these signals mean and obey them.

589 Mark *one* answer
What does this arm signal mean?

- ☐ **A** The driver is slowing down
- ☐ **B** The driver intends to turn right
- ☐ **C** The driver wishes to overtake
- ☐ **D** The driver intends to turn left

There might be an occasion where another driver uses an arm signal. This may be because the vehicle's indicators are obscured by other traffic. In order for such signals to be effective, all drivers should know their meaning. Be aware that the 'left turn' signal might look similar to the 'slowing down' signal.

590 Mark *one* answer
What does this motorway sign mean?

- ☐ **A** Change to the lane on your left
- ☐ **B** Leave the motorway at the next exit
- ☐ **C** Change to the opposite carriageway
- ☐ **D** Pull up on the hard shoulder

On the motorway, signs sometimes show temporary warnings due to traffic or weather conditions. They may be used to indicate
- lane closures
- temporary speed limits
- weather warnings.

591 Mark *one* answer
What does this motorway sign mean?

- ☐ **A** Temporary minimum speed 50 mph
- ☐ **B** No services for 50 miles
- ☐ **C** Obstruction 50 metres (164 feet) ahead
- ☐ **D** Temporary maximum speed 50 mph

Look out for signs above your lane or on the central reservation. These will give you important information or warnings about the road ahead. To allow for the high speed of motorway traffic, these signs may light up some distance from any hazard. Don't ignore the signs just because the road looks clear to you.

592 Mark *one* answer
What does this sign mean?

- ☐ **A** Through traffic to use left lane
- ☐ **B** Right-hand lane T-junction only
- ☐ **C** Right-hand lane closed ahead
- ☐ **D** 11 tonne weight limit

You should change lanes as directed by the sign. Here, the right-hand lane is closed but the left-hand and centre lanes are available. Merging in turn is recommended when it's safe and traffic is going slowly; for example, at roadworks or a road traffic incident. When vehicles are travelling at speed, this isn't advisable and you should move into the appropriate lane in good time.

593 Mark *one* answer
What does '25' mean on this motorway sign?

- ☐ **A** The distance to the nearest town
- ☐ **B** The route number of the road
- ☐ **C** The number of the next junction
- ☐ **D** The speed limit on the slip road

Before you set out on your journey, use a road map to plan your route. When you see an advance warning of your junction, make sure you get into the correct lane in plenty of time. Last-minute harsh braking and cutting across lanes at speed is extremely hazardous.

594 Mark *one* answer
How should the right-hand lane of a three-lane motorway be used?

- ☐ **A** As a high-speed lane
- ☐ **B** As an overtaking lane
- ☐ **C** As a right-turn lane
- ☐ **D** As an acceleration lane

You should stay in the left-hand lane of a motorway unless you're overtaking another vehicle. The right-hand lane of a motorway is an overtaking lane; it isn't the 'fast lane'. After overtaking, move back to the left when it's safe to do so.

595 Mark *one* answer
Where can you find reflective amber studs on a motorway?

☐ **A** Separating the slip road from the motorway
☐ **B** On the left-hand edge of the road
☐ **C** On the right-hand edge of the road
☐ **D** Separating the lanes

At night or in poor visibility, reflective studs on the road help you to judge your position on the carriageway.

596 Mark *one* answer
Where would you find green reflective studs on a motorway?

☐ **A** Separating driving lanes
☐ **B** Between the hard shoulder and the carriageway
☐ **C** At slip-road entrances and exits
☐ **D** Between the carriageway and the central reservation

Knowing the colours of the reflective studs on the road will help you judge your position, especially at night, in foggy conditions or when visibility is poor.

597 Mark *one* answer
What should you do when you see this sign as you travel along a motorway?

☐ **A** Leave the motorway at the next exit
☐ **B** Turn left immediately
☐ **C** Change lane
☐ **D** Move onto the hard shoulder

You'll see this sign if the motorway is closed ahead. Pull into the left-hand lane as soon as it's safe to do so. Don't wait until the last moment before you move across, because the lane may be busy and you'll have to rely on another driver making room for you.

598 Mark *one* answer
What does this sign mean?

☐ **A** No motor vehicles
☐ **B** End of motorway
☐ **C** No through road
☐ **D** End of bus lane

When you leave the motorway, make sure that you check your speedometer. You may be going faster than you realise. Slow down and look for speed-limit signs.

599 Mark *one* answer

Which sign means that the national speed limit applies?

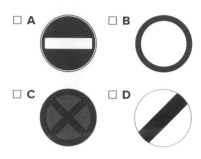

☐ A

☐ B

☐ C

☐ D

You should know the speed limit for the road on which you're travelling and for your vehicle. The different speed limits are shown in *The Highway Code*.

600 Mark *one* answer

What's the national speed limit on a single carriageway road?

☐ **A** 50 mph
☐ **B** 60 mph
☐ **C** 40 mph
☐ **D** 70 mph

If you're travelling on a dual carriageway that becomes a single carriageway road, reduce your speed gradually so that you aren't exceeding the limit as you enter. There might not be a sign to remind you of the limit, so make sure you know the speed limits for different types of road and vehicle.

601 Mark *one* answer

What does this sign mean?

☐ **A** End of motorway
☐ **B** End of restriction
☐ **C** Lane ends ahead
☐ **D** Free recovery ends

Temporary restrictions on motorways are shown on signs that have flashing amber lights. At the end of the restriction, you'll see this sign without any flashing lights.

602 Mark *one* answer

What does this sign indicate?

☐ **A** A diversion route
☐ **B** A picnic area
☐ **C** A pedestrian zone
☐ **D** A cycle route

When a diversion route has been put in place, drivers are advised to follow a symbol, which may be a black triangle, square, circle or diamond shape on a yellow background.

603 Mark *one* answer
What does this traffic sign mean?

- ☐ **A** Compulsory maximum speed limit
- ☐ **B** Advisory maximum speed limit
- ☐ **C** Compulsory minimum speed limit
- ☐ **D** Advised separation distance

The sign gives you an early warning of a speed restriction. If you're travelling at a higher speed, slow down in good time. You could come across queuing traffic due to roadworks or a temporary obstruction.

604 Mark *one* answer
What should you do when you see this sign at a crossroads?

- ☐ **A** Maintain the same speed
- ☐ **B** Carry on with great care
- ☐ **C** Find another route
- ☐ **D** Telephone the police

When traffic lights are out of order, treat the junction as an unmarked crossroads. Be very careful and be prepared to stop; no-one has priority.

605 Mark *one* answer
What does this sign mean?

- ☐ **A** Motorcycles only
- ☐ **B** No cars
- ☐ **C** Cars only
- ☐ **D** No motorcycles

You must comply with all traffic signs and be especially aware of those signs that apply specifically to the type of vehicle you're using.

606 Mark *one* answer
You're on a motorway. A lorry has stopped in the right-hand lane. What should you do when you see this sign on the lorry?

- ☐ **A** Move into the right-hand lane
- ☐ **B** Stop behind the flashing lights
- ☐ **C** Pass the lorry on the left
- ☐ **D** Leave the motorway at the next exit

Sometimes work is carried out on the motorway without closing the lanes. When this happens, signs are mounted on the back of lorries to warn other road users of the roadworks ahead.

607 Mark *one* answer
You're on a motorway. What should you do if there's a red cross showing on the signs above your lane only?

- ☐ **A** Continue in that lane and look for further information
- ☐ **B** Don't continue in that lane
- ☐ **C** Pull onto the hard shoulder
- ☐ **D** Stop and wait for an instruction to proceed

A red cross above your lane shows that your lane is closed. You should move into another lane as soon as you can do so safely.

608 Mark *one* answer
When may you sound your vehicle's horn?

- ☐ **A** To give you right of way
- ☐ **B** To attract a friend's attention
- ☐ **C** To warn others of your presence
- ☐ **D** To make slower drivers move over

Never sound your vehicle's horn aggressively. You mustn't sound it in a built-up area between 11.30 pm and 7.00 am, or when you're stationary, unless another road user poses a danger. Don't scare animals by sounding your horn.

609 Mark *one* answer
Your vehicle is stationary. When may you use its horn?

- ☐ **A** When another road user poses a danger
- ☐ **B** When the road is blocked by queuing traffic
- ☐ **C** When it's used only briefly
- ☐ **D** When signalling that you've just arrived

When your vehicle is stationary, only sound the horn if you think there's a risk of danger from another road user. Don't use it just to attract someone's attention. This causes unnecessary noise and could be misleading.

610 Mark *one* answer
What does this sign mean?

- ☐ **A** You can park on the days and times shown
- ☐ **B** No parking on the days and times shown
- ☐ **C** No parking at all from Monday to Friday
- ☐ **D** End of the urban clearway restrictions

Urban clearways are provided to keep traffic flowing at busy times. You may stop only briefly to set down or pick up passengers. Times of operation will vary from place to place, so always check the signs.

611 Mark *one* answer
What does this sign mean?

- ☐ **A** Quayside or river bank
- ☐ **B** Steep hill downwards
- ☐ **C** Uneven road surface
- ☐ **D** Road liable to flooding

You should be careful in these locations, as the road surface is likely to be wet and slippery. There may be a steep drop to the water, and there may not be a barrier along the edge of the road.

612 Mark *one* answer
Which sign means you have priority over oncoming vehicles?

☐ A   ☐ B

☐ C   ☐ D

Even though you have priority, be prepared to give way if other drivers don't. This will help to avoid congestion, confrontation or even a collision.

613 Mark *one* answer
What do the long white lines along the centre of the road mean?

- ☐ **A** Bus lane
- ☐ **B** Hazard warning
- ☐ **C** Give way
- ☐ **D** Lane marking

The centre of the road is usually marked by a broken white line, with lines that are shorter than the gaps. When the lines become longer than the gaps, this is a hazard warning line. Look well ahead for these, especially when you're planning to overtake or turn off.

614 Mark *one* answer
What's the reason for the hatched area along the centre of this road?

- ☐ **A** It separates traffic flowing in opposite directions
- ☐ **B** It marks an area to be used by overtaking motorcyclists
- ☐ **C** It's a temporary marking to warn of the roadworks
- ☐ **D** It separates the two sides of the dual carriageway

Areas of 'hatched markings' such as these separate traffic streams that could be a danger to each other. They're often seen on bends or where the road becomes narrow. If the area is bordered by a solid white line, you mustn't enter it except in an emergency.

615 Mark *one* answer
Other drivers may sometimes flash their headlights at you. What's the official meaning of this signal?

- ☐ **A** There's a radar speed trap ahead
- ☐ **B** They're giving way to you
- ☐ **C** They're warning you of their presence
- ☐ **D** There's a fault with your vehicle

If other drivers flash their headlights, this isn't a signal to show priority. The flashing of headlights has the same meaning as sounding the horn: it's a warning of their presence.

616 Mark *one* answer
What does this signal mean?

- ☐ **A** Cars must stop
- ☐ **B** Trams must stop
- ☐ **C** Both trams and cars must stop
- ☐ **D** Both trams and cars can continue

The white light shows that trams must stop. The green light shows that other vehicles can go if the way is clear. Trams are being introduced into more cities, so you're likely to come across them and you should learn which signs apply to them.

617 Mark *one* answer
Where would you find these road markings?

- ☐ **A** At a railway crossing
- ☐ **B** At a mini-roundabout
- ☐ **C** On a motorway
- ☐ **D** On a pedestrian crossing

These markings show the direction in which the traffic should go at a mini-roundabout.

618 Mark *one* answer
A police car is following you. What should you do if the police officer flashes the headlights and points to the left?

☐ **A** Turn left at the next junction
☐ **B** Pull up on the left
☐ **C** Stop immediately
☐ **D** Move over to the left

You must pull up on the left as soon as it's safe to do so and switch off your engine.

619 Mark *one* answer
You see this amber traffic light ahead. Which light, or lights, will come on next?

☐ **A** Red alone
☐ **B** Red and amber together
☐ **C** Green and amber together
☐ **D** Green alone

At junctions controlled by traffic lights, you must stop behind the white line until the lights change to green. A red light, an amber light, and red and amber lights showing together all mean stop. You may proceed when the light is green unless your exit road is blocked or pedestrians are crossing in front of you. If you're approaching traffic lights that are visible from a distance and the light has been green for some time, be ready to slow down and stop, because the lights are likely to change.

620 Mark *one* answer
What does it mean if you see this signal on the motorway?

☐ **A** Leave the motorway at the next exit
☐ **B** All vehicles use the hard shoulder
☐ **C** Sharp bend to the left ahead
☐ **D** Stop: all lanes ahead closed

You'll see this sign if there has been an incident ahead and the motorway is closed. You must obey the sign. Make sure that you prepare to leave in good time. Don't cause drivers to take avoiding action by cutting in at the last moment.

621 Mark *one* answer
What must you do when you see this sign?

☐ **A** Stop only if traffic is approaching
☐ **B** Stop even if the road is clear
☐ **C** Stop only if children are waiting to cross
☐ **D** Stop only if a red light is showing

'Stop' signs are situated at junctions where visibility is restricted or where there's heavy traffic. They must be obeyed: you must stop. Look carefully before moving off.

622 Mark *one* answer
Which shape is used for a 'give way' sign?

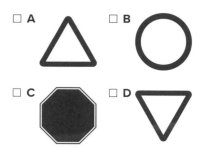

☐ **A** ☐ **B** ☐ **C** ☐ **D**

Other warning signs are the same shape and colour, but the 'give way' triangle points downwards. When you see this sign, you must give way to traffic on the road that you're about to enter.

623 Mark *one* answer
What does this sign mean?

☐ **A** Buses turning
☐ **B** Ring road
☐ **C** Mini-roundabout
☐ **D** Keep right

When you see this sign, look out for any direction signs and judge whether you need to signal your intentions. Do this in good time so that other road users approaching the roundabout know what you're planning to do.

624 Mark *one* answer
What does this sign mean?

☐ **A** Two-way traffic straight ahead
☐ **B** Two-way traffic crosses a one-way road
☐ **C** Two-way traffic over a bridge
☐ **D** Two-way traffic crosses a two-way road

Be prepared for traffic approaching from junctions on either side of you. Try to avoid unnecessary changing of lanes just before the junction.

625 Mark *one* answer
What does this sign mean?

☐ **A** Two-way traffic crosses a one-way road
☐ **B** Traffic approaching you has priority
☐ **C** Two-way traffic straight ahead
☐ **D** Motorway contraflow system ahead

This sign may be at the end of a dual carriageway or a one-way street. It's there to warn you of oncoming traffic.

626 Mark *one* answer
What does this sign mean?

- ☐ **A** Hump bridge
- ☐ **B** Traffic-calming hump
- ☐ **C** Low bridge
- ☐ **D** Uneven road

You'll need to slow down. At hump bridges, your view ahead will be restricted and the road will often be narrow. If the bridge is very steep, sound your horn to warn others of your approach. Going over the bridge too fast is highly dangerous to other road users and could even cause your wheels to leave the road, with a resulting loss of control.

627 Mark *one* answer
Which sign informs you that you're coming to a 'no through road'?

☐ **A**   ☐ **B**

☐ **C**   ☐ **D**

This sign is found at the entrance to a road that can only be used for access.

628 Mark *one* answer
What does this sign mean?

- ☐ **A** Direction to park-and-ride car park
- ☐ **B** No parking for buses or coaches
- ☐ **C** Direction to bus and coach park
- ☐ **D** Parking area for cars and coaches

To ease the congestion in town centres, some cities and towns provide park-and-ride schemes. These allow you to park in a designated area and ride by bus into the centre. Park-and-ride schemes are usually cheaper and easier than car parking in the town centre.

629 Mark *one* answer
What should you do when you're approaching traffic lights that have red and amber showing together?

- ☐ **A** Pass the lights if the road is clear
- ☐ **B** Take care because there's a fault with the lights
- ☐ **C** Wait for the green light
- ☐ **D** Stop because the lights are changing to red

Be aware that other traffic might still be clearing the junction as you approach. A green light means you may go on, but only if the way is clear.

630 Mark *one* answer

You've stopped at a railway level crossing. What should you do if the red lights continue to flash after a train has gone by?

☐ **A** Phone the signal operator
☐ **B** Alert drivers behind you
☐ **C** Wait
☐ **D** Proceed with caution

You must always obey red flashing stop lights. If a train passes but the lights continue to flash, another train will be passing soon. Cross only when the lights go off and the barriers open.

---

631 Mark *one* answer

You're in a tunnel and you see this sign. What does it mean?

☐ **A** Direction to an emergency pedestrian exit
☐ **B** Beware of pedestrians: no footpath ahead
☐ **C** No access for pedestrians
☐ **D** Beware of pedestrians crossing ahead

If you have to leave your vehicle and get out of a tunnel by an emergency exit, do so as quickly as you can. Follow the signs directing you to the nearest exit point.
If there are several people using the exit, don't panic but try to leave in a calm and orderly manner.

632 Mark *one* answer

Which sign shows that you're entering a one-way system?

☐ A   ☐ B

☐ C   ☐ D

If the road has two lanes, you can use either lane and overtake on either side. Use the lane that's more convenient for your destination unless signs or road markings indicate otherwise.

633 Mark *one* answer
What does this sign mean?

- ☐ **A** With-flow bus and cycle lane
- ☐ **B** Contraflow bus and cycle lane
- ☐ **C** No buses and cycles allowed
- ☐ **D** No waiting for buses and cycles

Buses and cycles can travel in this lane. In this example, they'll flow in the same direction as other traffic. If it's busy, they may be passing you on the left, so watch out for them. Times on the sign will show the lane's hours of operation; if no times are shown, or there's no sign at all, this means the lane is in operation 24 hours a day. In some areas, other vehicles, such as taxis and motorcycles, are allowed to use bus lanes. The sign will show if this is the case.

634 Mark *one* answer
Which of these signs warns you of a zebra crossing?

☐ **A**   ☐ **B**

☐ **C** ☐ **D**

Look well ahead and check the pavements and surrounding areas for pedestrians. Look for anyone walking towards the crossing. Check your mirrors for traffic behind, in case you have to slow down or stop.

635 Mark *one* answer
What does this sign mean?

- ☐ **A** School crossing patrol
- ☐ **B** No pedestrians allowed
- ☐ **C** Pedestrian zone – no vehicles
- ☐ **D** Zebra crossing ahead

Look well ahead and be ready to stop for any pedestrians crossing, or about to cross, the road. Also check the pavements for anyone who looks like they might step or run into the road.

636 Mark *one* answer
Which sign means there will be two-way traffic crossing your route ahead?

This sign is found in or at the end of a one-way system. It warns you that traffic will be crossing your path from both directions.

---

637 Mark *one* answer
Which arm signal tells you that the car you're following is going to pull up?

There may be occasions when drivers need to give an arm signal to confirm their intentions. This could include in bright sunshine, at a complex road layout, when stopping at a pedestrian crossing or when turning right just after passing a parked vehicle. You should understand what each arm signal means. If you give arm signals, make them clear, correct and decisive.

638 Mark *one* answer
Which sign means turn left ahead?

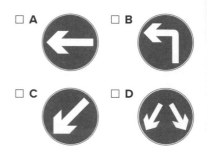

Blue circles tell you what you must do and this sign gives a clear instruction to turn left ahead. You should be looking out for signs at all times and know what they mean.

---

639 Mark *one* answer
What should you be aware of if you've just passed this sign?

- [ ] **A** This is a single-track road
- [ ] **B** You can't stop on this road
- [ ] **C** Only one lane is in use
- [ ] **D** All traffic is going one way

In a one-way system, traffic may pass you on either side. Always be aware of all traffic signs and understand their meaning. Look well ahead and react to them in good time.

640 Mark *one* answer
You're approaching traffic lights and the red light is showing. What signal will show next?

☐ **A** Red and amber
☐ **B** Green alone
☐ **C** Amber alone
☐ **D** Green and amber

If you know which light is going to show next, you can plan your approach accordingly. This can help prevent excessive braking or hesitation at the junction.

641 Mark *one* answer
What does this sign mean?

☐ **A** Low bridge ahead
☐ **B** Tunnel ahead
☐ **C** Ancient monument ahead
☐ **D** Traffic danger spot ahead

When approaching a tunnel, switch on your dipped headlights. Be aware that your eyes might need to adjust to the sudden darkness. You may need to reduce your speed.

642 Mark *one* answer
What does the white line along the side of the road indicate?

☐ **A** The edge of the carriageway
☐ **B** The approach to a hazard
☐ **C** No parking
☐ **D** No overtaking

A continuous white line is used on many roads to indicate the edge of the carriageway. This can be useful when visibility is restricted. The line is discontinued at junctions, lay-bys, and entrances to or exits from private drives.

643 Mark *one* answer
What does this white arrow on the road mean?

☐ **A** Entrance on the left
☐ **B** All vehicles turn left
☐ **C** Return to your side of the road
☐ **D** Road bends to the left

The arrow indicates the direction in which to pass hatch markings or double white lines. If you're overtaking, you must return to the left-hand side of the road.

644 Mark *one* answer

How should you give an arm signal to turn left?

☐ A

☐ B

☐ C

☐ D

There may be occasions when other road users are unable to see your indicator, such as in bright sunlight or at a busy, complicated junction. In these cases, an arm signal will help others to understand your intentions.

645 Mark *one* answer

You're waiting at a T-junction. What should you do if a vehicle is coming from the right, with its left indicator flashing?

☐ **A** Move out and accelerate hard

☐ **B** Wait until the vehicle starts to turn in

☐ **C** Pull out before the vehicle reaches the junction

☐ **D** Move out slowly

Other road users may give misleading signals. When you're waiting at a junction, don't emerge until you're sure of their intentions.

646 Mark *one* answer
When may you use hazard warning lights while you're driving?

☐ **A** Instead of sounding the horn in a built-up area between 11.30 pm and 7.00 am

☐ **B** On a motorway or unrestricted dual carriageway, to warn of a hazard ahead

☐ **C** On rural routes, after a sign warning of animals

☐ **D** On the approach to toucan crossings, where cyclists are waiting to cross

When there's queuing traffic ahead and you have to slow down or even stop, briefly showing your hazard warning lights will help alert the traffic behind to the hazard.

647 Mark *one* answer
Why should you make sure that your indicators are cancelled after turning at a junction?

☐ **A** To avoid flattening the battery

☐ **B** To avoid misleading other road users

☐ **C** To avoid dazzling other road users

☐ **D** To avoid damage to the indicator relay

Leaving your indicators on could confuse other road users and may even lead to a crash. Be aware that if you haven't turned sharply, your indicators may not self-cancel and you'll need to turn them off manually.

648 Mark *one* answer
You're driving in busy traffic. You want to pull up just after a junction on the left. When should you signal?

☐ **A** As you're passing or just after the junction

☐ **B** Just before you reach the junction

☐ **C** Well before you reach the junction

☐ **D** It would be better not to signal at all

You need to signal to let other drivers know your intentions. However, if you indicate too early, they may think you're turning left into the junction. Correct timing of the signal is very important to avoid misleading others.

649 Mark *one* answer
For how long is an MOT certificate normally valid?

☐ **A** Three years after the date it was issued
☐ **B** 10,000 miles
☐ **C** One year after the date it was issued
☐ **D** 30,000 miles

Some garages will remind you that your vehicle is due for its annual MOT test, but not all do. To ensure continuous cover, you may take your vehicle for its MOT up to one month before its existing MOT certificate expires. The expiry date on the new certificate will be 12 months after the expiry date on the old certificate.

650 Mark *one* answer
What's a cover note?

☐ **A** A document issued before you receive your driving licence
☐ **B** A document issued before you receive your insurance certificate
☐ **C** A document issued before you receive your registration document
☐ **D** A document issued before you receive your MOT certificate

Sometimes an insurance company will issue a temporary insurance certificate called a cover note. It gives you the same insurance cover as your certificate but lasts for a limited period, usually one month.

651 Mark *one* answer
You've just passed your first practical driving test. What will you have to do if you get six penalty points on your licence in the next two years?

☐ **A** Retake only your theory test
☐ **B** Retake your theory and practical tests
☐ **C** Retake only your practical test
☐ **D** Reapply for your full licence immediately

If you accumulate six or more penalty points within two years of gaining your first full licence, it will be revoked. The six or more points include any gained due to offences you committed before passing your test. If this happens, you may only drive as a learner until you pass both the theory and practical tests again.

652 Mark *one* answer
For how long is a Statutory Off-Road Notification (SORN) valid?

☐ **A** Until the vehicle is taxed, sold or scrapped
☐ **B** Until the vehicle is insured and MOT'd
☐ **C** Until the vehicle is repaired or modified
☐ **D** Until the vehicle is used on the road

A SORN allows you to keep a vehicle off-road and untaxed. SORN will end when the vehicle is taxed, sold or scrapped.

653 Mark *one* answer
What's a Statutory Off-Road Notification (SORN)?

☐ **A** A notification to tell DVSA that a vehicle doesn't have a current MOT
☐ **B** Information kept by the police about the owner of a vehicle
☐ **C** A notification to tell DVLA that a vehicle isn't being used on the road
☐ **D** Information held by insurance companies to check a vehicle is insured

If you want to keep a vehicle untaxed and off the public road, you must make a SORN. It's an offence not to do so. Your SORN is valid until your vehicle is taxed, sold or scrapped.

654 Mark *one* answer   **NI**
What's the maximum fine for driving or riding without insurance?

☐ **A** Unlimited
☐ **B** £500
☐ **C** £1000
☐ **D** £5000

Driving or riding without insurance is a serious offence. As well as an unlimited fine, you may be disqualified or incur penalty points.

655 Mark *one* answer
Who's legally responsible for ensuring that a vehicle registration certificate (V5C) is updated?

☐ **A** The registered vehicle keeper
☐ **B** The vehicle manufacturer
☐ **C** Your insurance company
☐ **D** The licensing authority

It's your legal responsibility to keep the details on your vehicle registration certificate (V5C) up to date. You should tell the licensing authority about any changes. These include your name, address or vehicle details. If you don't do this, you may have problems when you try to sell your vehicle.

656 Mark *one* answer
Your insurer will issue you with an insurance certificate. When must you produce this document for inspection?

☐ **A** When making a SORN
☐ **B** When buying or selling a vehicle
☐ **C** When a police officer asks you for it
☐ **D** When your vehicle is having an MOT test

You must produce a valid insurance certificate when requested by a police officer. If you can't do this immediately, you may be asked to take it to a police station. Other documents you may be asked to produce are your driving licence and the vehicle's MOT certificate.

657 Mark *one* answer
When must your vehicle have valid insurance cover?

☐ **A** Before you can make a SORN
☐ **B** Before you can sell the vehicle
☐ **C** Before you can scrap the vehicle
☐ **D** Before you can tax the vehicle

Your vehicle must have valid insurance cover before you can tax it. If required, it will also need to have a valid MOT certificate. You can tax your vehicle online, by phone or at certain post offices.

658 Mark *one* answer
What do you need before you can legally use a motor vehicle on the road?

☐ **A** An appropriate driving licence
☐ **B** Breakdown cover
☐ **C** Proof of your identity
☐ **D** A vehicle handbook

Using a motor vehicle on the road illegally carries a heavy fine and can lead to penalty points on your driving licence. You must
• hold a valid driving licence for the class of vehicle you're using
• be insured to drive the vehicle.

If required, the vehicle must have a current MOT test certificate and be taxed for use on the road.

659 Mark *one* answer
What must you have when you apply to renew your vehicle tax?

☐ **A** Valid insurance
☐ **B** The vehicle's chassis number
☐ **C** The handbook
☐ **D** A valid driving licence

You can renew your vehicle tax online, at post offices and by phone using the DVLA vehicle tax service. When applying, make sure you have all the relevant valid documents, including a valid MOT test certificate where applicable.

660 Mark *one* answer
A police officer asks to see your documents. You don't have them with you. How many days do you have to produce them at a police station?

☐ **A** 5 days
☐ **B** 7 days
☐ **C** 14 days
☐ **D** 21 days

You don't have to carry your vehicle's documents wherever you go. If a police officer asks to see them and you don't have them with you, you may be asked to produce them at a police station within 7 days.

661 Mark *one* answer

When should you update your vehicle registration certificate?

☐ **A** When you pass your driving test
☐ **B** When you move house
☐ **C** When your vehicle needs an MOT
☐ **D** When you have a collision

As the registered keeper of a vehicle, it's up to you to inform DVLA of any changes in your details; for example, your name or address. You do this by completing and sending off the relevant section of the registration certificate.

662 Mark *one* answer

What must you check before you drive someone else's vehicle?

☐ **A** That the vehicle owner has third-party insurance cover
☐ **B** That your own vehicle has insurance cover
☐ **C** That the vehicle is insured for your use
☐ **D** That the insurance documents are in the vehicle

Driving a vehicle without insurance cover is illegal, so be sure that, whoever's car you drive, you're insured – whether on their policy or on your own. If you need to take out insurance, it's worth comparing several quotes before you decide which insurance provider best meets your needs.

663 Mark *one* answer

Your car needs to pass an MOT test. What may be invalidated if you drive the car without a current MOT certificate?

☐ **A** The vehicle service record
☐ **B** The vehicle insurance
☐ **C** The vehicle tax
☐ **D** The vehicle registration document

If your vehicle requires an MOT certificate, it's illegal to drive it without one and your insurance may be invalid if you do so. The only exceptions are that you may drive to a pre-arranged MOT test appointment, or to a garage for repairs required for the test.

664 Mark *one* answer

What legal requirement must be met by a newly qualified driver?

☐ **A** They must display green L plates
☐ **B** They must have a new photograph taken for their full licence
☐ **C** They must be accompanied on their first motorway journey
☐ **D** They must have valid motor insurance

It's your responsibility to make sure you're properly insured for the vehicle you're driving. This is the case regardless of whether you're a newly qualified driver or one with more experience.

665 Mark *one* answer
What's covered by third-party insurance?

☐ **A** Damage to your vehicle
☐ **B** Fire damage to your vehicle
☐ **C** Flood damage to your vehicle
☐ **D** Damage to other vehicles

Third-party insurance doesn't cover damage to your own vehicle or injury to yourself. If you have a crash and your vehicle is damaged, you might have to carry out the repairs at your own expense.

666 Mark *one* answer
Who's responsible for paying the vehicle tax?

☐ **A** The driver of the vehicle
☐ **B** The registered keeper of the vehicle
☐ **C** The car dealer
☐ **D** The Driver and Vehicle Licensing Agency (DVLA)

The registered keeper of the vehicle is responsible for paying the vehicle tax or making a Statutory Off-Road Notification (SORN) if the vehicle is to be kept untaxed and off the road.

667 Mark *one* answer
What information is found on a vehicle registration document?

☐ **A** The registered keeper
☐ **B** The type of insurance cover
☐ **C** The service history details
☐ **D** The date of the MOT

Every vehicle used on the road has a registration document. This shows the vehicle's details, including date of first registration, registration number, registered keeper, previous keeper, make of vehicle, engine size, chassis number, year of manufacture and colour.

668 Mark *one* answer
When must you contact the Driver and Vehicle Licensing Agency (DVLA)?

☐ **A** When you get a parking ticket
☐ **B** When you change your vehicle
☐ **C** When you use your vehicle for work
☐ **D** When your vehicle's insurance is due

DVLA needs to keep its records up to date. It sends out a reminder when a vehicle's tax is due for renewal. To do this, it needs to know the name and address of the registered keeper. Every vehicle in the country is registered, so it's possible to trace its history.

669 Mark *one* answer
What circumstances require you to notify the Driver and Vehicle Licensing Agency (DVLA)?

- [ ] **A** When your health affects your driving
- [ ] **B** When you have to work abroad
- [ ] **C** When you lend your vehicle to someone
- [ ] **D** When your vehicle needs an MOT certificate

DVLA holds the records of all vehicles, drivers and riders in Great Britain and Northern Ireland. They need to know if you have a medical condition that might affect your ability to drive safely. You must tell them if your health deteriorates and you become unfit to drive.

670 Mark *one* answer   NI
When could the cost of your insurance be reduced?

- [ ] **A** When you're under 25 years old
- [ ] **B** When you don't wear glasses
- [ ] **C** When you pass the driving test first time
- [ ] **D** When you complete the Pass Plus scheme

The cost of insurance varies with your age and how long you've been driving. Usually, the younger you are, the more expensive it is, especially if you're under 25. Pass Plus provides additional training to newly qualified drivers. The scheme is recognised by many insurance companies, and taking this extra training could give you reduced insurance premiums, as well as improving your skills and experience.

671 Mark *one* answer
In order to supervise a learner driver you need to have held a full driving licence for the same category of vehicle, for at least three years. What other requirement must you meet?

- [ ] **A** To have a car with dual controls
- [ ] **B** To be at least 21 years old
- [ ] **C** To be an approved driving instructor
- [ ] **D** To hold an advanced driving certificate

Learner drivers benefit by combining professional driving lessons with private practice. However, you need to be at least 21 years old and have held your driving licence for at least 3 years before you can supervise a learner driver.

672 Mark *one* answer

Your car requires an MOT certificate. When is it legal to drive it without an MOT certificate?

☐ **A** Up to seven days after the old certificate has run out
☐ **B** When driving to an MOT centre to arrange an appointment
☐ **C** When driving the car with the owner's permission
☐ **D** When driving to an appointment at an MOT centre

When a car is three years old (four years old in Northern Ireland), it must pass an MOT test and have a valid MOT certificate before it can be used on the road. Exceptionally, you may
- drive to a pre-arranged test appointment or to a garage for repairs required for the test
- drive vehicles that are more than 40 years old without an MOT test, but they must be in a roadworthy condition before being used on the road. See GOV.UK for more details.

673 Mark *one* answer   NI

When will a new car need its first MOT test?

☐ **A** When it's one year old
☐ **B** When it's three years old
☐ **C** When it's five years old
☐ **D** When it's seven years old

The vehicle you drive must be roadworthy and in good condition. If it's over three years old, it must pass an MOT test to remain in use on the road (unless it's exempt from the MOT test – see GOV.UK).

674 Mark *one* answer

What does third-party insurance cover?

☐ **A** Damage to your vehicle
☐ **B** Damage to other vehicles
☐ **C** Injury to yourself
☐ **D** All damage and injury

Third-party insurance cover is usually cheaper than comprehensive cover. However, it doesn't cover any damage caused to your own vehicle or property. It only covers damage and injury you cause to others.

675 Mark *one* answer
What's the legal minimum insurance cover you must have to drive on public roads?

☐ **A** Third party, fire and theft
☐ **B** Comprehensive
☐ **C** Third party only
☐ **D** Personal injury cover

The minimum insurance required by law is third-party cover. This covers your liability to others involved in a collision but not damage to your vehicle. Basic third-party insurance also won't cover theft or fire damage. Ask your insurance company for advice on the best cover for you and make sure that you read the policy carefully.

676 Mark *one* answer
What does it mean if your insurance policy has an excess of £500?

☐ **A** The insurance company will pay the first £500 of any claim
☐ **B** You'll be paid £500 if you don't claim within one year
☐ **C** Your vehicle is insured for a value of £500 if it's stolen
☐ **D** You'll have to pay the first £500 of the cost of any claim

Having an excess on your policy will help to keep the premium down. However, if you make a claim, you'll have to pay the excess yourself – in this case, £500.

677 Mark *one* answer
When are you allowed to use hazard warning lights?

- ☐ **A** When stopped and temporarily obstructing traffic
- ☐ **B** When travelling during darkness without headlights
- ☐ **C** When parked on double yellow lines to visit a shop
- ☐ **D** When travelling slowly because you're lost

You mustn't use hazard warning lights while moving, except to warn traffic behind when you slow suddenly on a motorway or unrestricted dual carriageway. Never use hazard warning lights to excuse dangerous or illegal parking.

678 Mark *one* answer
What should you do if you have to stop while you're going through a congested tunnel?

- ☐ **A** Pull up very close to the vehicle in front to save space
- ☐ **B** Ignore any message signs, as they're never up to date
- ☐ **C** Keep a safe distance from the vehicle in front
- ☐ **D** Make a U-turn and find another route

It's important to keep a safe distance from the vehicle in front at all times. This still applies in congested tunnels, even if you're moving very slowly or have stopped. If the vehicle in front breaks down, you may need room to manoeuvre past it.

679 Mark *one* answer
You arrive at the scene of a crash where someone is bleeding heavily from a wound in their arm. Nothing is embedded in the wound. What could you do to help?

- ☐ **A** Walk them around and keep them talking
- ☐ **B** Dab the wound
- ☐ **C** Get them a drink
- ☐ **D** Apply pressure over the wound

If possible, lay the casualty down. Protect yourself from exposure to blood and, when you're sure there's nothing in the wound, apply firm pressure using clean material.

680 Mark *one* answer
You're at an incident. What could you do to help an unconscious casualty?

- ☐ **A** Take photographs of the scene
- ☐ **B** Check that they're breathing normally
- ☐ **C** Move them to somewhere more comfortable
- ☐ **D** Splash their face with cool water

If a casualty is unconscious, you need to check that they're breathing normally. Look for chest movements, look and listen for breathing, and feel for breath on your cheek.

681 Mark *one* answer

A casualty isn't breathing normally and needs CPR. At what rate should you press down and release on the centre of their chest?

- ☐ **A** 10 times per minute
- ☐ **B** 120 times per minute
- ☐ **C** 60 times per minute
- ☐ **D** 240 times per minute

If a casualty isn't breathing normally, cardiopulmonary resuscitation (CPR) may be needed to maintain circulation. Place two hands on the centre of the chest and press down hard and fast – around 5–6 centimetres and about twice a second.

682 Mark *one* answer

Following a collision, a person has been injured. What would be a warning sign for shock?

- ☐ **A** Flushed complexion
- ☐ **B** Warm dry skin
- ☐ **C** Slow pulse
- ☐ **D** Rapid shallow breathing

The effects of shock may not be immediately obvious. Warning signs to look for include
- a rapid pulse
- sweating
- pale grey skin
- rapid shallow breathing.

683 Mark *one* answer

An injured person has been placed in the recovery position. They're unconscious but breathing normally. What else should be done?

- ☐ **A** Press firmly between their shoulders
- ☐ **B** Place their arms by their side
- ☐ **C** Give them a hot sweet drink
- ☐ **D** Check their airway remains open

After a casualty has been placed in the recovery position, make sure their airway remains open and monitor their condition until medical help arrives. Where possible, don't move a casualty unless there's further danger.

684 Mark *one* answer

An injured motorcyclist is lying unconscious in the road. The traffic has stopped and there's no further danger. What could you do to help?

- ☐ **A** Remove their safety helmet
- ☐ **B** Seek medical assistance
- ☐ **C** Move the person off the road
- ☐ **D** Remove their leather jacket

If someone has been injured, the sooner proper medical attention is given the better. Ask someone to phone for help or do it yourself. An injured person should only be moved if they're in further danger. An injured motorcyclist's helmet shouldn't be removed unless it's essential.

685 Mark *one* answer
What should you do if you see a large box fall from a lorry onto the motorway?

- ☐ **A** Go to the next emergency telephone and report the hazard
- ☐ **B** Catch up with the lorry and try to get the driver's attention
- ☐ **C** Stop close to the box until the police arrive
- ☐ **D** Pull over to the hard shoulder, then remove the box

Lorry drivers can be unaware of objects falling from their vehicles. If you see something fall onto a motorway, look to see if the driver pulls over. If they don't stop, don't attempt to retrieve the object yourself. Pull onto the hard shoulder near an emergency telephone and report the hazard.

686 Mark *one* answer
You're going through a long tunnel. What will warn you of congestion or an incident ahead?

- ☐ **A** Hazard warning lines
- ☐ **B** Other drivers flashing their lights
- ☐ **C** Variable message signs
- ☐ **D** Areas with hatch markings

Follow the instructions given by the signs or by tunnel officials. In congested tunnels, a minor incident can soon turn into a major one, with serious or even fatal results.

687 Mark *one* answer
An adult casualty isn't breathing. To maintain circulation, CPR should be given. What's the correct depth to press down on their chest?

- ☐ **A** 1 to 2 centimetres
- ☐ **B** 5 to 6 centimetres
- ☐ **C** 10 to 15 centimetres
- ☐ **D** 15 to 20 centimetres

An adult casualty isn't breathing normally. To maintain circulation, place two hands on the centre of the chest. Then press down hard and fast – around 5–6 centimetres and about twice a second.

688 Mark *one* answer
You're the first person to arrive at an incident where people are badly injured. You've switched on your hazard warning lights and checked all engines are stopped. What else should you do?

- ☐ **A** Make sure that an ambulance has been called
- ☐ **B** Stop other cars and ask the drivers for help
- ☐ **C** Try and get people who are injured to drink something
- ☐ **D** Move the people who are injured clear of their vehicles

If you're the first to arrive at a crash scene, the first concerns are the risk of further collision and fire. Ensuring that vehicle engines are switched off will reduce the risk of fire. Use hazard warning lights so that other traffic knows there's a need for caution. Make sure the emergency services are contacted; don't assume it's already been done.

689 Mark *one* answer

You arrive at the scene of a motorcycle crash. The rider is injured. When should their helmet be removed?

- ☐ **A** Only when it's essential
- ☐ **B** Always straight away
- ☐ **C** Only when the motorcyclist asks
- ☐ **D** Always, unless they're in shock

Don't remove a motorcyclist's helmet unless it's essential. Remember they may be suffering from shock. Don't give them anything to eat or drink, but do reassure them confidently.

690 Mark *one* answer

You arrive at an incident. There's no danger from fire or further collisions and the emergency services have been called. What's your first priority when attending to an unconscious motorcyclist?

- ☐ **A** Check whether they're breathing normally
- ☐ **B** Check whether they're bleeding
- ☐ **C** Check whether they have any broken bones
- ☐ **D** Check whether they have any bruising

At the scene of an incident, always be aware of danger from further collisions or fire. The first priority when dealing with an unconscious person is to ensure they can breathe. This may involve clearing their airway if you can see an obstruction or if they're having difficulty breathing.

691 Mark *one* answer

At an incident, someone is unconscious and you want to help. What would be the first thing to check?

- ☐ **A** Whether their vehicle is insured
- ☐ **B** Whether they have any allergies
- ☐ **C** Whether they're comfortable
- ☐ **D** Whether their airway is open

Remember this procedure by saying DR ABC. This stands for Danger, Response, Airway, Breathing, Circulation. Give whatever first aid you can and stay with the injured person until a medical professional takes over.

692 Mark *one* answer

What could you do to help injured people at an incident?

- ☐ **A** Keep them warm and comfortable
- ☐ **B** Give them something to eat
- ☐ **C** Keep them on the move by walking them around
- ☐ **D** Give them a warm drink

There are a number of things you can do to help, even without expert training. Be aware of further danger from other traffic and fire; make sure the area is safe. People may be in shock. Don't give them anything to eat or drink. Keep them warm and comfortable and reassure them. Don't move injured people unless there's a risk of further danger.

693 Mark *one* answer
There's been a collision. How can you help a driver who's suffering from shock?

☐ **A** Give them a drink
☐ **B** Reassure them confidently
☐ **C** Ask who caused the incident
☐ **D** Offer them a cigarette

A casualty suffering from shock may have injuries that aren't immediately obvious. Call the emergency services, then stay with the person in shock, offering reassurance until the experts arrive.

694 Mark *one* answer
You arrive at the scene of a motorcycle crash. No other vehicle is involved. The rider is unconscious and lying in the middle of the road. What's the first thing you should do at the scene?

☐ **A** Move the rider out of the road
☐ **B** Warn other traffic
☐ **C** Clear the road of debris
☐ **D** Give the rider reassurance

The motorcyclist is in an extremely vulnerable position, exposed to further danger from traffic. Approaching vehicles need advance warning in order to slow down and safely take avoiding action or stop. Don't put yourself or anyone else at risk. Use the hazard warning lights on your vehicle to alert other road users to the danger.

695 Mark *one* answer
At an incident, how could you help a small child who isn't breathing?

☐ **A** Find their parents and explain what's happening
☐ **B** Open their airway and begin CPR
☐ **C** Put them in the recovery position and slap their back
☐ **D** Talk to them confidently until an ambulance arrives

If a young child has stopped breathing, first check that their airway is open and then begin CPR. With a young child, you may only need to use one hand and you shouldn't press down as far as you would with an adult. Continue the procedure until the child is breathing again or until a medical professional takes over.

696 Mark *one* answer
At an incident, a casualty isn't breathing. What should you do while helping them to start breathing again?

☐ **A** Put their arms across their chest
☐ **B** Shake them firmly
☐ **C** Roll them onto their side
☐ **D** Open their airway

It's important to ensure that the airway is open before you start CPR. To open the casualty's airway, place your fingers under their chin and lift it forward.

697 Mark *one* answer
At an incident, someone is suffering from severe burns. How could you help them?

☐ **A** Apply lotions to the injury
☐ **B** Burst any blisters
☐ **C** Remove anything sticking to the burns
☐ **D** Douse the burns with clean, cool water

Your priority is to cool the burns with clean, cool water. Its coolness will help take the heat out of the burns and relieve the pain. Keep the wound doused for at least 20 minutes. If blisters appear, don't attempt to burst them, as this could lead to infection.

698 Mark *one* answer
You arrive at an incident. A pedestrian is bleeding heavily from a leg wound. The leg isn't broken and there's nothing in the wound. How could you help?

☐ **A** Dab the wound to stop the bleeding
☐ **B** Keep the casualty's legs flat on the ground
☐ **C** Give them a warm drink
☐ **D** Apply firm pressure over the wound

You should protect yourself from exposure to blood, and then apply firm pressure over the wound to stem the flow of blood. As soon as practical, fasten a pad to the wound with a bandage or length of cloth. Use the cleanest material available.

699 Mark *one* answer
At an incident, a casualty is unconscious but breathing. When should you move them?

☐ **A** When an ambulance is on its way
☐ **B** When bystanders tell you to move them
☐ **C** When there's a risk of further danger
☐ **D** When bystanders offer to help you

Don't move a casualty unless there's further danger; for example, from other traffic or fire. They may have unseen or internal injuries. Moving them unnecessarily could cause further injury. Don't remove a motorcyclist's helmet unless it's essential.

700 Mark *one* answer
At an incident, it's important to look after any casualties. What should you do with them when the area is safe?

☐ **A** Move them away from the vehicles
☐ **B** Ask them how it happened
☐ **C** Give them something to eat
☐ **D** Keep them where they are

When the area is safe and there's no danger from other traffic or fire, it's better not to move casualties. Moving them may cause further injury.

701 Mark *one* answer
Which sign shows that a tanker is carrying dangerous goods?

□ **A**

LONG VEHICLE

□ **B**

2YE
1089

□ **C**

□ **D**

Tankers will display a hazard warning plate on the side and rear of the vehicle. Details of hazard warning symbols are given in *The Highway Code*. If a tanker is involved in a collision, you may need to report the tanker's hazard labelling to the emergency services.

702 Mark *one* answer
Which document may the police ask you to produce after you've been involved in a collision?

□ **A** Your vehicle registration document
□ **B** Your driving licence
□ **C** Your theory test certificate
□ **D** Your vehicle service record

You must stop if you've been involved in a collision that results in injury or damage. The police may ask to see your driving licence and insurance details at the time or later at a police station.

703 Mark *one* answer
After a collision, someone is unconscious in their vehicle. When should you call the emergency services?

□ **A** Only as a last resort
□ **B** As soon as possible
□ **C** After you've woken them up
□ **D** After checking for broken bones

It's important to make sure that the emergency services arrive as soon as possible. When a person is unconscious, they could have serious injuries that aren't immediately obvious.

704 Mark *one* answer
A collision has just happened. An injured person is lying in a busy road. What's the first thing you should do?

□ **A** Treat the person for shock
□ **B** Warn other traffic
□ **C** Place them in the recovery position
□ **D** Make sure the injured person is kept warm

The most immediate danger is further collisions and fire. You could warn other traffic by switching on hazard warning lights, displaying an advance warning triangle or sign (but not on a motorway), or by any other means that doesn't put you or others at risk.

705 Mark *one* answer

At an incident, how could you help a casualty who has stopped breathing?

☐ **A** Keep their head tilted forwards as far as possible
☐ **B** Follow the DR ABC code
☐ **C** Raise their legs to help with circulation
☐ **D** Try to give them something to drink

The DR ABC code has been devised by medical experts to give the best outcome until the emergency services arrive and take care of casualties.

706 Mark *one* answer

You're at the scene of an incident. How could you help someone who's suffering from shock?

☐ **A** Reassure them confidently
☐ **B** Offer them a cigarette
☐ **C** Give them a warm drink
☐ **D** Offer them some food

If someone is suffering from shock, try to keep them warm and as comfortable as you can. Don't give them anything to eat or drink but reassure them confidently and try not to leave them alone.

707 Mark *one* answer

There's been a collision. A motorcyclist is lying injured and unconscious. Why should you only remove their helmet if it's essential?

☐ **A** They might not want you to remove it
☐ **B** Removing it could make any injuries worse
☐ **C** Removing it could let them get cold
☐ **D** You could scratch the helmet as you remove it

When someone is injured, any movement that isn't absolutely necessary should be avoided, since it could make the injuries worse. Unless it's essential to remove a motorcyclist's helmet, it's generally safer to leave it in place.

708 Mark *one* answer

You're on a motorway. When can you use hazard warning lights?

☐ **A** When a vehicle is following too closely
☐ **B** When you slow down quickly because of danger ahead
☐ **C** When you're being towed by another vehicle
☐ **D** When you're riding on the hard shoulder

Briefly using your hazard warning lights will warn the traffic behind you that there's a hazard ahead. Turn them off again when following drivers have seen and responded to your signal.

709 Mark *one* answer

You've broken down on a two-way road. You have a warning triangle. At least how far from your vehicle should you place the warning triangle?

- ☐ **A** 5 metres (16 feet)
- ☐ **B** 25 metres (82 feet)
- ☐ **C** 45 metres (147 feet)
- ☐ **D** 100 metres (328 feet)

Advance warning triangles fold flat and don't take up much room. Use one to warn other road users if your vehicle has broken down or if there has been an incident. Place it at least **45 metres (147 feet)** behind your vehicle (or the incident), on the same side of the road or verge. Place it further back if the scene is hidden by, for example, a bend, hill or dip in the road. Don't use warning triangles on motorways.

710 Mark *one* answer

Your car breaks down on a level crossing. What's the first thing you should do?

- ☐ **A** Tell drivers behind what's happened
- ☐ **B** Leave your vehicle and get everyone clear
- ☐ **C** Walk down the track and signal the next train
- ☐ **D** Stay in your car until you're told to move

If your vehicle breaks down on a level crossing, your first priority is to get everyone out of the vehicle and clear of the crossing. Then use the railway telephone, if there is one, to tell the signal operator. If you have time before the train arrives, move the vehicle clear of the crossing, but only do this if the alarm signals aren't activated.

711 Mark *one* answer
What should you do if a tyre bursts while you're driving?

- ☐ **A** Pull on the parking brake
- ☐ **B** Brake as quickly as possible
- ☐ **C** Pull up slowly at the side of the road
- ☐ **D** Continue on at a normal speed

A tyre bursting can lead to a loss of control, especially if you're travelling at high speed. Using the correct procedure should help you to stop the vehicle safely.

712 Mark *one* answer
What should you do if your vehicle has a puncture on a motorway?

- ☐ **A** Drive slowly to the next service area to get assistance
- ☐ **B** Pull up on the hard shoulder or in an emergency refuge area. Change the wheel as quickly as possible
- ☐ **C** Pull up on the hard shoulder or in an emergency refuge area and call for assistance
- ☐ **D** Switch on your hazard warning lights. Stop in your lane

Pull up on the hard shoulder or in an emergency refuge area and call for assistance. Don't attempt to repair your vehicle while it's on the hard shoulder, because of the risk posed by traffic passing at high speeds.

713 Mark *one* answer
Your vehicle has stalled in the middle of a level crossing. What should you do if the warning bells start to ring while you're trying to restart the engine?

- ☐ **A** Get out of the car and clear of the crossing
- ☐ **B** Run down the track to warn the signal operator
- ☐ **C** Carry on trying to restart the engine
- ☐ **D** Push the vehicle clear of the crossing

If the warning bells ring, leave the vehicle and get any passengers well clear of the crossing immediately.

714 Mark *one* answer
What should you do before driving into a tunnel?

- ☐ **A** Switch off your radio
- ☐ **B** Take off your sunglasses
- ☐ **C** Close your sunroof
- ☐ **D** Switch on your windscreen wipers

If you're wearing sunglasses, you should remove them before driving into a tunnel. If you don't, your vision will be restricted, even in tunnels that appear to be well lit.

715 Mark *one* answer
Which lights should you use when you're driving in a tunnel?

☐ **A** Sidelights
☐ **B** Front spotlights
☐ **C** Dipped headlights
☐ **D** Rear fog lights

Before entering a tunnel, you should switch on your dipped headlights, as this will allow you to see and be seen. In many tunnels, it's a legal requirement. Don't wear sunglasses while you're driving in a tunnel.

716 Mark *one* answer
What should you do to reduce the risk of your vehicle catching fire?

☐ **A** Keep water levels above maximum
☐ **B** Check out any strong smell of fuel
☐ **C** Avoid driving with a full tank of fuel
☐ **D** Use fuel additives

The fuel in your vehicle can be a dangerous fire hazard. If you smell fuel, check out where it's coming from. Never
- use a naked flame near the vehicle if you can smell fuel
- smoke when refuelling your vehicle.

717 Mark *one* answer
You're driving on the motorway. What should you do if luggage falls from your vehicle?

☐ **A** Stop at the next emergency telephone and report the incident
☐ **B** Stop on the motorway and switch on hazard warning lights while you pick it up
☐ **C** Walk back up the motorway to pick it up
☐ **D** Pull up on the hard shoulder and wave traffic down

If any object falls onto the motorway carriageway from your vehicle, pull onto the hard shoulder near an emergency telephone and call for assistance. Don't stop on the carriageway or attempt to retrieve anything.

718 Mark *one* answer
What should you do if an instrument panel warning light comes on while you're driving?

☐ **A** Continue if the engine sounds all right
☐ **B** Hope that it's just a temporary electrical fault
☐ **C** Deal with the problem when there's more time
☐ **D** Check out the problem quickly and safely

Make sure you know what the different warning lights mean. An illuminated warning light could mean that your car is unsafe to drive. If you aren't sure about the problem, get a qualified mechanic to check it.

719 Mark *one* answer
What should you do if your vehicle breaks down in a tunnel?

☐ **A** Stay in your vehicle and wait for the police
☐ **B** Stand in the lane behind your vehicle to warn others
☐ **C** Stand in front of your vehicle to warn oncoming drivers
☐ **D** Switch on hazard warning lights, then go and call for help

A broken-down vehicle in a tunnel can cause serious congestion and danger to other road users. If your vehicle breaks down, get help without delay. Switch on your hazard warning lights, then go to an emergency telephone to call for help.

720 Mark *one* answer
What should you do if your vehicle catches fire while you're driving through a tunnel?

☐ **A** Leave it where it is, with the engine running
☐ **B** Pull up, then walk to an emergency telephone
☐ **C** Park it away from the carriageway
☐ **D** Drive it out of the tunnel if it's safe to do so

If it's possible, and you can do so without causing further danger, it may be safer to drive a vehicle that's on fire out of a tunnel. The greatest danger in a tunnel fire is smoke and suffocation.

721 Mark *one* answer
What should you do first if your vehicle has broken down on an automatic railway level crossing?

☐ **A** Get everyone out of the vehicle and clear of the crossing
☐ **B** Telephone your vehicle recovery service to move it
☐ **C** Walk along the track to give warning to any approaching trains
☐ **D** Try to push the vehicle clear of the crossing as soon as possible

First, get yourself and anyone else well away from the crossing. If there's a railway telephone, use that to get instructions from the signal operator. Then, if there's time, move the vehicle clear of the crossing.

722 Mark *one* answer
What's the first thing you must do if you have a collision while you're driving your car?

☐ **A** Stop only if someone waves at you
☐ **B** Call the emergency services
☐ **C** Stop at the scene of the incident
☐ **D** Call your insurance company

If you're in a collision that causes damage or injury to any other person, vehicle, animal or property, by law you must stop. Give your name, the vehicle owner's name and address, and the vehicle's registration number to anyone who has reasonable grounds for requesting them.

723 Mark *one* answer
What information should you share if you're involved in a collision that causes damage to another vehicle?

☐ **A** Your occupation and reason for your journey
☐ **B** Your name, address and vehicle registration number
☐ **C** Your national insurance number
☐ **D** Your internet service provider

Try to keep calm and don't rush. Make sure that you've shared all the relevant details with the other driver before you leave the scene. If possible, take pictures and note the positions of all the vehicles involved.

724 Mark *one* answer   NI
You lose control of your car and damage a garden wall. What must you do if the property owner isn't available?

☐ **A** Report the incident to the police within 24 hours
☐ **B** Go back to tell the house owner the next day
☐ **C** Report the incident to your insurance company when you get home
☐ **D** Find someone in the area to tell them about it immediately

If the property owner isn't available at the time, you must inform the police about the incident. This should be done as soon as possible, and in any case within 24 hours.

725 Mark *one* answer
What restrictions apply if you're towing a trailer on a three-lane motorway?

- ☐ **A** You mustn't exceed 50 mph
- ☐ **B** You mustn't overtake
- ☐ **C** You must have a stabiliser fitted
- ☐ **D** You mustn't use the right-hand lane

The motorway regulations for towing a trailer state that you mustn't

- use the right-hand lane of a three-lane motorway unless directed to do so (for example, at roadworks or due to a lane closure)
- exceed 60 mph.

726 Mark *one* answer
What should you do if you're towing a trailer and it starts to swing from side to side?

- ☐ **A** Ease off the accelerator to reduce your speed
- ☐ **B** Let go of the steering wheel and let it correct itself
- ☐ **C** Brake hard and hold the pedal down
- ☐ **D** Accelerate until it stabilises

Strong winds or buffeting from large vehicles can cause a trailer or caravan to swing from side to side ('snake'). If this happens, ease off the accelerator. Don't brake harshly, steer sharply or increase your speed.

727 Mark *one* answer
When would you increase the pressure in your tyres so that it's above the normal value?

- ☐ **A** When the roads are slippery
- ☐ **B** When the vehicle is fitted with anti-lock brakes
- ☐ **C** When the tyre tread is worn below 2 mm
- ☐ **D** When carrying a heavy load

Check the vehicle handbook. This should give you guidance on the correct tyre pressures for your vehicle and when you may need to adjust them. If you're carrying a heavy load, you may need to adjust the headlights as well. Most cars have a switch on the dashboard to do this.

728 Mark *one* answer
How will a heavy load on your roof rack affect your vehicle's handling?

☐ **A** It will improve the road holding
☐ **B** It will reduce the stopping distance
☐ **C** It will make the steering lighter
☐ **D** It will reduce stability

A heavy load on your roof rack will reduce the stability of the vehicle because it moves the centre of gravity away from that designed by the manufacturer. Be aware of this when you drive round bends and corners. If you change direction at speed, your vehicle and/or load could become unstable and you could lose control.

729 Mark *one* answer
What would be affected if you carry a very heavy load on your vehicle?

☐ **A** The vehicle's gearbox
☐ **B** The vehicle's ventilation
☐ **C** The vehicle's handling
☐ **D** The vehicle's battery

Any load will have an effect on the handling of your vehicle, and this becomes worse as you increase the load. You need to be aware of this when carrying passengers or heavy loads, fitting a roof rack or towing a trailer.

730 Mark *one* answer
Who's responsible for making sure that a vehicle isn't overloaded?

☐ **A** The driver of the vehicle
☐ **B** The owner of the items being carried
☐ **C** The person who loaded the vehicle
☐ **D** The licensing authority

Carrying heavy loads will affect control and the vehicle's handling characteristics. If the vehicle you're driving is overloaded, you'll be held responsible.

731 Mark *one* answer
You're planning to tow a caravan. What will help the handling of the combination?

- ☐ **A** A jockey wheel fitted to the tow bar
- ☐ **B** Power steering fitted to the towing vehicle
- ☐ **C** Anti-lock brakes fitted to the towing vehicle
- ☐ **D** A stabiliser fitted to the tow bar

Towing a caravan or trailer affects the way the towing vehicle handles. A stabiliser device isn't designed to overcome instability caused by incorrect loading but it can give added security in side winds and from buffeting caused by large vehicles.

732 Mark *one* answer
Are passengers allowed to ride in a caravan that's being towed?

- ☐ **A** Yes, if they're over 14
- ☐ **B** No, not at any time
- ☐ **C** Only if all the seats in the towing vehicle are full
- ☐ **D** Only if a stabiliser is fitted

Riding in a towed caravan is highly dangerous. The safety of the entire unit is dependent on the stability of the trailer. Moving passengers would make the caravan unstable and could cause loss of control.

733 Mark *one* answer
What safety device must be fitted to a trailer braking system?

- ☐ **A** Stabiliser
- ☐ **B** Jockey wheel
- ☐ **C** Corner steadies
- ☐ **D** Breakaway cable

In the event that the trailer becomes detached from the towing vehicle, the breakaway cable activates the trailer brakes before snapping. This allows the towing vehicle to get free of the trailer and out of danger.

734 Mark *one* answer

You wish to tow a trailer. Where would you find the maximum noseweight for your vehicle's tow hitch?

☐ **A** In the vehicle handbook
☐ **B** In *The Highway Code*
☐ **C** In your vehicle registration certificate
☐ **D** In your licence documents

You must know how to load your trailer or caravan so that the hitch exerts an appropriate downward force on the tow ball. Information about the maximum permitted noseweight can be found in your vehicle handbook or obtained from your vehicle manufacturer's agent.

735 Mark *one* answer

How should a load be carried on your roof rack?

☐ **A** Securely fastened with
   suitable restraints
☐ **B** Loaded towards the rear of the vehicle
☐ **C** Visible in your exterior mirror
☐ **D** Covered with plastic sheeting

Any load must be securely fastened to the vehicle. The safest way to carry items on the roof is in a specially designed roof box. This will help to keep your luggage secure and dry, and it also has less wind resistance than loads carried exposed on a roof rack.

736 Mark *one* answer

You're carrying a child under three years old in your car. Which restraint is suitable for a child of this age?

☐ **A** A child seat
☐ **B** An adult holding a child
☐ **C** An adult seat belt
☐ **D** An adult lap belt

It's your responsibility to ensure that all children in your car are secure. Suitable restraints include a child seat, baby seat, booster seat or booster cushion. It's essential that any restraint used is suitable for the child's size and weight, and fitted according to the manufacturer's instructions.

PART 4:
ANSWERS TO
QUESTIONS

Section 1 – **Alertness**

1 C	2 B	3 D	4 C	5 C	6 C
7 C	8 B	9 C	10 B	11 A	12 A
13 D	14 B	15 A	16 B	17 B	18 B
19 C	20 D	21 D	22 D	23 D	24 C
25 C	26 D				

Section 2 – **Attitude**

27 D	28 A	29 C	30 D	31 D	32 B
33 B	34 A	35 D	36 A	37 B	38 A
39 A	40 C	41 A	42 D	43 D	44 D
45 B	46 C	47 B	48 C	49 A	50 C
51 A	52 C	53 C	54 B	55 D	56 B
57 C	58 B	59 A	60 B	61 B	62 C
63 B	64 D	65 C			

Section 3 – **Safety and your vehicle**

66 A	67 C	68 C	69 B	70 D	71 C
72 D	73 A	74 C	75 D	76 B	77 B
78 D	79 B	80 D	81 C	82 A	83 D
84 A	85 A	86 B	87 B	88 D	89 A
90 B	91 D	92 D	93 D	94 B	95 B
96 B	97 B	98 A	99 C	100 D	101 D
102 B	103 B	104 B	105 D	106 C	107 D
108 D	109 C	110 A	111 A	112 B	113 D
114 C	115 A	116 A	117 D	118 C	119 B
120 B	121 B	122 D	123 C	124 A	125 D
126 A	127 B	128 D	129 C	130 D	131 D
132 B	133 B	134 C	135 D	136 C	137 D
138 B	139 C	140 A	141 A	142 D	

Section 4 – **Safety margins**

143 D	144 D	145 A	146 B	147 D	148 B
149 C	150 A	151 D	152 A	153 A	154 B
155 D	156 B	157 B	158 D	159 A	160 C
161 A	162 C	163 B	164 D	165 D	166 B
167 D	168 A	169 A	170 A	171 C	172 B
173 C	174 C	175 C	176 A		

Section 5 – **Hazard awareness**

177 C	178 C	179 A	180 D	181 C	182 C
183 C	184 D	185 B	186 A	187 A	188 A
189 C	190 B	191 C	192 D	193 B	194 B
195 C	196 A	197 D	198 D	199 C	200 B
201 C	202 B	203 A	204 A	205 A	206 C
207 A	208 D	209 B	210 C	211 C	212 A
213 B	214 B	215 B	216 D	217 A	218 C
219 D	220 B	221 B	222 C	223 D	224 C
225 C	226 A	227 B	228 A	229 B	230 C
231 C	232 A	233 C	234 D	235 C	236 C
237 D	238 B	239 C	240 B	241 D	242 A
243 A	244 D	245 D	246 B	247 D	248 D
249 A	250 A	251 B	252 D	253 A	254 B

Section 6 – **Vulnerable road users**

255 D	256 D	257 B	258 D	259 D	260 C
261 D	262 D	263 D	264 B	265 D	266 D
267 C	268 C	269 C	270 A	271 D	272 D
273 D	274 C	275 D	276 A	277 D	278 C
279 C	280 D	281 D	282 B	283 A	284 C
285 C	286 A	287 D	288 A	289 B	290 B
291 A	292 A	293 C	294 B	295 D	296 A
297 D	298 D	299 D	300 C	301 B	302 B
303 D	304 C	305 B	306 A	307 D	308 B
309 B	310 D	311 C	312 B	313 C	314 A
315 C	316 C	317 B	318 B	319 D	320 B
321 B	322 C	323 D	324 A	325 D	

Section 7 – **Other types of vehicle**

326 A	327 A	328 B	329 B	330 D	331 B
332 B	333 A	334 B	335 B	336 D	337 D
338 A	339 D	340 A	341 B	342 C	343 B
344 D	345 B	346 D	347 D		

Section 8 – **Vehicle handling**

348 A	349 A	350 D	351 D	352 A	353 C
354 C	355 D	356 C	357 D	358 D	359 C
360 C	361 B	362 B	363 D	364 D	365 B
366 C	367 A	368 B	369 A	370 B	371 D
372 C	373 C	374 A	375 C	376 D	377 B
378 D	379 D	380 C	381 C	382 C	383 D
384 C	385 A	386 A	387 C	388 D	389 B
390 D	391 C				

Section 9 – **Motorway rules**

392 D	393 D	394 A	395 C	396 C	397 C
398 A	399 C	400 C	401 C	402 C	403 C
404 C	405 B	406 B	407 A	408 B	409 D
410 C	411 A	412 A	413 D	414 B	415 A
416 A	417 C	418 B	419 B	420 D	421 A
422 D	423 D	424 B	425 D	426 A	427 D
428 C	429 B	430 D	431 B	432 D	433 B
434 A	435 A	436 C	437 D	438 A	439 B
440 B	441 A	442 D	443 C	444 B	445 C
446 D	447 A	448 B			

Section 10 – **Rules of the road**

449 C	450 D	451 B	452 A	453 C	454 D
455 D	456 A	457 B	458 A	459 B	460 A
461 D	462 A	463 D	464 C	465 A	466 C
467 C	468 B	469 A	470 C	471 A	472 D
473 B	474 A	475 B	476 A	477 B	478 A
479 D	480 A	481 D	482 B	483 C	484 B
485 B	486 B	487 D	488 D	489 C	490 D
491 D	492 D	493 D	494 C	495 C	496 D
497 A	498 A	499 C	500 B	501 A	502 D
503 A	504 A	505 D	506 D	507 D	508 A
509 A	510 A	511 D	512 D	513 A	514 A
515 A					

Section 11 – **Road and traffic signs**

516 D	517 D	518 A	519 A	520 D	521 B
522 D	523 D	524 D	525 A	526 C	527 B
528 D	529 A	530 B	531 B	532 C	533 A
534 C	535 B	536 C	537 D	538 C	539 C
540 D	541 A	542 D	543 D	544 B	545 A
546 A	547 A	548 B	549 B	550 A	551 D
552 A	553 C	554 A	555 B	556 C	557 B
558 D	559 A	560 A	561 C	562 D	563 A
564 C	565 B	566 D	567 B	568 B	569 C
570 D	571 C	572 B	573 C	574 D	575 B
576 A	577 A	578 C	579 D	580 A	581 C
582 C	583 B	584 A	585 C	586 A	587 A
588 D	589 D	590 A	591 D	592 C	593 C
594 B	595 C	596 C	597 A	598 B	599 D
600 B	601 B	602 A	603 A	604 B	605 D
606 C	607 B	608 C	609 A	610 B	611 A
612 C	613 B	614 A	615 C	616 B	617 B
618 B	619 A	620 A	621 B	622 D	623 C
624 B	625 C	626 A	627 C	628 A	629 C
630 C	631 A	632 B	633 A	634 A	635 D
636 B	637 C	638 B	639 D	640 A	641 B
642 A	643 C	644 C	645 B	646 B	647 B
648 A					

Section 12 – **Documents**

649 C	650 B	651 B	652 A	653 C	654 A
655 A	656 C	657 D	658 A	659 A	660 B
661 B	662 C	663 B	664 D	665 D	666 B
667 A	668 B	669 A	670 D	671 B	672 D
673 B	674 B	675 C	676 D		

Section 13 – **Incidents, accidents and emergencies**

677 A	678 C	679 D	680 B	681 B	682 D
683 D	684 B	685 A	686 C	687 B	688 A
689 A	690 A	691 D	692 A	693 B	694 B
695 B	696 D	697 D	698 D	699 C	700 D
701 B	702 B	703 B	704 B	705 B	706 A
707 B	708 B	709 C	710 B	711 C	712 C
713 A	714 B	715 C	716 B	717 A	718 D
719 D	720 D	721 A	722 C	723 B	724 A

Section 14 – **Vehicle loading**

725 D	726 A	727 D	728 D	729 C	730 A
731 D	732 B	733 D	734 A	735 A	736 A

PART 5: GLOSSARY

Glossary

Accelerate
To make the vehicle move faster by pressing the right-hand pedal.

Advanced stop lines
A marked area on the road at traffic lights, which permits cyclists or buses to wait in front of other traffic.

Adverse weather
Bad weather that makes driving difficult or dangerous.

Alert
Quick to notice possible hazards.

Anticipation
Looking out for hazards and taking action before a problem starts.

Anti-lock brakes
Brakes that stop the wheels locking so that you are less likely to skid on a slippery road.

Aquaplane
To slide out of control on a wet road surface.

Articulated vehicle
A long vehicle that is divided into two or more sections joined by cables.

Attitude
The way you think or feel, which affects the way you drive. Especially, whether you are patient and polite, or impatient and aggressive.

Automatic
A vehicle with gears that change by themselves as you speed up or slow down.

Awareness
Taking notice of the road and traffic conditions around you at all times.

Black ice
An invisible film of ice that forms over the road surface, creating very dangerous driving conditions.

Blind spot
The section of road behind you that you cannot see in your mirrors. You 'cover' your blind spot by looking over your shoulder before moving off or overtaking.

Brake fade
Loss of power to the brakes when you have been using them for a long time without taking your foot off the brake pedal. For example, when driving down a steep hill. The brakes will overheat and not work properly.

Braking distance
The distance you must allow to slow the vehicle in order to come to a stop.

Brow
The highest point of a hill.

Built-up area
A town, or place with lots of buildings.

Carriageway
One side of a road or motorway. A 'dual carriageway' has a central reservation.

Catalytic converter
A piece of equipment fitted in the exhaust system that changes harmful gases into less harmful ones.

Chicane
A sharp double bend that has been put into a road to make traffic slow down.

Child restraint
A child seat or special seat belt for children. It keeps them safe and stops them moving around in the car.

Clearway
A road where no stopping is allowed at any time. The sign for a clearway is a red cross in a red circle on a blue background.

Coasting

Driving a vehicle without using any of the gears. That is, with your foot on the clutch pedal and the car in neutral.

Commentary driving

Talking to yourself about what you see on the road ahead and what action you are going to take – an aid to concentration.

Comprehensive insurance

A motor insurance policy that pays for all repairs even if you cause an accident.

Concentration

Keeping all your attention on your driving.

Conditions

How good or bad the road surface is, volume of traffic on the road, and what the weather is like.

Congestion

Heavy traffic that makes it difficult to get to where you want to go.

Consideration

Thinking about other road users and not just yourself. For example, letting another driver go first at a junction.

Contraflow

When traffic on a motorway follows signs to move to the opposite carriageway for a short distance because of roadworks. (During a contraflow, there is traffic driving in both directions on the same side of the motorway.)

Coolant

Liquid in the radiator that removes heat from the engine.

Defensive driving

Driving safely without taking risks, looking out for hazards and thinking for others.

Disqualified

Stopped from doing something (eg driving) by law, because you have broken the law.

Distraction

Anything that stops you concentrating on your driving, such as talking to passengers or using your mobile phone.

Document

An official paper or card, eg your driving licence.

Dual carriageway

A road or motorway with a central reservation.

Engine braking – *see also* gears

Using the low gears to keep your speed down. For example, when you are driving down a steep hill and you want to stop the vehicle running away. Using the gears instead of braking will help to prevent brake fade.

Environment

The world around us and the air we breathe.

Equestrian crossing

An unusual kind of crossing. It has a button high up for horse riders to push.

Exceed

Go higher than an upper limit.

Exhaust emissions

Gases that come out of the exhaust pipe to form part of the outside air.

Field of vision

How far you can see in front and around you when you are driving.

Filler cap

Provides access to the vehicle's fuel tank, for filling up with petrol or diesel.

Glossary

Fog lights

Extra bright rear (and sometimes front) lights that may be used in very poor visibility due to fog. You must remember to switch them off when visibility improves, as they can dazzle and distract other drivers.

Ford

A place in a stream or river that is shallow enough to drive across with care.

Four-wheel drive (4WD)

On a conventional vehicle, steering and engine speed affect just two 'drive' wheels. On 4WD, they affect all four wheels, ensuring optimum grip on loose ground.

Frustration

Feeling annoyed because you cannot drive as fast as you want to because of other drivers or heavy traffic.

Fuel consumption

The amount of fuel (petrol or diesel) that your vehicle uses. Different vehicles have different rates of consumption. Increased fuel consumption means using more fuel. Decreased fuel consumption means using less fuel.

Fuel gauge

A display or dial on the instrument panel that tells you how much fuel (petrol or diesel) you have left.

Gantry

An overhead platform like a high narrow bridge that displays electric signs on a motorway.

Gears

Control the speed of the engine in relation to the vehicle's speed. May be hand operated (manual) or automatically controlled. In a low gear (such as first or second), the engine runs more slowly. In a high gear (such as fourth or fifth), it runs more quickly. Putting the car into a lower gear as you drive can create the effect of engine braking – forcing the engine to run more slowly.

Handling

How well your vehicle moves or responds when you steer or brake.

Harass

To drive in a way that makes other road users afraid.

Hard shoulder

The single lane to the left of the inside lane on a motorway, which is for emergency use only. You should not drive on the hard shoulder except in an emergency, or when there are signs telling you to use the hard shoulder because of roadworks.

Harsh braking (or harsh acceleration)

Using the brake (or accelerator) too hard so as to cause wear on the engine.

Hazard warning lights

Flashing amber lights that you should use only when you have broken down. On a motorway, you can use them to warn other drivers behind you of a hazard ahead.

High-sided vehicle

A van or truck with tall sides, or a tall trailer such as a caravan or horse-box, that is at risk of being blown off-course in strong winds.

Impatient
Not wanting to wait for pedestrians and other road users.

Inflate
To blow up – to put air in your tyres until they are at the right pressures.

Instrument panel
The car's electrical controls and gauges, set behind the steering wheel. Also called the dashboard.

Intimidate
To make someone feel afraid.

Involved
Being part of something. For example, being one of the drivers in an accident.

Jump leads
A pair of thick electric cables with clips at either end. You use it to charge a flat battery by connecting it to the live battery in another vehicle.

Junction
A place where two or more roads join.

Liability
Being legally responsible.

Manoeuvre
Using the controls to make your car move in a particular direction. For example, when turning, reversing or parking.

Manual
By hand. In a car that is a 'manual' or has manual gears, you have to change the gears yourself.

Maximum
The largest possible; 'maximum speed' is the highest speed allowed.

Minimum
The smallest possible.

Mirrors
Cars have a minimum of three rear view mirrors: one in the centre of the windscreen, and one on each front door. Additional mirrors may be required on longer vehicles, or when towing a high trailer such as a caravan. Some mirrors may be curved (convex or concave) to increase the field of vision. The mirror on the windscreen can be turned to anti-dazzle position, if glare from headlights behind creates a distraction.

Mobility
The ability to move around easily.

Monotonous
Boring. For example, a long stretch of motorway with no variety and nothing interesting to see.

MOT
The test that proves your car is safe to drive. Your MOT certificate is one of the important documents for your vehicle.

Motorway
A fast road that has two or more lanes on each side and a hard shoulder. Drivers must join or leave it on the left, via a motorway junction. Many kinds of slower vehicles – such as bicycles – are not allowed on motorways.

Multiple-choice questions
Questions with several possible answers where you have to try to choose the right one.

Observation
The ability to notice important information, such as hazards developing ahead.

Obstruct
To get in the way of another road user.

Octagonal
Having eight sides.

Glossary

Oil level

The amount of oil needed for the engine to run effectively. The oil level should be checked as part of your regular maintenance routine, and the oil replaced as necessary.

Pedestrian

A person walking.

Pelican crossing

A crossing with traffic lights that pedestrians can use by pushing a button. Cars must give way to pedestrians on the crossing while the amber light is flashing. You must give pedestrians enough time to get to the other side of the road.

Perception

Seeing or noticing (as in Hazard Perception).

Peripheral vision

The area around the edges of your field of vision.

Positive attitude

Being sensible and obeying the law when you drive.

Priority

The vehicle or other road user that is allowed by law to go first is the one that has priority.

Provisional licence

A first driving licence. All learner drivers must get one before they start having lessons.

Puffin crossing

A type of pedestrian crossing that does not have a flashing amber light phase.

Reaction time

The amount of time it takes you to see a hazard and decide what to do about it.

Red route

You see these in London and some other cities. Double red lines at the edge of the road tell you that you must not stop or park there at any time. Single red lines have notices with times when you must not stop or park. Some red routes have marked bays for either parking or loading at certain times.

Red warning triangle

An item of safety equipment to carry in your car in case you break down. You can place the triangle 45m behind your car on the same side of the road. It warns traffic that your vehicle is causing an obstruction. (Do not use these on motorways.)

Residential areas

Areas of housing where people live. The speed limit is 30mph or sometimes 20mph.

Road hump

A low bump built across the road to slow vehicles down. Also called 'sleeping policemen'.

Rumble strips

Raised strips across the road near a roundabout or junction that change the sound the tyres make on the road surface, warning drivers to slow down. They are also used on motorways to separate the main carriageway from the hard shoulder.

Safety margin

The amount of space you need to leave between your vehicle and the one in front so that you are not in danger of crashing into it if the driver slows down suddenly or stops. Safety margins have to be longer in wet or icy conditions.

Separation distance
The amount of space you need to leave between your vehicle and the one in front so that you are not in danger of crashing into it if the driver slows down suddenly or stops. The separation distance must be longer in wet or icy conditions.

Security coded radio
To deter thieves, a radio or CD unit that requires a security code (or pin number) to operate it.

Single carriageway
Generally, a road with one lane in each direction.

Skid
When the tyres fail to grip the surface of the road, the subsequent loss of control of the vehicle's movement is called a skid. Usually caused by harsh or fierce braking, steering or acceleration.

Snaking
Moving from side to side. This sometimes happens with caravans or trailers when you drive too fast, or they are not properly loaded.

Staggered junction
Where you drive cross another road. Instead of going straight across, you have to go a bit to the right or left.

Steering
Control of the direction of the vehicle. May be affected by road surface conditions: when the steering wheel turns very easily, steering is 'light', and when you have to pull hard on the wheel it is described as 'heavy'.

Sterile
Clean and free from bacteria.

Stopping distance
The time it takes for you to stop your vehicle – made up of 'thinking distance' and 'braking distance'.

Supervisor
Someone who sits in the passenger seat with a learner driver. They must be over 21 and have held a full driving licence for at least three years.

Tailgating
Driving too closely behind another vehicle – usually to harass the driver in front.

Thinking distance
The time it takes you to notice something and take the right action. You need to add thinking distance to your braking distance to make up your total stopping distance.

Third party insurance
An insurance policy that insures you against any claim by passengers or other persons for damage or injury to their person or property.

Toucan crossing
A type of pedestrian crossing that does not have a flashing amber light phase, and cyclists are allowed to ride across.

Tow
To pull something behind your vehicle. It could be a caravan or trailer.

Traffic-calming measures
Speed humps, chicanes and other devices placed in roads to slow traffic down.

Tram
A public transport vehicle that moves along the streets on fixed rails, usually electrically powered by overhead lines.

Tread depth
The depth of the grooves in a car's tyres that help them grip the road surface. The grooves must all be at least 1.6mm deep.

Glossary

Turbulence

Strong movement of air. For example, when a large vehicle passes a much smaller one.

Two-second rule

In normal driving, the ideal minimum distance between you and the vehicle in front can be timed using the 'two-second' rule. As the vehicle in front passes a fixed object (such as a signpost), say to yourself 'Only a fool breaks the two second rule'. It takes two seconds to say it. If you have passed the same object before you finish, you are too close – pull back.

Tyre pressures

The amount of air that must be pumped into a tyre in order for it to be correctly blown up.

Vehicle Excise Duty

The tax you pay for your vehicle so that you may drive it on public roads, also known as road tax.

Vehicle Registration Certificate

A record of details about a vehicle and its owner, also known as a log book.

Vehicle watch scheme

A system for identifying vehicles that may have been stolen.

Vulnerable

At risk of harm or injury.

Waiting restrictions

Times when you may not park or load your vehicle in a particular area.

Wheel balancing

To ensure smooth rotation at all speeds, wheels need to be 'balanced' correctly. This is a procedure done at a garage or tyre centre, when each wheel is removed for testing. Balancing may involve minor adjustment with the addition of small weights, to avoid wheel wobble.

Wheel-spin

When the vehicle's wheels spin round out of control with no grip on the road surface.

Zebra crossing

A pedestrian crossing without traffic lights. It has an orange light, and is marked by black and white stripes on the road. Drivers must stop for pedestrians to cross.

PART 6: THE PRACTICAL TEST QUESTIONS AND ANSWERS

The practical test

CONTENTS

Good defensive driving depends on adopting the right attitude from the start. These questions will test your knowledge of what is required before you even sit in the driver's seat.

1

What do you need before you can drive on a public road?

Fill in the missing words

P__ __ __ __ __ __ __ __ __ __

__ __ __ __ __ __ __

2

The best way to learn is to have regular planned tuition with an Approved Driving Instructor (ADI).

An ADI is someone who has taken and passed all three driving instructor's e __ __ __ __ __ __ __ __ __ __ __ __ and is on the official r__ __ __ __ __ __ __

Complete the sentence

HINTS & TIPS

A fully qualified ADI should display a green certificate on the windscreen of their car. Ask to see it.

3

Anyone supervising a learner must be at least __ __ years old and must have held (and still hold) a full driving licence (motor car) for at least t__ __ __ __ years

Complete the sentence

4

Your tuition vehicle must display L plates. Where should they be placed?

Answer _____

_____

_____

5

Young and inexperienced drivers are more vulnerable. Is this true or false?

Tick the correct box **True** ☐ **False** ☐

6

Showing responsibility to yourself and others is the key to being a safe driver. Ask yourself, would you ...

Tick the correct box

1 Want to drive with someone who has been drinking? **YES** ☐ **NO** ☐

2 Want to drive with someone who takes risks and puts other lives at risk? **YES** ☐ **NO** ☐

3 Want to drive with someone who does not concentrate? **YES** ☐ **NO** ☐

4 Want to drive with someone who drives too fast? **YES** ☐ **NO** ☐

7

Do you want to be a safe and responsible driver?

Tick the correct box **YES** ☐ **NO** ☐

8

You must pass a theory test before you can take the practical test. When would be the best time to sit this test?

Mark two answers

1 Before applying for a provisional licence. ☐

2 Just before taking the practical test. ☐

3 Some time during the early weeks of your driving lessons. ☐

4 After full study of available training materials. ☐

9

To use the controls safely you need to adopt a suitable driving position. There are a number of checks you should make.

Fill in the missing words

1 Check the h _ _ _ _ _ _ _ _ _ is on.

2 Check the d _ _ _ _ are shut.

3 Check your s _ _ _ is in the correct position.

4 Check the h _ _ _ r _ _ _ _ _ _ _ _ is adjusted to give maximum protection.

5 Check the driving m _ _ _ _ _ _ are adjusted to give maximum rear view.

6 Check your s _ _ b _ _ _ is securely fastened.

10

Here is a list of functions and a list of controls.

Match each function to its control by placing the appropriate letter in the box

THE FUNCTIONS	THE CONTROLS
A To control the direction in which you want to travel	☐ The handbrake
B To slow or stop the vehicle	☐ The driving mirrors
C To increase or decrease the engine's speed	☐ The gear lever
D To give you a clear view behind	☐ The clutch
E To hold the vehicle still when it is stationary	☐ The steering wheel
F To enable you to change gear	☐ The foot-brake
G To enable you to make or break contact between the engine and the wheels	☐ The accelerator

Fill in the missing word
The accelerator can also be called the g _ _ pedal

11

Which foot should you use for each of these controls (in cars with a manual gearbox)?

R = Right foot   **L** = Left foot
The foot-brake ☐
The clutch ☐
The accelerator ☐

12

Are the following statements about steering true or false?

Tick the appropriate boxes

	True	False
1 I must keep both hands on the wheel at all times.	☐	☐
2 To keep good control I should feed the wheel through my hands.	☐	☐
3 I can place my hands at any position as long as I am comfortable.	☐	☐
4 When going round corners, it is best to cross my hands (hand over hand).	☐	☐
5 I should never take both hands off the wheel when the vehicle is moving.	☐	☐
6 To straighten up I should feed the wheel back through my hands.	☐	☐

13

Match each of the following functions to its control.

THE FUNCTIONS

A To enable you to see the road ahead and other road users to see you without causing dazzle

B To show other road users which way you intend to turn

C To use only when visibility is 100 metres/ 328 feet or less

D To enable you to see further, but not to be used when there is oncoming traffic

E To warn other road users of your presence

F To warn other road users when you are temporarily obstructing traffic

THE CONTROLS

☐ The direction indicators

☐ Dipped beam

☐ Main beam

☐ Rear fog lamp

☐ Horn

☐ Hazard lights

1

**The following is a list of actions involved in moving off from rest.
Number the boxes 1 to 9 to show the correct sequence**

The first box has been filled in to give you a start

☐1 **A** Press the clutch down fully

☐ **F** Let the clutch come to biting point and hold it steady

☐ **B** Check your mirrors

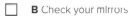

☐ **G** Check your blind spot

☐ **C** Set the accelerator pedal

☐ **H** If safe, release the handbrake and let the clutch up a little more

☐ **D** Move the gear lever into 1st gear

☐ **I** Press the accelerator pedal a little more and let the clutch up fully

☐ **E** Decide whether you need to give a signal

2

**The following is a list of actions required for stopping normally.
Number the boxes 1 to 9 to show the correct sequence.**

The first box has been filled in to give you a start

[1] **A** Check your mirrors

B Take your foot off the accelerator pedal

C Decide whether you need to signal and, if necessary, do so

D Press the brake pedal, lightly at first and then more firmly

E As the car stops, ease the pressure off the foot-brake (except when you are on a slope)

F Just before the car stops, press the clutch pedal right down

G Put the gear lever into neutral

H Apply the handbrake fully

I Take both feet off the pedals

HINTS & TIPS
In your driving test, you will be expected to show that you can control the car smoothly. If you should stall, put the gears in neutral and the handbrake on, and start again.

Gears enable you to select the power you need from the engine to perform a particular task.

3

Which gear gives you the most pulling power?

Answer ☐

4

If you were travelling at 60mph on a clear road, from the image above, which gear would you most likely select?

Answer ☐

5

When approaching and turning a corner, as shown in the diagram, which gear would you most likely use?

Answer ☐

6

You need to change gear to match your e__ __ __ __ __ speed to the speed at which your v__ __ __ __ __ __ is travelling. The s__ __ __ __ the engine is making will help you know w__ __ __ to change gear.

Complete the sentences

7

Number the boxes to show the correct sequence of actions required when changing up.

The first box has been filled in for you

1
☐ **A** Place your left hand on the gear lever

☐ **B** Move the gear lever to the next highest position

☐ **C** Press the clutch pedal down fully and ease off the accelerator pedal

☐ **D** Let the clutch pedal come up fully and, at the same time, press the accelerator pedal

☐ **E** Put your left hand back on the steering wheel

8

Are the following statements about changing down true or false?

Tick the appropriate boxes   **True False**

1 I would stay in the highest gear as long as possible, even if my engine started to labour ☐ ☐

2 I would change down early so that the engine helps to slow the car down ☐ ☐

3 I would avoid using the foot-brake as much as possible ☐ ☐

4 I would usually slow the car down by using the foot-brake first. Then, when I am at the required speed, I would change down to the appropriate gear ☐ ☐

5 I would always change down through the gears so that I do not miss out any intermediate gears ☐ ☐

4 Use the brakes, where necessary, to reduce speed before changing down ☐ ☐

5 Listen to the sound of the engine ☐ ☐

6 Take your eyes off the road when changing gear ☐ ☐

7 Hold the gear lever longer than necessary ☐ ☐

8 Coast with the clutch down or the gear lever in neutral ☐ ☐

11

Which wheels turn when you turn the steering wheel?

A The front wheels

B The back wheels

Answer ☐

9

When changing gear, I should look ...

1 Ahead ☐

2 At the gear lever ☐

3 At my feet ☐

Which is correct?

12

When you turn your steering wheel to the right, which way do your wheels turn?

A To the right

B To the left

Answer ☐

10

Do's and don'ts

Tick the appropriate boxes   **Do Don't**

1 Force the gear lever if there is any resistance ☐ ☐

2 Rush the gear changes ☐ ☐

3 Match your speed with the correct gear ☐ ☐

13

The steering lock is ...

A The locking mechanism that stops the steering wheel from moving when the ignition key is removed

B The angle through which the wheels turn when the steering wheel is turned

Answer ☐

14

Which wheels follow the shorter pathway?

Put letter A or B in the box

A The front wheels
B The back wheels

Answer ☐

15

Which is the correct position for normal driving?

Put letter A, B or C in the box

Answer ☐

A   B   C

16

Which diagram shows the correct pathway when driving normally?

Put letter A or B in the box

Answer ☐

A   B

17

Pushing the clutch pedal down ...

Put letter A or B in the box

A Releases the engine from the wheels
B Engages the engine with the wheels

Answer ☐

18

The point where the clutch plates meet is called the b__ __ __ __ __ point.

Fill in the missing word

19

By controlling the amount of contact between the clutch plates, it is possible to control the speed of the car.

Would you use this control ...

Tick the appropriate boxes   **YES**   **NO**

1 When moving away from rest? ☐ ☐

2 When manoeuvring the car in reverse gear? ☐ ☐

3 When slowing down to turn a corner? ☐ ☐

4 In very slow moving traffic? ☐ ☐

5 To slow the car down? ☐ ☐

HINTS & TIPS

Remember: MSM stands for Mirror, Signal, Manoeuvre. Always use this routine when moving off, turning or overtaking.

1

A junction is a point where t __ __ o__ m__ __ __ r__ __ __ __ __ meet.

Complete the sentence

2

Here are five types of junction. Name them

A

_____

B

_____

C

_____

D

_____

E

_____

3

Match these road signs to the junctions shown opposite.

Put letters A, B, C, D and E in the boxes

1 ☐

2 ☐

3 ☐

4 ☐

5 ☐

4

What do these signs mean?

1 Stop and give way
2 Slow down, look, and proceed if safe
3 Give way to traffic on the major road
Put a number in each box

A ☐

B ☐

5

At every junction you should follow a safe routine.

Put the following into the correct order by numbering the boxes 1 to 5

Signal ☐   Speed ☐   Position ☐
Mirrors ☐   Look ☐

6

The diagram below shows a car turning right into a minor road. The boxes are numbered to show the correct sequence of actions.

Complete the sentence
At point 5 you should look and
a _ _ _ _ _ the situation,
d _ _ _ _ _ to go or wait,
and a _ _ accordingly.

7

Turning left into a minor road. Which diagram below shows the best path to follow when driving a motor car A, B, C or D?

Answer ☐

8

You turn into a side road. Pedestrians are already crossing it. Should you ...

Tick the appropriate box

A Sound your horn ☐

B Slow down and give way ☐

C Flash your lights ☐

D Wave them across ☐

9

Turning right into a minor road.

Which diagram shows the best path to follow: A, B, C or D?

Answer ☐

10

These are the golden rules for emerging from junctions.

Complete the sentences

1 Always use your m__ __ __ __ __ __ to check the speed and p __ __ __ __ __ __ __ of vehicles behind.

2 Always cancel your s__ __ __ __ __ .

3 Speed up to a s__ __ __ speed after joining the new road.

4 Keep a s__ __ __ d__ __ __ __ __ __ __ between you and the vehicle ahead.

5 Do not attempt to o__ __ __ __ __ __ __ until you can assess the new road.

HINTS & TIPS
At an unmarked crossroads, no one has priority. Be extra-cautious at these junctions.

11

All crossroads must be approached with caution.

Match actions 1, 2 and 3 listed below with these diagrams

Actions

1 Approach with caution, look well ahead and be prepared to stop. Remember other drivers may assume they have priority.

2 Look well ahead, slow down and be prepared to give way to traffic on the major road.

3 Look well ahead and into the side roads for approaching vehicles. Remember other drivers may not give you priority.

Answer ☐

Answer ☐

Answer ☐

12

Which of the following statements describes the correct procedure when approaching a roundabout?

Put letter A, B or C in the box

A The broken white line at a roundabout means I must stop and give way to traffic already on the roundabout.

B The broken white line at a roundabout means I must give priority to traffic already on the roundabout.

C The broken white line means I should give way to any traffic approaching from my immediate right.

Answer ☐

13

The following sentences give guidance on lane discipline on a roundabout.

Fill in the missing words

1 When turning left at a roundabout, I should stay in the __ __ __ __ hand lane and should stay in that lane throughout.

2 When going ahead at a roundabout, I should be in the __ __ __ __ hand lane, and should stay in that lane throughout, unless conditions dictate otherwise.

3 When turning right at a roundabout, I should approach in the r__ __ __ __ hand lane, or approach as if turning right at a junction, and stay in that lane throughout.

14

The letters A, B and C in the diagram mark places where you should signal.

Complete the sentences

1 I would signal at **A** when turning __ __ __ __.

2 I would signal at **B** when g__ __ __ __ __ __ __ __ __.

3 I would signal at **A** and at **C** when turning __ __ __ __ __.

15

At a roundabout you should always use a safe routine.

Fill in the missing words

M__ __ __ __ __ __, s __ __ __ __ __, p__ __ __ __ __ __ __, s__ __ __ __, l__ __ __.

16

What does this sign mean?

Write 1, 2 or 3 in the box

1 Roundabout

2 Mini-roundabout

3 Vehicles may pass either side.

Answer ☐

HINTS & TIPS
Be careful at roundabouts where destinations are marked for each lane. Make sure you are in the correct lane for your destination.

1

It is safest to park off the road or in a car park whenever possible. If you have to park on the road, think ...

Fill in the missing words

1 Is it s___ ___ ___ ?

2 Is it c___ ___ ___ ___ ___ ___ ___ ___ ___ ___?

3 Is it l___ ___ ___ ___ ?

2

In this diagram below four of the cars are parked illegally or without consideration of others.

Put the numbers of these cars in the boxes

☐ ☐ ☐ ☐

3

Check how well you know the rules about where you may and may not park.

Are the following statements true or false?

Tick the appropriate boxes   **True**   **False**

1 In a narrow street, I should park with two wheels up on the pavement to leave more room for other traffic.   ☐   ☐

2 I am allowed to park in a 'Disabled' space if all other spaces are full.   ☐   ☐

3 I should not park on the zig-zag lines near a zebra crossing.   ☐   ☐

4 Red lines painted on the road mean 'No Stopping'.   ☐   ☐

5 I should never park on the opposite side of the road to my direction of travel.   ☐   ☐

4

List three places not mentioned in Question 3 where you should *not* park.

1 _____
_____
_____
_____
_____
_____

2 _____
_____
_____
_____
_____
_____

3 _____
_____
_____
_____
_____

HINTS & TIPS
Use your *Highway Code* to find out more about parking regulations

1

The diagram shows a stationary vehicle on the left-hand side of the road.

Which should have priority, vehicle 1 or vehicle 2?

Answer ☐

2

This diagram shows a steep downward hill with an obstruction on the right-hand side of the road.

Which vehicle should be given priority, vehicle 1 or vehicle 2?

Answer ☐

3

The diagram shows two vehicles, travelling in opposite directions, turning right at a crossroads. Are these statements true or false?

Tick the appropriate boxes   **True**   **False**

1 The safest route is to pass each other offside to offside. ☐ ☐

2 If the approaching vehicle flashes its headlamps, I should turn as quickly as possible. ☐ ☐

3 I should always try to get eye-to-eye contact with the driver of the other vehicle to determine which course to take. ☐ ☐

4

Which of the following factors, illustrated in the diagram, should be taken into consideration when turning right into a side road?

Tick the appropriate boxes   **YES**   **NO**

1 The speed of the approaching vehicle (A) ☐ ☐

2 The roadworks ☐ ☐

3 The speed of vehicle B ☐ ☐

4 The cyclist ☐ ☐

5 Your speed (vehicle C) ☐ ☐

6 The pedestrians ☐ ☐

7 The car waiting to turn right (D) ☐ ☐

1

Are the following statements true or false when stopping in an emergency?

Tick the appropriate boxes   True   False

1 Stopping in an emergency increases the risk of skidding. ☐ ☐

2 I should push the brake pedal down harder as I slow down. ☐ ☐

3 It is important to. react quickly ☐ ☐

4 I should always remember to look in my mirrors as I slow down. ☐ ☐

5 I should signal left to tell other road users what I am doing. ☐ ☐

6 I should keep both hands on the wheel. ☐ ☐

7 I should always check my mirrors and look round before moving off. ☐ ☐

2

Is the following statement true or false?

An emergency stop will be carried out on every driving test

Tick the correct box   **YES** ☐ **NO** ☐

3

Cadence braking is a technique which can be used in very slippery conditions in an emergency.

Fill in the missing words
The technique requires you to p_ _ _ the brake pedal.
The procedure to follow is:

1 Apply m_ _ _ _ _ pressure.

2 Release the brake pedal just as the wheels are about to l_ _ _.

3 Then q_ _ _ _ _ _ apply the brakes again. Apply and release the brakes until the vehicle has stopped. This technique should only be used in emergency situations.

4

Anti-lock braking systems (ABS)* work in a similar way to cadence braking.

Fill in the missing words
When braking in an emergency, ABS brakes allow you to s_ _ _ _ and b_ _ _ _ _ at the same time. You do not have to p_ _ _ the brakes as you would in cadence braking. When using ABS you keep the p_ _ _ _ _ _ _ applied.

HINTS & TIPS
If a vehicle is travelling too close behind you, then increase the gap you have ahead. Always think for the driver behind.

Are these statements about ABS braking true or false?

Tick the appropriate boxes   **True**   **False**

1 Cars fitted with ABS braking cannot skid. ☐ ☐

2 I do not need to leave as much room between me and the car in front if I have ABS brakes because I know I can stop in a shorter distance. ☐ ☐

*ABS is a registered trade mark of Bosch (Germany). ABS stands for Anti-Blockiersystem. The English translation is Anti-lock Braking System

The distance taken for a car to reach stopping point divides into thinking distance and braking distance.

5
Could these factors affect thinking distance?

Tick the appropriate boxes   **YES**   **NO**

1 The condition of your tyres ☐ ☐

2 Feeling tired or unwell ☐ ☐

3 Speed of reaction ☐ ☐

4 Going downhill ☐ ☐

6
Most drivers' reaction time is well over ...

Tick the appropriate box

½ second ☐

1 second ☐

5 seconds ☐

7
Stopping distance depends partly on the speed at which the car is travelling.

Complete the sentences

1 At 30mph your overall stopping distance will be __ __ metres or __ __ feet.

2 At 50mph your thinking distance will be __ __ metres or __ __ feet.

3 At 70mph your overall stopping distance will be __ __ metres or __ __ __feet.

8
Stopping distance also varies according to road conditions.

Complete the sentences
In wet weather your vehicle will take l __ __ __ __ __ to stop. You should therefore allow m __ __ __ time.

9
Too many accidents are caused by drivers driving too close to the vehicle in front. A safe gap between you and the vehicle in front can be measured by noting a stationary object and counting in seconds the time that lapses between the vehicle in front passing that object and your own vehicle passing that object.

Complete the sentence
Only a fool b __ __ __ __ __ the t __ __ s __ __ __ __ __ rule.

1

Are these statements about moving off at an angle true or false?

Tick the appropriate boxes — True — False

1 I should check my mirrors as I am pulling out. ☐ ☐

2 I should check my mirrors and blindspot before I pull out. ☐ ☐

3 I should move out as quickly as possible. ☐ ☐

4 The amount of steering required will depend on how close I am to the vehicle in front. ☐ ☐

5 I should look for oncoming traffic. ☐ ☐

6 As long as I am signalling, people will know what I am doing. I will be able to pull out because somebody will let me in. ☐ ☐

2

Are these statements about moving off uphill true or false?

Tick the appropriate boxes — True — False

1 On an uphill gradient the car will tend to roll back. ☐ ☐

2 To stop the car rolling back I need to use more acceleration. ☐ ☐

3 I do not need to use the handbrake. ☐ ☐

4 The biting point may be slightly higher. ☐ ☐

5 I need to press the accelerator pedal further down than when moving off on the level. ☐ ☐

6 I need to allow more time to pull away. ☐ ☐

7 The main controls I use will be the clutch pedal, the accelerator pedal and the handbrake. ☐ ☐

3

Are these statements about moving off downhill true or false?

Tick the appropriate boxes

	True	False
1 The car will tend to roll forwards.	☐	☐
2 The main controls I use will be the handbrake, the clutch pedal and the accelerator pedal.	☐	☐
3 The only gear I can move off in is 1st gear.	☐	☐
4 I should release the handbrake while keeping the foot-brake applied.	☐	☐
5 I should look round just before moving off.	☐	☐
6 I must not have my foot on the foot-brake as I start to release the clutch.	☐	☐

4

The following statements are about approaching a junction when going uphill or downhill. With which do you agree?

When going downhill ...   YES   NO

1 It is more difficult to slow down ☐ ☐

2 Putting the clutch down will help slow the car down ☐ ☐

3 The higher the gear, the greater the control ☐ ☐

4 When changing gear you may need to use the foot-brake at the same time as the clutch ☐ ☐

When going uphill ...   YES   NO

5 Early use of mirrors, signals, brakes, gears and steering will help to position the car correctly ☐ ☐

6 You may need to use your handbrake more often ☐ ☐

7 When you change gear, the car tends to slow down ☐ ☐

1

Before reversing there are three things to consider.

Fill in the missing words

1 Is it s__ __ __?

2 Is it c__ __ __ __ __ __ __ __ __ __?

3 Is it within the l__ __?

2

Are the following statements about reversing true or false?

Tick the appropriate boxes   **True**   **False**

1 Other road users should see what I am doing and wait for me. ☐ ☐

2 I should wave pedestrians on, so that I can get on with the manoeuvre more quickly. ☐ ☐

3 I should avoid being too hesitant. ☐ ☐

4 I should avoid making other road users slow down or change course. ☐ ☐

3

How should you hold the steering wheel when reversing left?

Which is correct?   Answer ☐

A   B   C

4

These statements are all about reversing.

Tick those which you think are correct

     True   **False**

1 My car will respond differently in reverse gear. ☐ ☐

2 My car will feel no different. ☐ ☐

3 Steering is not affected. The car responds the same as when going forward. ☐ ☐

4 The steering will feel different. I will have to wait for the steering to take effect. ☐ ☐

5

Which way will the rear of the car go when it is reversed? Left or right?

A   B

Answer   Answer

_____   _____

6

It is important to move the vehicle slowly when reversing.

Complete the sentence

Moving the vehicle slowly is safer because I have control and it allows me to carry out good o_ _ _ _ _ _ _ _ _ _ checks.

7

When reversing, good observation is vital. Where should you look?

Tick the correct answer

1 At the kerb ☐

2 Ahead ☐

3 Where your car is going ☐

4 Out of the back window ☐

8

Are these statements about reversing round a corner true or false?

Tick the correct boxes	True	False
1 If the corner is sharp, I need to be further away from the kerb.	☐	☐
2 The distance from the kerb makes no difference.	☐	☐
3 I should try to stay reasonably close to the kerb all the way round.	☐	☐

9

Before reversing I should check ...

Tick the correct box

1 Behind me ☐

2 Ahead and to the rear ☐

3 My door mirrors ☐

4 All round ☐

10

Which position is the correct one in which to start steering?

A, B, C or D? Answer ☐

11

Which way should you steer?

Answer _____

12

What will happen to the front of the car?

Answer _____

13

Are these statements about steering when reversing round a corner true or false?

Tick the appropriate boxes   True   False

1 The more gradual, ☐ ☐
the corner the less
I have to steer.

2 I need to steer the same ☐ ☐
for every corner.

3 The sharper the corner, ☐ ☐
the more I have to steer.

14

As I enter the new road, I should continue to keep a look-out for
p__ __ __ __ __ __ __ __ __ __ __ __ and
other r__ __ __ u__ __ __ __ __.

I should s__ __ __ if necessary.

Complete the sentences

15

True or false? When reversing from a major road into a side road on the right, I have to move to the wrong side of the road.

Tick the correct box   True ☐ False ☐

16

Which diagram shows the correct path to follow when moving to the right-hand side of the road? A or B?

Answer ☐

A

B

17

Which of the following correctly describes your sitting position for reversing to the right?

1 I will need to sit so that I can see over my right shoulder.

2 I will need to sit so that I can see over my right shoulder, ahead and to the left.

3 My position is the same as when reversing to the left.
Which statement is correct? 1, 2 or 3

Answer ☐

18

True or false? I may need to change my hand position on the wheel.

Tick the correct box **True** ☐ **False** ☐

19

True or false? It is easier to judge my position from the kerb when reversing to the right than when reversing to the left.

Tick the correct box **True** ☐ **False** ☐

20

Reversing to the right is more dangerous than reversing to the left because ...

1 I cannot see as well

2 I am on the wrong side of the road

3 I might get in the way of vehicles emerging from the side road
Which statement is correct – 1, 2 or 3?

Answer ☐

21

How far down the side road would you reverse before moving over to the left-hand side?

Which diagram is correct? A or B?

Answer ☐

A

B

22

Look at the diagrams and decide which is safer.

A Reversing into a side road

B Turning round in the road

Answer ☐

23

The secret of turning in the road is to move the vehicle s__ __ __ __ __ and steer b__ __ __ __ __ __.

Complete the sentence

24

I must be able to complete the manoeuvre in three moves: 1 forward, 2 reverse, 3 forward. True or false?

Tick the correct box **True** ☐ **False** ☐

25

Before manoeuvring what should you take into consideration?

Tick the correct boxes

1 The size of your engine ☐

2 The width of the road ☐

3 The road camber ☐

4 The steering circle of your vehicle ☐

5 Parking restrictions ☐

26

Before moving forward, it is important to check a__ __ r__ __ __ __ for other road users.

Complete the sentence

HINTS & TIPS
When taking your test, you will be assessed on how well you can control the car; so don't rush your manoeuvres.

27

Turning in the road requires proper use of the steering wheel.

Answer the following questions...

1 When going forwards, which way should you steer?

Answer _____

2 Before you reach the kerb ahead, what should you do?

Answer _____

3 When reversing, which way should you steer?

Answer _____

4 Before you reach the kerb behind you, what should you do?

Answer _____

5 As you move forward again, which way should you steer to straighten up?

Answer _____

28

Reversing is a potentially dangerous manoeuvre. Good observation is essential.

Answer the following questions

1 If you are steering left when reversing, which shoulder should you look over?

Answer _____

2 As you begin to steer to the right, where should you look?

Answer _____

29

When parking between two cars ...

1 The car is more manoeuvrable when driving forwards

2 The car is more manoeuvrable when reversing

3 There is no difference between going into the space forwards or reversing into it

Which statement is correct? 1, 2 or 3?

Answer ☐

HINTS & TIPS
In your driving test you may be asked to reverse into a parking bay at the test centre, or to park behind another car, using reverse gear. So make sure you practise these manoeuvres.

30

The diagram shows a car preparing to reverse into a parking space. Which position is the correct one in which to start steering left, A, B, C or D?

Answer ☐

31

With practice you should be able to park in a gap ...

1 Your own car length

2 1½ times your own car length

3 2 times your own car length

4 2½ times your own car length

Answer ☐

32

Use the diagram to help you answer the following questions.

1 Which way would you steer?

Answer _____

2 At this point what would you try to line up with the offside (right-hand side) of your vehicle?

Answer _____

3 As you straighten up what do you have to be careful of?

Answer _____

4 What do you need to do to straighten up?

Answer _____

5 What would you need to do in order to position the vehicle parallel to the kerb?

Answer _____

33

True or false? During my driving test ...

Tick the correct boxes

	True	False
1 I will certainly be asked to perform the manoeuvre in Question 32	☐	☐
2 I have to be able to park in atight space between two cars	☐	☐

34

When carrying out this manoeuvre, where is it important to look?

Answer _____

_____

35

Look at the diagram and answer the following question.

Which bay should you use and why?

Answer _____

_____

36

Why, wherever possible, should you choose to reverse into a parking bay?

Answer _____

_____

_____

_____

37

As well as being very aware of how c_ _ _ _ I am to the parked cars

on either side, I should also be alert for cars moving near me from all d_ _ _ _ _ _ _ _ _, as well as the possibility of p_ _ _ _ _ _ _ _ _ walking around my car.

Complete the sentence

38

True or false? During my driving test ...

Tick the correct boxes

	True	False
1 I will certainly be asked to perform a bay parking manoeuvre	☐	☐
2 I may be asked to forward park in a parking bay	☐	☐
3 My instructor will tell me what's expected of me	☐	☐

39

When might you choose to forward park in a parking bay?

Answer _____
_____
_____

40

When reversing out of a parking bay, I should be careful to o __ __ __ __ __ __ behind me before and during the manoeuvre, and be vigilant of p __ __ __ __ __ __ __ __ __ __ and other cars.

Complete the sentence

_____

41

During your test you may be asked to pull up on the right hand side of the road and reverse for two car lengths before rejoining traffic. Can you think of a situation when this might be necessary?

Answer _____
_____
_____

1

Traffic lights have three lights, red, amber, and green, which change from one to the other in a set order. Number the boxes 1 to 5 to show the correct order. The first answer has been filled in to give you a start.

☐ Amber [1] Red ☐ Red and amber
☐ Red ☐ Green

2

What do the colours mean?

Fill in the correct colour for each of the following

1 Go ahead if the way is clear.

Colour _____

2 Stop and wait.

Colour _____

3 Stop unless you have crossed the stop line or you are so close to it that stopping might cause an accident.

Colour _____

4 Stop and wait at the stop line.

Colour _____

3

Which of the following statements are true?

On approach to traffic lights you should ...

Tick the appropriate boxes

1 Speed up to get through before they change ☐

2 Be ready to stop ☐

3 Look for pedestrians ☐

4 Sound your horn to urge pedestrians to cross quickly ☐

4

Some traffic lights have green filters. Do they mean ...

1 You can filter in the direction of the arrow only when the main light is showing green?

2 You can filter even when the main light is not showing green?

Answer ☐

5

The diagram shows the three lanes at a set of traffic lights.

Which lane would you use for ...

1 Going ahead
Answer _____

2 Turning right
Answer _____

3 Turning left
Answer _____

6

At some traffic lights and junctions you will see yellow criss-cross lines (box junctions). Can you ...

Tick the correct boxes

	YES	NO
1 Wait within them when going ahead if your exit is not clear?	☐	☐
2 Wait within them when going right if your exit is not clear?	☐	☐
3 Wait within them if there is oncoming traffic stopping you turning right but your exit is clear?	☐	☐

Pedestrians have certain rights of way at pedestrian crossings.

7

On approaching a zebra crossing, drivers will notice four features. Name them

1 _____

2 _____

3 _____

4 _____

8

Are these statements about pedestrian crossings true or false?

Tick the correct boxes

	True	False
1 I cannot park or wait on the zig-zag lines on the approach to a zebra crossing.	☐	☐
2 I cannot park or wait on the zig-zag lines on either side of the crossing.	☐	☐
3 I can overtake on the zig-zag lines on the approach to a crossing as long as the other vehicle is travelling slowly.	☐	☐
4 I must give way to a pedestrian once he/she has stepped on to the crossing.	☐	☐

5 If, on approach to a crossing, I intend to slow down or stop, I may use a slowing-down arm signal. ☐ ☐

9

On approaching a pelican crossing, drivers will notice three key features.

Name them

1 _____
_____
_____
_____

2 _____
_____
_____
_____

3 _____
_____
_____

10

If you see a pedestrian at a zebra crossing or pelican crossing carrying a white stick, do you think ...

Tick the correct box

1 He/she has difficulty walking? ☐

2 He/she is visually impaired? ☐

11

The traffic lights at a pelican crossing have the same meaning as ordinary traffic lights, but they do not have a red and amber phase.

1 What do they show instead of the red and amber phase?
Answer _____
_____

2 What does the light mean?
Answer _____
_____

12

What sound is usually heard at a pelican crossing when the green man is shown to pedestrians?

Answer _____
_____
_____
_____

13

Toucan and puffin crossings are similar to pelican crossings but with one main difference. Name it.

Answer _____
_____
_____
_____

14

As well as pedestrians, what other type of road users should you watch for at a toucan crossing?

Answer _____
_____
_____
_____

A level crossing is where the road crosses at a railway line. It is potentially dangerous and should be approached with caution.

15

Match each traffic sign below with its correct meaning.

1 Level crossing without gates or barriers ☐

2 Level crossing with lights ☐

3 Level crossing with gates or barriers ☐

4 Level crossing without lights ☐

A   B

C

D

16

If you break down on a level crossing, should you ...

Tick the appropriate boxes

1 Tell your passengers to wait in the vehicle while you go to get help? ☐

2 Get everybody out and clear of the crossing? ☐

3 Telephone the police? ☐

4 Telephone the signal operator? ☐

5 If there is still time, push your car clear of the crossing? ☐

One-way systems are where all traffic flows in the same direction.

1

Which of these signs means one-way traffic?

A   B

Answer ☐

2

Are these statements about one-way systems true or false?

Tick the correct boxes

	True	False
1 In one-way streets traffic can pass me on both sides.	☐	☐
2 Roundabouts are one-way systems.	☐	☐
3 For normal driving I should stay on the left.	☐	☐
4 I should look out for road markings and get in lane early.	☐	☐

As a rule, the more paint on the road, the more important the message.

3

Road markings are divided into three categories.

Fill in the missing words

1 Those which give
i __ __ __ __ __ __ __ __ __ __.

2 Those which give
w __ __ __ __ __ __ __.

3 Those which give o __ __ __ __ __

4

There are two main advantages which road markings have over other traffic signs. Name them.

1 _____
_____

2 _____
_____

5

What do these lines across the road mean?

1 Stop and give way.

2 Give priority to traffic coming from the immediate right.

3 Give way to traffic coming from the right.

Answer ☐

1 Give way to traffic on the major road.

2 Stop at the line and give way to traffic on the major road.

Answer ☐

6

Where you see double solid white lines painted along the centre of the road, what does this mean?

Tick any boxes you think are appropriate. More than one answer may be correct.

1 I must not park or wait on the carriageway. ☐

2 I can park between 7pm and 7am. ☐

3 I must not overtake. ☐

4 I must not cross the white line except to turn right or in circumstances beyond my control. ☐

7

What is the purpose of these hatched markings (chevrons)?

Answer _____
_____

8

What does it mean if the chevrons are edged with a solid white line?

Answer _____
_____

The shape and colour of a sign will help you understand what it means.

9

Look at the sign shapes below and say whether each gives an order, a warning or information.

1

Answer _____   2

Answer _____

3

Answer _____

10

Complete the sentences

1 A circular sign with a blue background tells you what you m__ __ __ do.

2 A circular sign with a red border tells you what you m__ __ __ n__ __ do.

11

What do these signs mean?

GIVE WAY

Answer _____
_____
_____
_____

STOP

Answer _____
_____
_____
_____

12

Some junctions have a stop sign, others have a give way sign.

Complete the sentence
A stop sign is usually placed at a junction where v__ __ __ __ __ is l__ __ __ __ __ __.

13

Information signs are colour-coded.

Match each of the following signs to its colouring.

A White letters on a brown background

B Black letters on a white background

C Black letters on a white background with a blue border

D White letters on a blue background with a white border

E White letters on a green background, yellow route numbers with a white border

☐ Motorway signs

☐ Primary routes

☐ Other routes

☐ Local places

☐ Tourist signs

1

Good observation is vital in today's busy traffic.

Complete the sentence

When using my mirrors I should try to make a mental note of the s_ _ _ _,
b_ _ _ _ _ _ _ _ and
i_ _ _ _ _ _ _ _ _ of the driver behind.

2

Driving in built-up areas is potentially dangerous.

Look at the diagram opposite

1 What action should the driver of car **A** take?

List four options

A _____
B _____
C _____
D _____

2 What action should the driver of car **B** take?

List four options

A _____
B _____
C _____
D _____

HINTS & TIPS

Observation means looking all around and seeing anything that matters. Don't stare at just one thing – keep your eyes moving.

3

Motorcyclists are often less visible than other road users.

Complete this well-known phrase
Think once, think twice, think b__ __ __.

4

When you observe traffic following too close behind you, would you

Tick the correct box

1 Speed up to create a bigger gap? ☐

2 Touch your brake lights to warn the following driver? ☐

3 Keep to a safe speed, and keep checking the behaviour and intentions of the following driver? ☐

5

Some hazards are potential, others are actual and there all the time, such as a bend in the road.

A Name five more actual hazards

1 _____

2 _____

3 _____

4 _____

5 _____

B Name five potential hazards, such as a dog off its lead

1 _____

2 _____

3 _____

4 _____

5 _____

6

Modern driving requires full concentration. Are the following statements true or false?

Tick the correct boxes

	True	False
1 Carrying a mobile phone can reduce the stress of a long journey.	☐	☐
2 It is illegal to use a hand-held mobile phone while driving.	☐	☐
3 Conversation on a hands-free phone can still distract my attention.	☐	☐
4 I should pull up in a safe place to make or receive calls.	☐	☐
5 I should programme my satnav before setting off on my journey.	☐	☐
6 It's safe to adjust my satnav whilst driving.	☐	☐

7

When driving, all the following actions have something in common.

What is it?

Reading a map

Eating

Changing a cd

Listening to loud music

Setting a satnav

Answer _____

_____

_____

_____

One of the features of driving on the open road is taking bends properly.

_____

8

As a rule you should be travelling at the correct s_ _ _ _, using the correct g_ _ _, and be in the correct p_ _ _ _ _ _ _.

_____

9

Should you brake ...

Tick the appropriate box

1 Before you enter the bend? ☐

2 As you enter the bend? ☐

3 While negotiating the bend? ☐

10

Which way does force push a car on a bend?

A Inwards or **B** Outwards

Answer ☐

11

What happens to the weight of the car when you use the brakes?

A It is thrown forwards

B It remains even

C It is thrown back

Answer ☐

12

When you approach a bend, what position should you be in?

Complete the sentences

A On a right-hand bend I should keep to the _____

_____

B On a left-hand bend I should keep to the _____

_____

Overtaking is a potentially dangerous manoeuvre.

13

Before overtaking, consider whether it is really n__ __ __ __ __ __ __ __.

Fill in the missing word

Always use the safety routine when overtaking.

Put these actions into their correct sequence by putting numbers 1 to 7, as seen in the diagram, in the boxes

☐ Signal   ☐ Mirrors   ☐ Look
☐ Position ☐ Mirrors   ☐ Speed
☐ Manoeuvre

14

What is the minimum amount of clearance you should give a cyclist or motor cyclist?

Answer _____

_____

15

There are four situations in which you may, with caution, overtake on the left-hand side of the car in front.

Name them

1 _____
   _____
   _____

2 _____
   _____
   _____

3 _____
   _____
   _____

4 _____
   _____
   _____

16

List four places where it would be dangerous to overtake.

1 _____
   _____
   _____

2 _____
   _____
   _____

3 _____
   _____
   _____

4 _____
   _____
   _____

17

Dual carriageways can appear similar to motorways, but there are important differences. Which of the following statements apply to dual carriageways?

Tick the relevant boxes

1 Reflective studs are not used. ☐

2 Cyclists are allowed. ☐

3 The speed limit is always 60mph. ☐

4 You cannot turn right to enter or leave a dual carriageway. ☐

5 Milk floats and slow moving farm vehicles are prohibited. ☐

18

When turning right from a minor road on to a dual carriageway, where would you wait …

A When there is a wide central reserve?
Answer _____
   _____
   _____

B When the central reserve is too narrow for your car?
Answer _____
   _____
   _____

19

When travelling at 70mph on a dual carriageway, which lane would you use?

Answer _____

20
What do these signs mean?

A

Answer _____

B

Answer _____

C

Answer _____

21
Which of the signs in Question 20 would you expect to see on a dual carriageway?

Answer _____
_____
_____
_____
_____

22
Why is it important to plan your movements especially early when leaving a dual carriageway to the right (see diagram below)?

Answer _____
_____
_____
_____
_____

23

Motorways are designed to enable traffic to travel faster in greater safety.

Compared to other roads, are they statistically ...

Tick the correct box

1 Safer? ☐

2 Less safe? ☐

3 No different? ☐

24

Are the following groups allowed on the motorway?

Tick the correct boxes

1 Provisional licence holders supervised by a qualified driver ☐

2 Provisional licence holders supervised by an Approved Driving Instructor (ADI) ☐

3 Motor cycles over 50cc ☐

4 Pedestrians ☐

5 HGV learner drivers ☐

6 Newly qualified drivers with less than three months' experience ☐

7 Motor cycles under 125cc ☐

8 Cyclists ☐

25

There are some routine checks you should carry out on your car before driving on the motorway.

Name four of them

1 _____
_____
_____

2 _____
_____
_____

3 _____
_____
_____

4 _____
_____
_____

26

On the motorway, if something falls from either your own or another vehicle, should you ...

Tick the correct box

1 Flash your headlights to inform other drivers? ☐

2 Pull over, put your hazard warning lights on and quickly run on to the motorway to collect the object? ☐

3 Pull over on to the hard shoulder, use the emergency telephone to call the police? ☐

4 Flag another motorist down to get help? ☐

27

Which colour do you associate with motorway signs?

Tick the correct box

1 Black lettering on a white background ☐

2 White lettering on a green background ☐

3 White lettering on a blue background ☐

28

At night or in poor weather conditions, your headlights will pick out reflective studs. Match the colour of the studs to their function by placing the appropriate letter in the box.

A Amber **B** Red **C** Green **D** White

1 Marks the edge of the hard shoulder ☐

2 Marks the edge of the central reservation ☐

3 Marks the lane lines ☐

4 Marks exits and entrances ☐

29

Do the broken lines at the end of the acceleration lane mean ...

Tick the correct box

1 The edge of the carriageway? ☐

2 Other traffic should let you in? ☐

3 Give way to traffic already on the carriageway? ☐

30

If you see congestion ahead, is it legal to use your hazard warning lights to warn drivers behind you?

Tick the correct box **YES** ☐ **NO** ☐

31

What is the most common cause of accidents on motorways?

Tick the correct box

1 Vehicles breaking down ☐

2 Drivers falling asleep ☐

3 Drivers travelling too fast, too close to the vehicle in front ☐

4 Fog ☐

32

Are the following statements true or false?

I can use the hard shoulder ...

Tick the correct boxes	True	False
1 To take a short break	☐	☐
2 To stop and read a map	☐	☐
3 To allow the children to stretch their legs	☐	☐
4 To pull over in an emergency	☐	☐
5 To answer a phone call	☐	☐

33

In normal driving on the motorway, you should overtake ...

Tick the correct box

1 On the right ☐

2 On the left ☐

3 On either side ☐

1

Cars fitted with automatic transmission select the gear depending on the road speed and the load on the engine. They therefore have no c__ __ __ __ __ pedal.

Fill in the missing word

_____

2

The advantages of an automatic car are ...

1 _____
_____

2 _____
_____

3

The gear selector has the same function as a manual selector, but what function do each of the following have?

Park _____
_____
Reverse_____
_____
Neutral_____
_____
Drive_____
_____
3rd_____
_____
2nd_____
_____
1st_____
_____

4

Automatic cars have a device called a kickdown. Is its function ...

Tick the correct box

1 To select a higher gear? ☐

2 To select a lower gear manually? ☐

3 To provide quick acceleration when needed? ☐

5

When driving an automatic car, would you select a lower gear ...

Tick the appropriate boxes	YES	NO
1 To control speed when going down a steep hill?	☐	☐
2 To slow the car down in normal driving?	☐	☐
3 When going uphill?	☐	☐
4 To overtake, in certain circumstances?	☐	☐
5 When manoeuvring?	☐	☐
6 Before stopping?	☐	☐

6

An automatic car has two foot pedals, the foot-brake and the accelerator.

For normal driving, which foot would you use ...

1 For the brake?
Answer _____

2 For the accelerator?
Answer _____

7

When you are driving an automatic car, using one foot to control both pedals is preferable to using both the left and the right foot. Why?

Answer _____

_____

_____

8

Some cars with automatic transmission have a tendency to 'creep'.

Which gears allow the car to creep?

Answer _____

_____

9

When driving an automatic car, would you use the handbrake ...

Tick the correct box

1 More than in a manual car? ☐

2 The same? ☐

3 Less? ☐

HINTS & TIPS

Remember – if you haven't got your foot on the brake when you select Drive in an automatic car, the vehicle may begin to move forward.

10

In which position should the gear selector be when you are starting the engine?

Answer _____

or _____

11

As you approach a bend, an automatic car will sometimes change up because there is less pressure on the accelerator.

What should you do to prevent this happening?

Tick the correct box

1 Slow down before the bend and accelerate gently as you turn. ☐

2 Brake as you go round the bend. ☐

3 Brake and accelerate at the same time. ☐

1

There are many myths and misunderstandings surrounding the driving test.

Are the following true or false?

Tick the correct boxes   **True**   **False**

1 The driving test is designed ☐ ☐
to see whether I can drive
around a test route without
making any mistakes.

2 The driving test is designed ☐ ☐
to see whether I can drive
safely under various traffic
conditions.

3 I do not need to know any ☐ ☐
of *The Highway Code*.

4 The examiner has a set ☐ ☐
allocation of passes
each week.

5 I may be expected to drive ☐ ☐
up to the maximum national
speed limit, where appropriate.

2

The length of the normal driving test is approximately ...

Tick the correct box

1 60 minutes ☐

2 90 minutes ☐

3 40 minutes ☐

3

If, during the test, you do not understand what the examiner says to you, you would take a guess because you must not talk to him or her.

Is this statement true or false?
Tick the correct box **True** ☐ **False** ☐

4

You may have heard people say that it is easier to pass the driving test in certain parts of the country.

Tick the correct box   **YES**   **NO**
Do you agree with   ☐   ☐
this statement?

5

If you fail your test, you can take it again. Which of the following statements is correct?

Tick the correct box(es)

1 If you fail the test, you can apply straight
away for another appointment. ☐

2 If you fail the test you have to wait a
month before you can apply for another
appointment. ☐

3 You can re-take your test, subject to
appointment availability, any time. ☐

4 You have to wait 10 working days before
you can re-take the test. ☐

6

Before the practical part of your test, the examiner will test your eyesight.

This is done by asking you to read a new-style number plate at a distance of ...

Tick the correct box

1 30.5 metres (100 feet) ☐

2 20 metres (66 feet) ☐

3 40.5 metres (133 feet) ☐

7

What will happen if you fail your eyesight test?

Answer _____

_____

_____

8

It is essential that you take both sections of your

p__ __ __ __ __ __ __ __ __ __
l__ __ __ __ __ __ **to the test centre.**

9

The examiner will expect you to drive without making any mistakes.

Do you think this statement is true or false?

Tick the correct box **True** ☐ **False** ☐

10

When reversing, are you allowed to undo your seat belt?

Tick the correct box **YES** ☐ **NO** ☐

11

If you fail your test, what will the examiner do?

1 _____

_____

2 _____

_____

12

When you have passed your driving test, what are you entitled to do?

1 _____

_____

2 _____

_____

13

I have within the last month passed my test.

Can I supervise a learner driver?

Tick the correct box **YES** ☐ **NO** ☐

14

When you have passed your test, what will the Examiner do with your provisional licence?

Answer _____

_____

15

While you are waiting for your full licence to be sent to you, can you drive legally?

Tick the correct box **YES** ☐ **NO** ☐

16

While taking your driving test, you should drive ...

Tick the correct box

1 Especially carefully, keeping about 5mph below the speed limit ☐

2 As you would normally drive with your instructor ☐

3 With confidence, keeping at or just over the speed limit, to show that you can really drive ☐

17

Can you take a driving test if you are deaf?

Tick the correct box **YES** ☐ **NO** ☐

The driving test ensures that all drivers reach a minimum standard.

1
Do you think that learning to drive ends with passing the test?

Tick the correct box **YES** ☐ **NO** ☐

2
What knowledge and skills are not necessarily assessed in the present driving test?

List three

1 _____
_____

2 _____
_____

3 _____
_____

3
Which of these statements do you think best describes advanced driving?

Tick the correct box

1 Advanced driving is learning to handle your car to its maximum performance. ☐

2 Advanced driving is learning to drive defensively with courtesy and consideration to others. ☐

3 Advanced driving is learning to drive fast. ☐

4
There are particular circumstances under which you are required to take a driving test again. Name them

Answer _____
_____
_____

5
Once you have passed your driving test, your licence is usually valid until you reach __ __ years of age.

Complete the sentence

HINTS & TIPS
Driving is a skill you can improve for the rest of your life; consider further training after the test.

Driving at night can cause problems.

6

Some people have difficulty in driving at night.

Which age group would you expect, in general, to experience most difficulties?

Tick the correct box

1 Older people ☐

2 Younger people ☐

7

Which of these statements do you think is correct?

Tick the correct box

1 Street lighting and my car's headlights mean that I can see just as well as in the daylight. Therefore driving at night is just like driving in the daylight. ☐

2 At night I have to rely on my car's headlights and any additional lighting. Therefore I cannot see as far or drive as fast as in the daylight. ☐

8

At dusk and dawn what action should you take to compensate for driving a dark coloured car?

Answer _____

_____

9

When driving after dark in a built-up area, should you use ...

Tick the correct box

1 Dipped headlights? ☐

2 Side or dim-dipped lights? ☐

10

***The Highway Code* says you should not use your horn in a built-up area between 11.30pm and 7am.**

What is the exception to that rule?

Answer _____

_____

11

The diagram below illustrates two vehicles parked at night on a two-way road.

Which one is parked correctly?

Tick the correct box

A ☐   B ☐

12

Certain groups of road users are particularly vulnerable at night.

Name two of them

1 _____

2 _____

_____

13

Under what circumstances would you use dipped headlights during the day?

Answer _____

_____

and then complete the sentence
S__ __ and b__ s__ __ __.

_____

14

When you are waiting at a junction after dark, your brake lights might d__ __ __ __ __ the driver behind. It is better to use your h__ __ __ __ __ __ __ __.

Complete the sentences

Certain weather conditions can create hazardous driving conditions in the summer as well as in the winter.

_____

15

Which of the following causes greatest danger to drivers?

Tick the correct box

1 Snow ☐

2 Ice ☐

3 Heavy rain ☐

4 Not being able to see properly ☐

_____

16

In wet weather conditions your tyres can lose their grip.

You should allow at least d__ __ __ __ __ the distance between you and the car in front that you allow on a dry road.

Fill in the missing word

17

In very wet conditions there is a danger of a build-up of water between your tyres and the road.

This is called

a__ __ __ __ __ __ __ __ __ __.

Fill in the missing word

18

How can you prevent a build-up of water occurring?

S__ __ __ d__ __ __

19

How should you deal with floods?

Tick the correct box

1 Drive through as fast as possible to avoid stopping ☐

2 Drive through slowly in 1st gear, slipping the clutch to keep the engine speed high ☐

3 Drive through in the highest gear possible, slipping the clutch to keep the engine speed high ☐

20

Will less tread on your tyres ...

Tick the correct box

1 Increase your braking distance? ☐

2 Decrease your braking distance? ☐

21

When the tyres lose contact with the road, the steering will feel v__ __ __ l__ __ __ __.

Complete the sentence

22

After you have driven through a flood, should you check ...

Tick the correct box

1 Your speedometer? ☐

2 Your brakes? ☐

3 Your oil? ☐

23

There are certain key precautions you should take when driving in fog.

Complete the following sentences

1 S__ __ __ d__ __ __.

2 Ensure you are able to s__ __ __ within the distance you can see to be clear.

3 Use your w__ __ __ __ __ __ __ __ __ __ w__ __ __ __ __.

4 Use your d__ __ __ __ __ __ __ and your h__ __ __ __ __ r__ __ __ w__ __ __ __ __ __ __ __ __.

24

Under what circumstances should you use your rear fog lights?

When visibility is less than _____ metres/feet.

Fill in the correct number

25

When you are following another vehicle in fog, should you ...

Tick the correct box

1 Follow closely behind because it will help you see where you are going? ☐

2 Leave plenty of room between you and the vehicle in front? ☐

26

When you are following another vehicle in fog, should you use ...

Tick the correct box

1 Main beam headlights? ☐

2 Dipped headlights? ☐

27

Extra precautions are needed when dealing with a junction in fog.

Complete the following sentences

1 Open your w__ __ __ __ __ __ and switch off your a__ __ __ __ s__ __ __ __ __. L__ __ __ __ __ for other vehicles.

2 Signal e__ __ __ __ .

3 Use your b__ __ __ __ __. The light will a__ __ __ __ following vehicles.

4 Use your h__ __ __ if you think it will w__ __ __ other road users.

28

Is the following statement about anti-lock brakes true or false?

Anti-lock brakes will stop me skidding when driving on snow or ice.

Tick the correct box   **True** ☐ **False** ☐

29

When driving in snow or ice you should gently test your b_ _ _ _ _ from time to time.

Fill in the missing word

30

In order to slow down when driving on snow or ice you should ...

Fill in the missing words

1 Use your brakes g_ _ _ _ _ .

2 Get into a l_ _ _ _ g_ _ _ earlier than normal.

3 Allow your speed to d_ _ _ and use b_ _ _ _ _ gently and early

31

On snow or ice, braking distances can increase by ...

Tick the correct box

1 10 times ☐

2 5 times ☐

3 20 times ☐

4 15 times ☐

32

When going downhill in snow, what would you do to help you slow down?

Answer _____

_____

33

When cornering in snow or ice, what should you avoid doing?

Answer _____

_____

34
How can you reduce the risk of wheel spin?

Answer _____

_____

_____

35
Three important factors cause a skid.

Name them.

1 _____

_____

2 _____

_____

3 _____

_____

36
Some everyday driving actions, especially in poor weather, can increase the risk of skidding.

Fill in the missing words

1 S__ __ __ __ __ __ down.

2 S__ __ __ __ __ __ __ up.

3 T__ __ __ __ __ __ corners.

4 Driving u__ __ __ __ __ and
   d__ __ __ __ __ __ __.

HINTS & TIPS

If you realise that your car is starting to skid, ease off the brake and accelerator, then steer smoothly in the same direction as the skid.

All vehicles need routine attention and maintenance to keep them in good working order. Neglecting maintenance can be costly and dangerous.

1

With which of these statements do you agree?

Tick the correct box

1 Allowing the fuel gauge to drop too low is bad for the engine. ☐

2 In modern cars the fuel level makes little difference. ☐

2

What do you put into the engine to lubricate the moving parts?

Answer _____

_____

_____

3

How frequently should you check your oil level?

Tick the correct box

1 Once a month ☐

2 Once a year ☐

3 Every time you fill up with fuel ☐

4

The engine is often cooled by a mixture of w_ _ _ _ and a_ _ _ _ f_ _ _ _ _.

Some engines are a_ _ cooled.

Complete the sentence

5

How frequently should you test your brakes?

Tick the correct box

1 Daily ☐

2 Monthly ☐

3 Weekly ☐

4 When I use them ☐

6

Incorrectly adjusted headlamps can cause d_ _ _ _ _ to other road users.

Complete the sentence

7

All headlamps, indicators and brake lights should be kept in good working order. It is also important that they are kept c_ _ _ _ .

Fill in the missing word

8

Tyres should be checked for u__ __ __ __ __ wear and tyre walls for b__ __ __ __ __ and c__ __ __.

Complete the sentence

_____

9

The legal requirement for tread depth is not less than ...

Tick the correct box

1 1.4mm ☐

2 1.6mm ☐

3 2mm ☐

10

What should you do if your brakes feel slack or spongy?

Answer _____

_____

_____

11

Vehicle breakdowns could result from ...

Fill in the missing words

1 N__ __ __ __ __ of the vehicle

2 Lack of r__ __ __ __ __ __
c__ __ __ __ __

3 Little or no
p__ __ __ __ __ __ __ __ __ __ __
maintenance

4 A__ __ __ __ of the vehicle

12

It is advisable to carry a warning triangle.

1 On a straight road how far back should it be placed?

Tick the correct box

45 metres (148 feet) ☐

200 metres (656 feet) ☐

150 metres (492 feet) ☐

2 On a dual carriageway, how far back should it be placed? At least ...

Tick the correct box

200 metres (656 feet) ☐

150 metres (492 feet) ☐

450 metres (1476 feet) ☐

13

If you use a warning triangle, is it worth putting your hazard lights on as well?

Tick the correct box **YES** ☐ **NO** ☐

14

If your vehicle breaks down on a motorway, should you ...

Tick the correct box

1 Gently brake, put your hazard lights on and seek assistance? ☐

2 Pull over to the central reservation as far to the right as possible? ☐

3 Pull over safely on to the hard shoulder as far away from the carriageway as possible? ☐

15

If your vehicle has broken down on the motorway, should you tell your passengers to ...

Tick the correct box

1 Stay in the vehicle while you seek assistance? ☐

2 Wait by the car on the hard shoulder but watch for other vehicles? ☐

3 Get out of the vehicle and wait on the embankment away from the hard shoulder? ☐

16

The marker posts at the side of all motorways have a picture of a telephone handset.

How can you tell which way to walk to reach the nearest telephone?

Answer _____

_____

_____

17

When you use the emergency telephone on a motorway, what will the operator ask you?

1 _____
_____
_____

2 _____
_____
_____

3 _____
_____
_____

4 _____
_____
_____

18

Disabled drivers cannot easily get to an emergency telephone. How can they summon help?

1 _____
_____
_____

2 _____
_____
_____

19

If you break down when travelling alone, there are three things you are advised NOT to do.

Complete the sentences

1 Do not ask p__ __ __ __ __ __
m__ __ __ __ __ __ __ __ for help.

2 Do not accept help from anyone you
d__ n__ __ k__ __ __ (except the emergency services or a breakdown service).

3 Do not l__ __ __ __ you vehicle
l__ __ __ __ __ than necessary.

20

If I am first or one of the first to arrive at the scene of an accident, should I ...

Tick the correct boxes

	True	False
1 Always move injured people away from vehicles?	☐	☐
2 Tell the ambulance personnel or paramedics what I think is wrong with those injured?	☐	☐
3 Give casualties something warm to drink?	☐	☐
4 Switch off hazard warning lights?	☐	☐
5 Switch off vehicle engines?	☐	☐
6 Inform the police of the accident?	☐	☐

21

If you are involved in an accident, what MUST you do?

Answer _____
_____
_____

_____

22

If you are involved in an accident and nobody is injured, do you have to call the police?

Tick the correct box   **YES** ☐ **NO** ☐

23

What information do you need to exchange if you are involved in an accident?

1 _____
_____
_____

2 _____
_____
_____

3 _____
_____
_____

4 _____
_____
_____

5 _____
_____
_____

24

If you thought you had a fire in your car's engine, what action would you take?

1 _____

_____

_____

2 _____

_____

_____

3 _____

_____

_____

25

There are three items of emergency equipment it is wise to carry in your car.

Fill in the missing words

1 F__ __ __ __ A__ __ kit

2 F__ __ __
e__ __ __ __ __ __ __ __ __ __

3 W__ __ __ __ __ __ t__ __ __ __ __ __

26

When you rejoin a motorway from the hard shoulder, should you ...

Tick the correct box

1 Signal right and join when there is safe gap? ☐

2 Keep your hazard lights on and drive down the hard shoulder until there is a safe gap? ☐

3 Use the hard shoulder to build up speed and join the carriageway when safe? ☐

27

**Fuel combustion causes waste products. One of these is a gas called c__ __ __ __ __ __ d__ __ __ __ __ __.
This is a major cause of the g__ __ __ __ __ __ __ __ __ __ effect.**

Complete the sentences

28

How much does transport contribute to the production of carbon dioxide in the country (expressed as a percentage of the total production)?

Tick the correct box

1 10 per cent ☐

2 25 per cent ☐

3 50 per cent ☐

4 20 per cent ☐

29

The MOT test checks the roadworthiness of a vehicle.

Does it include an exhaust emission test?

Tick the correct box YES ☐ NO ☐

30

A catalytic convertor stops the emission of carbon dioxide.

Tick the correct box True ☐ False ☐

31

Which uses up more fuel?

Tick the correct box

1 A car travelling at 50mph ☐

2 A car travelling at 70mph ☐

32

There are some measures car drivers can take to help reduce damage to the environment.

List five

1 _____
_____

2 _____
_____

3 _____
_____

4 _____
_____

5 _____
_____

Before buying a used car it is best to decide what you want the car for and how much you can afford.

33

There are three main sources of supply for used vehicles. You can buy from a d__ __ __ __ __, at an a__ __ __ __ __ __ or p__ __ __ __ __ __ __ __.

Complete the sentence

34

When reading a glowing description of a used car, what should you first consider?

Answer _____
_____
_____

35

Are these statements about buying a used car through a dealer or at an auction true or false?

Tick the correct boxes   **True**   **False**

1 It is often cheaper to buy a   ☐   ☐
car at an auction than
through a dealer.

2 I have the same legal rights   ☐   ☐
when I buy at an auction as
when I buy from a dealer.

3 I should always read the   ☐   ☐
terms and conditions of
trade before I buy a car
at an auction.

4 The best way to select a   ☐   ☐
used car dealer is by
recommendation.

36

Cars bought through a dealer often have a warranty.

What should you check?

1 _____
_____

2 _____
_____

37

When you test drive a vehicle, you should make sure that it is t__ __ __ __, has a current M__ __ certificate (if applicable) and that all i__ __ __ __ __ __ __ __ requirements are complied with.

Complete the sentence

_____

38

There are some important items that you should check on before you buy a used car.

List three

1 _____
_____

2 _____
_____

3 _____
_____

39

Do you think the following statement is true or false?

It is advisable to have my vehicle examined by a competent and unbiased expert before I buy.

Tick the correct box   **True** ☐   **False** ☐

Particular difficulties are encountered when towing a caravan or trailer. There are some very good courses which will help you master the skills required.

1

People can underestimate the length of the total combination of car and caravan or trailer.

Is the overall length usually ...

Tick the correct box

1 Twice the length of a normal car? ☐

2 Three times the length of a normal car? ☐

2

What additional fixtures should you attach to your car to help you see more clearly?

Answer _____

_____

_____

3

When towing you will need more distance than normal to overtake. Is it ...

Tick the correct box

1 Twice the normal distance? ☐

2 Three times the normal distance? ☐

3 Four times the normal distance? ☐

4

A device called a s__ __ __ __ __ __ __ __ __ will make the combination safer to handle.

Fill in the missing word

5

The stability of the caravan will depend on how you load it. Should heavy items be loaded ...

Tick the correct box

1 At the front? ☐

2 At the rear? ☐

3 Over the axle(s)? ☐

6

There are special restrictions for vehicles which are towing.

A What is the speed limit on a dual carriageway?

Tick the correct box

1 50mph ☐

2 60mph ☐

3 70mph ☐

B What is the speed on a single carriageway?

Tick the correct box

1 40mph ☐

2 50mph ☐

3 60mph ☐

7

There are some important checks you should make before starting off.

List four

_____
_____
_____

2 _____
_____
_____

3 _____
_____
_____

4 _____
_____
_____

8

If you decide to stop to take a break, before allowing anyone to enter the caravan you should lower the j__ __ __ __ __ w__ __ __ __ and c__ __ __ __ __ s__ __ __ __ __ __ __.

Fill in the missing words

Many people now take their car abroad or hire a vehicle when on holiday.

9

Motoring organisations such as the Automobile Association can help you plan and organise your trip.

The AA can provide advice on travel and v__ __ __ __ __ __ insurance.

They will also help you organise the d__ __ __ __ __ __ __ __ that you will need.

Fill in the missing words

10

Before travelling to Europe, you should always ...

Complete the sentences

1 Plan the r__ __ __ __ __ you wish to take.

2 Know the local m__ __ __ __ __ __ __ __
  r__ __ __ __ __ __ __ __ __ __.

11

It is essential that your vehicle should be checked thoroughly.

List four of the routine checks you should make

1 _____
_____
_____

2 _____
_____
_____

3 _____
_____
_____

4 _____
_____
_____

12

In most European countries you are advised to carry your
d__ __ __ __ __ __
l__ __ __ __ __ __ on you.

Complete the sentence

_____

13

What do the letters IDP stand for?

Answer _____
_____
_____

14

Where might you need an IDP?

Answer _____
_____
_____

_____

15

In most European countries what age do you have to be to drive?

Tick the correct box
1 ☐ 21 **2** ☐ 18 **3** ☐ 16

_____

16

Some European countries can require you to carry additional emergency equipment.

List four of the items you are recommended to carry

1 _____
_____
_____

2 _____
_____
_____

3 _____
_____
_____

4 _____
_____
_____

ANSWERS TO QUESTIONS

Answers to questions

Section 1

Introduction to learning to drive

A1 A current, signed, full or provisional licence for the category of vehicle that you are driving

A2 examinations
register

A3 21 years old
three years

A4 To the front and rear. It is important not to place them in windows where they could restrict good vision.

A5 True

A6 You should have answered No to all the questions.

A7 Yes. This should be the ambition of every driver.

A8 3, 4

Adjusting your driving position

A9
  1 handbrake
  2 doors
  3 seat
  4 head restraint
  5 mirrors
  6 seat belt

Introduction to vehicle controls

A10 The handbrake E
The driving mirrors D
The gear lever F
The clutch G
The steering wheel A
The foot-brake B
The accelerator C
gas

A11 The foot-brake R
The clutch L
The accelerator R

A12 **1** False. You will need one hand to change gear or use other controls.
2 True
3 False. The best position is quarter to three or ten to two.
4 False. It is safest to feed the wheel through your hands.
5 True
6 True

A13 The direction indicators B
Dipped beam A
Main beam D
Rear fog lamp C
Horn E
Hazard lights F

Section 2

Moving off

A1	A 1
	B 5
	C 3
	D 2
	E 6
	F 4
	G 7
	H 8
	I 9

Stopping (normally)

A2	A 1
	B 3
	C 2
	D 4
	E 6
	F 5
	G 8
	H 7
	I 9

Gear changing

A3	1st gear
A4	5th, or 4th if the car has a 4-speed gear box
A5	Usually 2nd gear, but 1st if you need to go very slowly or 3rd if the corner is sweeping and you can take it safely at a higher speed
A6	engine
	vehicle
	sound
	when
A7	A 1
	B 3

	C 2
	D 4
	E 5
A8	**1** False. This will cause the engine to labour.
	2 False. It is good practice to use the brakes to slow the car down. Using the transmission causes wear and tear which can be very costly. Also, the brakes are more effective.
	3 False
	4 True
	5 False. It is good practice to miss out the unwanted gears and select the gear most appropriate to your road speed.
A9	**1**
A10	**1** Don't
	2 Don't
	3 Do
	4 Do
	5 Do
	6 Don't
	7 Don't
	8 Don't

Steering

A11	**A** except in a few cars fitted with four-wheel steering (in which case all four wheels will move)
A12	**A**
A13	**B**
A14	**B**

Road positioning

A15 **C** well to the left but not too close to the kerb

A16 **B** Avoid swerving in and out. It is unnecessary and confuses other drivers.

Clutch control

A17 **A**

A18 biting

A19 **1** Yes
2 Yes
3 No
4 Yes
5 No

Section 3

Junctions

A1 two or more roads

A2 **A** T-junction
B Y-junction
C Roundabout
D Staggered crossroads
E Crossroads

A3 **1** E
2 C
3 B
4 D
5 A

A4 **A** 1
B 3

A5 **1** Mirrors
2 Signal
3 Position
4 Speed
5 Look

A6 assess
decide
act

A7 **A**

A8 **B**

A9 **D**

A10 **1** mirrors, position
2 signal
3 safe
4 safe distance
5 overtake

Crossroads

A11 **A 3** Crossroads. Priority for traffic on the major road. Never assume other drivers will give you priority.
B 1 Unmarked crossroads
C 2 Crossroads with give way lines at the end of your road. Give way to traffic on the major road.

Roundabouts

A12 **C**

A13 1 Left
2 Left
3 Right. Remember to use the MSM routine before signalling left to turn off.

A14 **1** Left
2 Going ahead
3 Right

A15 **mirrors**
signal
position
speed
look

A16 **2**

Section 4

Parking (on the road)

A1 **1** safe
2 considerate
3 legal
A2 Cars 1, 2, 3, 6
A3 **1** False
2 False
3 True
4 True
5 False. Although not best practice, it's fine to park on the opposite side of the road as long as it's safe to do so.
A4 Any of the following:
at a bus stop
at a school entrance
opposite a junction
on a bend
on the brow of a hill
on a Clearway
on a motorway
at night facing oncoming traffic
in a residents' parking zone.

Section 5

Passing stationary vehicles and obstructions

A1 Vehicle 2
A2 Vehicle 2, even though the obstruction is on the right. Where safe, when travelling downhill be prepared to give priority to vehicles (especially heavy vehicles) that are coming uphill.

Meeting other vehicles

A3 **1** True
2 False. Always consider whether it is safe. Are there dangers the other driver cannot see? Remember, flashing headlamps has the same meaning as sounding the horn. It is a warning: 'I am here!' Sometimes it is taken to mean: 'I am here and I am letting you pass.'
3 True
A4 **1** Yes
2 Yes
3 No
4 Yes
5 Yes
6 Yes
7 Yes

Section 6

Stopping in an emergency

A1 **1** True
2 True
3 True
4 False. Looking in the mirror should not be necessary. You should know what is behind you.
5 False
6 True
7 True
A2 False. An emergency stop will be conducted randomly on only some tests. You must always know how to stop safely in an emergency.
A3 pump
1 maximum
2 lock
3 quickly

A4 steer
brake
pump
pressure
1 False. Other elements beyond braking can cause skidding e.g. acceleration or going too fast into a bend.
2 False. Although you may stop in a shorter distance, you still need to leave the correct distance to allow yourself time to react and vehicles behind you time to stop.

Stopping distances

A5 **1** No
2 Yes
3 Yes
4 No
A6 ½ second
A7 **1** 23 metres/75 feet
2 15 metres/50 feet
3 96 metres/315 feet
A8 longer
more
A9 breaks
two-second

Section 7

Moving off at an angle

A1 **1** False. You should check your mirrors and blindspot before moving out. Keep alert for other traffic as you pull out and stop if necessary.
2 True
3 False. Move out slowly and carefully.
4 True. The closer you are, the greater the angle.
5 True. As you move out, you are likely to move on to the right-hand side of the road and into conflict with oncoming vehicles.
6 False. You should signal only if it helps or warns other road users. Signalling gives you no right to pull out.

Moving off uphill

A2 **1** True
2 False. Using the accelerator pedal will not move the car forwards.
3 False. As your feet will be using the clutch pedal and the accelerator pedal you need to use the handbrake to stop the car rolling back.
4 True
5 True
6 True
7 True

Moving off downhill

A3 **1** True
2 False. Almost certainly you will need to use the foot-brake.
3 False. It is often better to move off in 2nd gear.
4 True. This will stop the car rolling forwards.
5 True
6 False. You will need to have your foot on the foot-brake to stop the car rolling forwards.

Approaching junctions

A4 The following statements are correct: 1, 4, 5, 6, 7

Section 8

Reversing

A1 safe
convenient
law
A2 **1** False
2 False
3 True
4 True
A3 A
A4 1, 4
A5 Car A: to the left
Car B: to the right
A6 observation

Reversing into a side road on the left

A7 3
A8 **1** True
2 False
3 True
A9 4
A10 C
A11 Left
A12 The front of the car will swing out to the right
A13 **1** True
2 False
3 True
A14 pedestrians
road users
stop

Reversing into a side road on the right

A15 True
A16 B
A17 2
A18 True. You may need to place your left hand at 12 o'clock and lower your right hand.
A19 True
A20 2
A21 B

Answers to questions

Turning in the road

A22 **A**

A23 slowly
briskly

A24 False, but you should try to complete the manoeuvre in as few moves as possible.

A25 **2, 3, 4**

A26 **all** round

A27 **1** Right
2 Steer briskly left
3 Left
4 Steer briskly right
5 Right

A28 **1** Left
2 Over your right shoulder to where the car is going

Reverse parallel parking

A29 **2**

A30 **C** in line with the rear of the parked vehicle

A31 **2**

A32 **1** To the left
2 The nearside headlamp of the vehicle towards which you are reversing
3 Clipping the rear offside of the lead car
4 Take off the left lock
5 Steer to the right and then take off the right lock as you get straight

A33 **1** False
2 False

A34 **All** round, particularly for pedestrians and oncoming vehicles

A35 **C.** The other bay widths are reduced by parked vehicles. This may make opening doors a squeeze.

A36 Allows you to make best use of the area in front of the bay. Gives you a better view when driving out of the space

A37 close
directions
pedestrians

A38 **1** False
2 True
3 True

A39 Answers might include to remove things from the boot, or when using a pushchair

A40 observe
pedestrians

A41 Answers might include when making a delivery or pulling into an on-street parking bay on the opposite side of the road

Section 9

Traffic lights and yellow box junctions

A1 **1** red
2 red and amber
3 green
4 amber
5 red

A2 **1** green
2 red and amber
3 amber
4 red

A3 **1** False
2 True
3 True
4 False. Pedestrians who are already crossing have priority.

A4 **2**

A5 **1** Lane A or B
2 Lane C
3 Lane A

A6 **1** No. If your exit is blocked
you should not enter a
yellow box junction.
2 No. If your exit is blocked
you should not enter a
yellow box junction.
3 Yes

Pedestrian crossings

A7 **1** Zig-zag lines
2 Flashing yellow beacons on
both sides of the road
3 Black and white stripes on
the crossing
4 A give way line

A8 **1** True
2 True. You must not park or wait
on the zig-zag lines on either side
of the crossing.
3 False. You must not overtake on the
zig-zag lines on approach to
the crossing.
4 True
5 True. A slowing down arm signal
should be used. It helps pedestrians
understand what you intend to do.
They cannot see your brake lights.

A9 **1** Traffic lights
2 Zig-zag lines
3 A white stop line

A10 **2** A white stick means the pedestrian
is visually impaired. A white stick
with two reflector bands means the
pedestrian may be deaf as well as
visually impaired.

A11 **1** Flashing amber
2 You must give way to pedestrians on
the crossing, but if it is clear you may
go on.

A12 A bleeping tone. This sounds when
the red light shows to drivers and
helps visually impaired pedestrians
know when it is safe to cross.

A13 There is no flashing amber light
sequence. The light sequence is the
same as normal traffic lights.

A14 cyclists

Level crossings

A15 **A** 3
B 1
C 2
D 4

A16 **2**
4
5

Section 10

One-way systems

A1 **A** is the correct sign for a
one-way street.
B tells you 'Ahead only'.

A2 **1** True
2 True
3 True
4 True

Answers to questions

Road markings

A3 information
warnings
orders

A4 **1** They can be seen when other signs may be hidden
2 They give a continuing message

A5 **A** 2
B 2

A6 1, 4

A7 They are used to separate potentially dangerous streams of traffic.

A8 You must not enter the hatched area.

Traffic signs

A9 **1** Warning
2 Order
3 Information

A10 **1** must
2 must not

A11 **1** You must give way to traffic on the major road. Delay your entry until it is safe to join the major road.
2 You must stop (even if the road is clear). Wait until you can enter the new road safely.

A12 vision is limited

A13 Motorway signs D
Primary routes E
Other routes B
Local places C
Tourist signs A

Section 11

Road observation

A1 speed
behaviour
intentions

A2 **1** Observe that the view into the new road is restricted.
The driver should ...
Move forward slowly, to get a better view.
Note the pedestrian who may walk in front of or behind car **A**.
Note the pedestrian waiting to cross.
Allow the cyclist to pass.
Once in position to see car **B**, stop and give way.
2 Observe that the parked car restricts the view into and out of the side road.
The driver should ...
Slow down on approach to parked car **P**.
Take up position to gain a better view and be more visible to car **A** and the pedestrian.
Slow down in case the pedestrian walks out from behind the parked car **P**.
Consider signal to pass parked car **P**.
Look carefully into minor road.
Note the actions of car **A**. Be prepared to stop.

A3 bike

A4 **3**

A5 **A**
1 Junctions
2 Hump-back bridges
3 Concealed entrances
4 Dead ground
5 Narrow lanes
B
1 Children playing
2 Horses
3 Pedestrians
4 Especially elderly and young cyclists
5 Other vehicles

A6 1 True. The ability to advise those at your destination of delays can help to reduce the worry of late arrivals
2 True. This applies even if you're stopped at traffic lights or queueing in traffic
3 True
4 True
5 True
6 False

A7 All are distracting and upset concentration, and should not be carried out while driving.

Dealing with bends

A8 speed
gear
position

A9 1

A10 B

A11 A

A12 A On a right-hand bend keep to the left. This will help to improve your view.
B On a left-hand bend keep to the centre of the lane. Do not move to the centre of the road to get a better view. A vehicle travelling in the opposite direction may be taking the bend wide.

Overtaking

A13 necessary
1 Mirrors
2 Position
3 Speed
4 Look
5 Mirrors
6 Signal
7 Manoeuvre

A14 About the width of a small car, more in windy or poor weather conditions

A15 1 The vehicle in front is signalling and positioned to turn right
2 You are using the correct lane to turn left at a junction
3 Traffic is moving slowly in queues and the traffic on the right is moving more slowly than you are
4 You are in a one-way street

A16 1 On approach to a junction
2 The brow of a hill
3 The approach to a bend
4 Where there is dead ground.
NB These are examples. Be guided by *The Highway Code*.

Answers to questions

Dual carriageways

A17 **2** Statements 1, 3, 4 and 5 do
not apply:
1 Reflective studs are used on some
dual carriageways.
3 The speed limit is subject to local
conditions and may vary from 40mph
up to the national speed limit.
4 You can turn right on to and off dual
carriageways unlike motorways, where
all traffic enters and leaves on the left.
5 You may find slow moving vehicles
sometimes displaying a flashing
amber light.

A18 **A** You would cross over the first
carriageway then wait in the gap in
the central reservation. Be careful, if
you are towing or if your vehicle is
long, that you do not cause other road
users to change course or slow down.
B You would wait until there is a gap in
the traffic long enough for you safely
to clear the first carriageway and
emerge into the second.

A19 The speed limit applies to all lanes.
Use the first lane to travel in and the
second for overtaking.

A20 **A** Dual carriageway ends
B Road narrows on both sides
C Two-way traffic straight ahead

A21 **A** and **C**

A22 Traffic is moving much faster, and one
or more lanes will have to be crossed.

Motorway driving

A23 **1**

A24 **1** No
2 Yes, as long as the car has
dual controls
3 Yes
4 No
5 Yes
6 Yes
7 Yes
8 No

A25 **1** Oil
2 Water
3 Fuel
4 Tyre pressures
These are just some of the checks;
for more information, refer to your
car's manual.

A26 **3** You should never attempt to
retrieve anything from the
carriageway.

A27 **3**

A28 **B** Amber
A Red
D Green
C White

A29 **3**

A30 Yes

A31 **3**

A32 **1** False
2 False
3 False
4 True
5 False

A33 **1** except when traffic is moving slowly
in queues and the queue on the right
is travelling more slowly

Section 12

Driving an automatic car

A1   Clutch

A2   **1** Driving is easier
        2 There is more time to concentrate on the road

A3   Park – Locks the transmission. This should be selected only when the vehicle is stationary.
        Reverse – Enables the car to go backwards, as in a manual car.
        Neutral – Has the same function as in a manual car. The engine is not in contact with the driving wheels.
        Drive – Is used for driving forwards. It automatically selects the most appropriate gear.
        3rd – Has the same function as manual gears
        2nd – Has the same function as manual gears
        1st – Has the same function as manual gears

A4   3

A5   **1** Yes
        2 No
        3 Yes, if you needed extra control
        4 You would probably use kickdown, but possibly in certain circumstances you would manually select a lower gear
        5 Yes, maybe using 1st gear
        6 No. Use the brakes

A6   **1** The right foot
        2 The right foot

A7   It stops you trying to control the brake and accelerator at the same time.
        It encourages early release of the accelerator and progressive braking.

A8   Drive, reverse, all forward gears.

A9   **1** You should apply the handbrake every time you stop. Otherwise you have to keep your foot on the foot-brake.

A10 Park (P) or Neutral (N)

A11 **1**

Section 13

The driving test

A1   **1** False
        2 True
        3 False
        4 False
        5 True

A2   3

A3   False. If you did not hear clearly or did not understand what the examiner said, you should ask him or her to repeat the instruction. If you have any problem with your hearing, it is advisable to tell the examiner at the start of the test.

A4   No. The standard test does not vary. The test result should be the same wherever it is taken.

A5   1, 4

A6   2

A7   The test will not proceed. You have failed not only the eyesight section, but the whole test. Remember, if you wear glasses or contact lenses, to wear them for the eyesight test and for the rest of the driving test.

Answers to questions

A8 Provisional licence

A9 False. You can make some less serious faults and still reach the required standard.

A10 Yes, but remember to do it up again when you have completed the exercise.

A11 **1** Give you a verbal explanation of the main reasons for failure
2 Write out a form for you to take away showing you your main errors

A12 **1** Drive unsupervised
2 Drive without L plates

A13 No. You must have had at least three years' driving experience (and be over 21 years of age).

A14 The Examiner will keep your provisional licence and arrange for DVLA to send your full licence to you.

A15 Yes. It is a good idea to keep a note of your driver number and the date you passed your test.

A16 **2** The examiner will expect you to drive normally. You should abide by all speed limits and drive according to road and traffic conditions.

A17 Yes. The examiner will be skilled in giving instructions and directions to deaf candidates.

Section 14

Beyond the test

A1 No

A2 **1** Bad weather driving
2 Night-time driving
3 Motorway driving
4 Skid control ... and more

A3 **2**

A4 There are certain serious driving offences which carry the penalty of disqualification. In order to regain a full licence, the disqualified driver has to apply for a provisional licence and take an extended test. If, because of certain illnesses, you have been unable to drive for 10 years, you will be required to take the test again in order to gain a full licence.
For new drivers: the accumulation of six or more penalty points within two years of passing the test will mean reverting to a provisional licence and re-sitting the test.

A5 70

Safe night driving

A6 **1** although people of any age can find it difficult to drive at night

A7 **2**

A8 Switch on earlier, switch off later.

A9 **1** It helps others to see you.

A10 If you are stationary, to avoid danger from a moving vehicle.

A11 **A** Always park with the flow of traffic. You will show red reflectors to vehicles travelling in your direction.

A12 **1** Pedestrians
2 Cyclists } two of these
3 Motorcyclists

A13 In poor weather conditions – see and be seen

A14 dazzle
handbrake

All-weather driving

A15 4

A16 double

A17 aquaplaning

A18 Slow down
Allow time for the tread patterns to disperse the water.

A19 2

A20 1

A21 very light

A22 2

A23 **1** Slow down
2 stop
3 windscreen wipers
4 demister, heated rear windscreen

A24 100 metres/328 feet

A25 2

A26 2

A27 **1** windows, audio system.
Listen
2 early
3 brakes, alert
4 horn, warn

A28 False, because your tyres are not in contact with the road

A29 brakes

A30 **1** gently
2 lower gear
3 drop, brakes

A31 1

A32 If possible, control your speed before reaching the hill. Select a low gear early.

A33 Using your brakes

A34 Avoid harsh acceleration

A35 **1** The driver
2 The vehicle
3 The road conditions

A36 **1** Slowing
2 Speeding
3 Turning
4 Uphill, downhill

Answers to questions

Section 15

Vehicle care

A1   1
A2   Oil
A3   3
A4   Water, anti-freeze, air
A5   1
A6   dazzle
A7   clean
A8   uneven, bulges, cuts
A9   2
A10   Get them checked as quickly as possible

Breakdowns, accidents and emergencies

A11   **1** Neglect
      2 routine checks
      3 preventative
      4 abuse
A12   **1** 45 metres/148 feet
      2 At least 150 metres/492 feet
A13   Yes. Try to give as much warning as possible.
A14   3
A15   3
A16   Under the drawing of the handset is an arrow which points to the nearest telephone.

A17   **1** The emergency number (painted on the box)
      2 Vehicle details (make, registration mark, colour)
      3 Membership details of your motoring organisation
      4 Details of the fault
A18   **1** By displaying a Help pennant
      2 By using a mobile telephone
A19   **1** passing motorists
      2 do not know
      3 leave, longer
A20   **1** False. Do not move injured people unless they are in danger.
      2 False. Tell them the facts, not what you think is wrong.
      3 False. Do not give those injured anything to eat or drink. Keep them warm and reassure them.
      4 False. Keep hazard lights on to warn other drivers.
      5 True. Switch off engines. Put out cigarettes.
      6 True, in the case of injury.
A21   Stop
A22   No
A23   **1** The other driver's name, address and contact number
      2 The registration numbers of all vehicles involved
      3 The make of the other car
      4 The other driver's insurance details
      5 If the driver is not the owner, the owner's details.

A24   **1** Pull up quickly
        2 Get all passengers out
        3 Call assistance
A25   **1** First aid
        2 Fire extinguisher
        3 Warning triangle
A26   **3**

The motor car and the environment

A27   carbon dioxide, greenhouse
A28   **4**
A29   Yes
A30   False. A catalytic convertor reduces
        the level of carbon monoxide,
        nitrogen oxide and hydrocarbons
        by up to 90 per cent. Carbon dioxide
        is still produced.
A31   **2**
A32   Eight measures are listed here:
        1 Make sure your vehicle is in good
        condition and regularly serviced.
        2 Make sure tyres are correctly
        inflated. Under inflated tyres
        waste fuel.
        3 Avoid harsh braking.
        4 Buy a fuel-efficient vehicle.
        5 Use the most appropriate gear.
        6 Use your accelerator sensibly and
        avoid harsh acceleration.
        7 Use unleaded fuel.
        8 Dispose of waste oil, old batteries
        and used tyres sensibly.

Buying a used car

A33   dealer, auction, privately
A34   Why is it being sold?
A35   **1** True
        2 False
        3 True
        4 True
A36   **1** What is covered
        2 The length of the agreement
A37   taxed, MOT, insurance
A38   Four items to check are listed here:
        1 Mileage
        2 Has it been involved in
        any accidents?
        3 Number of owners
        4 Is there any hire purchase or finance
        agreement outstanding?
A39   True. The AA offers a national
        inspection scheme.

Answers to questions

Section 16

Towing a caravan or trailer

A1   1

A2   Exterior towing mirrors, to give you a good view

A3   2

A4   stabilizer

A5   3

A6   **A** 2

      B 2

A7   Seven checks are listed here:
   1 Is the caravan or trailer loaded correctly?
   2 Is it correctly hitched up to your vehicle?
   3 Are the lights and indicators working properly?
   4 Is the braking system working correctly?
   5 Is the jockey wheel assembly fully retracted?
   6 Are tyre pressures correct?
   7 Are all windows, doors and roof lights closed?

A8   jockey wheel, corner steadies

Driving in Europe

A9   vehicle, documents

A10   **1** route
   2 motoring regulations

A11   Here are five routine checks:
   1 Tyres, including spare. Always carry a spare tyre.
   2 Tool kit and jack.
   3 Lamps and brake lights.
   4 Fit deflectors to your headlamps to prevent dazzle to other drivers approaching on the left.
   5 Check you have an extra exterior mirror on the left.

A12   driving licence

A13   International Driving Permit

A14   Some non-EU countries

A15   2

A16   Five items are listed here:
   1 Spare lamps and bulbs
   2 Warning triangle
   3 First aid kit
   4 Fire extinguisher
   5 Reflective jacket

PART 7: THE HIGHWAY CODE

INTRODUCTION

This Highway Code applies to England, Scotland and Wales. *The Highway Code* is essential reading for everyone.

The aim of *The Highway Code* is to promote safety on the road, whilst also supporting a healthy, sustainable and efficient transport system.

Wording of the Highway Code

Many of the rules in the Code are legal requirements, and if you disobey these rules you are committing a criminal offence. You may be fined, given penalty points on your licence or be disqualified from driving. In the most serious cases you may be sent to prison. Such rules are identified by the use of the words **'MUST/MUST NOT'**. In addition, the rule includes an abbreviated reference to the legislation which creates the offence.

Although failure to comply with the other rules of the Code will not, in itself, cause a person to be prosecuted, *The Highway Code* may be used in evidence in any court proceedings under the Traffic Acts (see The road user and the law on page 125) to establish liability. This includes rules which use advisory wording such as 'should/should not' or 'do/do not'.

Knowing and applying the rules

Knowing and applying the rules contained in The Highway Code could significantly reduce road casualties. Cutting the number of deaths and injuries that occur on our roads every day is a responsibility we all share. The Highway Code can help us discharge that responsibility. Further information on driving/riding techniques can be found in 'The Official DVSA Guide to Driving - the essential skills' and 'The Official DVSA Guide to Riding - the essential skills'.

HIERARCHY OF ROAD USERS

The 'hierarchy of road users' is a concept that places those road users most at risk in the event of a collision at the top of the hierarchy. The hierarchy does not remove the need for everyone to behave responsibly. The road users most likely to be injured in the event of a collision are pedestrians, cyclists, horse riders and motorcyclists, with children, older adults and disabled people being more at risk. The following H rules clarify this concept.

Rule H1

It is important that ALL road users are aware of *The Highway Code*, are considerate to other road users and understand their responsibility for the safety of others.

Everyone suffers when road collisions occur, whether they are physically injured or not. But those in charge of vehicles that can cause the greatest harm in the event of a collision bear the greatest responsibility to take care and reduce the danger they pose to others. This principle applies most strongly to drivers of large goods and passenger vehicles, vans/minibuses, cars/taxis and motorcycles.

Cyclists, horse riders and drivers of horse drawn vehicles likewise have a responsibility to reduce danger to pedestrians.

None of this detracts from the responsibility of ALL road users, including pedestrians, cyclists and horse riders, to have regard for their own and other road users' safety.

Always remember that the people you encounter may have impaired sight, hearing or mobility and that this may not be obvious.

Rule H2 - Rule for drivers, motorcyclists, horse drawn vehicles, horse riders and cyclists

At a junction you should give way to pedestrians crossing or waiting to cross a road into which or from which you are turning.

You **MUST** give way to pedestrians on a zebra crossing, and to pedestrians and cyclists on a parallel crossing (see Rule 195).

Pedestrians have priority when on a zebra crossing, on a parallel crossing or at light controlled crossings when they have a green signal.

You should give way to pedestrians waiting to cross a zebra crossing, and to pedestrians and cyclists waiting to cross a parallel crossing.

Horse riders should also give way to pedestrians on a zebra crossing, and to pedestrians and cyclists on a parallel crossing.

Cyclists should give way to pedestrians on shared use cycle tracks and to horse riders on bridleways.

Only pedestrians may use the pavement. Pedestrians include wheelchair and mobility scooter users.

Pedestrians may use any part of the road and use cycle tracks as well as the pavement, unless there are signs prohibiting pedestrians.

Rule H2: Wait for the pedestrian to cross the junction before turning.
This applies if you are turning right or left into the junction.

Laws TSRGD Schedule 14 part 1 and part 5 & HA 1835 sect 72, R(S)A 1984, sect 129 & Countryside Act 1968 Sect 1 part 30

Rule H3 - Rule for drivers and motorcyclists

You should not cut across cyclists, horse riders or horse drawn vehicles going ahead when you are turning into or out of a junction or changing direction or lane, just as you would not turn across the path of another motor vehicle. This applies whether they are using a cycle lane, a cycle track, or riding ahead on the road and you should give way to them.

Do not turn at a junction if to do so would cause the cyclist, horse rider or horse drawn vehicle going straight ahead to stop or swerve.

You should stop and wait for a safe gap in the flow of cyclists if necessary. This includes when cyclists are:
- approaching, passing or moving off from a junction
- moving past or waiting alongside stationary or slow-moving traffic
- travelling around a roundabout

Rule H3: Wait for the cyclist to pass the junction before turning.
This also applies if there is a cycle lane or cycle track
and if you are turning right or left into the junction.

RULES FOR PEDESTRIANS

General guidance

1. Pavements and footways (including any path along the side of a road) should be used if provided. Where possible, avoid being next to the kerb with your back to the traffic. If you have to step into the road, look both ways first. Always remain aware of your environment and avoid unnecessary distractions. Always show due care and consideration for others.

2. If there is no pavement keep to the right-hand side of the road so that you can see oncoming traffic. You should take extra care and
- be prepared to walk in single file, especially on narrow roads or in poor light
- keep close to the side of the road.

It may be safer to cross the road well before a sharp right-hand bend so that oncoming traffic has a better chance of seeing you. Cross back after the bend.

3. Help other road users to see you. Wear or carry something light-coloured, bright or fluorescent in poor daylight conditions. When it is dark, use reflective materials (e.g. armbands, sashes, waistcoats, jackets, footwear), which can be seen by drivers using headlights up to three times as far away as non-reflective materials.

Rule 3: Help yourself to be seen

4. Young children should not be out alone on the pavement or road (see Rule 7). When taking children out, keep between them and the traffic and hold their hands firmly. Strap very young children into pushchairs or use reins. When pushing a young child in a buggy, do not push the buggy into the road when checking to see if it is clear to cross, particularly from between parked vehicles.

5. Organised walks or parades involving large groups of people walking along a road should use a pavement if available; if one is not, they should keep to the left. Look-outs should be positioned at the front and back of the group, and they should wear fluorescent clothes in daylight and reflective clothes in the dark. At night, the look-out in front should show a white light and the one at the back a red light. People on the outside of large groups should also carry lights and wear reflective clothing.

6. Motorways. Pedestrians **MUST NOT** be on motorways or slip roads except in an emergency (see Rules 272 and 277).

Laws RTRA sect 17, MT(E&W)R 1982 as amended, reg 15(1)(b) & MT(S)R reg 13

Crossing the road

7. The Green Cross Code. The advice given below on crossing the road is for all pedestrians. Children should be taught the Code and should not be allowed out alone until they can understand and use it properly. The age when they can do this is different for each child. Many children cannot judge how fast vehicles are going or how far away they are. Children learn by example, so parents and carers should always use the Code in full when out with their children. They are responsible for deciding at what age children can use it safely by themselves.

A. First find a safe place to cross and where there is space to reach the pavement on the other side. Where there is a crossing nearby, use it. It is safer to cross using a subway, a footbridge, an island, a zebra, pelican, toucan or puffin crossing, or where there is a crossing point controlled by a police officer, a school crossing patrol or a traffic warden. Otherwise choose a place where you can see clearly in all directions. Try to avoid crossing between parked cars (see Rule 14), on a blind bend, or close to the brow of a hill. Move to a space where drivers and riders can see you clearly. Do not cross the road diagonally.

Rule 7: Look all around and listen for traffic before crossing

B. Stop just before you get to the kerb, where you can see if anything is coming. Do not get too close to the traffic. If there's no pavement, keep back from the edge of the road but make sure you can still see approaching traffic.

C. Look all around for traffic and listen. Traffic could come from any direction. Listen as well, because you can sometimes hear traffic before you see it.

D. If traffic is coming, let it pass. Look all around again and listen. Do not cross until there is a safe gap in the traffic and you are certain that there is plenty of time. Remember, even if traffic is a long way off, it may be approaching very quickly.

E. When it is safe, go straight across the road – do not run. Keep looking and listening for traffic while you cross, in case there is any traffic you did not see, or in case other traffic appears suddenly. Look out for cyclists and motorcyclists travelling between lanes of traffic. Do not walk diagonally across the road.

8. At a junction. When you are crossing or waiting to cross the road, other traffic should give way. Look out for traffic turning into the road, especially from behind you, and cross at a place where drivers can see you. If you have started crossing and traffic wants to turn into the road, you have priority and they should give way (see Rules H2 and 170).

9. Pedestrian Safety Barriers. Where there are barriers, cross the road only at the gaps provided for pedestrians. Do not climb over the barriers or walk between them and the road.

10. Tactile paving. Raised surfaces that can be felt underfoot provide warning and guidance to blind or partially sighted people. The most common surfaces are a series of raised studs, which are used at crossing points with a dropped kerb, or a series of rounded raised bars which are used at level crossings, at the top and bottom of steps and at some other hazards.

11. One-way streets. Check which way the traffic is moving. Do not cross until it is safe to do so without stopping. Bus and cycle lanes may operate in the opposite direction to the rest of the traffic.

12. Bus and cycle lanes. Take care when crossing these lanes as traffic may be moving faster than in the other lanes, or against the flow of traffic.

13. Routes shared with cyclists. Cycle tracks may run alongside footpaths or pavements and be separated from them by a feature such as a change of material, a verge, a kerb or a white line. Such routes may also incorporate short lengths of tactile paving to help visually impaired people stay on the correct side. On the pedestrian side this may comprise a series of flat-topped bars running across the direction of travel (ladder pattern). On the cyclist side the same bars are orientated in the direction of travel (tramline pattern).

Some routes shared with cyclists will not be separated by such a feature allowing cyclists and pedestrians to share the same space. Cyclists should respect your safety (see Rule 62) but you should also take care not to obstruct or endanger them. Always remain aware of your environment and avoid unnecessary distractions.

Where signs indicate, some routes are shared between pedestrians, cyclists, horse riders and horse drawn vehicles. Cyclists, horse riders and drivers of horse drawn vehicles should respect your safety, but you should take care not to obstruct or endanger them. Always remain aware of your environment and avoid unnecessary distractions.

14. Parked vehicles. If you have to cross between parked vehicles, use the outside edges of the vehicles as if they were the kerb. Stop there and make sure you can see all around and that the traffic can see you. Make sure there is a gap between any parked vehicles on the other side, so you can reach the pavement. Never cross the road in front of, or behind, any vehicle with its engine running, especially a large vehicle, as the driver may not be able to see you.

15. Reversing vehicles. Never cross behind a vehicle which is reversing, showing white reversing lights or sounding a warning.

16. Moving vehicles. You **MUST NOT** get onto or hold onto a moving vehicle.
Law RTA 1988 sect 26

17. At night. Wear something reflective to make it easier for others to see you (see Rule 3). If there is no pedestrian crossing nearby, cross the road near a street light so that traffic can see you more easily.

Crossings

18. At all crossings. When using any type of crossing you should
- always check that the traffic has stopped before you start to cross or push a pram onto a crossing
- always cross between the studs or over the zebra markings. Do not cross at the side of the crossing or on the zig-zag lines, as it can be dangerous.
You **MUST NOT** loiter on any type of crossing.
Laws ZPPPCRGD reg 19 & RTRA sect 25(5)

19. Zebra crossings. Give traffic plenty of time to see you and to stop before you start to cross. Vehicles will need more time when the road is slippery. Wait until traffic has stopped from both directions or the road is clear before crossing. Remember that traffic does not have to stop until someone has moved onto the crossing. Drivers and riders should give way to pedestrians waiting to cross and **MUST** give way to pedestrians on a zebra crossing (see Rule H2). Keep looking both ways, and listening, in case a driver or rider has not seen you and attempts to overtake a vehicle that has stopped.

Rule 19: Zebra crossings have flashing beacons

A zebra crossing with a central island is two separate crossings (see Rule 20).
Law TSRGD Schedule 14 part 5

20. Where there is an island in the middle of a zebra crossing, wait on the island and follow Rule 19 before you cross the second half of the road – it is a separate crossing.

Rule 20: Zebra crossings with a central island are two separate crossings

21. At traffic lights. There may be special signals for pedestrians. You should only start to cross the road when the green figure shows. If you have started to cross the road and the green figure goes out, you should still have time to reach the other side, but do not delay. If no pedestrian signals have been provided, watch carefully and do not cross until the traffic lights are red and the traffic has stopped. Keep looking and check for traffic that may be turning the corner. Remember that traffic lights may let traffic move in some lanes while traffic in other lanes has stopped.

Rule 21: At traffic lights, puffin and pelican crossings *At pelican crossings only

The Highway Code

22. Pelican crossings. These are signal-controlled crossings operated by pedestrians. Push the control button to activate the traffic signals. When the red figure shows, do not cross. When a steady green figure shows, check the traffic has stopped then cross with care. When the green figure begins to flash you should not start to cross. If you have already started you should have time to finish crossing safely.

23. Puffin crossings differ from pelican crossings as the red and green figures are above the control box on your side of the road and there is no flashing green figure phase. Press the button and wait for the green figure to show.

24. When the road is congested, traffic on your side of the road may be forced to stop even though their lights are green. Traffic may still be moving on the other side of the road, so press the button and wait for the signal to cross.

25. Toucan crossings are light-controlled crossings which allow cyclists and pedestrians to share crossing space and cross at the same time. They are push-button operated. Pedestrians and cyclists will see the green signal together. Cyclists are permitted to ride across.

Rule 25: Toucan crossings can be used by both cyclists and pedestrians

26. At some crossings there is a bleeping sound or voice signal to indicate to blind or partially sighted people when the steady green figure is showing, and there may be a tactile signal to help deafblind people.

27. Equestrian crossings are for horse riders. They have pavement barriers, wider crossing spaces, horse and rider figures in the light panels and either two sets of controls (one higher), or just one higher control panel.

Rule 27: Equestrian crossings are used by horse riders.
There is often a parallel crossing

28. 'Staggered' pelican or puffin crossings. When the crossings on each side of the central refuge are not in line they are two separate crossings. On reaching the central island, press the button again and wait for a steady green figure.

Rule 28: Staggered crossings (with an island in the middle)
are two separate crossings

29. Crossings controlled by an authorised person. Do not cross the road unless you are signalled to do so by a police officer, traffic warden or school crossing patrol. Always cross in front of them.

30. Where there are no controlled crossing points available it is advisable to cross where there is an island in the middle of the road. Use the Green Cross Code (see Rule 7) to cross to the island and then stop and use it again to cross the second half of the road.

Situations needing extra care

31. Emergency vehicles. If an ambulance, fire engine, police or other emergency vehicle approaches using flashing blue lights, headlights and/or sirens, keep off the road.

32. Buses. Get on or off a bus only when it has stopped to allow you to do so. Watch out for cyclists when you are getting off. Never cross the road directly behind or in front of a bus. Wait until it has moved off and you can see clearly in both directions.

33. Tramways. These may run through pedestrian areas. Their path will be marked out by shallow kerbs, changes in the paving or other road surface, white lines or yellow dots. Cross at designated crossings where provided. Elsewhere treat trams as you would other road vehicles and look both ways along the track before crossing. Do not walk along the track as trams may come up behind you. Trams move quietly and cannot steer to avoid you.

34. Railway level crossings. You **MUST NOT** cross or pass a stop line when the red lights show, (including a red pedestrian figure). Also do not cross if an alarm is sounding or the barriers are being lowered. The tone of the alarm may change if another train is approaching. If there are no lights, alarms or barriers, stop, look both ways and listen before crossing. A tactile surface comprising rounded bars running across the direction of pedestrian travel may be installed on the footpath approaching a level crossing to warn visually impaired people of its presence. The tactile surface should extend across the full width of the footway and should be located at an appropriate distance from the barrier or projected line of the barrier.

Law TSRGD, reg 52

35. Street and pavement repairs. A pavement may be closed temporarily because it is not safe to use. Take extra care if you are directed to walk in or to cross the road.

RULES FOR USERS OF POWERED WHEELCHAIRS AND POWERED MOBILITY SCOOTERS

Powered wheelchairs and mobility scooters (Called Invalid Carriages in law)

36. There is one class of manual wheelchair (called a Class 1 invalid carriage) and two classes of powered wheelchairs and powered mobility scooters. Manual wheelchairs and Class 2 vehicles are those with an upper speed limit of 4mph (6km/h) and are designed to be used on pavements. Class 3 vehicles are those with an upper speed limit of 8mph (12km/h) and are equipped to be used on the road as well as the pavement.

37. When you are on the road you should obey the guidance and rules for other vehicles; when on the pavement you should follow the guidance and rules for pedestrians.

On pavements

38. Pavements are safer than roads and should be used when available. You should give pedestrians priority and show consideration for other pavement users, particularly those with a hearing or visual impairment who may not be aware that you are there.

39. Powered wheelchairs and scooters **MUST NOT** travel faster than 4mph (6km/h) on pavements or in pedestrian areas. You may need to reduce your speed to adjust to other pavement users who may not be able to move out of your way quickly enough or where the pavement is too narrow.

Law UICHR reg 4

40. When moving off the pavement onto the road, you should take special care. Before moving off, always look round and make sure it's safe to join the traffic. Always try to use dropped kerbs when moving off the pavement, even if this means travelling further to locate one.

If you have to climb or descend a kerb, always approach it at right angles and don't try to negotiate a kerb higher than the vehicle manufacturer's recommendations.

On the road

41. You should take care when travelling on the road as you may be travelling more slowly than other traffic (your machine is restricted to 8mph (12km/h) and may be less visible).

42. When on the road, Class 3 vehicles should travel in the direction of the traffic. Class 2 users should always use the pavement when it is available. When there is no pavement, you should use caution when on the road. Class 2 users should, where possible, travel in the direction of the traffic. If you are travelling at night when lights **MUST** be used, you should travel in the direction of the traffic to avoid confusing other road users.

Law UICHR reg 9

43. You **MUST** follow the same rules about using lights, indicators and horns as for other road vehicles, if your vehicle is fitted with them. At night, lights **MUST** be used. Be aware that other road users may not see you and you should make yourself more visible – even in the daytime and also at dusk – by, for instance, wearing a reflective jacket or reflective strips on the back of the vehicle.

Law UICHR reg 9

44. Take extra care at road junctions. When going straight ahead, check to make sure there are no vehicles about to cross your path from the left, the right, or overtaking you and turning left. There are several options for dealing with right turns, especially turning from a major road. If moving into the middle of the road is difficult or dangerous, you can
- stop on the left-hand side of the road and wait for a safe gap in the traffic
- negotiate the turn as a pedestrian, i.e. travel along the pavement and cross the road between pavements where it is safe to do so. Class 3 users should switch the vehicle to the lower speed limit when on pavements.

If the junction is too hazardous, it may be worth considering an alternative route. Similarly, when negotiating major roundabouts (i.e. with two or more lanes) it may be safer for you to use the pavement or find a route which avoids the roundabout altogether.

45. All normal parking restrictions should be observed. Your vehicle should not be left unattended if it causes an obstruction to other pedestrians – especially those in wheelchairs. Parking concessions provided under the Blue Badge scheme (see Further reading) will apply to those vehicles displaying a valid badge.

46. These vehicles **MUST NOT** be used on motorways (see Rule 253). They should not be used on unrestricted dual carriageways where the speed limit exceeds 50mph (80km/h) but if they are used on these dual carriageways, they **MUST** have a flashing amber beacon. A flashing amber beacon should be used on all other dual carriageways (see Rule 220).

Laws RTRA sect 17(2) & (3), & RVLR reg 17(1) & 26

RULES ABOUT ANIMALS
Horse-drawn vehicles

47. Horse-drawn vehicles used on the highway should be operated and maintained in accordance with standards set out in the Department for Transport's *Code of Practice for Horse-Drawn Vehicles*. This Code lays down the requirements for a road driving assessment and includes a comprehensive list of safety checks to ensure that a carriage and its fittings are safe and in good working order. The standards set out in the Road Driving Assessment may be required to be met by a Local Authority if an operator wishes to obtain a local authority licence to operate a passenger-carrying service.

48. Safety equipment and clothing. All horse-drawn vehicles should have two red rear reflectors. It is safer not to drive at night but if you do, a light showing white to the front and red to the rear **MUST** be fitted.

Law RVLR reg 4

Horse riders

49. Safety equipment. Children under the age of 14 **MUST** wear a helmet which complies with the Regulations. It **MUST** be fastened securely. Other riders should also follow these requirements. These requirements do not apply to a child who is a follower of the Sikh religion while wearing a turban.

Laws H(PHYR)A sect 1 & H(PHYR)R reg 3

50. Other clothing. You should wear
- boots or shoes with hard soles and heels
- light-coloured or fluorescent clothing in daylight
- reflective clothing if you have to ride at night or in poor visibility.

Rule 50: Help yourself to be seen

51. At night. It is safer not to ride on the road at night or in poor visibility, but if you do, make sure you wear reflective clothing and your horse has reflective bands above the fetlock joints. A light which shows white to the front and red to the rear should be fitted, with a band, to the rider's right arm and/or leg/riding boot. If you are leading a horse at night, carry a light in your right hand, showing white to the front and red to the rear, and wear reflective clothing on both you and your horse. It is strongly recommended that a fluorescent/reflective tail guard is also worn by your horse.

Riding

52. Before you take a horse or horse drawn vehicle on to the road, you should
- ensure all tack fits well and is in good condition
- make sure you can control the horse.

If you are an inexperienced horse rider or have not ridden for a while, consider taking the Ride Safe Award from the British Horse Society. The Ride Safe Award provides a foundation for any horse rider to be safe and knowledgeable when riding in all environments but particularly on the road. For more information, see www.bhs.org.uk

Always ride with other, less nervous horses if you think that your horse will be nervous of traffic. Never ride a horse without both a saddle and bridle.

53. Before riding off or turning, look behind you to make sure it is safe, then give a clear arm signal.

When riding on the road you should
- keep to the left
- keep both hands on the reins unless you are signalling
- keep both feet in the stirrups
- not carry another person
- not carry anything which might affect your balance or get tangled up with the reins
- keep a horse you are leading to your left
- move in the direction of the traffic flow in a one-way street
- never ride more than two abreast, and ride in single file on narrow or busy roads and when riding round bends.

54. You **MUST NOT** take a horse onto a footpath or pavement, and you should not take a horse onto a cycle track. Use a bridleway where possible. Equestrian crossings may be provided for horse riders to cross the road and you should use these where available (see Rule 27). You should dismount at level crossings where a 'horse rider dismount' sign is displayed.

Laws HA 1835 sect 72, R(S)A, sect 129(5)

55. Avoid roundabouts wherever possible. If you use them you should
- keep to the left and watch out for vehicles crossing your path to leave or join the roundabout
- signal right when riding across exits to show you are not leaving
- signal left just before you leave the roundabout.

Other animals

56. Dogs. Do not let a dog out on the road on its own. Keep it on a short lead when walking on the pavement, road or path shared with cyclists or horse riders.

57. When in a vehicle make sure dogs or other animals are suitably restrained so they cannot distract you while you are driving or injure you, or themselves, if you stop quickly. A seat belt harness, pet carrier, dog cage or dog guard are ways of restraining animals in cars.

58. Animals being herded. These should be kept under control at all times. You should, if possible, send another person along the road in front to warn other road users, especially at a bend or the brow of a hill. It is safer not to move animals after dark, but if you do, then wear reflective clothing and ensure that lights are carried (white at the front and red at the rear of the herd).

RULES FOR CYCLISTS

Overview

These rules are in addition to those in the following sections, which apply to all vehicles (except the Motorway section). See also Annex 1 – You and your bicycle.

59. Clothing. You should avoid clothes that may get tangled in the chain, or in a wheel or may obscure your lights when you are cycling.

Light-coloured or fluorescent clothing can help other road users to see you in daylight and poor light, while reflective clothing and/or accessories (belt, arm or ankle bands) can increase your visibility in the dark.

You should wear a cycle helmet that conforms to current regulations, is the correct size and securely fastened. Evidence suggests that a correctly fitted helmet will reduce your risk of sustaining a head injury in certain circumstances.

Rule 59: Help yourself to be seen

60. At night your cycle **MUST** have white front and red rear lights lit. It **MUST** also be fitted with a red rear reflector (and amber pedal reflectors, if manufactured after 1/10/85). White front reflectors and spoke reflectors will also help you to be seen. Flashing lights are permitted but it is recommended that cyclists who are riding in areas without street lighting use a steady front lamp.

Law RVLR regs 13, 18 & 24

61. Cycle Routes and Other Facilities. Cycle lanes are marked by a white line (which may be broken) along the carriageway (see Rule 140). Use facilities such as cycle lanes and tracks, advanced stop lines and toucan crossings (see Rules 62 and 73) where they make your journey safer and easier. This will depend on your experience and skills and the situation at the time. While such facilities are provided for reasons of safety, cyclists may exercise their judgement and are not obliged to use them.

62. Cycle Tracks. These are routes for cyclists that are physically protected or located away from motor traffic, other than where they cross side roads (see Rule 206). Cycle tracks may run alongside footpaths or pavements and be separated by a feature such as a change of material, a verge, a kerb or a white line. You **MUST** keep to the side intended for cyclists as the pedestrian side remains a pavement or footpath.

Some cycle tracks shared with pedestrians will not be separated by such a feature. On such shared use routes, you should always take care when passing pedestrians, especially children, older or disabled people, and allow them plenty of room. Always be prepared to slow down and stop if necessary (see Rule H2).
Law HA 1835 sect 72

63. Sharing space with pedestrians, horse riders and horse drawn vehicles. When riding in places where sharing with pedestrians, horse riders or horse drawn vehicles is permitted, take care when passing pedestrians and horse riders, especially children, older adults or disabled people. Slow down when necessary and let them know you are there; for example, by ringing your bell (it is recommended that a bell is fitted to your bike), or by calling out politely.

Remember that pedestrians may be deaf, blind or partially sighted and that this may not be obvious.

Do not pass pedestrians, horse riders or horse drawn vehicles closely or at high speed, particularly from behind. You should not pass a horse on their left. Remember that horses can be startled if passed without warning. Always be prepared to slow down and stop when necessary.

64. You **MUST NOT** cycle on a pavement.
Laws HA 1835 sect 72 & R(S)A, sect 129

65. Bus Lanes. Most bus lanes may be used by cyclists as indicated on signs. Watch out for people getting on or off a bus. Be very careful when overtaking a bus or leaving a bus lane as you will be entering a busier traffic flow. Do not pass between the kerb and a bus when it is at a stop.

66. You should
- avoid any actions that could reduce your control of your cycle
- be considerate of the needs of other road users when riding in groups. You can ride two abreast and it can be safer to do so, particularly in larger groups or when accompanying children or less experienced riders. Be aware of drivers behind you and allow them to overtake (for example, by moving into single file or stopping) when you feel it is safe to let them do so
- not ride close behind another vehicle in case it stops suddenly
- not carry anything which will affect your balance or may get tangled up with your wheels or chain

- be considerate of other road users, particularly blind and partially sighted pedestrians, and horse riders (see Rule H1). Let them know you are there when necessary, for example, by calling out or ringing your bell if you have one. It is recommended that a bell be fitted.

67. You should
- look all around to make sure it is safe before moving away from the kerb, when pulling out to overtake or to pass stationary vehicles, or when turning at junctions or stopping
- watch out for obstructions in the road, such as drains, service covers and potholes, positioning yourself so you can move to the left (as well as to the right) to avoid them safely
- take care when passing parked vehicles, leaving enough room (a door's width or 1 metre) to avoid being hit if a car door is opened, and watch out for pedestrians stepping into your path
- be aware of traffic coming up behind you, including other cyclists, and give a clear signal to show other road users what you intend to do (see 'Signals to other road users')
- take extra care near road humps, narrowings and other traffic calming features
- when cycling on the road, only pass to the left of large vehicles when they are stationary or slow moving and you should proceed with caution as the driver may not be able to see you. Be particularly careful on the approach to junctions or where a large vehicle could change lanes to the left.

68. You **MUST NOT**
- carry a passenger unless your cycle has been built or adapted to carry one
- hold onto a moving vehicle or trailer
- ride in a dangerous, careless or inconsiderate manner
- ride when under the influence of drink or drugs, including medicine.

Law RTA 1988 sects 24, 26, 28, 29 & 30 as amended by RTA 1991

69. You **MUST** obey all traffic signs and traffic light signals.

Laws RTA 1988 sect 36 & TSRGD Schedule 3 pt 3, sch7 pt4, sch9 pts 4 and 6, sch 13 pt 6, sch 14 pt 2

70. When parking your cycle
- find a conspicuous location where it can be seen by passers-by
- use cycle stands or other cycle parking facilities wherever possible
- do not leave it where it would cause an obstruction or hazard to other road users
- secure it well so that it will not fall over and become an obstruction or hazard.

71. At traffic light junctions and at cycle-only crossings with traffic lights, you **MUST NOT** cross the stop line when the traffic lights are red.

Some junctions have an advanced stop line to enable you to position yourself ahead of other traffic and wait (see Rule 178). When the traffic lights are red, you may cross the first stop line, but you **MUST NOT** cross the final stop line.
Laws RTA 1988 sect 36 & TSRGD Schedule 14 part 1

Road junctions

72. Road positioning. When riding on the roads, there are two basic road positions you should adopt, depending on the situation.

1) Ride in the centre of your lane, to make yourself as clearly visible as possible, in the following situations
- on quiet roads or streets – if a faster vehicle comes up behind you, move to the left to enable them to overtake, if you can do so safely
- in slower-moving traffic – when the traffic around you starts to flow more freely, move over to the left if you can do so safely so that faster vehicles behind you can overtake
- at the approach to junctions or road narrowings where it would be unsafe for drivers to overtake you

2) When riding on busy roads, with vehicles moving faster than you, allow them to overtake where it is safe to do so whilst keeping at least 0.5 metres away, and further where it is safer, from the kerb edge. Remember that traffic on most dual carriageways moves quickly. Take extra care crossing slip roads.

73. Junctions. Some junctions, particularly those with traffic lights, have special cycle facilities, including small cycle traffic lights at eye-level height, which may allow you to move or cross separately from or ahead of other traffic. Use these facilities where they make your journey safer and easier.

At junctions with no separate cyclist facilities, it is recommended that you proceed as if you were driving a motor vehicle (see Rules 170 to 190).

Position yourself in the centre of your chosen lane, where you feel able to do this safely, to make yourself as visible as possible and to avoid being overtaken where this would be dangerous. If you do not feel safe to proceed in this way, you may prefer to dismount and wheel your bike across the junction.

74. Turning. When approaching a junction on the left, watch out for vehicles turning in front of you, out of or into the side road. If you intend to turn left, check first for other cyclists or motorcyclists before signalling. Do not ride on the inside of vehicles signalling or slowing down to turn left.

If you are turning right, check the traffic to ensure it is safe, then signal and move to the centre of the road. Wait until there is a safe gap in the oncoming traffic and give a final look before completing the turn. It may be safer to wait on the left until there is a safe gap or to dismount and push your cycle across the road.

When turning into or out of a side road, you should give way to pedestrians crossing or waiting to cross (see Rule H2).

75. Two Stage Turns. At some signal-controlled junctions there may be signs and markings informing cyclists to turn right in two stages:

Stage 1: When the traffic lights turn green, cyclists wishing to make the turn should go straight ahead to the location marked by a cycle symbol and turn arrow on the carriageway; then stop and wait there

Stage 2: When the traffic lights on the far side of the junction, now facing the cyclists, turn green, they should then complete the manoeuvre

Roundabouts

76. Going straight ahead. If you are going straight ahead at a junction, you have priority over traffic waiting to turn into or out of the side road, unless road signs or markings indicate otherwise (see Rule H3). Check that you can proceed safely, particularly when approaching junctions on the left alongside stationary or slow-moving traffic. Watch out for drivers intending to turn across your path. Remember the driver ahead may not be able to see you, so bear in mind your speed and position in the road.

Take great care when deciding whether it is safe to pass stationary or slow-moving lorries and other long vehicles, especially at the approach to junctions, as their drivers may not be able to see you. Remember that they may have to move over to the right before turning left, and that their rear wheels may then come very close to the kerb while turning (see Rule 67).

77. Busy roads. When crossing faster or busy main roads, you may find it safer and easier to
- dismount and push your cycle across
- wait for a safe gap in the traffic before doing so, especially on faster roads and dual carriageways
- make use of traffic islands or central reservations to help you where appropriate.

78. Full details about the correct procedure at roundabouts without cycle facilities are contained in Rules 184 to 190.

Watch out for vehicles crossing your path to leave or join the roundabout, remembering that drivers may not easily see you.

79. If you are turning right, you can ride in the left or right-hand lanes and move left when approaching your exit. Position yourself in the centre of your lane if it is safe to do so (see Rule 72) and signal right to indicate that you are not leaving the roundabout. Alternatively, you may feel safer walking your cycle round on the pavement or verge.

If you decide to ride round keeping to the left-hand lane you should
- be aware that drivers may not easily see you
- take extra care when cycling across exits. You should signal right to show you are not leaving the roundabout
- watch out for vehicles crossing your path to leave or join the roundabout.

Where a roundabout has separate cycle facilities, you should use these facilities where they make your journey safer and easier although you are not obliged to use them. This will depend on your experience and skills and the situation at the time.

80. Give plenty of room to long vehicles on the roundabout as they need more space to manoeuvre. Do not ride in the space they need to get round the roundabout. It may be safer to wait until they have cleared the roundabout.

Crossing the road

81. Do not ride across equestrian crossings, as they are for horse riders only. Do not ride across a pelican, puffin or zebra crossing. Dismount and wheel your cycle across.

82. Crossings. Toucan crossings are light-controlled crossings which allow cyclists and pedestrians to share crossing space and cross at the same time. They are push-button operated. Pedestrians and cyclists will see the green signal together. Cyclists are permitted to ride across.

Cycle tracks on opposite sides of the road may be linked by cycle-only signalled crossings. You may ride across but you **MUST NOT** cross until the green cycle symbol is showing.

Cycle track crossings can be in spacious pedestrian environments. Cyclists should look out and be prepared to stop for pedestrians crossing the track informally as well as at these designated points.

Take extra care when crossing level crossings and tramways (see Rule 306). You should dismount at level crossings where a 'cyclist dismount' sign is displayed.

Law TSRGD Schedule 14 part 1

RULES FOR MOTORCYCLISTS
General guidance

These Rules are in addition to those in the following sections which apply to all vehicles. See also Annex 2 – Motorcycle licence requirements.

83. On all journeys, the rider and pillion passenger on a motorcycle, scooter or moped **MUST** wear a protective helmet. This does not apply to a follower of the Sikh religion while wearing a turban. Helmets **MUST** comply with the Regulations and they **MUST** be fastened securely. Riders and passengers of motor tricycles and quadricycles, also called quadbikes, should also wear a protective helmet. Before each journey check that your helmet visor is clean and in good condition.

Laws RTA 1988 sects 16 & 17 & MC(PH)R as amended reg 4

84. It is also advisable to wear eye protectors, which **MUST** comply with the Regulations. Scratched or poorly fitting eye protectors can limit your view when riding, particularly in bright sunshine and the hours of darkness. Consider wearing ear protection. Strong boots, gloves and suitable clothing may help to protect you if you are involved in a collision.

Laws RTA 1988 sect 18 & MC(EP)R as amended reg 4

85. You **MUST NOT** carry more than one pillion passenger who **MUST** sit astride the machine on a proper seat. They should face forward with both feet on the footrests. You **MUST NOT** carry a pillion passenger unless your motorcycle is designed to do so. Provisional licence holders **MUST NOT** carry a pillion passenger.

Laws RTA 1988 sect 23, MV(DL)R reg 16(6) & CUR reg 102

86. Daylight riding. Make yourself as visible as possible from the side as well as the front and rear. You could wear a light or brightly coloured helmet and fluorescent clothing or strips. Dipped headlights, even in good daylight, may also make you more conspicuous. However, be aware that other vehicle drivers may still not have seen you, or judged your distance or speed correctly, especially at junctions.

Rule 86: Help yourself to be seen

87. Riding in the dark. Wear reflective clothing or strips to improve your visibility in the dark. These reflect light from the headlamps of other vehicles, making you visible from a longer distance. See Rules 113 to 116 for lighting requirements.

88. Manoeuvring. You should be aware of what is behind and to the sides before manoeuvring. Look behind you; use mirrors if they are fitted. When in traffic queues look out for pedestrians crossing between vehicles and vehicles emerging from junctions or changing lanes. Position yourself so that drivers in front can see you in their mirrors. Additionally, when filtering in slow-moving traffic, take care and keep your speed low.

Remember: Observation – Signal – Manoeuvre

RULES FOR DRIVERS AND MOTORCYCLISTS

Vehicle condition

89. Vehicle condition. You **MUST** ensure your vehicle and trailer comply with the full requirements of the Road Vehicles (Construction and Use) Regulations and Road Vehicles Lighting Regulations (see Annex 4 – The road user and the law).

Fitness to drive

90. Make sure that you are fit to drive. You **MUST** report to the Driver and Vehicle Licensing Agency (DVLA) any health condition likely to affect your driving.
Law RTA 1988 sect 94

91. Driving when you are tired greatly increases your risk of collision. To minimise this risk
- make sure you are fit to drive. Do not begin a journey if you are tired. Get sufficient sleep before embarking on a long journey
- avoid undertaking long journeys between midnight and 6 am, when natural alertness is at a minimum
- plan your journey to take sufficient breaks. A minimum break of at least 15 minutes after every two hours of driving is recommended
- if you feel sleepy, stop in a safe place. Do not stop in an emergency area or on a hard shoulder of a motorway (see Rule 262 for guidance on places to take a break when travelling on motorways).

92. Vision. You **MUST** be able to read a vehicle number plate, in good daylight, from a distance of 20 metres (or 20.5 metres where the old style number plate is used). If you need to wear glasses (or contact lenses) to do this, you **MUST** wear them at all times while driving. The police have the power to require a driver to undertake an eyesight test.
Laws RTA 1988 sect 96 & MV(DL)R reg 40 & sched 8

93. Slow down, and if necessary stop, if you are dazzled by bright sunlight.

94. At night or in poor visibility, do not use tinted glasses, lenses or visors if they restrict your vision.

Alcohol and drugs

95. Do not drink and drive as it will seriously affect your judgement and abilities.

In England and Wales you **MUST NOT** drive with a breath alcohol level higher than 35 microgrammes/100 millilitres of breath or a blood alcohol level of more than 80 milligrammes/100 millilitres of blood.

In Scotland the legal limits are lower. You **MUST NOT** drive with a breath alcohol level higher than 22 microgrammes/100 millilitres of breath or a blood alcohol level of more than 50 milligrammes/100 millilitres of blood.

Alcohol will
- give a false sense of confidence
- reduce co-ordination and slow down reactions
- affect judgement of speed, distance and risk
- reduce your driving ability, even if you're below the legal limit
- take time to leave your body; you may be unfit to drive in the evening after drinking at lunchtime, or in the morning after drinking the previous evening.

The best solution is not to drink at all when planning to drive because any amount of alcohol affects your ability to drive safely. If you are going to drink, arrange another means of transport.

Laws RTA 1988 sects 4, 5 & 11(2) & PLSR

96. You **MUST NOT** drive under the influence of drugs or medicine. For medicines, check with your doctor or pharmacist and do not drive if you are advised that you may be impaired.

You **MUST NOT** drive if you have illegal drugs or certain medicines in your blood above specified limits. It is highly dangerous so never take illegal drugs if you intend to drive; the effects are unpredictable, but can be even more severe than alcohol and result in fatal or serious road crashes. Illegal drugs have been specified at very low levels so even small amounts of use could be above the specified limits. The limits for certain medicines have been specified at higher levels, above the levels generally found in the blood of patients who have taken normal therapeutic doses. If you are found to have a concentration of a drug above its specified limit in your blood because you have been prescribed or legitimately supplied a particularly high dose of medicine, then you can raise a statutory medical defence, provided your driving was not impaired by the medicine you are taking.

Law RTA 1988 sects 4 & 5

Before setting off

97. Before setting off. You **MUST** ensure that

- you have a valid licence and insurance to drive the vehicle you intend to use (see Annex 3)
- your vehicle is legal and roadworthy (see Annexes 3 and 6 for important vehicle maintenance and safety checks).

You **SHOULD** ensure that

- you have planned your route and allowed sufficient time for breaks and possible delays
- you have sufficient fuel or charge for your journey, especially if it includes motorway driving
- you know where all the controls are and how to use them
- clothing and footwear do not prevent you using the controls in the correct manner
- your mirrors and seat are adjusted correctly to ensure comfort, full control and maximum vision
- head restraints are properly adjusted to reduce the risk of neck and spine injuries in the event of a collision.

It is recommended for emergency use that

- you have a mobile telephone containing emergency contacts (e.g. breakdown assistance)
- you have high-visibility clothing.

Laws RTA 1988 sects 42, 45, 47, 49, 53, 87, 99(4) & 143, MV(DL)R reg 16, 40 & sched 4, VERA sect 29, RVLR 1989 regs 23 & 27, & CUR regs 27, 30, 32 & 61

Rule 97: Make sure head restraints are properly adjusted

Vehicle towing and loading

98. Before towing. As a driver

- you **MUST NOT** tow more than your licence permits. If you passed your car driving test on or after 1 January 1997, you are restricted on the weight of trailer you can tow
- you **MUST** ensure that both your vehicle and your trailer are in a roadworthy condition. This includes checking that all tyres are legal, the trailer braking system is in full working order and all trailer lights are working correctly
- you **MUST NOT** overload your vehicle or trailer. You should not tow a weight greater than that recommended by the manufacturer of your vehicle
- you should distribute the weight in your caravan or trailer evenly with heavy items over the axle(s) and ensure a downward load on the tow ball. The manufacturer's recommended weight and tow ball load should not be exceeded. This should minimise the possibility of swerving or snaking and loss of control
- you **MUST** secure your load and it **MUST NOT** stick out dangerously. Make sure any heavy or sharp objects and any animals are secured safely. If there is a collision, they might hit someone inside the vehicle and cause serious injury
- if your vehicle is narrower than your trailer or load, or your trailer or load obstructs your rearward view, then towing mirrors **MUST** be used
- your trailer **MUST** be fitted with a secondary coupling device, such as a safety chain
- carrying a load or pulling a trailer may require you to adjust your headlights.

During towing. As a driver

- you should be aware that reduced speed limits apply (see Rule 124)
- you should be aware that your stopping distance may increase significantly when towing (see Rule 126)
- you **MUST NOT** drive in the right-hand lane on motorways with three or more lanes (see Rule 265)
- if the trailer starts to swerve or snake, or you lose control, ease off the accelerator and reduce speed gently to regain control. Do not brake harshly.

Breakdowns. In the event of a breakdown, be aware

- that towing a vehicle on a tow rope is potentially dangerous. You should consider using a solid tow bar or professional recovery
- it may take longer to build up speed when rejoining a carriageway (see also Rule 278).

For additional advice about towing safely, see Further reading.

Laws CUR regs 27, 33, 86a & 100, RVLR reg 18, MT(E&W)R reg 12 & MV(DL)R reg 6, 7, 76 & sched 2

Seat belts and child restraints

99. You **MUST** wear a seat belt in cars, vans and other goods vehicles if one is fitted (see table below). Adults, and children aged 14 years and over, **MUST** use a seat belt or child restraint, where fitted, when seated in minibuses, buses and coaches. Exemptions are allowed for the holders of medical exemption certificates and those making deliveries or collections in goods vehicles when travelling less than 50 metres (approx 162 feet).

Laws RTA 1988 sects 14 & 15, MV(WSB)R, MV(WSBCFS)R & MV(WSB)(A)R 2005 & 2006

Seat Belt Requirements.
This table summarises the main legal requirements for wearing seat belts in cars, vans and other goods vehicles.

	Front seat	Rear seat	Who is responsible?
Driver	Seat belt **MUST** be worn if fitted		**Driver**
Child under 3 years of age	Correct child restraint **MUST** be used	Correct child restraint **MUST** be used. If one is not available in a taxi, may travel unrestrained.	**Driver**
Child from 3rd birthday up to 1.35 metres (approx 4ft 5ins) in height (or 12th birthday, whichever they reach first)	Correct child restraint **MUST** be used	Correct child restraint **MUST** be used where seat belts fitted. **MUST** use adult belt if correct child restraint is not available in a licensed taxi or private hire vehicle, or for reasons of unexpected necessity over a short distance, or if two occupied restraints prevent fitment of a third.	**Driver**
Child over 1.35 metres (approx 4ft 5ins) in height or 12 or 13 years	Seat belt **MUST** be worn if available	Seat belt **MUST** be worn if available	**Driver**
Adult passengers aged 14 and over	Seat belt **MUST** be worn if available	Seat belt **MUST** be worn if available	**Passenger**

100. The driver **MUST** ensure that all children under 14 years of age in cars, vans and other goods vehicles wear seat belts or sit in an approved child restraint where required (see table on previous page). If a child is under 1.35 metres (approx 4 feet 5 inches) tall, a baby seat, child seat, booster seat or booster cushion **MUST** be used suitable for the child's weight and fitted to the manufacturer's instructions.

Laws RTA 1988 sects 14 & 15, MV(WSB)R, MV(WSBCFS)R & MV(WSB)(A)R 2006

Rule 100: Make sure that a child uses a suitable restraint
which is correctly adjusted

101. A rear-facing baby seat **MUST NOT** be fitted into a seat protected by an active frontal airbag, as in a crash it can cause serious injury or death to the child.

Laws RTA 1988 sects 14 & 15, MV(WSB)R, MV(WSBCFS)R & MV(WSB)(A)R 2006

102. Children in cars, vans and other goods vehicles. Drivers who are carrying children in cars, vans and other goods vehicles should also ensure that

- children should get into the vehicle through the door nearest the kerb
- child restraints are properly fitted to manufacturer's instructions
- children do not sit behind the rear seats in an estate car or hatchback, unless a special child seat has been fitted
- the child safety door locks, where fitted, are used when children are in the vehicle
- children are kept under control.

GENERAL RULES, TECHNIQUES AND ADVICE FOR ALL DRIVERS AND RIDERS

Overview

This section should be read by all drivers, motorcyclists, cyclists and horse riders. The rules in *The Highway Code* do not give you the right of way in any circumstance, but they advise you when you should give way to others. Always give way if it can help to avoid an incident.

Signals

103. Signals warn and inform other road users, including pedestrians (see Signals to other road users), of your intended actions. You should always

- give clear signals in plenty of time, having checked it is not misleading to signal at that time
- use them to advise other road users before changing course or direction, stopping or moving off
- cancel them after use
- make sure your signals will not confuse others. If, for instance, you want to stop after a side road, do not signal until you are passing the road. If you signal earlier it may give the impression that you intend to turn into the road. Your brake lights will warn traffic behind you that you are slowing down
- use an arm signal to emphasise or reinforce your signal if necessary. Remember that signalling does not give you priority.

104. You should also

- watch out for signals given by other road users and proceed only when you are satisfied that it is safe
- be aware that an indicator on another vehicle may not have been cancelled.

105. You **MUST** obey signals given by police officers, traffic officers, traffic wardens (see Signals by authorised persons) and signs used by school crossing patrols.

Laws RTRA sect 28, RTA 1988 sect 35, TMA sect 6, & FTWO art 3

106. Police stopping procedures. If the police want to stop your vehicle they will, where possible, attract your attention by

- flashing blue lights, headlights or sounding their siren or horn, usually from behind
- directing you to pull over to the side by pointing and/or using the left indicator.

You **MUST** then pull over and stop as soon as it is safe to do so. Then switch off your engine.

Law RTA 1988 sect 163

Other stopping procedures

107. Driver and Vehicle Standards Agency Officers have powers to stop vehicles on all roads, including motorways and trunk roads. They will attract your attention by flashing amber lights
- either from the front requesting you to follow them to a safe place to stop
- or from behind directing you to pull over to the side by pointing and/or using the left indicator.

It is an offence not to comply with their directions. You **MUST** obey any signals given (see Signals by authorised persons).

Laws RTA 1988 sect 67, PRA sect 41 & sched 5(8)

108. Traffic Officers have powers to stop vehicles on most motorways and some 'A' class roads, in England and Wales. If traffic officers in uniform want to stop your vehicle on safety grounds (e.g. an insecure load) they will, where possible, attract your attention by
- flashing amber lights, usually from behind
- directing you to pull over to the side by pointing and/or using the left indicator.

You **MUST** then pull over and stop as soon as it is safe to do so. Then switch off your engine. It is an offence not to comply with their directions (see Signals by authorised persons).

Law RTA 1988, sects 35 & 163 as amended by TMA, sect 6

109. Traffic light signals and traffic signs
You **MUST** obey all traffic light signals (see Light signals controlling traffic) and traffic signs giving orders, including temporary signals & signs (see Traffic signs). Make sure you know, understand and act on all other traffic and information signs and road markings (see Traffic signs, Road markings and Vehicle markings).

Laws RTA 1988 sect 36 & TSRGD Schedule 3 part 4, Schedule 9 parts 7 and 8, Schedule 14 parts 1 and 5, Schedule 7 part 6, Schedule 15 part 1

110. Flashing headlights. Only flash your headlights to let other road users know that you are there. Do not flash your headlights to convey any other message or intimidate other road users.

111. Never assume that flashing headlights is a signal inviting you to proceed. Use your own judgement and proceed carefully.

112. The horn. Use only while your vehicle is moving and you need to warn other road users of your presence. Never sound your horn aggressively. You **MUST NOT** use your horn
- while stationary on the road
- when driving in a built-up area between the hours of 11.30pm and 7am

except when another road user poses a danger.

Law CUR reg 99

Lighting requirements

113. You **MUST**
- ensure all sidelights and rear registration plate lights are lit between sunset and sunrise
- use headlights at night, except on a road which has lit street lighting. These roads are generally restricted to a speed limit of 30mph (48km/h) unless otherwise specified
- use headlights when visibility is seriously reduced (see Rule 226).

Night (the hours of darkness) is defined as the period between half an hour after sunset and half an hour before sunrise.

Laws RVLR regs 3, 24, & 25, (In Scotland – RTRA sect 82 (as amended by NRSWA, para 59 of sched 8))

114. You **MUST NOT**
- use any lights in a way that would dazzle or cause discomfort to other road users, including pedestrians, cyclists and horse riders
- use front or rear fog lights unless visibility is seriously reduced. You **MUST** switch them off when visibility improves to avoid dazzling other road users (see Rule 226).

In stationary queues of traffic, drivers should apply the parking brake and, once the following traffic has stopped, take their foot off the footbrake to deactivate the vehicle brake lights. This will minimise glare to road users behind until the traffic moves again.

Law RVLR reg 27

115. You should also
- use dipped headlights, or dim-dip if fitted, at night in built-up areas and in dull daytime weather, to ensure that you can be seen
- keep your headlights dipped when overtaking until you are level with the other vehicle and then change to main beam if necessary, unless this would dazzle oncoming road users
- slow down, and if necessary stop, if you are dazzled by oncoming headlights.

116. Hazard warning lights. These may be used when your vehicle is stationary, to warn that it is temporarily obstructing traffic. Never use them as an excuse for dangerous or illegal parking. You **MUST NOT** use hazard warning lights while driving or being towed unless you are on a motorway or unrestricted dual carriageway and you need to warn drivers behind you of a hazard or obstruction ahead. Only use them for long enough to ensure that your warning has been observed.

Law RVLR reg 27

Control of the vehicle

Braking

117. In normal circumstances. The safest way to brake is to do so early and lightly. Brake more firmly as you begin to stop. Ease the pressure off just before the vehicle comes to rest to avoid a jerky stop.

118. In an emergency. Brake immediately. Try to avoid braking so harshly that you lock your wheels. Locked wheels can lead to loss of control.

119. Skids. Skidding is usually caused by the driver braking, accelerating or steering too harshly or driving too fast for the road conditions. If skidding occurs, remove the cause by releasing the brake pedal fully or easing off the accelerator. Turn the steering wheel in the direction of the skid. For example, if the rear of the vehicle skids to the right, steer immediately to the right to recover.

Rule 119: Rear of the car skids to the right. Driver steers to the right.

120. ABS. If your vehicle is fitted with anti-lock brakes, you should follow the advice given in the vehicle handbook. However, in the case of an emergency, apply the footbrake firmly; do not release the pressure until the vehicle has slowed to the desired speed. The ABS should ensure that steering control will be retained, but do not assume that a vehicle with ABS will stop in a shorter distance.

121. Brakes affected by water. If you have driven through deep water your brakes may be less effective. Test them at the first safe opportunity by pushing gently on the brake pedal to make sure that they work. If they are not fully effective, gently apply light pressure while driving slowly. This will help to dry them out.

122. Coasting. This term describes a vehicle travelling in neutral or with the clutch pressed down. It can reduce driver control because

- engine braking is eliminated
- vehicle speed downhill will increase quickly
- increased use of the footbrake can reduce its effectiveness
- steering response will be affected, particularly on bends and corners
- it may be more difficult to select the appropriate gear when needed.

123. The Driver and the Environment

You **MUST NOT** leave a parked vehicle unattended with the engine running or leave a vehicle engine running unnecessarily while that vehicle is stationary on a public road. Generally, if the vehicle is stationary and is likely to remain so for more than a couple of minutes, you should apply the parking brake and switch off the engine to reduce emissions and noise pollution. However it is permissible to leave the engine running if the vehicle is stationary in traffic or for diagnosing faults.

Law CUR regs 98 & 107

124. Speed limits

You **MUST NOT** exceed the maximum speed limits for the road and for your vehicle (see the Speed Limits table, on next page). A speed limit of 30 mph (48 km/h) generally applies to all roads with street lights (excluding motorways) unless signs show otherwise.

Locally set speed limits may apply, for example

- 20 mph (32 km/h) in some built-up areas
- 50 mph (80 km/h) on single carriageways with known hazards
- variable speed limit signs are used on some motorways and dual carriageways to change the maximum speed limit.

Speed limits are enforced by the police.

Law RTRA sects 81, 86, 89 & sched 6 as amended by MV(VSL)(E&W)

Rule 124: Examples of speed enforcement

Speed Limits

Types of vehicle	Built up areas MPH (km/h)	Single carriageways MPH (km/h)	Dual carriageways MPH (km/h)	Motorways MPH (km/h)
Cars & motorcycles (including car derived vans up to 2 tonnes maximum laden weight)	30 (48)	60 (96)	70 (112)	70 (112)
Cars towing caravans or trailers (including car derived vans and motorcycles)	30 (48)	50 (80)	60 (96)	60 (96)
Motorhomes or motor caravans (not exceeding 3.05 tonnes maximum unladen weight)	30 (48)	60 (96)	70 (112)	70 (112)
Motorhomes or motor caravans (exceeding 3.05 tonnes maximum unladen weight)	30 (48)	50 (80)	60 (96)	70 (112)
Buses, coaches and minibuses (not exceeding 12 metres in overall length)	30 (48)	50 (80)	60 (96)	70† (112)
Goods vehicles (not exceeding 7.5 tonnes maximum laden weight)	30 (48)	50 (80)	60 (96)	70†† (112)
Goods vehicles (exceeding 7.5 tonnes maximum laden weight) in England and Wales	30 (48)	50 (80)	60 (96)	60 (96)
Goods vehicles (exceeding 7.5 tonnes maximum laden weight) in Scotland	30 (48)	40 (64)	50 (80)	60 (96)

† 60 mph (96 km/h) if exceeding 12 metres in overall length.

†† 60 mph (96 km/h) if articulated or towing a trailer.

For speed limits that apply to special types of vehicles, such as oversized vehicles, see Further reading.

125. The speed limit is the absolute maximum and does not mean it is safe to drive at that speed irrespective of conditions. Unsafe speed increases the chances of causing a collision (or being unable to avoid one), as well as its severity. Inappropriate speeds are also intimidating, deterring people from walking, cycling or riding horses. Driving at speeds too fast for the road and traffic conditions is dangerous. You should always reduce your speed when

- the road layout or condition presents hazards, such as bends
- sharing the road with pedestrians, particularly children, older adults or disabled people, cyclists and horse riders, horse drawn vehicles and motorcyclists
- weather conditions make it safer to do so
- driving at night as it is more difficult to see other road users.

126. Stopping distances. Drive at a speed that will allow you to stop well within the distance you can see to be clear. You should

- leave enough space between you and the vehicle in front so that you can pull up safely if it suddenly slows down or stops. The safe rule is never to get closer than the overall stopping distance (see Typical Stopping Distances diagram on next page)
- allow at least a two-second gap between you and the vehicle in front on high-speed roads and in tunnels where visibility is reduced. The gap should be at least doubled on wet roads and up to ten times greater on icy roads
- remember, large vehicles and motorcycles need a greater distance to stop. If driving a large vehicle in a tunnel, you should allow a four-second gap between you and the vehicle in front

If you have to stop in a tunnel, leave at least a 5-metre gap between you and the vehicle in front.

Rule 126: Use a fixed point such as a sign to help measure a two-second gap

Tailgating is where the gap between you and the vehicle in front is too small for you to be able to stop safely if the vehicle in front suddenly brakes.

Tailgating is dangerous, intimidating and can cause collisions, especially when driving at speed. Keeping a safe distance from the vehicle in front gives you time to react and stop if necessary. Dangerous and careless driving offences, such as tailgating, are enforced by the police.

TYPICAL STOPPING DISTANCES

The distances below are a general guide. The distance will depend on your attention (thinking distance), the road surface, the weather and the condition of your vehicle at the time.

Thinking Distance	Braking Distance
	Average car length = 4 metres (13 feet)

20mph (32km/h)
6m | 6m = **12 metres (40 feet)** or three car lengths

30mph (48km/h)
9m | 14m = **23 metres (75 feet)** or six car lengths

40mph (64km/h)
12m | 24m = **36 metres (118 feet)** or nine car lengths

50mph (80km/h)
15m | 38m = **53 metres (175 feet)** or thirteen car lengths

60mph (96km/h)
18m | 55m = **73 metres (240 feet)** or eighteen car lengths

70mph (112km/h)
21m | 75m = **96 metres (315 feet)** or twenty-four car lengths

Lines and lane markings on the road

Diagrams of all lines are shown in Road markings.

127. A broken white line. This marks the centre of the road. When this line lengthens and the gaps shorten, it means that there is a hazard ahead. Do not cross it unless you can see the road is clear and wish to overtake or turn off.

128. Double white lines where the line nearest to you is broken. This means you may cross the lines to overtake if it is safe, provided you can complete the manoeuvre before reaching a solid white line on your side. White direction arrows on the road indicate that you need to get back onto your side of the road.

129. Double white lines where the line nearest you is solid. This means you **MUST NOT** cross or straddle it unless it is safe and you need to enter adjoining premises or a side road. You may cross the line if necessary, provided the road is clear, to pass a stationary vehicle, or overtake a pedal cycle, horse or road maintenance vehicle, if they are travelling at 10mph (16km/h) or less.

Laws RTA 1988 sect 36 & TSRGD Schedule 9 part 8

130. Areas of white diagonal stripes or chevrons painted on the road. These are to separate traffic lanes or to protect traffic turning right.

- If the area is bordered by a broken white line, you should not enter the area unless it is necessary and you can see that it is safe to do so.
- If the area is marked with chevrons and bordered by solid white lines you **MUST NOT** enter it except in an emergency.

Laws MT(E&W)R regs 5, 9, 10 & 16, MT(S)R regs 4, 8, 9 & 14, RTA 1988 sect 36 & TSRGD Schedule 9 part 8

131. Lane dividers. These are short, broken white lines which are used on wide carriageways to divide them into lanes. You should keep between them.

132. Reflective road studs may be used with white lines.
White studs mark the lanes or the middle of the road.

- Red studs mark the left edge of the road.
- Amber studs mark the central reservation of a dual carriageway or motorway.
- Green studs mark the edge of the main carriageway at lay-bys and slip roads.
- Green/yellow studs indicate temporary adjustments to lane layouts, e.g. where road works are taking place.

Rule 132: Reflective road studs mark the lanes
and edges of the carriageway

Multi-lane carriageways

Lane discipline

133. If you need to change lane, first use your mirrors and if necessary take a quick sideways glance to make sure you will not force another road user to change course or speed. When it is safe to do so, signal to indicate your intentions to other road users and when clear, move over.

134. You should follow the signs and road markings and get into the lane as directed. In congested road conditions do not change lanes unnecessarily. Merging in turn is recommended but only if safe and appropriate when vehicles are travelling at a very low speed, e.g. when approaching roadworks or a road traffic incident. It is not recommended at high speed.

Single carriageway

135. Where a single carriageway has three lanes and the road markings or signs do not give priority to traffic in either direction
- use the middle lane only for overtaking or turning right. Remember, you have no more right to use the middle lane than a driver coming from the opposite direction
- do not use the right-hand lane.

136. Where a single carriageway has four or more lanes, use only the lanes that signs or markings indicate.

Dual carriageways

A dual carriageway is a road which has a central reservation to separate the carriageways.

137. On a two-lane dual carriageway you should stay in the left-hand lane. Use the right-hand lane for overtaking or turning right. After overtaking, move back to the left-hand lane when it is safe to do so.

138. On a dual carriageway with three or more lanes, you may use the middle lanes or the right-hand lane to overtake but you should return to the middle lanes and then the left-hand lane when it is safe to do so.

139. Climbing and crawler lanes. These are provided on some hills. Use this lane if you are driving a slow-moving vehicle or if there are vehicles behind you wishing to overtake. Be aware of the signs and road markings which indicate the lane is about to end.

140. Cycle lanes and cycle tracks. Cycle lanes are shown by road markings and signs. You **MUST NOT** drive or park in a cycle lane marked by a solid white line during its times of operation. Do not drive or park in a cycle lane marked by a broken white line unless it is unavoidable. You **MUST NOT** park in any cycle lane whilst waiting restrictions apply.

You should give way to any cyclists in a cycle lane, including when they are approaching from behind you – do not cut across them when you are turning or when you are changing lane (see Rule H3). Be prepared to stop and wait for a safe gap in the flow of cyclists before crossing the cycle lane.

Cycle tracks are routes for cyclists that are physically protected or located away from motor traffic, other than where they cross side roads. Cycle tracks may be shared with pedestrians.

You should give way to cyclists approaching or using the cycle track when you are turning into or out of a junction (see Rule H3). Be prepared to stop and wait for a safe gap in the flow of cyclists before crossing the cycle track, which may be used by cyclists travelling in both directions.

Bear in mind that cyclists are not obliged to use cycle lanes or cycle tracks.
Law RTRA sects 5 & 8

141. Bus lanes. These are shown by road markings and signs that indicate which (if any) other vehicles are permitted to use the bus lane. Unless otherwise indicated, you should not drive in a bus lane during its period of operation. You may enter a bus lane to stop, to load or unload where this is not prohibited.

142. High-occupancy vehicle lanes and other designated vehicle lanes. Lanes may be restricted for use by particular types of vehicle; these restrictions may apply some or all of the time. The operating times and vehicle types will be indicated on the accompanying traffic signs. You **MUST NOT** drive in such lanes during their times of operation unless signs indicate that your vehicle is permitted (see Traffic signs).

Vehicles permitted to use designated lanes may or may not include cycles, buses, taxis, licensed private hire vehicles, motorcycles, heavy goods vehicles (HGVs) and high-occupancy vehicles (HOVs).
Where HOV lanes are in operation, they **MUST ONLY** be used by
• vehicles containing at least the minimum number of people indicated on the traffic signs
• any other vehicles, such as buses and motorcycles, as indicated on signs prior to the start of the lane, irrespective of the number of occupants.
Laws RTRA sects 5 & 8, & RTA 1988, sect 36

143. One-way streets. Traffic **MUST** travel in the direction indicated by signs. Buses and/or cycles may have a contraflow lane. Choose the correct lane for your exit as soon as you can. Do not change lanes suddenly. Unless road signs or markings indicate otherwise, you should use
- the left-hand lane when going left
- the right-hand lane when going right
- the most appropriate lane when going straight ahead. Remember – traffic could be passing on both sides.

Laws RTA 1988 sect 36 & RTRA sects 5 & 8

General advice

144. You **MUST NOT**
- drive dangerously
- drive without due care and attention
- drive without reasonable consideration for other road users.

Driving requires focus and attention at all times. Remember, you may be driving dangerously or travelling too fast even if you don't mean to.

Law RTA 1988 sects 2 & 3 as amended by RTA 1991

145. You **MUST NOT** drive on or over a pavement, footpath or bridleway except to gain lawful access to property, or in the case of an emergency.

Laws HA 1835 sect 72 & RTA 1988 sect 34

146. Adapt your driving to the appropriate type and condition of road you are on. In particular
- do not treat speed limits as a target. It is often not appropriate or safe to drive at the maximum speed limit
- take the road and traffic conditions into account. Be prepared for unexpected or difficult situations, for example, the road being blocked beyond a blind bend. Be prepared to adjust your speed as a precaution
- where there are junctions, be prepared for road users emerging
- in side roads and country lanes look out for unmarked junctions where nobody has priority
- be prepared to stop at traffic control systems, roadworks, pedestrian crossings or traffic lights as necessary
- try to anticipate what pedestrians and cyclists might do. If pedestrians, particularly children, are looking the other way, they may step out into the road without seeing you.

147. Be considerate. Be careful of and considerate towards all types of road users, especially those requiring extra care (see Rule 204).

- you **MUST NOT** throw anything out of a vehicle; for example, food or food packaging, cigarette ends, cans, paper or carrier bags. This can endanger other road users, particularly motorcyclists and cyclists
- try to be understanding if other road users cause problems; they may be inexperienced or not know the area well
- be patient; remember that anyone can make a mistake
- do not allow yourself to become agitated or involved if someone is behaving badly on the road. This will only make the situation worse. Pull over, calm down and, when you feel relaxed, continue your journey
- slow down and hold back if a road user pulls out into your path at a junction. Allow them to get clear. Do not over-react by driving too close behind to intimidate them.

Law EPA sect 87

148. Safe driving and riding needs concentration.
Avoid distractions when driving or riding such as
- loud music (this may mask other sounds)
- trying to read maps
- starting or adjusting any music or radio
- arguing with your passengers or other road users
- eating and drinking
- smoking.

You **MUST NOT** smoke in public transport vehicles or in vehicles used for work purposes in certain prescribed circumstances. Separate regulations apply to England, Wales and Scotland. In England and Wales, the driver **MUST NOT** smoke or allow anyone to smoke in an enclosed private vehicle carrying someone under 18, including motor caravans. In Scotland it is an offence for anyone aged 18 or over to smoke in a private motor vehicle (unless it is parked and being used as living accommodation) when there is someone under 18 in the vehicle and the vehicle is in a public place.

Laws TSf(EV) R, TSfP(W) R, TPSCP(S)R, S-f(PV)R, S-f(W)R & SP(CIMV)(S)A

Mobile phones and in-vehicle technology

149. You **MUST** exercise proper control of your vehicle at all times. You **MUST NOT** use a hand-held mobile phone, or similar device, capable of interactive communication (such as a tablet) for any purpose when driving or when supervising a learner driver. This ban covers all use of a hand-held interactive communication device and it applies even when the interactive communication capability is turned off or unavailable. You **MUST NOT** pick up the phone or similar device while driving to dial a number and then put it in the cradle for the duration of the conversation. You **MUST NOT** pick up and use your hand-held phone or similar device while stationary in traffic.

There is an exception to call 999 or 112 in a genuine emergency when it is unsafe or impractical to stop. There is also an exception if you are using a hand-held mobile phone or similar device to make a contactless payment at a contactless payment terminal. Your vehicle **MUST** be stationary, and the goods or services **MUST** be received at the same time as, or after, the contactless payment

Never use a hand-held microphone when driving. Using hands-free equipment is also likely to distract your attention from the road. It is far safer not to use any telephone or similar device while you are driving or riding – find a safe place to stop first or use the voicemail facility and listen to messages later.

You may park your vehicle using a handheld remote control app or device. The app or device **MUST** be legal, and you should not put other people in danger when you use it.

Laws RTA 1988 sects 2 & 3, & CUR regs 104 & 110

150. There is a danger of driver distraction being caused by in-vehicle systems such as satellite navigation systems, congestion warning systems, PCs, multi-media, etc. You **MUST** exercise proper control of your vehicle at all times. Do not rely on driver assistance systems such as motorway assist, lane departure warnings, or remote control parking. They are available to assist but you should not reduce your concentration levels. Do not be distracted by maps or screen-based information (such as navigation or vehicle management systems) while driving or riding. If necessary find a safe place to stop.

As the driver, you are still responsible for the vehicle if you use a driver assistance system (like motorway assist). This is also the case if you use a hand-held remote control parking app or device. You **MUST** have full control over these systems at all times.

Laws RTA 1988 sects 2 & 3 & CUR reg 104 & 110

151. In slow-moving traffic. You should
- reduce the distance between you and the vehicle ahead to maintain traffic flow
- never get so close to the vehicle in front that you cannot stop safely
- leave enough space to be able to manoeuvre if the vehicle in front breaks down or an emergency vehicle needs to get past
- not change lanes to the left to overtake
- allow access into and from side roads, as blocking these will add to congestion
- allow pedestrians and cyclists to cross in front of you
- be aware of cyclists and motorcyclists who may be passing on either side.

Rule 151: Do not block access to a side road

Driving in built-up areas

152. Residential streets. You should drive slowly and carefully on streets where there are likely to be pedestrians, cyclists and parked cars. In some areas a 20mph (32km/h) maximum speed limit may be in force. Look out for

- vehicles emerging from junctions or driveways
- vehicles moving off
- car doors opening
- pedestrians
- children running out from between parked cars
- cyclists and motorcyclists.

153. Traffic-calming measures. On some roads there are features such as road humps, chicanes and narrowings which are intended to slow you down. When you approach these features reduce your speed. Allow cyclists and motorcyclists room to pass through them. Maintain a reduced speed along the whole of the stretch of road within the calming measures. Give way to oncoming road users if directed to do so by signs. You should not overtake other moving road users while in these areas.

Rule 153: Chicanes may be used to slow traffic down

Country roads

154. Take extra care on country roads and reduce your speed at approaches to bends, which can be sharper than they appear, and at junctions and turnings, which may be partially hidden. Be prepared for pedestrians, horse riders, cyclists, slow-moving farm vehicles or mud on the road surface. Make sure you can stop within the distance you can see to be clear. You should also reduce your speed where country roads enter villages.

155. Single-track roads. These are only wide enough for one vehicle. They may have special passing places. If you see a vehicle coming towards you, or the driver behind wants to overtake, pull into a passing place on your left, or wait opposite a passing place on your right. Give way to vehicles coming uphill whenever you can. If necessary, reverse until you reach a passing place to let the other vehicle pass. Slow down when passing pedestrians, cyclists and horse riders.

156. Do not park in passing places.

Vehicles prohibited from using roads and pavements

157. Certain motorised vehicles do not meet the construction and technical requirements for road vehicles and are generally not intended, not suitable and not legal for road, pavement, footpath, cycle path or bridleway use. These include most types of miniature motorcycles, also called mini motos, and motorised scooters, also called go peds, which are powered by electric or internal combustion engines. These types of vehicle **MUST NOT** be used on roads, pavements, footpaths or bridleways.

Laws RTA 1988 sects 34, 41a, 42, 47, 63 & 66, HA 1835, sect 72, & R(S)A sect 129

158. Certain models of motorcycles, motor tricycles and quadricycles, also called quad bikes, are suitable only for off-road use and do not meet legal standards for use on roads. Vehicles that do not meet these standards **MUST NOT** be used on roads. They **MUST NOT** be used on pavements, footpaths, cycle paths or bridleways either. You **MUST** make sure that any motorcycle, motor tricycle, quadricycle or any other motor vehicle meets legal standards and is properly registered, taxed and insured before using it on the roads. Even when registered, taxed and insured for the road, vehicles **MUST NOT** be used on pavements.

Laws RTA 1988 sects 34, 41a, 42, 47, 63, 66 & 156, HA 1835 sect 72, R(S)A sect 129 & VERA sects 1, 29, 31A & 43A

USING THE ROAD
General rules

159. Before moving off you should
* use all mirrors to check the road is clear
* look round to check the blind spots (the areas you are unable to see in the mirrors)
* signal if necessary before moving out
* look round for a final check.

Move off only when it is safe to do so.

Rule 159: Check the blind spot before moving off

160. Once moving you should
* keep to the left, unless road signs or markings indicate otherwise. The exceptions are when you want to overtake, turn right or pass parked vehicles or pedestrians in the road
* keep well to the left on right-hand bends. This will improve your view of the road and help avoid the risk of colliding with traffic approaching from the opposite direction
* drive or ride with both hands on the wheel or handlebars where possible. This will help you to remain in full control of the vehicle at all times. You may use driver assistance systems while you are driving. Make sure you use any system according to the manufacturer's instructions.
* be aware of other road users, especially cycles and motorcycles who may be filtering through the traffic. These are more difficult to see than larger vehicles and their riders are particularly vulnerable. Give them plenty of room, especially if you are driving a long vehicle or towing a trailer. You should give way to cyclists when you are changing direction or lane – do not cut across them.
* select a lower gear before you reach a long downhill slope. This will help to control your speed
* when towing, remember the extra length will affect overtaking and manoeuvring. The extra weight will also affect the braking and acceleration.

161. Mirrors. All mirrors should be used effectively throughout your journey. You should

- use your mirrors frequently so that you always know what is behind and to each side of you
- use them in good time before you signal or change direction or speed
- be aware that mirrors do not cover all areas and there will be blind spots. You will need to look round and check.

Remember: Mirrors – Signal – Manoeuvre

Overtaking

162. Before overtaking you should make sure
- the road is sufficiently clear ahead
- road users are not beginning to overtake you
- there is a suitable gap in front of the road user you plan to overtake.

163. Overtake only when it is safe and legal to do so. You should
- not get too close to the vehicle you intend to overtake
- use your mirrors, signal when it is safe to do so, take a quick sideways glance if necessary into the blind spot area and then start to move out
- not assume that you can simply follow a vehicle ahead which is overtaking; there may only be enough room for one vehicle
- move quickly past the vehicle you are overtaking, once you have started to overtake. Allow plenty of room. Move back to the left as soon as you can but do not cut in
- take extra care at night and in poor visibility when it is harder to judge speed and distance
- give way to oncoming vehicles before passing parked vehicles or other obstructions on your side of the road
- only overtake on the left if the vehicle in front is signalling to turn right, and there is room to do so
- stay in your lane if traffic is moving slowly in queues. If the queue on your right is moving more slowly than you are, you may pass on the left. Cyclists may pass slower moving or stationary traffic on their right or left and should proceed with caution as the driver may not be able to see you. Be careful about doing so, particularly on the approach to junctions, and especially when deciding whether it is safe to pass lorries or other large vehicles.
- give motorcyclists, cyclists and horse riders and horse drawn vehicles at least as much room as you would when overtaking a car (see Rules 211 to 215). As a guide:
- leave at least 1.5 metres when overtaking cyclists at speeds of up to 30mph, and give them more space when overtaking at higher speeds
- pass horse riders and horse-drawn vehicles at speeds under 10 mph and allow at least 2 metres of space

- allow at least 2 metres of space and keep to a low speed when passing a pedestrian who is walking in the road (for example, where there is no pavement)
- take extra care and give more space when overtaking motorcyclists, cyclists, horse riders, horse drawn vehicles and pedestrians in bad weather (including high winds) and at night
- you should wait behind the motorcyclist, cyclist, horse rider, horse drawn vehicle or pedestrian and not overtake if it is unsafe or not possible to meet these clearances.

Remember: Mirrors – Signal – Manoeuvre

Rule 163: Give vulnerable road users at least as much space as you would a car

164. Large vehicles. Overtaking these is more difficult. You should
- drop back. This will increase your ability to see ahead and should allow the driver of the large vehicle to see you in their mirrors. Getting too close to large vehicles, including agricultural vehicles such as a tractor with a trailer or other fixed equipment, will obscure your view of the road ahead and there may be another slow-moving vehicle in front
- make sure that you have enough room to complete your overtaking manoeuvre before committing yourself. It takes longer to pass a large vehicle. If in doubt do not overtake
- not assume you can follow a vehicle ahead which is overtaking a long vehicle. If a problem develops, they may abort overtaking and pull back in.

Rule 164: Do not cut in too quickly

165. You **MUST NOT** overtake
- if you would have to cross or straddle double white lines with a solid line nearest to you (but see Rule 129)
- if you would have to enter an area designed to divide traffic, if it is surrounded by a solid white line
- the nearest vehicle to a pedestrian crossing, especially when it has stopped to let pedestrians cross
- if you would have to enter a lane reserved for buses, trams or cycles during its hours of operation
- after a 'No Overtaking' sign and until you pass a sign cancelling the restriction.

Laws RTA 1988 sect 36, TSRGD Schedule 1, Schedule 9 part 7, Schedule 14 part 1

166. DO NOT overtake if there is any doubt, or where you cannot see far enough ahead to be sure it is safe. For example, when you are approaching
- a corner or bend
- a hump bridge
- the brow of a hill.

167. DO NOT overtake where you might come into conflict with other road users. For example
approaching or at a road junction on either side of the road
- where the road narrows
- when approaching a school crossing patrol
- on the approach to crossing facilities
- where a vehicle ahead is slowing to stop for a pedestrian that is crossing from a pedestrian island (see Rule 165)
- between the kerb and a bus or tram when it is at a stop
- where traffic is queuing at junctions or road works
- when you would force another road user to swerve or slow down
- at a level crossing
- when a road user is indicating right, even if you believe the signal should have been cancelled. Do not take a risk; wait for the signal to be cancelled
- stay behind if you are following a cyclist approaching a roundabout or junction, and you intend to turn left. Do not cut across cyclists going ahead, including those using cycle lanes and cycle tracks (see Rule H3)
- stay behind if you are following a horse rider or horse drawn vehicle approaching a roundabout or junction, and you intend to turn left. Do not cut across a horse rider or horse drawn vehicle going ahead
- when a tram is standing at a kerbside tram stop and there is no clearly marked passing lane for other traffic.

168. Being overtaken. If a driver is trying to overtake you, maintain a steady course and speed, slowing down if necessary to let the vehicle pass. Never obstruct drivers who wish to pass. Speeding up or driving unpredictably while someone is overtaking you is dangerous. Drop back to maintain a two-second gap if someone overtakes and pulls into the gap in front of you.

169. Do not hold up a long queue of traffic, especially if you are driving a large or slow-moving vehicle. Check your mirrors frequently, and if necessary, pull in where it is safe and let traffic pass.

Road junctions

170. Take extra care at junctions. You should

- watch out for cyclists, motorcyclists and pedestrians including powered wheelchairs/mobility scooter users as they are not always easy to see. Be aware that they may not have seen or heard you if you are approaching from behind
- give way to pedestrians crossing or waiting to cross a road into which or from which you are turning. If they have started to cross they have priority, so give way (see Rule H2)
- remain behind cyclists, horse riders, horse drawn vehicles and motorcyclists at junctions even if they are waiting to turn and are positioned close to the kerb
- watch out for long vehicles which may be turning at a junction ahead; they may have to use the whole width of the road to make the turn (see Rule 221)
- watch out for horse riders who may take a different line on the road from that which you would expect
- not assume, when waiting at a junction, that a vehicle coming from the right and signalling left will actually turn. Wait and make sure
- look all around before emerging. Do not cross or join a road until there is a gap large enough for you to do so safely.

Rule 170: Give way to pedestrians who have started to cross

171. You **MUST** stop behind the line at a junction with a 'Stop' sign and a solid white line across the road. Wait for a safe gap in the traffic before you move off.
Laws RTA 1988 sect 36 & TSRGD Schedule 9 parts 7 and 8

172. The approach to a junction may have a 'Give Way' sign or a triangle marked on the road. You **MUST** give way to traffic on the main road when emerging from a junction with broken white lines across the road.

Laws RTA 1988 sect 36 & TSRGD Schedule 9 parts 7 and 8

173. Dual carriageways. When crossing or turning right, first assess whether the central reservation is deep enough to protect the full length of your vehicle.

- If it is, then you should treat each half of the carriageway as a separate road. Wait in the central reservation until there is a safe gap in the traffic on the second half of the road.
- If the central reservation is too shallow for the length of your vehicle, wait until you can cross both carriageways in one go.

Rule 173: Assess your vehicle's length and do not obstruct traffic

174. Box junctions. These have criss-cross yellow lines painted on the road (see Road markings). You **MUST NOT** enter the box until your exit road or lane is clear. However, you may enter the box and wait when you want to turn right, and are only stopped from doing so by oncoming traffic, or by other vehicles waiting to turn right. At signalled roundabouts you **MUST NOT** enter the box unless you can cross over it completely without stopping.

Law TSRGD Schedule 9 parts 7 and 8

Rule 174: Enter a box junction only if your exit road is clear

Junctions controlled by traffic lights

175. You **MUST** stop behind the white 'Stop' line across your side of the road unless the light is green. If the amber light appears you may go on only if you have already crossed the stop line or are so close to it that to stop might cause a collision.

Laws RTA 1988 sect 36 & TSRGD Schedule 14 parts 1 and 4

176. You **MUST NOT** move forward over the white line when the red light is showing. Only go forward when the traffic lights are green if there is room for you to clear the junction safely or you are taking up a position to turn right. If the traffic lights are not working, treat the situation as you would an unmarked junction and proceed with great care.

Laws RTA 1988 sect 36 & TSRGD Schedule 14 parts 1 and 4

177. Green filter arrow. This indicates a filter lane only. Do not enter that lane unless you want to go in the direction of the arrow. You may proceed in the direction of the green arrow when it, or the full green light shows. Give other traffic, especially cyclists, time and room to move into the correct lane.

178. Advanced stop lines. Some signal-controlled junctions have advanced stop lines to allow cyclists to be positioned ahead of other traffic. Motorists, including motorcyclists, **MUST** stop at the first white line reached if the lights are amber or red and should avoid blocking the way or encroaching on the marked area at other times, e.g. if the junction ahead is blocked. If your vehicle has proceeded over the first white line at the time that the signal goes red, you should stop as soon as possible and **MUST** stop at the second white line. Allow cyclists, including any moving or waiting alongside you, enough time and space to move off when the green signal shows.

Drivers of large vehicles should stop sufficiently far behind the first white line so that they can see the whole area where cyclists may be waiting, allowing for any blind spot in front of the vehicle.

Laws RTA 1988 sect 36 & TSRGD Schedule 14 part 1

Rule 178: Do not unnecessarily encroach on the cyclists' waiting area

Turning right

179. Well before you turn right you should
- use your mirrors to make sure you know the position and movement of traffic behind you
- give a right-turn signal
- take up a position just left of the middle of the road or in the space marked for traffic turning right
- leave room for other vehicles to pass on the left, if possible.

180. Wait until there is a safe gap between you and any oncoming vehicle. Watch out for cyclists, motorcyclists, pedestrians and other road users. Check your mirrors and blind spot again to make sure you are not being overtaken, then make the turn. Do not cut the corner. Take great care when turning into a main road; you will need to watch for traffic in both directions and wait for a safe gap.

Remember: Mirrors – Signal – Manoeuvre

Rule 180: Position your vehicle correctly to avoid obstructing traffic

181. When turning right at crossroads where an oncoming vehicle is also turning right, there is a choice of two methods
- turn right side to right side; keep the other vehicle on your right and turn behind it. This is generally the safer method as you have a clear view of any approaching traffic when completing your turn
- left side to left side, turning in front of each other. This can block your view of oncoming vehicles, so take extra care. Cyclists and motorcyclists in particular may be hidden from your view. Road layout, markings or how the other vehicle is positioned can determine which course should be taken.

Rule 181: Left – Turning right side to right side.
Right – Turning left side to left side.

Turning left

182. Use your mirrors and give a left-turn signal well before you turn left. Do not overtake just before you turn left and watch out for traffic coming up on your left before you make the turn, especially if driving a large vehicle. Cyclists, motorcyclists and other road users in particular may be hidden from your view.

Rule 182: Do not cut in on cyclists

183. When turning
- keep as close to the left as is safe and practicable
- give way to any vehicles using a bus lane, cycle lane, cycle track or tramway from either direction, including when they are passing slow moving or stationary vehicles on either side.

Roundabouts

184. On approaching a roundabout take notice and act on all the information available to you, including traffic signs, traffic lights and lane markings which direct you into the correct lane. You should

- use **Mirrors – Signal – Manoeuvre** at all stages
- decide as early as possible which exit you need to take
- give an appropriate signal (see Rule 186). Time your signals so as not to confuse other road users
- get into the correct lane
- adjust your speed and position to fit in with traffic conditions
- be aware of the speed and position of all the road users around you.

185. When reaching the roundabout you should

- give priority to traffic approaching from your right, unless directed otherwise by signs, road markings or traffic lights
- check whether road markings allow you to enter the roundabout without giving way. If so, proceed, but still look to the right before joining
- watch out for all other road users already on the roundabout; be aware they may not be signalling correctly or at all
- look forward before moving off to make sure traffic in front has moved off.

Rule 185: Follow the correct procedure at roundabouts

186. Signals and position. When taking the first exit to the left, unless signs or markings indicate otherwise

- signal left and approach in the left-hand lane
- keep to the left on the roundabout and continue signalling left to leave.

When taking an exit to the right or going full circle, unless signs or markings indicate otherwise

* signal right and approach in the right-hand lane
* keep to the right on the roundabout until you need to change lanes to exit the roundabout
* signal left after you have passed the exit before the one you want.

When taking any intermediate exit, unless signs or markings indicate otherwise

* select the appropriate lane on approach to the roundabout
* you should not normally need to signal on approach
* stay in this lane until you need to alter course to exit the roundabout
* signal left after you have passed the exit before the one you want.

When there are more than three lanes at the entrance to a roundabout, use the most appropriate lane on approach and through it.

You should give priority to cyclists on the roundabout. They will be travelling more slowly than motorised traffic. Give them plenty of room and do not attempt to overtake them within their lane. Allow them to move across your path as they travel around the roundabout.

Cyclists, horse riders and horse drawn vehicles may stay in the left-hand lane when they intend to continue across or around the roundabout and should signal right to show you they are not leaving the roundabout. Drivers should take extra care when entering a roundabout to ensure that they do not cut across cyclists, horse riders or horse drawn vehicles in the left-hand lane, who are continuing around the roundabout.

187. In all cases watch out for and give plenty of room to

* pedestrians who may be crossing the approach and exit roads
* traffic crossing in front of you on the roundabout, especially vehicles intending to leave by the next exit
* traffic which may be straddling lanes or positioned incorrectly
* motorcyclists
* long vehicles (including those towing trailers). These might have to take a different course or straddle lanes either approaching or on the roundabout because of their length. Watch out for their signals.

188. Mini-roundabouts. Approach these in the same way as normal roundabouts. All vehicles **MUST** pass round the central markings except large vehicles which are physically incapable of doing so. Remember, there is less space to manoeuvre and less time to signal. Avoid making U-turns at mini-roundabouts. Beware of others doing this.
Laws RTA 1988 sect 36 & TSRGD Schedule 9 parts 7 and 8

189. At double mini-roundabouts treat each roundabout separately and give way to traffic from the right.

190. Multiple roundabouts. At some complex junctions, there may be a series of mini-roundabouts at each intersection. Treat each mini-roundabout separately and follow the normal rules.

Rule 190: Treat each roundabout separately

Pedestrian crossings

191. You **MUST NOT** park on a crossing or in the area covered by the zig-zag lines. You **MUST NOT** overtake the moving vehicle nearest the crossing or the vehicle nearest the crossing which has stopped to give way to pedestrians.

Laws RTRA sect 25(5) & TSRGD Schedule 14 parts 1 and 5

192. In slow-moving and queuing traffic you should keep crossings completely clear, as blocking these makes it difficult and dangerous for pedestrians to cross. You should not enter a pedestrian crossing if you are unable to completely clear the crossing. Nor should you block advanced stop lines for cycles.

Rule 192: Keep the crossing clear

193. You should take extra care where the view of either side of the crossing is blocked by queuing traffic or incorrectly parked vehicles. Pedestrians may be crossing between stationary vehicles.

194. Allow pedestrians plenty of time to cross and do not harass them by revving your engine or edging forward.

195. Zebra and parallel crossings. As you approach a zebra crossing
- look out for pedestrians waiting to cross and be ready to slow down or stop to let them cross
- you should give way to pedestrians waiting to cross
- you **MUST** give way when a pedestrian has moved onto a crossing
- allow more time for stopping on wet or icy roads
- do not wave, flash your lights or use your horn to invite pedestrians across; this could be dangerous if another vehicle is approaching
- be patient, do not sound your horn or rev your engine as this can be intimidating
- be aware of pedestrians approaching from the side of the crossing.

A zebra crossing with a central island is two separate crossings (see Rules 19 and 20).

Parallel crossings are similar to zebra crossings, but include a cycle route alongside the black and white stripes.

As you approach a parallel crossing
- look out for pedestrians or cyclists waiting to cross and slow down or stop
- you should give way to pedestrians or cyclists waiting to cross
- you **MUST** give way when a pedestrian or cyclist has moved onto a crossing
- allow more time for stopping on wet or icy roads
- do not wave, flash your lights or use your horn to invite pedestrians or cyclists across; this could be dangerous if another vehicle is approaching
- be patient, do not sound your horn or rev your engine as this can be intimidating
- be aware of pedestrians or cyclists approaching from the side of the crossing.

A parallel crossing with a central island is two separate crossings (see Rules 19 and 20).
Law TSRGD Schedule 14 part 5

Signal-controlled crossings

196. Pelican crossings. These are signal-controlled crossings where flashing amber follows the red 'Stop' light. You **MUST** stop when the red light shows. When the amber light is flashing, you **MUST** give way to any pedestrians on the crossing. If the amber light is flashing and there are no pedestrians on the crossing, you may proceed with caution.

Laws TSRGD reg 14 & RTRA sect 25(5)

Rule 196: Allow pedestrians to cross when the amber light is flashing

197. Pelican crossings which go straight across the road are one crossing, even when there is a central island. You **MUST** wait for pedestrians who are crossing from the other side of the island.

Law TSRGD reg 14

198. Give way to anyone still crossing after the signal for vehicles has changed to green. This advice applies to all crossings.

199. Toucan, puffin and equestrian crossings. These are similar to pelican crossings, but there is no flashing amber phase; the light sequence for traffic at these three crossings is the same as at traffic lights. If the signal-controlled crossing is not working, proceed with extreme caution. Do not enter the crossing if you are unable to completely clear it, to avoid obstructing pedestrians, cyclists or horse riders.

Reversing

200. Choose an appropriate place to manoeuvre. If you need to turn your vehicle around, wait until you find a safe place. Try not to reverse or turn round in a busy road; find a quiet side road or drive round a block of side streets.

201. Do not reverse from a side road into a main road. When using a driveway, reverse in and drive out if you can.

202. Look carefully before you start reversing. You should
- use all your mirrors
- check the 'blind spot' behind you (the part of the road you cannot see easily in the mirrors)
- check there are no pedestrians (particularly children), cyclists, other road users or obstructions in the road behind you.

Reverse slowly while
- checking all around
- looking mainly through the rear window
- being aware that the front of your vehicle will swing out as you turn.

Get someone to guide you if you cannot see clearly.

Rule 202: Check all round when reversing

203. You **MUST NOT** reverse your vehicle further than necessary.
Law CUR reg 106

ROAD USERS REQUIRING EXTRA CARE

Overview

204. The road users most at risk from road traffic are pedestrians, in particular children, older adults and disabled people, cyclists, horse riders and motorcyclists. It is particularly important to be aware of children, older adults and disabled people, and learner and inexperienced drivers and riders. In any interaction between road users, those who can cause the greatest harm have the greatest responsibility to reduce the danger or threat they pose to others.

Pedestrians

205. There is a risk of pedestrians, especially children, stepping unexpectedly into the road. You should drive with the safety of children in mind at a speed suitable for the conditions.

206. Drive carefully and slowly when

- in crowded shopping streets, Home Zones and Quiet Lanes (see Rule 218) or residential areas
- driving past bus and tram stops; pedestrians may emerge suddenly into the road
- passing parked vehicles, especially ice cream vans; children are more interested in ice cream than traffic and may run into the road unexpectedly
- needing to cross a pavement, cycle lane or cycle track; for example, to reach or leave a driveway or private access. Give way to pedestrians on the pavement and cyclists using a cycle lane or cycle track
- reversing into a side road; look all around the vehicle and give way to any pedestrians who may be crossing the road
- turning at road junctions; you should give way to pedestrians who are crossing or waiting to cross the road into which or from which you are turning
- going through road works or when passing roadside rescue and recovery vehicles, as there may be people working in or at the side of the road
- the pavement is closed due to street repairs and pedestrians are directed to use the road
- approaching pedestrians on narrow rural roads without a footway or footpath. Always slow down and be prepared to stop if necessary, giving them plenty of room as you drive past
- approaching zebra and parallel crossings as you **MUST** give way to pedestrians and cyclists on the crossing (see Rule 195)
- approaching pedestrians who have started to cross the road ahead of you. They have priority when crossing at a junction or side road so you should give way (see Rule H2).

Law TSRGD Schedule 14 Part 5

Rule 206: Watch out for children in busy areas

207. Particularly vulnerable pedestrians. These include
- children and older pedestrians who may not be able to judge your speed and could step into the road in front of you. At 40mph (64km/h) your vehicle will probably kill any pedestrians it hits. At 20mph (32km/h) there is only a 1 in 20 chance of the pedestrian being killed. So kill your speed
- older pedestrians who may need more time to cross the road. Be patient and allow them to cross in their own time. Do not hurry them by revving your engine or edging forward
- people with disabilities. People with hearing impairments may not be aware of your vehicle approaching. Those with walking difficulties require more time
- blind or partially sighted people, who may be carrying a white cane or using a guide dog. They may not be able to see you approaching
- deafblind people who may be carrying a white cane with a red band or using a dog with a red and white harness. They may not see or hear instructions or signals.

208. Near schools. Drive slowly and be particularly aware of young cyclists and pedestrians. In some places, there may be a flashing amber signal below the 'School' warning sign which tells you that there may be children crossing the road ahead. Drive very slowly until you are clear of the area.

209. Drive carefully and slowly when passing a stationary bus showing a 'School Bus' sign (see Vehicle markings) as children may be getting on or off.

School bus (displayed in front and rear window of bus or coach)

210. You **MUST** stop when a school crossing patrol shows a 'Stop for children' sign (see sections 'Signals by authorised persons' and 'Traffic signs').
Law RTRA sect 28

Motorcyclists and cyclists

211. It is often difficult to see motorcyclists and cyclists, especially when they are waiting alongside you, coming up from behind, coming out of or moving off from junctions, at roundabouts, overtaking you or filtering through traffic. Always look out for them before you emerge from a junction; they could be approaching faster than you think.

Do not turn at a junction if to do so would cause the cyclist going straight ahead to stop or swerve, just as you would do with a motor vehicle.

When turning right across a line of slow-moving or stationary traffic, look out for and give way to cyclists or motorcyclists on the inside of the traffic you are crossing. Be especially careful when moving off, turning, and when changing direction or lane. Be sure to check mirrors and blind spots carefully.

Rule 211: Look out for motorcyclists and cyclists at junctions

212. Give motorcyclists, cyclists, horse riders, horse drawn vehicles and pedestrians walking in the road (for example, where there is no pavement), at least as much room as you would when overtaking a car (see Rules 162 to 167). Drivers should take extra care and give more space when overtaking motorcyclists, cyclists, horse riders, horse drawn vehicles and pedestrians in bad weather (including high winds) and at night. If the rider looks over their shoulder it could mean that they intend to pull out, turn right or change direction. Give them time and space to do so.

213. On narrow sections of road, on quiet roads or streets, at road junctions and in slower-moving traffic, cyclists may sometimes ride in the centre of the lane, rather than towards the side of the road. It can be safer for groups of cyclists to ride two abreast in these situations. Allow them to do so for their own safety, to ensure they can see and be seen. Cyclists are also advised to ride at least a door's width or 1 metre from parked cars for their own safety.

On narrow sections of road, horse riders may ride in the centre of the lane. Allow them to do so for their own safety to ensure they can see and be seen.

Motorcyclists, cyclists, horse riders and horse drawn vehicles may suddenly need to avoid uneven road surfaces and obstacles such as drain covers or oily, wet or icy patches on the road. Give them plenty of room and pay particular attention to any sudden change of direction they may have to make.

Other road users

214. Animals. When passing animals, drive slowly. Give them plenty of room and be ready to stop. Do not scare animals by sounding your horn, revving your engine or accelerating rapidly once you have passed them. Look out for animals being led, driven or ridden on the road and take extra care. Keep your speed down at bends and on narrow country roads. If a road is blocked by a herd of animals, stop and switch off your engine until they have left the road. Watch out for animals on unfenced roads.

215. Horse riders and horse-drawn vehicles. Be particularly careful of horse riders and horse-drawn vehicles especially when approaching, overtaking, passing or moving away. Always pass wide and slowly. When you see a horse on a road, you should slow down to a maximum of 10 mph. Be patient, do not sound your horn or rev your engine. When safe to do so, pass wide and slow, allowing at least 2 metres of space.

Feral or semi feral ponies found in areas such as the New Forest, Exmoor and Dartmoor require the same consideration as ridden horses when approaching or passing.

Horse riders are often children, so take extra care and remember riders may ride in double file when escorting a young or inexperienced horse or rider. Look out for horse riders' and horse drivers' signals and heed a request to slow down or stop. Take great care and treat all horses as a potential hazard; they can be unpredictable, despite the efforts of their rider/driver. Remember there are three brains at work when you pass a horse; the rider's, the driver's and the horse's. Do not forget horses are flight animals and can move incredibly quickly if startled.

216. Older drivers. Their reactions may be slower than other drivers. Make allowance for this.

217. Learners and inexperienced drivers. They may not be so skilful at anticipating and responding to events. Be particularly patient with learner drivers and young drivers. Drivers who have recently passed their test may display a 'new driver' plate or sticker (see Safety code for new drivers).

218. Home Zones and Quiet Lanes. These are places where people could be using the whole of the road for a range of activities such as children playing or for a community event. You should drive slowly and carefully and be prepared to stop to allow people extra time to make space for you to pass them in safety.

Other vehicles

219. Emergency and Incident Support vehicles. You should look and listen for ambulances, fire engines, police, doctors or other emergency vehicles using flashing blue, red or green lights and sirens or flashing headlights, or traffic officer and incident support vehicles using flashing amber lights. When one approaches do not panic. Consider the route of such a vehicle and take appropriate action to let it pass, while complying with all traffic signs. If necessary, pull to the side of the road and stop, but try to avoid stopping before the brow of a hill, a bend or narrow section of road. Do not endanger yourself, other road users or pedestrians and avoid mounting the kerb. Do not brake harshly on approach to a junction or roundabout, as a following vehicle may not have the same view as you.

220. Powered vehicles used by disabled people. These small vehicles travel at a maximum speed of 8mph (12km/h). On a dual carriageway where the speed limit exceeds 50mph (80km/h) they **MUST** have a flashing amber beacon, but on other roads you may not have that advance warning (see Rules 36 to 46 inclusive).
Law RVLR reg 17(1) & 26

221. Large vehicles. These may need extra road space to turn or to deal with a hazard that you are not able to see. If you are following a large vehicle, such as a bus or articulated lorry, be aware that the driver may not be able to see you in the mirrors. Be prepared to stop and wait if it needs room or time to turn.

Rule 221: Large vehicles need extra room

222. Large vehicles can block your view. Your ability to see and to plan ahead will be improved if you pull back to increase your separation distance. Be patient, as larger vehicles are subject to lower speed limits than cars and motorcycles. Many large vehicles may be fitted with speed limiting devices which will restrict speed to 56mph (90km/h) even on a motorway.

223. Buses, coaches and trams. Give priority to these vehicles when you can do so safely, especially when they signal to pull away from stops. Look out for people getting off a bus or tram and crossing the road.

224. Electric vehicles. Be careful of electric vehicles such as milk floats and trams. Trams move quickly but silently and cannot steer to avoid you.

225. Vehicles with flashing amber beacons. These warn of a slow-moving or stationary vehicle (such as a traffic officer vehicle, salt spreader, snow plough or recovery vehicle) or abnormal loads, so approach with caution. On unrestricted dual carriageways, motor vehicles first used on or after 1 January 1947 with a maximum speed of 25mph (40km/h) or less (such as tractors) **MUST** use a flashing amber beacon (also see Rule 220).

Law RVLR, reg 17

DRIVING IN ADVERSE WEATHER CONDITIONS

Overview

226. You **MUST** use headlights when visibility is seriously reduced, generally when you cannot see for more than 100 metres (328 feet). You may also use front or rear fog lights but you **MUST** switch them off when visibility improves (see Rule 236).

Law RVLR regs 25 & 27

Wet weather

227. Wet weather. In wet weather, stopping distances will be at least double those required for stopping on dry roads (see Typical stopping distances). This is because your tyres have less grip on the road. In wet weather

- you should keep well back from the vehicle in front. This will increase your ability to see and plan ahead
- if the steering becomes unresponsive, it probably means that water is preventing the tyres from gripping the road. Ease off the accelerator and slow down gradually
- the rain and spray from vehicles may make it difficult to see and be seen
- be aware of the dangers of spilt diesel that will make the surface very slippery (see Annex 6: Vehicle maintenance, safety and security).
- take extra care around pedestrians, cyclists, motorcyclists and horse riders.

Icy and snowy weather

228. In winter check the local weather forecast for warnings of icy or snowy weather. **DO NOT** drive in these conditions unless your journey is essential. If it is, take great care and allow more time for your journey. Take an emergency kit of de-icer and ice scraper, torch, warm clothing and boots, first aid kit, jump leads and a shovel, together with a warm drink and emergency food in case you get stuck or your vehicle breaks down.

229. Before you set off

- you **MUST** be able to see, so clear all snow and ice from all your windows
- you **MUST** ensure that lights are clean and number plates are clearly visible and legible
- make sure the mirrors are clear and the windows are demisted thoroughly
- remove all snow that might fall off into the path of other road users
- check your planned route is clear of delays and that no further snowfalls or severe weather are predicted.

Laws CUR reg 30, RVLR reg 23, VERA sect 43 & RV(DRM)R reg 11

Rule 229: Make sure your windscreen is completely clear

230. When driving in icy or snowy weather
- drive with care, even if the roads have been treated
- keep well back from the road user in front as stopping distances can be ten times greater than on dry roads
- take care when overtaking vehicles spreading salt or other de-icer, particularly if you are riding a motorcycle or cycle
- watch out for snowploughs which may throw out snow on either side. Do not overtake them unless the lane you intend to use has been cleared
- be prepared for the road conditions to change over relatively short distances
- listen to travel bulletins and take note of variable message signs that may provide information about weather, road and traffic conditions ahead.

231. Drive extremely carefully when the roads are icy. Avoid sudden actions as these could cause loss of control. You should
- drive at a slow speed in as high a gear as possible; accelerate and brake very gently
- drive particularly slowly on bends where loss of control is more likely. Brake progressively on the straight before you reach a bend. Having slowed down, steer smoothly round the bend, avoiding sudden actions
- check your grip on the road surface when there is snow or ice by choosing a safe place to brake gently. If the steering feels unresponsive this may indicate ice and your vehicle losing its grip on the road. When travelling on ice, tyres make virtually no noise.

Windy weather

232. High-sided vehicles are most affected by windy weather, but strong gusts can also blow a car, cyclist, motorcyclist or horse rider off course. This can happen on open stretches of road exposed to strong crosswinds, or when passing bridges or gaps in hedges.

233. In very windy weather your vehicle may be affected by turbulence created by large vehicles. Motorcyclists are particularly affected, so keep well back from them when they are overtaking a high-sided vehicle.

Fog

234. Before entering fog check your mirrors then slow down.

If 'Fog' is shown on a sign but the road is clear, be prepared for a bank of fog or drifting patchy fog ahead. Even if it seems to be clearing, you can suddenly find yourself in thick fog.

235. When driving in fog you should
- use your lights as required (see Rule 226)
- keep a safe distance behind the vehicle in front. Rear lights can give a false sense of security
- be able to pull up well within the distance you can see clearly. This is particularly important on motorways and dual carriageways, as vehicles are travelling faster
- use your windscreen wipers and demisters
- beware of other drivers not using headlights
- not accelerate to get away from a vehicle which is too close behind you
- check your mirrors before you slow down. Then use your brakes so that your brake lights warn drivers behind you that you are slowing down
- stop in the correct position at a junction with limited visibility and listen for traffic. When you are sure it is safe to emerge, do so positively and do not hesitate in a position that puts you directly in the path of approaching vehicles.

236. You **MUST NOT** use front or rear fog lights unless visibility is seriously reduced (see Rule 226) as they dazzle other road users and can obscure your brake lights. You **MUST** switch them off when visibility improves.
Law RVLR regs 25 & 27

Hot weather

237. Keep your vehicle well ventilated to avoid drowsiness. Be aware that the road surface may become soft or if it rains after a dry spell it may become slippery. These conditions could affect your steering and braking. If you are dazzled by bright sunlight, slow down and if necessary, stop.

WAITING AND PARKING

Waiting and parking

238. You **MUST NOT** wait or park on yellow lines during the times of operation shown on nearby time plates (or zone entry signs if in a Controlled Parking Zone) – see 'Traffic signs' and 'Road markings'. Double yellow lines indicate a prohibition of waiting at any time even if there are no upright signs. You **MUST NOT** wait or park, or stop to set down and pick up passengers, on school entrance markings (see Road markings) when upright signs indicate a prohibition of stopping.

Law RTRA sects 5 & 8

Parking

239. Use off-street parking areas, or bays marked out with white lines on the road as parking places, wherever possible. If you have to stop on the roadside:

- do not park facing against the traffic flow
- stop as close as you can to the side
- do not stop too close to a vehicle displaying a Blue Badge: remember, the occupant may need more room to get in or out
- you **MUST** switch off the engine, headlights and fog lights
- you **MUST** apply the handbrake before leaving the vehicle
- you **MUST** ensure you do not hit anyone when you open your door. Check for cyclists or other traffic by looking all around and using your mirrors
- where you are able to do so, you should open the door using your hand on the opposite side to the door you are opening; for example, use your left hand to open a door on your right-hand side. This will make you turn your head to look over your shoulder. You are then more likely to avoid causing injury to cyclists or motorcyclists passing you on the road, or to people on the pavement
- it is safer for your passengers (especially children) to get out of the vehicle on the side next to the kerb
- put all valuables out of sight and make sure your vehicle is secure
- lock your vehicle.

Before using a hand-held device to help you to park, you **MUST** make sure it is safe to do so. Then, you should move the vehicle into the parking space in the safest way, and by the shortest route possible.

When you use a hand-held device to help you to park, you **MUST** remain in control of the vehicle at all times. Do not use the hand-held device for anything else while you are using it to help you park, and do not put anyone in danger. Use the hand-held device according to the manufacturer's instructions.

When using an electric vehicle charge point, you should park close to the charge point and avoid creating a trip hazard for pedestrians from trailing cables. Display a warning sign if you can. After using the charge point, you should return charging cables and connectors neatly to minimise the danger to pedestrians and avoid creating an obstacle for other road users.

Laws CUR regs 98, 105, 107 & 110, RVLR reg 27 & RTA 1988 sect 42

Rule 239: Check before opening your door

240. You **MUST NOT** stop or park on
- the carriageway, an emergency area or a hard shoulder of a motorway except in an emergency (see Rules 270 and 271)
- a pedestrian crossing, including the area marked by the zig-zag lines (see Rule 191)
- a clearway (see Traffic signs)
- taxi bays as indicated by upright signs and markings
- an urban clearway within its hours of operation, except to pick up or set down passengers (see Traffic signs)
- a road marked with double white lines, even when a broken white line is on your side of the road, except to pick up or set down passengers, or to load or unload goods
- a tram or cycle lane during its period of operation
- a cycle track
- red lines, in the case of specially designated 'red routes', unless otherwise indicated by signs. Any vehicle may enter a bus lane to stop, load or unload where this is not prohibited (see Rule 141).

Laws MT(E&W)R regs 7 & 9 as amended by MT(E&W)(A)(E)R, MT(S)R regs 6 & 8, RTRA sects 5, 6 & 8, TSRGD Schedule 7 parts 2,3,4,5 and 7, Schedule 9 part 6, Schedule 14 parts 1 and 5

241. You **MUST NOT** park in parking spaces reserved for specific users, such as Blue Badge holders, residents or motorcycles, unless entitled to do so.

Laws CSDPA sect 21 & RTRA sects 5 & 8

242. You **MUST NOT** leave your vehicle or trailer in a dangerous position or where it causes any unnecessary obstruction of the road.

Laws RTA 1988 sect 22 & CUR reg 103

243. DO NOT stop or park
- near a school entrance
- anywhere you would prevent access for Emergency Services
- at or near a bus or tram stop or taxi rank
- on the approach to a level crossing/tramway crossing
- opposite or within 10 metres (32 feet) of a junction, except in an authorised parking space
- near the brow of a hill or hump bridge
- opposite a traffic island or (if this would cause an obstruction) another parked vehicle
- where you would force other traffic to enter a tram lane
- where the kerb has been lowered to help wheelchair users and powered mobility vehicles
- in front of an entrance to a property
- on a bend
- where you would obstruct cyclists' use of cycle facilities **except** when forced to do so by stationary traffic.

244. You **MUST NOT** park partially or wholly on the pavement in London, and should not do so elsewhere unless signs permit it. Parking on the pavement can obstruct and seriously inconvenience pedestrians, people in wheelchairs or with visual impairments and people with prams or pushchairs.

Law GL(GP)A sect 15

245. Controlled Parking Zones. The zone entry signs indicate the times when the waiting restrictions within the zone are in force. Parking may be allowed in some places at other times. Otherwise parking will be within separately signed and marked bays.

246. Goods vehicles. Vehicles with a maximum laden weight of over 7.5 tonnes (including any trailer) **MUST NOT** be parked on a verge, pavement or any land situated between carriageways, without police permission. The only exception is when parking is essential for loading and unloading, in which case the vehicle **MUST NOT** be left unattended.

Law RTA 1988 sect 19

247. Loading and unloading. Do not load or unload where there are yellow markings on the kerb and upright signs advise restrictions are in place (see Road markings). This may be permitted where parking is otherwise restricted. On red routes, specially marked and signed bays indicate where and when loading and unloading is permitted.

Law RTRA sects 5 & 8

Parking at night

248. You **MUST NOT** park on a road at night facing against the direction of the traffic flow unless in a recognised parking space.

Laws CUR reg 101 & RVLR reg 24

249. All vehicles **MUST** display parking lights when parked on a road or a lay-by on a road with a speed limit greater than 30mph (48km/h).

Law RVLR reg 24

250. Cars, goods vehicles not exceeding 2500kg laden weight, invalid carriages, motorcycles and pedal cycles may be parked without lights on a road (or lay-by) with a speed limit of 30mph (48km/h) or less if they are

• at least 10 metres (32 feet) away from any junction, close to the kerb and facing in the direction of the traffic flow
• in a recognised parking place or lay-by.

Other vehicles and trailers, and all vehicles with projecting loads, **MUST NOT** be left on a road at night without lights.

Laws RVLR reg 24 & CUR reg 82(7)

251. Parking in fog. It is especially dangerous to park on the road in fog. If it is unavoidable, leave your parking lights or sidelights on.

252. Parking on hills. If you park on a hill you should
- park close to the kerb and apply the handbrake firmly
- select a forward gear and turn your steering wheel away from the kerb when facing uphill
- select reverse gear and turn your steering wheel towards the kerb when facing downhill
- use 'park' if your car has an automatic gearbox.

Rule 252: Turn your wheels away from the kerb when parking facing uphill.
Turn your wheels towards the kerb when parking downhill

Decriminalised Parking Enforcement (DPE)

DPE is becoming increasingly common as more authorities take on this role. The local traffic authority assumes responsibility for enforcing many parking contraventions in place of the police. Further details on DPE may be found at the following websites:

www.trafficpenaltytribunal.gov.uk (outside London)
www.londontribunals.gov.uk (inside London)

MOTORWAYS

General

A number of the rules for motorways also apply to other high-speed roads. Many other Rules apply to motorway driving, either wholly or in part: Rules 46, 57, 83 to 126, 130 to 134, 139, 144, 146 to 151, 160, 161, 219, 221 to 222, 225, 226 to 237, 274 to 278, 280 and 281 to 290.

253. Prohibited vehicles. Motorways **MUST NOT** be used by pedestrians, holders of provisional motorcycle licences, riders of motorcycles under 50 cc (4 kW), cyclists, horse riders, certain slow-moving vehicles and those carrying oversized loads (except by special permission), agricultural vehicles, and powered wheelchairs/powered mobility scooters (see Rules 36 to 46 inclusive).

Provisional car licence holders **MUST NOT** drive on the motorway unless they are accompanied by a DVSA Approved Driving Instructor (ADI) and are driving a car displaying red L plates (or D plates in Wales) with dual controls.

Laws HA 1980 sects 16, 17 & sched 4, MT(E&W)R regs 3(d), 4 & 11 as amended by MT(E&W)(A)R 2004 & MT(E&W)(A)R 2018, R(S)A sects 7, 8 & sched 3, RTRA sect 17 & MT(S)R reg 10 as amended by MT(S)(A)R 2018

254. Traffic on motorways usually travels faster than on other roads, so you have less time to react. It is especially important to use your mirrors earlier and look much further ahead than you would on other roads.

Motorway signals

255. Signs and signals (see 'Light signals controlling traffic') are used to warn you of hazards ahead. For example, there may be an incident, fog, a spillage or road workers on the carriageway which you may not immediately be able to see.

256. A single sign or signal can display advice, restrictions and warnings for all lanes.

Lane specific signs and signals can display advice, restrictions and warnings that apply to individual lanes.

257. Amber flashing lights. These signals warn of a hazard ahead. You should
- reduce your speed
- be prepared for the hazard
- only increase your speed when you pass a signal that is not flashing, or a sign displaying a national speed limit or the word 'END', and you are sure it is safe to do so.

Rule 257: Signal warning of a hazard

258. Red flashing light signals and a red 'X' on a sign identify a closed lane in which people, stopped vehicles or other hazards are present. You

- **MUST** follow the instructions on signs in advance of a closed lane to move safely to an open lane
- **MUST NOT** drive in a closed lane. A sign will inform you when the lane is no longer closed by displaying a speed limit or the word 'END'.

Rule 258: signals and signs indicating lane closures

Rule 258: signals and signs indicating lane closures

Be aware that
- there can be several hazards in a closed lane
- emergency services and traffic authorities use closed lanes to reach incidents and help people in need
- where the left lane is closed at an exit slip road, this means that the exit cannot be used.

Where **red flashing light** signals and closure of all lanes are shown on a sign, the road is closed. You

MUST NOT go beyond the sign in any lane or use the hard shoulder to avoid the road closure unless directed to do so by a police or traffic officer.

Rule 258: signals and signs indicating lane closures

Lane and road closures indicated by red flashing lights are enforced by the police.

Laws RTA 1988 sects 35 & 36 as amended by TMA sect 6, TSRGD reg 3 and sched 15, MT(E&W)R reg 9 & MT(S)R reg 8.

Joining the motorway

259. When you join the motorway you will normally approach it from a road on the left (a slip road) or from an adjoining motorway. You should
- give priority to traffic already on the motorway
- check the traffic on the motorway and match your speed to fit safely into the traffic flow in the left-hand lane
- not cross solid white lines that separate lanes or use the hard shoulder
- stay on the slip road if it continues as an extra lane on the motorway
- remain in the left-hand lane long enough to adjust to the speed of traffic before considering overtaking.

On the motorway

260. When you can see well ahead and the road conditions are good, you should
- drive at a steady cruising speed which you and your vehicle can handle safely and is within the speed limit (see Rule 124 and the Speed Limits table)
- keep a safe distance from the vehicle in front and increase the gap on wet or icy roads, or in fog (see Rules 126 and 235).

261. You **MUST NOT** exceed
- a speed limit displayed within a red circle on a sign
- the maximum speed limit for the road and for your vehicle (see Rule 124).

Speed limits are enforced by the police (see Rule 124).
Law RTRA sects 17, 86, 89 & sched 6

262. The monotony of driving on motorways and other high-speed roads can make you feel sleepy. To minimise the risk, follow the advice in Rule 91 about ensuring you are fit to drive and taking breaks.

Service areas are located along motorways to allow you to take breaks and to obtain refreshments. Refreshment and rest facilities on the local road network may also be accessible from motorway exits.

263. Unless directed to do so by a police or traffic officer, you **MUST NOT**
- reverse along any part of a motorway, including slip roads, hard shoulders and emergency areas
- cross the central reservation
- drive against the traffic flow.

If you have missed your exit, or have taken the wrong route, carry on to the next exit.
Laws RTA 1988 sect 35 as amended by TMA sect 6, MT(E&W)R regs 6, 8 & 10, & MT(S)R regs 4, 5, 7 & 9

Lane discipline

264. Keep in the left lane unless overtaking.
- If you are overtaking, you should return to the left lane when it is safe to do so (see also Rules 267 and 268).
- Be aware of emergency services, traffic officers, recovery workers and other people or vehicles stopped on the hard shoulder or in an emergency area. If you are driving in the left lane, and it is safe to do so, you should move into the adjacent lane to create more space between your vehicle and the people and stopped vehicles.

65. The right-hand lane of a motorway with three or more lanes **MUST NOT** be used (except in prescribed circumstances) if you are driving

- any vehicle drawing a trailer
- a goods vehicle with a maximum laden weight exceeding 3.5 tonnes but not exceeding 7.5 tonnes, which is required to be fitted with a speed limiter
- a goods vehicle with a maximum laden weight exceeding 7.5 tonnes
- a passenger vehicle with a maximum laden weight exceeding 7.5 tonnes constructed or adapted to carry more than eight seated passengers in addition to the driver
- a passenger vehicle with a maximum laden weight not exceeding 7.5 tonnes which is constructed or adapted to carry more than eight seated passengers in addition to the driver, which is required to be fitted with a speed limiter.

Laws MT(E&W)R reg 12, MT(E&W)(A)R, MT(S)R reg 11 & MT(S)(A)R

266. Approaching a junction. Look well ahead for signals, signs and road markings. Direction signs may be placed over the road. If you need to, you should change lanes well ahead of a junction. At some junctions, a lane may lead directly off the road. Only get in that lane if you wish to go in the direction indicated by signs or road markings.

Overtaking

267. Do not overtake unless you are sure it is safe and legal to do so. Overtake only on the right. You should

- check your mirrors
- take time to judge the speeds correctly
- make sure that the lane you will be joining is sufficiently clear ahead and behind
- take a quick sideways glance into the blind spot area to verify the position of a vehicle that may have disappeared from your view in the mirror
- remember that traffic may be coming up behind you very quickly. Check all your mirrors carefully. Look out for motorcyclists. When it is safe to do so, signal in plenty of time, then move out
- ensure you do not cut in on the vehicle you have overtaken
- be especially careful at night and in poor visibility when it is harder to judge speed and distance.

268. Do not overtake on the left or move to a lane on your left to overtake. In congested conditions, where adjacent lanes of traffic are moving at similar speeds, traffic in left-hand lanes may sometimes be moving faster than traffic to the right. In these conditions you may keep up with the traffic in your lane even if this means passing traffic in the lane to your right. Do not weave in and out of lanes to overtake.

269. Hard shoulder. (where present). You **MUST NOT** use a hard shoulder except in an emergency or if directed to do so by the police, traffic officers or a traffic sign.

Hard shoulder (where used as an extra lane). The hard shoulder is used as an extra lane on some motorways during periods of congestion. A red 'X' or blank sign above the hard shoulder means that you **MUST NOT** use the hard shoulder except in an emergency.

You can only use the hard shoulder as an extra lane when a speed limit is shown above the hard shoulder.

Where the hard shoulder is being used as an extra lane, emergency areas are provided for use in an emergency (see Rule 270).

Laws MT(E&W)R regs 5 & 9, MT(S)R regs 4 & 8, & RTA 1988 sects 35 & 36 as amended by TMA sect 6

Stopping

270. Emergency areas are located along motorways with no hard shoulder or where the hard shoulder can be used as an extra lane (see Rule 269) and **MUST** only be used in an emergency.

They are marked by blue signs with an orange SOS telephone symbol and may have orange surfacing.

Rule 270: emergency area

Rule 270: sign indicating distance to next emergency area

Follow the requirements and advice in
- Rule 277 if your vehicle develops a problem on the motorway
- Rule 278 to rejoin the carriageway from an emergency area.

Laws MT(E&W)R reg 9 as amended by MT(E&W)(A)(E)R, & MT(S)R reg 8

271. You **MUST NOT** stop on any carriageway, emergency area, hard shoulder, slip road, central reservation or verge except in an emergency, or when told to do so by the police, traffic officers, an emergency sign or by red flashing light signals.

Do not stop on any part of a motorway to make or receive mobile telephone calls, except in an emergency.

Laws MT(E&W)R regs 7, 9, 10 & 16 as amended by MT(E&W)(A)(E)R, MT(S)R regs 6(1), 8, 9 & 14, PRA sect 41 & sched 5(8), RTA 1988 sects 35, 36 & 163 as amended by TMA sect 6, & CUR reg 110 as amended by CUR(A)(No4)R

272. You **MUST NOT** pick up or set down anyone, or walk on a motorway, except in an emergency.

Laws RTRA sect 17 & MT(E&W)R reg 15

Leaving the motorway

273. Unless signs indicate that a lane leads directly off the motorway, you will normally leave the motorway by a slip road on your left. You should
- watch for the signs letting you know you are getting near your exit
- move into the left-hand lane well before reaching your exit
- signal left in good time and reduce your speed on the slip road as necessary.

274. On leaving the motorway or using a link road between motorways, your speed may be higher than you realise – 50mph (80km/h) may feel like 30mph (48km/h). Check your speedometer and adjust your speed accordingly. Some slip-roads and link roads have sharp bends, so you will need to slow down.

BREAKDOWNS AND INCIDENTS

Place of relative safety

275. If you need to stop your vehicle in the event of a breakdown or incident, try to stop in a place of relative safety. A place of relative safety is where you, your passengers and your vehicle are less likely to be at risk from moving traffic.

The safest place to stop is a location which is designed for parking. On motorways and other high-speed roads, the safest place to stop is a service area. Other places of relative safety include

- lay-bys
- emergency areas (see Rule 270)
- hard shoulders (see Rule 269).

Be aware that hard shoulders provide less protection than other places of relative safety because they are so close to high-speed traffic.

You and your passengers should, where possible, keep well away from your vehicle and moving traffic. Otherwise moving traffic could collide with your vehicle, forcing it into you and your passengers.

Breakdowns

276. If your vehicle breaks down, think first of all other road users and

- get your vehicle off the road if possible
- warn other traffic by using your hazard warning lights if your vehicle is causing an obstruction
- help other road users see you by wearing light-coloured or fluorescent clothing in daylight and reflective clothing at night or in poor visibility
- put a warning triangle on the road at least 45 metres (147 feet) behind your broken-down vehicle on the same side of the road, or use other permitted warning devices if you have them. Always take great care when placing or retrieving them, but never use them on motorways
- if possible, keep your sidelights on if it is dark or visibility is poor
- do not stand (or let anybody else stand) between your vehicle and oncoming traffic
- at night or in poor visibility do not stand where you will prevent other road users seeing your lights.

Additional rules for the motorway

277. If your vehicle develops a problem, leave the carriageway at the next exit or pull into a service area if possible (see Rule 275 for places of relative safety). If you cannot, you should

Go left

- move into the left lane
- pull into an emergency area or onto a hard shoulder if you can
- stop as far to the left as possible, leaving space to exit your vehicle and with your wheels turned to the left
- if you can, stop just beyond an emergency telephone
- switch your hazard warning lights on
- if it's dark or visibility is poor, use sidelights.

Get safe

- exit your vehicle by the side furthest from traffic, if it is safe and possible to do so, and ensure passengers do the same

If you can't
- get your vehicle to the left lane or a place of relative safety (see Rule 275), and
- exit your vehicle safely to get well away from it and moving traffic,

you should
- stay in your vehicle
- keep your seatbelts and hazard warning lights on
- call 999 immediately and ask for the police. Alternatively, press your SOS button if your vehicle has one and ask for the police.

- put on high-visibility clothing if you have it and it is within easy reach
- get behind a safety barrier where there is one, but be aware of any unseen hazards such as sudden drops, uneven ground or debris
- **DO NOT** stand in a place where your vehicle could be forced into you if moving traffic collides with it
- **DO NOT** return to your vehicle even if it's raining, cold or dark
- remain alert and aware of vehicles or debris coming towards you
- keep passengers away from the carriageway and children under control
- **DO NOT** attempt repairs on your vehicle
- **DO NOT** place a warning triangle on the carriageway
- animals **MUST** be kept in the vehicle or, in an emergency, under control on the verge.

Rule 277: Keep well away from your vehicle and moving traffic

Get help

- use the free emergency telephone to obtain advice and assistance
- contact a breakdown recovery service
- always face the traffic when you speak to remain aware of vehicles or debris coming towards you
- inform them if you are a vulnerable motorist such as disabled, older or travelling alone
- wait well away from your vehicle and moving traffic, behind the safety barrier where there is one
- if you are unable to exit your vehicle or if you have not stopped near a free emergency telephone, call 999 immediately and ask for the police. Alternatively, press your SOS button if your vehicle has one and ask for the police.

Communicating your location. How to identify your location to the emergency services.

eCall. Press the SOS button if your vehicle has one.

App. Use a mobile telephone mapping application.

Marker post or driver location sign. Quote the numbers and letters on marker posts or driver location signs which are located along the edge of the road.

Laws MT(E&W)R reg 14 & MT(S)R reg 12

278. To rejoin the carriageway after a breakdown from
- a hard shoulder, build up speed, indicate and watch for a safe gap in the traffic. Be aware that vehicles, obstructions or debris may be present on the hard shoulder
- an emergency area, you **MUST** use the emergency telephone provided and follow the operator's advice for exiting the emergency area. A lane may need to be closed so that you can rejoin the carriageway safely.

Rule 278: Emergency area information sign

Law RTA 1988 sect 36

279. Disabled drivers. If you have a disability that prevents you from following the above advice in Rules 277 and 278, you should

- switch on your hazard warning lights
- stay in your vehicle and keep your seat belt on
- call 999 immediately and ask for the police. Alternatively, press your SOS button if your vehicle has one and ask for the police.

If you are deaf, hard of hearing or speech impaired, it is recommended that you register for the 999 text service (emergencySMS.net) before making a journey.

Obstructions

280. If anything falls from a vehicle on to a motorway or other high-speed road, **DO NOT** remove the obstruction yourself. Stop in a place of relative safety (see Rule 275) and call the emergency services on 999.

On other roads, you should only remove obstructions if it is safe to do so.

Incidents

281. Warning signs or flashing lights. If you see emergency or incident support vehicles displaying flashing lights in the distance, be aware there may be an incident ahead (see Rule 219). You should slow down and be prepared to move safely into another lane or stop.

The emergency services, traffic officers and recovery workers may be required to work in the carriageway; for example, dealing with debris, collisions or conducting rolling roadblocks. You **MUST** follow any directions given by police or traffic officers as to whether you can safely pass the incident or obstruction.

Laws RTA 1988 sects 35 & 163 as amended by TMA sect 6

282. When passing the scene of an incident, remain alert for hazards (such as debris or slow-moving vehicles) and do not slow down unnecessarily (for example, if an incident is on the other side of a dual carriageway). You should focus on the road ahead when passing an incident because a lack of attention may cause a further incident, collision or congestion (see also Rule 283, below).

283. If you are involved in an incident or collision or stop to give assistance

- if possible, stop in a place of relative safety (see Rule 275)
- use your hazard warning lights to warn other traffic
- put on high-visibility clothing if you have it
- ask drivers to switch off their engines
- ask drivers and passengers to stop smoking
- contact the emergency services on 999 and provide full details of the incident location and any casualties. Use an emergency telephone, a mobile telephone, or press the SOS button if your vehicle has one (see Rule 277 on how to identify your location on a motorway or other high-speed road)
- move uninjured people away from the vehicles to a place of relative safety (see Rule 275)
- **DO NOT** move injured people from their vehicles unless they are in immediate danger
- **DO NOT** remove a motorcyclist's helmet unless it is essential and you are trained to do so
- be prepared to give first aid (see Annex 7 and Useful websites)
- stay at the scene until the emergency services arrive
- be prepared to exchange details (see Rule 286).

If you are involved in any other medical emergency, you should contact the emergency services in the same way.

Incidents involving dangerous goods

284. Vehicles carrying dangerous goods in packages will be marked with plain orange reflective plates. Road tankers and vehicles carrying tank containers of dangerous goods will have hazard warning plates (see Vehicle markings).

285. If an incident involves a vehicle containing dangerous goods, follow the advice in Rule 283 and, in particular

- switch off engines and **DO NOT SMOKE**
- keep well away from the vehicle and do not be tempted to try to rescue casualties as you yourself could become one
- call the emergency services and give as much information as possible about the labels and markings on the vehicle. **DO NOT** use a mobile phone close to a vehicle carrying flammable loads.

Documentation

286. If you are involved in a collision which causes damage or injury to any other person, vehicle, animal or property, you **MUST**
- stop. If possible, stop in a place of relative safety (see Rule 275)
- give your own and the vehicle owner's name and address, and the registration number of the vehicle, to anyone having reasonable grounds for requiring them
- if you do not give your name and address at the time of the collision, report it to the police as soon as reasonably practicable, and in any case within 24 hours.

Law RTA 1988 sect 170

287. If another person is injured and you do not produce your insurance certificate at the time of the crash to a police officer or to anyone having reasonable grounds to request it, you **MUST**
- report it to the police as soon as possible and in any case within 24 hours
- produce your insurance certificate for the police within seven days.

Law RTA 1988 sect 170

ROADWORKS, LEVEL CROSSINGS AND TRAMWAYS

Roadworks

288. When the 'Road Works Ahead' sign is displayed, take extra care and look for additional signs providing more specific instructions. Observe all signs – they are there for your safety and the safety of road workers.
- You **MUST NOT** exceed any temporary maximum speed limit.
- Keep a safe distance from the vehicle in front (see Rule 126).
- Use your mirrors and get into the correct lane for your vehicle in good time and as signs direct.
- Do not switch lanes to overtake queuing traffic.
- Take extra care near cyclists and motorcyclists as they are vulnerable to skidding on grit, mud or other debris at road works.
- Where lanes are restricted due to road works, merge in turn (see Rule 134).
- Do not drive through an area marked off by traffic cones.
- Watch out for vehicles entering or leaving the works area. Where vehicles are travelling in the road and are displaying amber warning lights, leave extra space and expect them to slow or turn into a works area.
- Concentrate on the road ahead, not the road works.
- Bear in mind that the road ahead may be obstructed by the works or by slow-moving or stationary traffic.

Law RTRA sect 16

Additional rules for high-speed roads

289. Take special care on motorways and other high-speed dual carriageways. Lanes may be closed to traffic and a lower speed limit may apply.

Works vehicles may be used to close lanes or carriageways for repairs. Where large 'Keep Left' or 'Keep Right' signs are displayed on the back, you **MUST** move over and pass the works vehicle on the side indicated and not return to the closed lane until you can see it is safe to do so.

Where a vehicle displays the sign 'CONVOY VEHICLE NO OVERTAKING', you **MUST NOT** pass the vehicle. A flashing light arrow or red 'X' may also be used to make the works vehicle more visible from a distance and give earlier warning to drivers.

Laws RTA 1988 sect 36, TSRGD reg 3 and sched 13

290. Road works may contain features that require extra care.
* **Narrow lanes.** Lanes may be narrower than normal and will be marked by studs or temporary road markings. Keep a safe distance (see Rule 126) from the vehicle in front and make sure you can clearly see the edges of the lane ahead.
* **Contraflow systems.** These mean that you may be travelling in a narrower lane than normal and with no permanent barrier between you and oncoming traffic. At the start and finish of contraflows, you should slow down and increase the distance to the vehicle in front because changes in the camber of the road may affect vehicle stability.
* **Breakdown advice.** If your vehicle breaks down in road works, follow Rules 275, 277 and 278 but be aware that areas marked off by cones contain significant hazards. Where available, you should move your vehicle into a signed road works refuge location. Signs indicate where dedicated recovery services are provided.

Level crossings

291. A level crossing is where a road crosses a railway or tramway line. Approach and cross it with care. Never drive onto a crossing until the road is clear on the other side and do not get too close to the car in front. Never stop or park on, or near, a crossing.

292. Overhead electric lines. It is dangerous to touch overhead electric lines. You **MUST** obey the safe height warning road signs and you should not continue forward onto the railway if your vehicle touches any height barrier or bells. The clearance available is usually 5 metres (16 feet 6 inches) but may be lower.

Laws RTA 1988 sect 36, TSRGD Schedule 2 part 7

293. Controlled Crossings. Most crossings have traffic light signals with a steady amber light, twin flashing red stop lights (see Light signals controlling traffic and Traffic signs) and an audible alarm for pedestrians. They may have full, half or no barriers.

- You **MUST** always obey the flashing red stop lights.
- You **MUST** stop behind the white line across the road.
- Keep going if you have already crossed the white line when the amber light comes on.
- Do not reverse onto or over a controlled crossing.
- You **MUST** wait if a train goes by and the red lights continue to flash. This means another train will be passing soon.
- Only cross when the lights go off and barriers open.
- Never zig-zag around half-barriers, they lower automatically because a train is approaching.
- At crossings where there are no barriers, a train is approaching when the lights show.

Laws RTA 1988 sect 36 & TSRGD Schedule 14 parts 1 and 4

Rule 293: Stop when the traffic lights show

294. Railway telephones. If you are driving a large or slow-moving vehicle, a long, low vehicle with a risk of grounding, or herding animals, a train could arrive before you are clear of the crossing. You **MUST** obey any sign instructing you to use the railway telephone to obtain permission to cross. You **MUST** also telephone when clear of the crossing if requested to do so.

Laws RTA 1988 sect 36 & TSRGD Schedule 9 parts 7 and 8

295. Crossings without traffic lights. Vehicles should stop and wait at the barrier or gate when it begins to close and not cross until the barrier or gate opens.

96. User-operated gates or barriers. Some crossings have 'Stop' signs and small red and green lights. You **MUST NOT** cross when the red light is showing, only cross if the green light is on. If crossing with a vehicle, you should
   open the gates or barriers on both sides of the crossing
   check that the green light is still on and cross quickly
   close the gates or barriers when you are clear of the crossing.
Laws TWA 1992 sect 55 & PC(SB)R 1996

297. If there are no lights, follow the procedure in Rule 296. Stop, look both ways and listen before you cross. If there is a railway telephone, always use it to contact the signal operator to make sure it is safe to cross. Inform the signal operator again when you are clear of the crossing.

298. Open crossings. These have no gates, barriers, attendant or traffic lights but will have a 'Give Way' sign. You should look both ways, listen and make sure there is no train coming before you cross.

299. Incidents and breakdowns. If your vehicle breaks down, or if you have an incident on a crossing you should
   get everyone out of the vehicle and clear of the crossing immediately
   use a railway telephone if available to tell the signal operator. Follow the instructions you are given
   move the vehicle clear of the crossing if there is time before a train arrives. If the alarm sounds, or the amber light comes on, leave the vehicle and get clear of the crossing immediately.

Tramways

300. You **MUST NOT** enter a road, lane or other route reserved for trams. Take extra care where trams run along the road. You should avoid driving directly on top of the rails and should take care where trams leave the main carriageway to enter the reserved route, to ensure you do not follow them. The width taken up by trams is often shown by tram lanes marked by white lines, yellow dots or by a different type of road surface. Diamond-shaped signs and white light signals give instructions to tram drivers only.
Law RTRA sects 5 & 8

301. Take extra care where the track crosses from one side of the road to the other and where the road narrows and the tracks come close to the kerb. Tram drivers usually have their own traffic signals and may be permitted to move when you are not. Always give way to trams. Do not try to race or overtake them or pass them on the inside, unless they are at tram stops or stopped by tram signals and there is a designated tram lane for you to pass.

The Highway Code

302. You **MUST NOT** park your vehicle where it would get in the way of trams or where it would force other drivers to do so. Do not stop on any part of a tram track, except in a designated bay where this has been provided alongside and clear of the track. When doing so, ensure that all parts of your vehicle are outside the delineated tram path. Remember that a tram cannot steer round an obstruction.

Law RTRA sects 5 & 8

303. Tram stops. Where the tram stops at a platform, either in the middle or at the side of the road, you **MUST** follow the route shown by the road signs and markings. At stops without platforms you **MUST NOT** drive between a tram and the left-hand kerb when a tram has stopped to pick up passengers. If there is no alternative route signed, do not overtake the tram – wait until it moves off.

Law RTRA sects 5 & 8

304. Look out for pedestrians, especially children, running to catch a tram approaching a stop.

305. Always give priority to trams, especially when they signal to pull away from stops, unless it would be unsafe to do so. Remember that they may be carrying large numbers of standing passengers who could be injured if the tram had to make an emergency stop. Look out for people getting off a bus or tram and crossing the road.

306. All road users, but particularly cyclists and motorcyclists, should take extra care when driving or riding close to or crossing the tracks, especially if the rails are wet. You should take particular care when crossing the rails at shallow angles, on bends and at junctions. It is safest to cross the tracks directly at right angles. Other road users should be aware that cyclists and motorcyclists may need more space to cross the tracks safely.

307. Overhead electric lines. Tramway overhead wires are normally 5.8 metres (19 feet) above any carriageway, but can be lower. You should ensure that you have sufficient clearance between the wire and your vehicle (including any load you are carrying) before driving under an overhead wire. Drivers of vehicles with extending cranes, booms, tipping apparatus or other types of variable height equipment should ensure that the equipment is fully lowered. Where overhead wires are set lower than 5.8 metres (19 feet), these will be indicated by height clearance markings – similar to 'low bridge' signs. The height clearances on these plates should be carefully noted and observed. If you are in any doubt as to whether your vehicle will pass safely under the wires, you should always contact the local police or the tramway operator. Never take a chance as this can be extremely hazardous.

LIGHT SIGNALS CONTROLLING TRAFFIC

Traffic Light Signals

RED means 'Stop'. Wait behind the stop line on the carriageway

RED AND AMBER also means 'Stop'. Do not pass through or start until GREEN shows

GREEN means you may go on if the way is clear. Take special care if you intend to turn left or right and give way to pedestrians who are crossing

AMBER means 'Stop' at the stop line. You may go on only if the AMBER appears after you have crossed the stop line or are so close to it that to pull up might cause an accident

A GREEN ARROW may be provided in addition to the full green signal if movement in a certain direction is allowed before or after the full green phase. If the way is clear you may go but only in the direction shown by the arrow. You may do this whatever other lights may be showing. White light signals may be provided for trams

Flashing red lights

**Alternately flashing red lights mean
YOU MUST STOP**

At level crossings, lifting bridges, airfields, fire stations, etc.

Motorway signals

You **MUST NOT** proceed further in this lane

Change lane

Reduced visibility ahead

Lane ahead closed

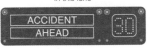

Temporary maximum speed advised and information message

You ****MUST NOT**** enter or proceed in the left lane, temporary mandatory maximum speed limit and information message

Temporary maximum speed advised

End of restriction

Lane control signals

Green arrow - lane available to traffic facing the sign
Red crosses - lane closed to traffic facing the sign
White diagonal arrow - change lanes in direction shown

SIGNALS TO OTHER ROAD USERS
Direction indicator signals

I intend to move out to the right
or turn right

I intend to move in to the left
or turn left or stop on the left

Brake light signals

I am applying the brakes

Reversing light signals

I intend to reverse

Hazard light signals

I am temporarily obstructing
traffic or warning of a hazard or
obstruction ahead (see Rule 116)

These signals should not be used except for the purposes described.

Arm signals

For use when direction indicator signals are not used, or when necessary to reinforce direction indicator signals
and stop lights. ***Also for use by pedal cyclists and those in charge of horses.***

I intend to move in to the left
or turn left

I intend to move out to the right
or turn right

I intend to slow down or stop

SIGNALS BY AUTHORISED PERSONS
Police officers
Stop

Traffic approaching
from the front

Traffic approaching from
both front and behind

Traffic approaching
from behind

To beckon traffic on

From the side

From the front

From behind*

Arm signals to persons controlling traffic

I want to go straight on

I want to turn left;
use either hand

I want to turn right

*In Wales, bilingual signs appear on emergency services vehicles and clothing

Driver & Vehicle Standards Agency (DVSA) officers and traffic officers

Traffic officer

DVSA officer

These officers now have new powers to stop/direct vehicles and will be using hand signals and light signals similar to those used by police. You **MUST** obey any signals given (see Rules 107 and 108).

School Crossing Patrols

Not ready to cross pedestrians

Barrier to stop pedestrians crossing

Ready to cross pedestrians, vehicles must be prepared to stop

All vehicles must stop

TRAFFIC SIGNS
Signs giving orders

Signs with red circles are mostly prohibitive.
Plates below signs qualify their message.

Entry to
20mph zone

End of
20mph zone

Maximum
speed

National
speed limit
applies

School
crossing
patrol

Stop and
give way

Give way to traffic
on major road

Manually operated temporary
STOP and GO signs

No entry for
vehicular traffic

No vehicles
except bicycles
being pushed

No cycling

No motor
vehicles

No buses (over 8
passenger seats)

No
overtaking

No towed
caravans

No vehicles
carrying
explosives

No vehicle or
combination of vehicles
over length shown

No vehicles
over height
shown

No vehicles
over width
shown

Give priority to
vehicles from
opposite direction

No right turn

No left turn

No U-turns

No goods vehicles over
maximum gross weight
shown (in tonnes) except
for loading and unloading

Note: Although **The Highway Code** shows many of the signs commonly in use, a comprehensive explanation of our signing system is given in the AA's booklet **Know Your Traffic Signs**, which is on sale at booksellers. The booklet also illustrates and explains the vast majority of signs the road user is likely to encounter. The signs illustrated in **The Highway Code** are not all drawn to the same scale. In Wales, bilingual versions of some signs are used including Welsh and English versions of place names. Some older designs of signs may still be seen on the roads.

No vehicles over maximum gross weight shown (in tonnes)

Parking restricted to permit holders

No stopping during period indicated except for buses

No stopping during times shown except for as long as necessary to set down or pick up passengers

No waiting

No stopping (Clearway)

Signs with blue circles but no red border mostly give positive instruction.

Ahead only

Turn left ahead (right if symbol reversed)

Turn left (right if symbol reversed)

Keep left (right if symbol reversed)

Vehicles may pass either side to reach same destination

Mini-roundabout (roundabout circulation - give way to vehicles from the immediate right)

Route to be used by pedal cycles only

Segregated pedal cycle and pedestrian route

Minimum speed

End of minimum speed

Buses and cycles only

Trams only

Pedestrian crossing point over tramway

One-way traffic (note: compare circular 'Ahead only' sign)

With-flow bus and cycle lane

Contraflow bus lane

With-flow pedal cycle lane

Warning signs

Distance to
'STOP' line
ahead

Dual carriageway
ends

Road narrows on
right (left if symbol
reversed)

Road narrows on
both sides

Distance to
'Give Way'
line ahead

Crossroads

Junction on
bend ahead

T-junction with
priority over vehicles
from the right

Staggered
junction

Traffic merging
from left ahead
**The priority through
route is indicated by
the broader line**

Double bend first
to left (symbol may
be reversed)

Bend to the
right (or left if
symbol reversed)

Roundabout

Uneven road

Plate below
some signs

Two-way
traffic crosses
one-way road

Two-way traffic
straight ahead

Opening or swing
bridge ahead

Low-flying
aircraft or sudden
aircraft noise

Falling or
fallen rocks

Traffic signals
not in use

Traffic signals

Slippery road

Steep hill
downwards

Steep hill
upwards

Gradients may be shown as a ratio i.e. 20% = 1:5

Tunnel ahead

Trams crossing
ahead

Level crossing
with barrier
or gate ahead

Level crossing
without barrier
or gate ahead

Level crossing
without barrier

Warning signs – continued

School crossing patrol ahead (some signs have amber lights which flash when crossings are in use)

School crossing patrol ahead (some signs have amber lights which flash when crossings are in use)

Frail (or blind or disabled if shown) pedestrians likely to cross road ahead

Pedestrians in road ahead

Zebra crossing

Overhead electric cable; plate indicates maximum height of vehicles which can pass safely

Available width of headroom indicated

Sharp deviation of route to left (or right if chevrons reversed)

Light signals ahead at level crossing, airfield or bridge

Minature warning lights at level crossings

Cattle

Wild animals

Wild horses or ponies

Accompanied horses or ponies

Cycle route ahead

Risk of ice

Traffic queues likely ahead

Distance over which road humps extend

Other danger; plate indicates nature of danger

Soft verges

Side winds

Hump bridge

Worded warning sign

Quayside or river bank

Risk of grounding

Direction signs

Mostly rectangular
Signs on motorways – blue backgrounds

At a junction leading directly into a motorway (junction number may be shown on a black background)

On approaches to junctions (junction number on black background)

Route confirmatory sign after junction

Downward pointing arrows mean 'Get in lane'
The left-hand lane leads to a different destination from the other lanes.

The panel with the inclined arrow indicates the destinations which can be reached by leaving the motorway at the next junction

Signs on primary routes – green backgrounds

On approaches to junctions

At the junction

Route confirmatory sign after the junction

On approaches to junctions

On approaches to junction in Wales (bilingual)

Blue panels indicate that the motorway starts at the junction ahead.
Motorways shown in brackets can also be reached along the route indicated. White panels indicate local or non-primary routes leading from the junction ahead. Brown panels show the route to tourist attractions.
The name of the junction may be shown at the top of the sign.
The aircraft symbol indicates the route to an airport.
A symbol may be included to warn of a hazard or restriction along that route.

Green background signs – continued

Primary route forming part of a ring road

Signs on non-primary and local routes – black borders

On approaches to junctions

At the junction

Direction to toilets with access for the disabled

Green panels indicate that the primary route starts at the junction ahead. Route numbers on a blue background show the direction to a motorway. Route numbers on a green background show the direction to a primary route.

Other direction signs

Picnic site

Ancient monument in the care of English Heritage

Direction to a car park

Tourist attraction

Direction to camping and caravan site

Advisory route for lorries

Route for pedal cycles forming part of a network

Recommended route for pedal cycles to place shown

Route for pedestrians

Symbols showing emergency diversion route for motorway and other main road traffic

Diversion route

Information signs

All rectangular

Entrance to controlled parking zone

Entrance to congestion charging zone

End of controlled parking zone

Advance warning of restriction or prohibition ahead

Parking place for solo motorcycles

With-flow bus lane ahead which pedal cycles and taxis may also use

Lane designated for use by high occupancy vehicles (HOV) - see Rule 142

Vehicles permitted to use an HOV lane ahead

End of motorway

Start of motorway and point from which motorway regulations apply

Appropriate traffic lanes at junction ahead

Variable speed limit with camera enforcement sign

Traffic on the main carriageway coming from right has priority over joining traffic

Additional traffic joining from left ahead. Traffic on main carriageway has priority over joining traffic from right hand lane of slip road

Traffic in right hand lane of slip road joining the main carriageway has priority over left hand lane

Motorway service area sign showing the operator's name

'Countdown' markers at exit from motorway (each bar represents 100 yards to the exit). Green-backed markers may be used on primary routes and white-backed markers with black bars on other routes. At approaches to concealed level crossings white-backed markers with red bars may be used. Although these will be erected at equal distances the bars do not represent 100 yard intervals.

Information signs – continued

Traffic has priority over oncoming vehicles

Hospital ahead with Accident and Emergency facilities

Tourist information point

No through road for vehicles

Recommended route for pedal cycles

Home Zone Entry

Area in which cameras are used to enforce traffic regulations

Bus lane on road at junction ahead

Roadworks signs

Road works

Loose chippings

Temporary hazard at roadworks

Temporary lane closure (the number and position of arrows and red bars may be varied according to lanes open and closed)

Slow-moving or stationary works vehicle blocking a traffic lane. Pass in the direction shown by the arrow.

Mandatory speed limit ahead

Roadworks 1 mile ahead

End of roadworks and any temporary restrictions including speed limits

Signs used on the back of slow-moving or stationary vehicles warning of a lane closed ahead by a works vehicle. There are no cones on the road

Lane restrictions at roadworks ahead

One lane crossover at contraflow roadworks

ROAD MARKINGS
Across the carriageway

Stop line at signals
or police control

Stop line at 'Stop' sign

Stop line for pedestrians
at a level crossing

Give way to traffic on major road (can
also be used at mini roundabouts)

Give way to traffic from the right
at a roundabout

Give way to traffic from the right
at a mini-roundabout

Along the carriageway

Edge line

Centre line
See Rule 127

Hazard
warning line
See Rule 127

Double white lines
See Rules 128 and 129

See Rule 130

Lane line
See Rule 131

Along the edge of the carriageway

Waiting restrictions

Waiting restrictions indicated by yellow lines apply to the carriageway, pavement and verge. You may stop to load or unload (unless there are also loading restrictions as described below) or while passengers board or alight. Double yellow lines mean no waiting at any time, unless there are signs that specifically indicate seasonal restrictions. The times at which the restrictions apply for other road markings are shown on nearby plates or on entry signs to controlled parking zones. If no days are shown on the signs, the restrictions are in force every day including Sundays and Bank Holidays. White bay markings and upright signs (see below) indicate where parking is allowed.

| No waiting at any time | No waiting during times shown on sign | Waiting is limited to the duration specified during the days and times shown |

Red Route stopping controls

Red lines are used on some roads instead of yellow lines. In London the double and single red lines used on Red Routes indicate that stopping to park, load/unload or to board and alight from a vehicle (except for a licensed taxi or if you hold a Blue Badge) is prohibited. The red lines apply to the carriageway, pavement and verge. The times that the red line prohibitions apply are shown on nearby signs, but the double red line ALWAYS means no stopping at any time. On Red Routes you may stop to park, load/unload in specially marked boxes and adjacent signs specify the times and purposes and duration allowed. A box MARKED IN RED indicates that it may only be available for the purpose specified for part of the day (e.g. between busy peak periods). A box MARKED IN WHITE means that it is available throughout the day.

RED AND SINGLE YELLOW LINES CAN ONLY GIVE A GUIDE TO THE RESTRICTIONS AND CONTROLS IN FORCE AND SIGNS, NEARBY OR AT A ZONE ENTRY, MUST BE CONSULTED.

| No stopping at any time | No stopping during times shown on sign | Parking is limited to the duration specified during the days and times shown | Only loading may take place at the times shown for up to a maximum duration of 20 mins |

On the kerb or at the edge of the carriageway

Loading restrictions on roads other than Red Routes

Yellow marks on the kerb or at the edge of the carriageway indicate that loading or unloading is prohibited at the times shown on the nearby black and white plates. You may stop while passengers board or alight. If no days are indicated on the signs the restrictions are in force every day including Sundays and Bank Holidays.

ALWAYS CHECK THE TIMES SHOWN ON THE PLATES.

Lengths of road reserved for vehicles loading and unloading are indicated by a white 'bay' marking with the words 'Loading Only' and a sign with the white on blue 'trolley' symbol. This sign also shows whether loading and unloading is restricted to goods vehicles and the times at which the bay can be used. If no times or days are shown it may be used at any time. Vehicles may not park here if they are not loading or unloading.

No loading or unloading
at any time

No loading or unloading
at the times shown

Loading bay

Other road markings

Keep entrance clear of stationary vehicles, even if picking up or setting down children

Warning of 'Give
Way' just ahead

Parking space reserved
for vehicles named

See Rule 243

See Rule 141

Box junction - See Rule 174

Do not block that part of
the carriageway indicated

Indication of traffic lanes

VEHICLE MARKINGS

Large goods vehicle rear markings

Motor vehicles over 7500 kilograms maximum gross weight and trailers over 3500 kilograms maximum gross weight

Left

Right

LONG VEHICLE

Central

The vertical markings are also required to be fitted to builders' skips placed in the road, commercial vehicles or combinations longer than 13 metres (optional on combinations between 11 and 13 metres)

Hazard warning plates

Certain tank vehicles carrying dangerous goods must display hazard information panels

The above panel will be displayed by vehicles carrying certain dangerous goods in packages

The panel illustrated is for flammable liquid. Diamond symbols indicating other risks include:

Toxic substance

Oxidizing substance

Non-flammable compressed gas

Radioactive substance

Spontaneously combustible substance

Corrosive substance

Projection markers

Side marker

End marker

Both required when load or equipment (eg crane jib) overhangs front or rear by more than two metres

Other

School bus (displayed in front or rear window of bus or coach)

ANNEXES

1. You and your bicycle

Make sure that you feel confident of your ability to ride safely on the road. Be sure that

- you have the right size and type of cycle for your comfort and safety
- the lights and reflectors are kept clean and in good working order
- the tyres are in good condition and inflated to the pressure shown on the tyre
- the wheels spin freely
- the gears are working correctly
- the chain is properly adjusted and oiled
- the saddle and handlebars are adjusted to the correct height.

You should fit a bell to your cycle.

You **MUST**

- ensure your brakes are efficient
- have white front and red rear lights lit when cycling at night.

Laws PCUR regs 6 & 10 & RVLR reg 18

Cycle training: If you are an inexperienced cyclist or have not ridden for a while, consider taking a cycle training course. Some councils offer national standard cycle training such as Bikeability and in certain areas, this is free of charge. It can help build up your skills and confidence.

There are three levels to Bikeability, starting with the basics of balancing, stopping and starting safely, through to handling complex and busy junctions. You will also learn about traffic signs and the rules of the road, planning routes, safe road positioning and signalling (particularly at junctions) and basic cycle maintenance. For more information, see www.bikeability.org.uk and www.cycling.scot.

2. Motorcycle licence requirements

If you have a provisional motorcycle licence, you **MUST** satisfactorily complete a Compulsory Basic Training (CBT) course.

You can then ride unaccompanied on the public road a motorcycle up to 125cc, with a power output not exceeding 11kW, with L plates (in Wales either D plates or L plates, or both, can be used), for up to two years.

Law RTA 1988 sect 97(3)

To ride a moped, learners **MUST**:

- be 16 or over
- have a provisional moped licence
- complete CBT training.

Law RTA 1988 sect 97(3) & 101

You can then ride unaccompanied on the public road a two-wheeled vehicle with a maximum design speed of 45km/h (28mph), with L plates (in Wales either D plates or L plates, or both, can be used), for up to two years.

You **MUST** first pass the theory test for motorcycles and then the moped practical test to obtain your full moped licence.

Law MV(DL)R reg 38(4)

If you passed your car driving test before 1 February 2001 you are qualified to ride a moped without L plates (and/or D plates in Wales), although it is recommended that you complete CBT before riding on the road. If you passed your car driving test after this date you **MUST** complete CBT before riding a moped on the road.
Law RTA 1988 sect 97(3)

Licence categories for mopeds and motorcycles

Category AM (moped) – minimum age 16
- two-wheeled vehicle with a maximum design speed of 45km/h (28mph)
- three- or four-wheeled vehicle with a maximum design speed over 25km/h (15.5mph), up to 50cc and with a power output not exceeding 4 kW.

Category A1 – minimum age 17
- motorcycles up to 125cc, with a power output not exceeding 11kW
- tricycles with a power output not exceeding 15kW.

Category A2 – minimum age 19
- motorcycles with a power output not exceeding 35kW.

Category A
- unrestricted motorcycles with a power output over 35kW (the minimum age you can obtain a category A licence is 21 under progressive access or 24 under direct access)
- tricycles with a power output over 15kW (minimum age 21).

Progressive access is a process that allows a rider to take a higher-category practical test if they already have at least two years' experience on a lower-category motorcycle. For example, if you have held a category A2 licence for a minimum of two years, you can take the category A practical test at age 21. There is no requirement to take another theory test.

If you want to learn to ride motorcycles larger than 125cc and with a power output over 11kW, you **MUST** meet the minimum age requirements, satisfactorily complete a CBT course and be accompanied by an approved instructor on another motorcycle in radio contact.
Laws MV(DL)R regs 9 & 16(7), & RTA 1988 sect 97(3)

To obtain your full moped or motorcycle licence you **MUST** pass a motorcycle theory test and modules 1 and 2 practical tests on a two-wheeled motorcycle.
Law MV(DL)R reg 38

You **MUST NOT** carry a pillion passenger or pull a trailer until you have passed your test. Also see Rule 253 covering vehicles prohibited from motorways.
Law MV(DL)R reg 16

3. Motor vehicle documentation and learner driver requirements
Documents
Driving licence. You **MUST** have a valid driving licence for the category of motor vehicle you are driving. You **MUST** inform the Driver and Vehicle Licensing Agency (DVLA) if you change your name and/or address.
Law RTA 1988 sects 87 & 99(4)

Holders of non-European Community licences who are now resident in the UK may only drive on that licence for a maximum of 12 months from the date they become resident in this country. To ensure continuous driving entitlement
- a British provisional licence should be obtained and a driving test(s) passed before the 12 month period elapses, or
- in the case of a driver who holds a licence from a country which has been designated in law for licence exchange purposes, the driver should exchange the licence for a British one.

MOT. Cars and motorcycles **MUST** normally pass an MOT test three years from the date of the first registration and every year after that. You **MUST NOT** drive a motor vehicle without an MOT certificate when it should have one. Exceptionally, you may drive to a pre-arranged test appointment or to a garage for repairs required for the test. Driving an unroadworthy motor vehicle may invalidate your insurance. From 20 May 2018, cars, vans, motorcycles and other light passenger vehicles manufactured or first registered over 40 years ago, will be exempt from the MOT test, unless the vehicle has been substantially changed within the previous 30 years. Guidance on what counts as a substantial change can be found at www.gov.uk/historic vehicles.

If a vehicle that's currently exempt from the MOT test is substantially changed, the vehicle keeper cannot continue to claim an exemption from the MOT test.
Law RTA 1988 sects 45, 47, 49 & 53

Insurance. To use a motor vehicle on the road, you **MUST** have a valid insurance policy. This **MUST** at least cover you for injury or damage to a third party while using that motor vehicle. Before driving any motor vehicle, make sure that it has this cover for your use or that your own insurance provides adequate cover. You **MUST NOT** drive a motor vehicle without insurance. Also, be aware that even if a road traffic incident is not your fault, you may still be held liable by insurance companies.
Law RTA 1988 sect 143

Uninsured drivers can now be automatically detected by roadside cameras. Further to the penalties for uninsured driving (see Penalty table, Annex 5), an offender's vehicle can now be seized by the Police, taken away and crushed.
Law RTA 1988, sects 165a & 165b

The Highway Code

The types of cover available are indicated below:

Third-Party insurance – this is often the cheapest form of insurance, and is the minimum cover required by law. It covers anyone you might injure or whose property you might damage. It does not cover damage to your own motor vehicle or injury to yourself.

Third-Party, Fire and Theft insurance – similar to third-party, but also covers you against your motor vehicle being stolen, or damaged by fire.

Comprehensive insurance – this is the most expensive but the best insurance. Apart from covering other persons and property against injury or damage, it also covers damage to your own motor vehicle, up to the market value of that vehicle, and personal injury to yourself.

Registration certificate. Registration certificates (also called harmonised registration certificates) are issued for all motor vehicles used on the road, describing them (make, model, etc) and giving details of the registered keeper. You **MUST** notify the Driver and Vehicle Licensing Agency in Swansea as soon as possible when you buy or sell a motor vehicle, or if you change your name or address.

The buyer and seller are responsible for completing the registration certificates. The seller is responsible for forwarding them to DVLA. The procedures are explained on the back of the registration certificates.
Law RV(R&L)R regs 21, 22, 23 & 24

Vehicle Excise Duty (VED). Vehicle Excise Duty **MUST** be paid on all motor vehicles used or kept on public roads.
Law VERA sects 29 and 33

Statutory Off-Road Notification (SORN). This is a notification to the DVLA that a motor vehicle is not being used on the road. If you are the vehicle keeper and want to keep a motor vehicle untaxed and off the public road you **MUST** declare SORN – it is an offence not to do so. The vehicle will remain SORN until you sell, tax or scrap it. If your vehicle is uninsured or off the road it **MUST** have either a SORN declaration or valid insurance.
Law RV(RL)R 2002, reg 26 sched 4

Production of documents. You **MUST** be able to produce your driving licence, a valid insurance certificate and (if appropriate) a valid MOT certificate, when requested by a police officer. If you cannot do this you may be asked to take them to a police station within seven days.
Law RTA 1988 sects 164 & 165

Learner drivers

Learners driving a car **MUST** hold a valid provisional licence. They **MUST** be supervised by someone at least 21 years old who holds a full EC/EEA licence for that type of car (automatic or manual) and has held one for at least three years.
Laws MV(DL)R reg 16 & RTA 1988 sect 87

Vehicles. Any vehicle driven by a learner **MUST** display red L plates. In Wales, either red D plates, red L plates, or both, can be used. Plates **MUST** conform to legal specifications and **MUST** be clearly visible to others from in front of the vehicle and from behind. Plates should be removed or covered when not being driven by a learner (except on driving school vehicles).
Law MV(DL)R reg 16 & sched 4

You **MUST** pass the theory test (if one is required) and then a practical driving test for the category of vehicle you wish to drive before driving unaccompanied.
Law MV(DL)R reg 40

4. The road user and the law
Road traffic law

The following list can be found abbreviated throughout the Code. It is not intended to be a comprehensive guide, but a guide to some of the important points of law. For the precise wording of the law, please refer to the various Acts and Regulations (as amended) indicated in the Code. Abbreviations are listed below.

Most of the provisions apply on all roads throughout Great Britain, although there are some exceptions. The definition of a road in England and Wales is 'any highway and any other road to which the public has access and includes bridges over which a road passes' (RTA 1988 sect 192(1)). In Scotland, there is a similar definition which is extended to include any way over which the public have a right of passage (R(S)A 1984 sect 151(1)).

It is important to note that references to 'road' therefore generally include footpaths, bridleways and cycle tracks, and many roadways and driveways on private land (including many car parks). In most cases, the law will apply to them and there may be additional rules for particular paths or ways. Some serious driving offences, including drink-driving offences, also apply to all public places, for example public car parks.

The reference to 'emergency area' in the Code is an 'emergency refuge area' as defined in the Motorways Traffic (England and Wales) Regulations 1982 as amended by the Motorways Traffic (England and Wales)(Amendment)(England) Regulations 2015.

Acts and regulations are available as enacted or as amended at www.legislation.gov.uk and are available in their original print format from The Stationery Office.

Acts and regulations prior to 1988

Chronically Sick & Disabled Persons Act 1970	CSDPA
Functions of Traffic Wardens Order 1970	FTWO
Greater London (General Powers) Act 1974	GL(GP)A
Highway Act 1835 or 1980 (as indicated)	HA
Motorways Traffic (England & Wales) Regulations 1982	MT(E&W)R
Pedal Cycles (Construction & Use) Regulations 1983	PCUR
Public Passenger Vehicles Act 1981	PPVA
Road Traffic Act 1984	RTA
Road Traffic Regulation Act 1984	RTRA
Road Vehicles (Construction & Use) Regulations 1986	CUR
Roads (Scotland) Act 1984	R(S)A

Acts and regulations from 1988 onwards

Environmental Protection Act 1990	EPA
Horses (Protective Headgear for Young Riders) Act 1990	H(PHYR)A
Horses (Protective Headgear for Young Riders) Regulations 1992	H(PHYR)R
Motor Cycles (Eye Protectors) Regulations 1999	MC(EP)R
Motor Cycles (Protective Helmets) Regulations 1998	MC(PH)R
Motorways Traffic (England & Wales) (Amendment) Regulations 2004 or 2018 (as indicated)	MT(E&W)(A)R
Motorways Traffic (England & Wales) (Amendment) (England) Regulations 2015	MT(E&W)(A)(E)R
Motorways Traffic (Scotland) Regulations 1995	MT(S)R
Motorways Traffic (Scotland) (Amendment) Regulations 2004 or 2018 (as indicated)	MT(S)(A)R
Motor Vehicles (Driving Licences) Regulations 1999	MV(DL)R
Motor Vehicles (Variation of Speed Limits) (England & Wales) Regulations 2014	MV(VSL)(E&W)
Motor Vehicles (Wearing of Seat Belts) Regulations 1993	MV(WSB)R
Motor Vehicles (Wearing of Seat Belts) (Amendment) Regulations 2006	MV(WSB)(A)R
Motor Vehicles (Wearing of Seat Belts by Children in Front Seats) Regulations 1993	MV(WSBCFS)R
New Roads and Streetworks Act 1991	NRSWA
Pedal Cycles (Construction & Use) Regulations 1983	PCUR
Powers of Criminal Courts (Sentencing) Act 2000	PCC(S)A
Police Reform Act 2002	PRA
Prohibition of Smoking in Certain Premises (Scotland) Regulations 2006. Scottish SI 2006/No 90	TPSCP(S)R*
Road Safety Act 2006	RSA
Road Traffic Act 1984, 1988 or 1991 as indicated	RTA
Road Traffic Act 1988 (Prescribed Limit)(Scotland) Regulations 2014	PLSR
Road Traffic (New Drivers) Act 1995	RT(ND)A
Road Traffic Offenders Act 1988	RTOA
Road Vehicles (Construction and Use)(Amendment)(No 4) Regulations 2003	CUR(A)(No4)R
Road Vehicles (Display of Registration Marks) Regulations 2001	RV(DRM)R
Road Vehicles Lighting Regulations 1989	RVLR
Road Vehicles (Registration & Licensing) Regulations 2002	RV(R&L)R
Smoke-free (Exemptions and Vehicles) Regulations 2007 SI 2007/765	TSf(EV)*
Smoke-free Premises etc (Wales) Regulations 2007 SI 2007/W787	TSfP(W)R*
Smoke-free (Private Vehicles) Regulations 2015	S-f(PV)R
Smoke-free Premises etc (Wales) (Amendment) Regulations 2015	S-f(W)R
Smoking Prohibition (Children in Motor Vehicles) (Scotland) Act 2016	SP(CIMV)(S)A
Traffic Management Act 2004	TMA
Traffic Signs Regulations & General Directions 2002	TSRGD
Traffic Signs Regulations & General Directions 2016	TSRGD 2016
Use of Invalid Carriages on Highways Regulations 1988	UICHR
Vehicle Excise and Registration Act 1994	VERA
Zebra, Pelican and Puffin Pedestrian Crossings Regulations and General Directions 1997	ZPPPCRGD

*Specific legislation applies to smoking in vehicles which constitute workplaces.

For information, visit:
www.smokefreeengland.co.uk
www.ashscotland.org.uk/go-smoke-free
www.gov.wales/smoking

5. Penalties and The Highway Code

Parliament sets the maximum penalties for road traffic offences. The seriousness of the offence is reflected in the maximum penalty. It is for the courts to decide what sentence to impose according to circumstances.

The penalty table on the next page indicates some of the main offences, and the associated penalties. There is a wide range of other more specific offences which, for the sake of simplicity, are not shown here. The penalty points and disqualification system is described on the next page.

Penalty points and disqualification

The penalty point system is intended to deter drivers and motorcyclists from following unsafe motoring practices. Certain non-motoring offences, e.g. failure to rectify vehicle defects, can also attract penalty points.

The court **MUST** order points to be endorsed on the licence according to the fixed number or the range set by Parliament. The accumulation of penalty points acts as a warning to drivers and motorcyclists that they risk disqualification if further offences are committed.
Law RTOA sects 44 & 45

A driver or motorcyclist who accumulates 12 or more penalty points within a three-year period **MUST** be disqualified. This will be for a minimum period of six months, or longer if the driver or motorcyclist has previously been disqualified.
Law RTOA sect 35

For every offence which carries penalty points the court has a discretionary power to order the licence holder to be disqualified. This may be for any period the court thinks fit, but will usually be between a week and a few months.

In the case of serious offences, such as dangerous driving and drink-driving, the court **MUST** order disqualification. The minimum period is 12 months, but for repeat offenders or where the alcohol level is high, it may be longer. For example, a second drink-drive offence in the space of 10 years will result in a minimum of three years' disqualification.
Law RTOA sect 34

The Highway Code

Penalty Table

Offence	Imprisonment	Fine	Disqualification	Penalty Points
*Causing death by dangerous driving	14 years	Unlimited	Obligatory – 2 years minimum	3–11 (if exceptionally not disqualified)
*Dangerous driving	2 years	Unlimited	Obligatory	3–11 (if exceptionally not disqualified)
*Causing death by careless driving under the influence of drink or drugs	14 years	Unlimited	Obligatory – 2 years minimum	3–11 (if exceptionally not disqualified)
Careless and inconsiderate driving	-	Unlimited	Discretionary	3–9
Driving while unfit through drink or drugs or with excess alcohol; or failing to provide a specimen for analysis	6 months	Unlimited	Obligatory	3–11 (if exceptionally not disqualified)
Failing to stop after an accident or failing to report an accident	6 months	Unlimited	Discretionary	5–10
Driving when disqualified	6 months (12 months in Scotland)	Unlimited	Discretionary	6
Driving after refusal or revocation of licence on medical grounds	6 months	Unlimited	Discretionary	3–6
Driving without insurance	-	Unlimited	Discretionary	6–8
Using a vehicle in a dangerous condition	-	£2,500 (Unlimited for LGV or PCV)	Obligatory within 3 years of previous conviction for similar offence– 6 months minimum. Otherwise discretionary	3 in each case
Failure to have proper control of vehicle or full view of the road and traffic ahead	-	£1,000 (£2,500 for PCV or goods vehicle)	Discretionary	3
Using a hand-held mobile phone when driving	-	£1,000 (£2,500 for PCV or goods vehicle)	Discretionary	6
Driving otherwise than in accordance with a licence	-	£1,000	Discretionary	3–6
Speeding	-	£1,000 (£2,500 for motorway offences)	Discretionary	3–6 or 3 (fixed penalty)
Traffic light offences	-	£1,000	Discretionary	3
No MOT certificate	-	£1,000	-	-
Seat belt offences	-	£500	-	-
Dangerous cycling	-	£2,500	-	-
Careless cycling	-	£1,000	-	-
Cycling on pavement	-	£500	-	-
Failing to identify driver of a vehicle	-	£1,000	Discretionary	-

*Where a court disqualifies a person on conviction for one of these offences, it must order an extended retest. The courts also have discretion to order a retest for any other offence which carries penalty points, an extended retest where disqualification is obligatory, and an ordinary test where disqualification is not obligatory.

Furthermore, in some serious cases, the court **MUST** (in addition to imposing a fixed period of disqualification) order the offender to be disqualified until they pass a driving test. In other cases the court has a discretionary power to order such disqualification. The test may be an ordinary length test or an extended test according to the nature of the offence.

Law RTOA sect 36

New drivers

Special rules as set out below apply for a period of two years from the date of passing their first driving test, to drivers and motorcyclists from

- the UK, EU/EEA, the Isle of Man, the Channel Islands or Gibraltar who passed their first driving test in any of those countries
- other foreign countries who have to pass a UK driving test to gain a UK licence, in which case the UK driving test is treated as their first driving test; and
- other foreign countries who (without needing a test) exchanged their licence for a UK licence and subsequently passed a UK driving test to drive another type of vehicle, in which case the UK driving test is treated as their first driving test. For example a driver who exchanges a foreign licence (car) for a UK licence (car) and who later passes a test to drive another type of vehicle (e.g. an HGV) will be subject to the special rules.

Where a person subject to the special rules accumulates six or more penalty points before the end of the two-year period (including any points acquired before passing the test) their licence will be revoked automatically. To regain the licence they must reapply for a provisional licence and may drive only as a learner until they pass a further driving test (also see Annex 8 – Safety code for new drivers.)

Law RT(ND)A

Note. This applies even if they pay for offences by fixed penalty. Drivers in the first group (UK, EU/EEA etc.) who already have a full licence for one type of vehicle are not affected by the special rules if they later pass a test to drive another type of vehicle.

Other consequences of offending

Where an offence is punishable by imprisonment then the vehicle used to commit the offence may be confiscated.

Law PCC(S)A, sect 143

In addition to the penalties a court may decide to impose, the cost of insurance is likely to rise considerably following conviction for a serious driving offence. This is because insurance companies consider such drivers are more likely to be involved in a collision.

Drivers disqualified for drinking and driving twice within 10 years, or once if they are over two and a half times the legal limit, or those who refused to give a specimen, also have to satisfy the Driver and Vehicle Licensing Agency's Medical Branch that they do not have an alcohol problem and are otherwise fit to drive before their licence is returned at the end of their period of disqualification. Persistent misuse of drugs or alcohol may lead to the withdrawal of a driving licence.

6. Vehicle maintenance, safety and security
Vehicle maintenance

Take special care that lights, brakes, steering, exhaust system, seat belts, demisters, wipers, washers and any audible warning systems are all working. Also

- lights, indicators, reflectors, and number plates **MUST** be kept clean and clear
- windscreens and windows **MUST** be kept clean and free from obstructions to vision
- lights **MUST** be properly adjusted to prevent dazzling other road users.
- extra attention needs to be paid to this if the vehicle is heavily loaded
- exhaust emissions **MUST NOT** exceed prescribed levels
- ensure your seat, seat belt, head restraint and mirrors are adjusted correctly before you drive
- ensure that items of luggage are securely stowed.

Laws RVLR 1989 regs 23 & 27, & CUR regs 30 & 61

Warning displays. Make sure that you understand the meaning of all warning displays on the vehicle instrument panel. Do not ignore warning signs, they could indicate a dangerous fault developing.

- When you turn the ignition key, warning lights will be illuminated but will go out when the engine starts (except the handbrake warning light). If they do not, or if they come on while you are driving, stop and investigate the problem, as you could have a serious fault.
- If the charge warning light comes on while you are driving, it may mean that the battery isn't charging. This should also be checked as soon as possible to avoid loss of power to lights and other electrical systems.

Window tints. You **MUST NOT** use a vehicle with excessively dark tinting applied to the windscreen, or to the glass in any front window to either side of the driver. Window tinting applied during manufacture complies with the Visual Light Transmittance (VLT) standards. There are no VLT limits for rear windscreens or rear passenger windows.

Laws RTA 1988 sect 42 & CUR reg 32

Tyres. Tyres **MUST** be correctly inflated to the vehicle manufacturer's specification for the load being carried. Always refer to the vehicle's handbook or data. Tyres should also be free from certain cuts and other defects.

Cars, light vans and light trailers MUST have a tread depth of at least 1.6 mm across the central three-quarters of the breadth of the tread and around the entire circumference.

Motorcycles, large vehicles and passenger-carrying vehicles MUST have a tread depth of at least 1 mm across three-quarters of the breadth of the tread and in a continuous band around the entire circumference.

Mopeds should have visible tread.

Be aware that some vehicle defects can attract penalty points.

Tyre age. Tyres over 10 years old **MUST NOT** be used on the front axles of:
- goods vehicles with a maximum gross weight of more than 3.5 tonnes
- passenger vehicles with more than 8 passenger seats

Additionally, they **MUST NOT** be used on the rear axles of passenger vehicles with 9 to 16 passenger seats, unless equipped with twin wheels.

To prove the age of a tyre, it is further required that the date of tyre manufacture marking **MUST** always be legible.

Vehicles currently excluded from tyre roadworthiness regulations and vehicles of historical interest which are not used for commercial purpose are exempt from these requirements. *Law CUR reg 27*

If a tyre bursts while you are driving, try to keep control of your vehicle. Grip the steering wheel firmly and allow the vehicle to roll to a stop at the side of the road.

If you have a flat tyre, stop as soon as it is safe to do so. Only change the tyre if you can do so without putting yourself or others at risk - otherwise call a breakdown service.

Tyre pressures. Check weekly. Do this before your journey, when tyres are cold. Warm or hot tyres may give a misleading reading.

Your brakes and steering will be adversely affected by under-inflated or over-inflated tyres. Excessive or uneven tyre wear may be caused by faults in the braking or suspension systems, or wheels which are out of alignment. Have these faults corrected as soon as possible.

Fluid levels. Check the fluid levels in your vehicle at least weekly. Low brake fluid may result in brake failure and a crash. Make sure you recognise the low fluid warning lights if your vehicle has them fitted.

Before winter. Ensure that the battery is well maintained and that there are appropriate anti freeze agents in your radiator and windscreen bottle.

Other problems. If your vehicle
- pulls to one side when braking, it is most likely to be a brake fault or incorrectly inflated tyres. Consult a garage or mechanic immediately
- continues to bounce after pushing down on the front or rear, its shock absorbers are worn. Worn shock absorbers can seriously affect the operation of a vehicle and should be replaced
- smells of anything unusual such as burning rubber, petrol or an electrical fault; investigate immediately. Do not risk a fire.

Overheated engines or fire. Most engines are water-cooled. If your engine overheats you should wait until it has cooled naturally. Only then remove the coolant filler cap and add water or other coolant.

If your vehicle catches fire, get the occupants out of the vehicle quickly and to a safe place. Do not attempt to extinguish a fire in the engine compartment, as opening the bonnet will make the fire flare. Call the fire brigade.

Petrol stations/fuel tank/fuel leaks. Ensure that, when filling up your vehicle's tank or any fuel cans you are carrying, you do not spill fuel on the forecourt. Any spilled fuel should be immediately reported to the petrol station attendant. Diesel spillage is dangerous to other road users, particularly motorcyclists, as it will significantly reduce the level of grip between the tyres and road surface. Double-check for fuel leaks and make sure that

* you do not overfill your fuel tank
* the fuel cap is fastened securely
* the seal in the cap is not torn, perished or missing
* there is no visual damage to the cap or the fuel tank

Emergency fuel caps, if fitted, should form a good seal.

Never smoke, or use a mobile phone, on the forecourt of petrol stations as these are major fire risks and could cause an explosion.

Undertake all aspects of the daily walkaround checks for commercial vehicles, as recommended by DVSA (www.gov.uk/dvsa/commercial-vehicle-safety) and the Fleet Operator Recognition Scheme (www.fors-online.org.uk).

Vehicle security
When you leave your vehicle you should
* remove the ignition key and engage the steering lock
* lock the car, even if you only leave it for a few minutes
* close the windows completely
* never leave children or pets in an unventilated car
* take all contents with you, or lock them in the boot. Remember, for all a thief knows a carrier bag may contain valuables
* never leave vehicle documents in the car.

For extra security fit an anti-theft device such as an alarm or immobiliser. If you are buying a new car it is a good idea to check the level of built-in security features. Consider having your registration number etched on all your car windows. This is a cheap and effective deterrent to professional thieves.

7. First Aid on the road
The following information was compiled with the help of St John Ambulance, the British Heart Foundation and the British Red Cross. It's intended as a general guide for those without first-aid training but shouldn't be considered a substitute for proper training. Any first aid given at the scene of an incident should be looked on only as a temporary measure until the emergency services arrive.

1. Deal with danger
Further collisions and fire are the main dangers following a crash. Approach any vehicle involved with care, watching out for spilt oil or broken glass. Switch off all engines and, if possible, warn other traffic. If you have a vehicle, switch on your hazard warning lights. Stop anyone from smoking, and put on the gloves from your first-aid kit if you have one.

2. Get help

If you can do so safely, try to get the help of bystanders. Get someone to call the appropriate emergency services on 999 or 112 as soon as possible. They'll need to know the exact location of the incident (including the direction of traffic, for example, northbound) and the number of vehicles involved. Try to give information about the condition of any casualties, for example, if anyone is having difficulty breathing, is bleeding heavily, is trapped in a vehicle or doesn't respond when spoken to.

3. Help those involved

DO NOT move casualties from their vehicles unless there's the threat of further danger. **DO NOT** remove a motorcyclist's helmet unless it's essential. **DO** try to keep casualties warm, dry and as comfortable as you can. **DO** give reassurance confidently and try not to leave them alone or let them wander into the path of other traffic. **DO NOT** give them anything to eat or drink.

4. Provide emergency care

Remember the letters **D R A B C:**

D Danger Check that it's safe to approach.

R Response Try to get a response by gently shaking the casualty's shoulders and asking loudly 'Are you alright?' If they respond, check for injuries.

A Airway If there's no response, open the casualty's airway by placing your fingers under their chin and lifting it forward.

If the casualty is unconscious and breathing,
place them in the recovery position until medical help arrives.

B Breathing Check that the casualty is breathing normally. Look for chest movements, look and listen for breathing, and feel for breath on your cheek.

If there are no signs of breathing, start CPR. Interlock your fingers, place them in the centre of the casualty's chest and press down hard and fast – around 5 to 6 centimetres and about twice a second. You may only need one hand for a child and shouldn't press down as far. For infants, use two fingers in the middle of the chest and press down about a third of the chest depth. Don't stop until the casualty starts breathing again or a medical professional takes over.

C Circulation If the casualty is responsive and breathing, check for signs of bleeding. Protect yourself from exposure to blood and check for anything that may be in the wound, such as glass. Don't remove anything that's stuck in the wound. Taking care not to press on the object, build up padding on either side of the object. If nothing is embedded, apply firm pressure over the wound to stem the flow of blood. As soon as practical, fasten a pad to the wound with a bandage or length of cloth. Use the cleanest material available.

Burns Put out any flames, taking care for your own safety. Cool the burn for at least 20 minutes with plenty of clean, cool water. Cover the burn with cling film if available. Don't try to remove anything that's sticking to the burn.

5. Be prepared

Always carry a first aid kit – you might never need it, but it could save a life. Learn first aid – you can get first aid training from a qualified organisation such as St John Ambulance, St Andrew's First Aid, British Red Cross, or any suitable, qualified body (see Useful websites for contact details).

8. Safety code for new drivers

Once you have passed the driving test you will be able to drive on your own. This will provide you with lots of opportunities but you need to remain safe. Even though you have shown you have the skills you need to drive safely, many newly qualified drivers lack experience. You need to continue to develop your skills, especially anticipating other road users' behaviour to avoid having a collision. As many as one driver in five has some kind of collision in their first year of driving. This code provides some assistance to help you get the through the first 12 months after passing the driving test, when you are most vulnerable, as safely as possible.

- Many of the worst collisions happen at night. Between midnight and 6am is a time of high risk for new drivers. Avoid driving then unless it's really necessary.
- If you are driving with passengers, you are responsible for their safety. Don't let them distract you or encourage you to take risks. Tell your passengers that you need to concentrate if you are to get to your destination safely.
- Never show off or try to compete with other drivers, particularly if they are driving badly.
- Don't drive if you have consumed any alcohol or taken drugs. Even over-the-counter medicines can affect your ability to drive safely – read the label to see if they may affect your driving.
- Make sure everyone's wearing a seat belt throughout the journey.
- Keep your speed down – many serious collisions happen because the driver loses control, particularly on bends.
- Most new drivers have no experience of driving high-powered or sporty cars. Unless you have learnt to drive in such a vehicle you need to get plenty of experience driving on your own before driving a more powerful car.
- Driving while uninsured is an offence. See Annex 3 for information on types of insurance cover.

EMEMBER that under the New Drivers Act you will have your licence revoked if you get six penalty points on your licence within two years of passing your first driving test. You will need to pass both the theory and practical tests again to get back your full licence.

You could consider taking further training such as Pass Plus, which could save you money on your insurance, as well as helping you reduce your risk of being involved in a collision.

There are three ways to find out more:
    internet – www.gov.uk
    telephone – 0115 936 6504
    email – passplus@dvsa.gov.uk

Other information
Metric conversions

The conversions given throughout *The Highway Code* are rounded but a detailed conversion chart is shown below.

Miles	Kilometres	Miles	Kilometres
1.00	1.61	40.00	64.37
5.00	8.05	45.00	72.42
10.00	16.09	50.00	80.47
15.00	24.14	55.00	88.51
20.00	32.19	60.00	96.56
25.00	40.23	65.00	104.60
30.00	48.28	70.00	112.65
35.00	56.33		

Useful websites

www.gov.uk
www.sja.org.uk (St John Ambulance)
www.firstaid.org.uk (St Andrew's First Aid)
www.redcross.org.uk (British Red Cross)
www.nationalhighways.co.uk
www.transport.gov.scot
www.gov.wales/roads-driving
www.trafficengland.com
www.trafficscotland.org
www.traffic.wales

www.roadsafetygb.org.uk
www.askthe.police.uk
www.trafficpenaltytribunal.gov.uk
    (outside London)
www.londontribunals.gov.uk (inside London)
www.traveline.info
ec.europa.eu/transport/road_safety/going_
    abroad/index_en.htm
www.euroncap.com/en

Further reading
Best practice
Further information about good driving and riding practice can be found in the Driver and Vehicle Standards Agency books 'The Official DVSA Guide to Driving - the essential skills' and 'The Official DVSA Guide to Riding - the essential skills'. Information specifically for drivers of large vehicles can be found in 'The Official DVSA Guide to Driving Goods Vehicles' and 'The Official DVSA Guide to Driving Buses and Coaches'.

The Blue Badge Scheme
Get information about the Blue Badge Scheme from your council: www.gov.uk/blue-badge-scheme-information-council.

Code of Practice for Horse-Drawn Vehicles
The Code of Practice is available from: **Department for Transport,** International Vehicle Standards, Great Minster House, 33 Horseferry Road, London SW1P 4DR. Tel 0300 330 3000 www.gov.uk/government/publications/code-of-practice-for-horse-drawn-vehicles

Special types of vehicles
Further information about the use of special types of vehicles under the authority of the Road Vehicles (Authorisation of Special Types) (General) Order 2003 (STGO) or Special Orders can be found at www.gov.uk/government/publications/special-types-enforcement-guide/special-types-enforcement-guide.

Towing
Further information about towing safely can be found at www.gov.uk/towing-with-car; www.gov.uk/government/publications/inf30-requirements-for-towing-trailers-in-great-britain; www.gov.uk/guidance/tow-a-trailer-with-a-car-safety-checks.

INDEX

References are to rule numbers, except numbers and text in blue, which refer to the signs and signals section and the annexes.

The Highway Code

The Highway Code